Madly Singing in the Mountains

Arthur Waley, Davos, middle fifties

Madly Singing
in the Mountains

An Appreciation and Anthology
of Arthur Waley

Edited with a Preface by
Ivan Morris

HARPER  TORCHBOOKS

Harper & Row, Publishers

New York, Evanston, San Francisco, London

This book was originally published in 1970 by Walker and Company and is here reprinted by arrangement

First HARPER TORCHBOOK edition published 1972

STANDARD BOOK NUMBER: 06-131640-7

To Anthony and Lady Violet Powell

Preface

by Ivan Morris

This collection of works by and about Arthur Waley is in part a tribute to the man who has been a great influence in my life and whose inspiring example first turned me to Japanese studies. It is something of a hybrid, neither memorial volume, nor biography, nor selection of representative writings, but a mixture of all three.

The first and shorter part consists of articles by people who had close knowledge of him and his work, including his widow, his younger brother, old friends, fellow authors, Sinologists, and students like myself. I am most grateful to them for their contributions and for the help they have given me as an editor. I must also thank the many people who have sent me letters about Arthur Waley, often enclosing copies of correspondence and other valuable material. This part of the book will, I think, be useful for any future biographer. His task will be a hard one; for Waley was a shy, unusually modest man who never wrote anything directly about himself except a short preface to one of his collections of Chinese poetry.

Inevitably there are overlaps in the essays. Occasionally I have used my editorial discretion to suggest cuts, and the contributors have usually agreed. Yet some repetition is inherent in the nature of the book; and it is not necessarily damaging, for certain points, such as the influence of Waley on a new generation of Far Eastern specialists, emerge with particular effect when they are discussed independently by different writers. The disproportionate length of my own article requires an explanation, and indeed an apology. In its original form (*Encounter*, December 1966) it was no longer than many of the others in this book; but as, in response to my requests, many people provided me with letters and miscellanea about Arthur Waley, I did my best to incorporate everything that seemed important. The bulk of my additions consists of quotations and paraphrases.

The second part is an anthology in which I have included many of my favourite writings of Arthur Waley and also some of his more obscure pieces such as an article on skiing and an original poem about war. He was incredibly prolific, and few readers, even among his devotees, can be familiar with all his work. Some of the articles are taken from journals that have long been defunct and are hard to obtain; and a number of pieces, including a long BBC interview and several Japanese poems, are published here for the first time. Confronted with the fantastic riches of Waley's work, I have unashamedly allowed my personal preference to be the sole criterion. Owing to this arbitrary procedure, certain famous books of Waley's such as *Monkey* (which I happen not to like) are not represented at all, whereas my favourites like *Yuan Mei* loom large. I realise that almost all admirers of Waley's who see this book will be disgruntled to find that some of their favourite poems and prose passages have been left out; I can only hope they will be compensated by the pleasure of discovering unfamiliar pieces which they might otherwise never have read.

Wherever possible I have given the dates of Waley's authorship or translation; they appear in italics at the end of each piece. The dates for the Chinese poets and other writers are those provided by Waley himself; sometimes there are differences of opinion about these dates, but they are not important. For all bibliographic details the reader is referred to Mr F. A. Johns's *A Bibliography of Arthur Waley* (Rutgers University Press, London, George Allen & Unwin, 1968). For mechanical convenience I have placed Waley's footnotes and mine together and have numbered them consecutively, my own notes being distinguished by the letters *Ed.*

I should perhaps add a word about the title, which is from one of Po Chü-i's finest poems, *Jen ko yu i pi*. A friend has warned me that it might lead some readers into believing that Arthur Waley was insane. I have boldly taken this risk since the line seems most beautifully to express an aspect of the man that is often over-looked: his joyfulness. For him a great work of literature was not, as it seems to be for many later specialists, an entrenched fortress bristling with 'problems' and challenges that must be grimly attacked with a battery of jargon and scholarly weapons, but an endless source of joy.

My particular gratitude is due to two people. Mrs. Alison Waley has given me invaluable co-operation in suggesting material for the first part of this book; she has provided me with letters written to Waley by Lytton Strachey, Edith Sitwell, and many other friends; it is, above all, thanks to her that I was able to obtain a more rounded picture of Arthur Waley than was possible for me during his lifetime. The late Sir Stanley Unwin, who was Waley's publisher from 1919, helped me with this book at every stage, and also provided me with many valuable details about Arthur Waley, which I was able to use in my article. My acknowledgements to various publishers for permission to reprint copyright material are given elsewhere.

Acknowledgements

Francis Sitwell for letter from Edith Sitwell to Arthur Waley. Julian Trevelyan and the Hogarth Press for extract from *Rimeless Numbers* by R. C. Trevelyan.

Mrs Alison Waley for unpublished translations of nineteen Japanese poems; review of *The World of the Shining Prince: Court Life in Ancient Japan* by Ivan Morris; translation of 'Myself' by Akutagawa Ryūnosuke; 'A Poem by Kubla Khan'; 'Notes on the "Lute Girl's Song" '; and 'Did Buddha Die of Eating Pork?'

Mrs Alison Waley and Allen & Unwin Ltd. for Ainu stories 'The Owl Speaks' and 'The Little Wolf'.

Atlantic Monthly for 'Notes on Translation', copyright © 1958 by the Atlantic Monthly Company, Boston, Mass.

Encounter for 'The Genius of Arthur Waley' by Ivan Morris.

Journal of the Royal Asiatic Society for 'Notes on Chinese Poetry' (1918).

The New Statesman for 'A Chinaman's Description of Brighton in 1877' (December 1923); 'Waiting for the New' (July 1937); 'More Than a Revival' (March 1947); and 'Et pourtant c'est triste quand meurent les empires' (November 1940).

Bulletin of the School of Asian and African Studies for 'Liebnitz and Fu Hsi' (1921).

Times Literary Supplement for 'Dr Waley's Translations' by J. M. Cohen (October 1950) and 'From the Chinese' by David Hawkes (March 1961).

Allen & Unwin Ltd., for translations of 'The Dancing Horses' by Cheng Ch'u-hui; 'The Two Lunatics' by Tuan Ch'eng-shih and 'The Lady Who Loved Insects' from *The Real Tripitaka and Other Pieces* (1952); 'The Wreath of Cloud' from *The Tale of Genji* (1927); 'Some Far Eastern Dreams', 'Blake the Taoist', 'Censorship', 'Blitz Poem', 'No Discharge', 'Song', and 'In the Gallery' from *The Secret History of the Mongols and Other Pieces* (1963).

11

Barnes & Noble Inc., for translations of 'Chuang Tzu on Death', 'Mencius on Human Nature' and Epilogue from *Three Ways of Thought in Ancient China*; and extract from *The Pillow-Book of Sei Shōnagon*.

Ernest Benn Ltd,. for 'Zen Buddhism and its Relation to Art' from *An Introduction to the Study of Chinese Painting*.

Dufour Editons, Inc., for 'The British Capture of Ting-hai in July 1840' from *The Opium War Through Chinese Eyes*.

Grove Press, Inc., for 'A Comparison of Nō with Greek Tragedy and Other Forms of Ancient Drama' and translations of 'The Damask Drum' and 'Kagekiyo' from *The Nō Plays of Japan*.

Alfred A. Knopf, Inc., for 'The Great Summons', 'Self-Abandonment', 'The Chrysanthemums in the Eastern Garden', 'A Mad Poem', 'Old Age', 'The Pitcher', 'Sailing Homeward', 'After Getting Drunk, Becoming Sober in the Night', 'The Little Cart', 'On Hearing Someone Sing a Poem by Yüan Chên', 'On Being Sixty', 'Madly Singing in the Mountains', 'Last Poem', 'Lao Tzu', 'The Hat Given to the Poet by Li Chien', 'Going to the Mountains with a Little Dancing Girl Aged Fifteen', 'A Dream of Mountaineering', 'Children', 'The Old Man with the Broken Arm', 'On Board Ship: Reading Yüan Chên's Poems', 'Fighting South of the Ramparts', 'On His Baldness', 'Dreaming that I Went with Li and Yu to Visit Yüan Chên', 'The Cranes', and excerpt from the Introduction; Copyright 1919 by Alfred A. Knopf, Inc., and renewed in 1947 by Arthur Waley. Reprinted from *Translations from the Chinese* by Arthur Waley, by permission of the publisher.

The Macmillan Company for extracts from *Yuan Mei*; © The Macmillan Company 1957.

Oxford University Press for Introduction to *The Originality of Japanese Civilization*, published for the British Group attending the Conference of the Institute of Pacific Relations at Kyoto in October 1929.

David Higham Associates for extract from *Some English Eccentrics* by Edith Sitwell; and extracts from *Noble Essences* (1950) and *Left Hand Right Hand* (1940) by Sir Osbert Sitwell.

Rutgers University Press for extracts from two letters from Arthur Waley to Beryl de Zoete.

Mr F. A. Johns for acceding to my wish to use material which he had assembled for a collection of Arthur Waley's hitherto unreprinted pieces.

Contents

14

Illustrations

Part I: APPRECIATION

Intent of Courtesy

by Carmen Blacker

S ome time towards the end of the war I called at the Ministry of Information to return to John Pilcher the copy of *The Tale of Genji* he had lent me. For several months I had been working very hard at Japanese, the Japanese of that peculiar wartime variety which those of my generation remember so well. We had to translate examples of deciphered messages from merchant ships, announcing their position, speed and cargo, or old newspaper articles laboriously put into Roman script by our teachers in order that we should thereby become more accustomed to dealing with the deciphered messages. The vocabulary of our first lessons included the words for submarines, radar, land mines, and obscure parts of machines like transmitter-oscillators. *The Tale of Genji* had been a blessed oasis in the midst of this barren waste, promising rewards to come from the language in happier times.

But it was not long since I had left a girls' boarding school, and for most of the time I was still paralysed with shyness. To talk to new people, especially men, was a severe ordeal. So when John Pilcher said, 'You must come and meet Arthur Waley. He works just down the corridor', my instant reaction was one of alarm. But my protests were ignored, and a moment later I was in a small room where, behind a desk piled high with Chinese newspapers, sat the illustrious scholar. Thinking desperately that I must say something which he would at least agree with, I ventured on the remark, 'I often find Japanese dreadfully ambiguous'. 'Oh really', he replied in a high, level tone. 'I have never come across a single case of ambiguity in my whole life.'

It was not for months afterwards that I realised that he had intended by this remark not the devastating snub I had understood. He had meant me to hear a friendly, encouraging overture to an academic discussion. How interesting. That hasn't been *my* experience, certainly, but I should be delighted to hear of yours. . . . At the time, however, this interview with him seemed likely to be my last. So utterly improbable did it seem that he should wish a second encounter that I was dumbfounded when, several months later, I received the friendliest of invitations to call and see his books.

I telephoned to ask when I could come, and he at once invited me to supper. That night I wrote in my diary: 'He led me up several flights of stairs to the living room, where he was in the midst of frying the cutlets and boiling the peas. As we ate these, he talked about clavichords and the musical modes of ancient China and how a Dr Picken in Cambridge had caused an untimely thunderstorm in May by playing his *ch'in* in the winter tuning. After supper he showed me up another flight of stairs to his study, a wonderful room with books covering the wall. He showed me a poem of the 4th century about a white poplar which had some blanks and corruptions in it, and asked if I would like to 'run through it' with him. We sat on the sofa, each with a copy, and he translated it on the spot, explaining how the blanks might be filled in. Then to my delight he suggested going through 'The Bones of Chuang Tzu',[1] which I had never seen before in Chinese. He said it was his favourite Chinese poem, and it was fascinating to see how he turned it into English then and there. He produced a Japanese story, 'The Lady Who Loved Insects',[2] which he had translated some years before but which I had never seen. He read it aloud, and I sat entranced by the story and by his reading. When I left he gave me a small volume of Po Chü-i's poems and walked with me all the way to Tottenham Court Road Underground. . . .'

Such imaginative kindness to a tongue-tied girl seems as remarkable in retrospect as it was overwhelming at the time. And

[1] See p. 178–80.   [2] See p. 248–55.

yet, despite so large an intent of courtesy on his part, it was not for years that I was able to feel relaxed and at ease in his presence. Further encounters, on his bicycle in Bloomsbury, eating sandwiches in Russell Square, left me in the same state of foolish incoherence. Nor was I alone in this discomfort. It was shared by several of my contemporaries engaged in the study of Chinese and Japanese after the war. It was arranged, for example, that he should come once a week to the School of Oriental Studies and give a 'seminar' in Chinese poetry to a picked group of students and staff. He sent us the poems a day or two in advance, which we prepared diligently. He would arrive at five o'clock, and someone would read the poems in Mandarin. Someone else would read the poems in Cantonese. Someone else would then translate, fairly faultlessly on account of the hard communal work we had all put in beforehand. He would then make a few relevant remarks about rhymes and tone values, and a comment or two on the translation, that the character *wei* in the last line, for example, meant not a lieutenant but a eunuch. After this, complete silence. It was by then usually not more than 5:20, and I remember wondering, as I stared at the grain of the wood of the table in front of me, how the next forty minutes were to be got through. There were a hundred questions we should have asked him but there was hardly a person in the room who was not thinking his question too stupid to put to such a scholar. The long silences must have been as puzzling to him as they were distressing to us. I repented afterwards of the idiocy of our behaviour in making no attempt to draw out so extraordinary a mind.

But to some extent our failure to respond to his obvious intent of kindness and friendship was justified by the remarks by which he from time to time chose to open the conversation. 'What do you think of this deep ploughing with oxen?' he enquired suddenly at a dinner party in the summer of 1945. Seeing me stare blankly at him, he explained that a ploughshare of the Han dynasty had recently been discovered in China, capable of excavating a furrow of hitherto unsuspected depth. His surprise that I was not as conversant as himself with the latest archaeological finds was quite genuine.

On another occasion he called on me unexpectedly in Cambridge, and, settling himself in a chair, announced, 'The verb "to say" in the *Tao-te ching* is never used transitively'. And once when he arrived for tea his opening gambit was, 'In the *Shik-shuo hsin-jü* a kind of tea is mentioned called *ming* which was always drunk cold'. After a breathless 'Oh really?' from me, there was usually a long silence.

But as the years went by, his friendship continued. He was never too busy to help with books and advice, to console in depression, to write letters of recommendation for scholarships, which with uncanny frequency produced the goods. My veneration for him as a scholar of almost magical insight and as a master of language made the tea parties in Gordon Square, the encounters in Cambridge when he came up for feasts in King's, unforgettable occasions.

It was not until the winter of 1962 that I came to realise that he also possessed a nobility of character, a tenderness, a courage in grief and adversity, which my circumscribed encounters with him had not revealed.

In February 1962 I heard that Beryl de Zoete was desperately ill. I went to London to visit her and found that, with hideous irony, she, who all her life had been a student of the dance and had written with such grace and insight about Indian and Balinese dancing, had fallen a victim to the obscure disease called Huntingdon's Chorea, a kind of St Vitus's Dance, which had been responsible for the strange outbreaks of dancing mania in the middle ages. She was kept comparatively quiet by narcotics, Arthur told me as we climbed the stairs, without which she would have been violent and possibly homicidal. Her mind was still conscious, though she was able to make no coherent sounds.

She was a tragic figure. She seemed to have shrunk strangely and lay screwed up in bed like a withered doll, with no teeth, hardly any hair, her face skeletally thin, one arm making convulsive movements round her head. With a tenderness I had never seen in him before, Arthur bent over her and said, 'Look what lovely flowers Carmen has brought, and some more beautiful ones have come from Walter in Germany'.

Downstairs I met Alison for the first time. While Arthur was out of the room, she told me that for six weeks he had nursed Beryl night and day, entirely alone. She had refused to have a trained nurse and insisted that Arthur do everything for her. This he had done down to the smallest detail, despite an accident to his right hand and despite the appalling difficulties of nursing a patient whose every muscle is out of control. To add to his anxieties he had been told that by the following year he must leave the flat where he had lived for forty years because London University intended to appropriate that entire side of Gordon Square. In face of the difficulties of moving his library and of the almost certain prospect that his right hand would never write again, he had decided to give up Oriental studies altogether. Yes, he said as he came into the room, the kind of scholarship he had always gone in for—'rather slapdash with very few footnotes' was his own description—was more and more a thing of the past. The time had come to retire. He would read Dickens's letters and Wilkie Collins and Gide's journals and all the other books he had never had time to read before.

A few weeks afterwards I heard that Beryl had died. His fortitude in the face of this triple loss—the loss of Beryl, of his home, and of the use of his right hand—was an inspiration to those who met him during the succeeding months. His subsequent profound happiness with Alison in the house in Highgate was likewise unforgettable to those who stayed there.

In April 1966 I heard that Arthur had broken his spine in a car accident. An operation had revealed that his spine was crumbling under an advanced cancerous growth. For three months he had lain in great agony, paralysed from the chest down. No pain-killing drugs seemed to have any effect, and bad nursing had caused further unnecessary tribulation. Only three days before,

Alison told me, a hired nurse had lifted him under the arms and broken his back in another place, so that they were unable to move him from the two armchairs in which he was lying. Strangely enough, when the nurse had first arrived, Arthur had asked her name. 'Mrs Straw', he was told. 'Oh,' he said, 'not the last straw that broke the camel's back?'

The last time I saw him was on 24 June, three days before he died. He was lying motionless on the bed in the room at the top of the house, pulled up close to the open window with its view right across London. He lay making low moans, his eyes unfocussed, yet his face more beautiful than I ever remembered it. Alison was leaning over him, talking to him and singing to him, and in a minute or two I found myself in tears.

He was in greater pain then he had been for many days, she told me, and morphia seemed to do nothing. But the day before he had woken up at five and talked steadily till eight. He kept saying what sounded like, 'sala, sala'. 'Does that mean limbo?' she asked. 'Yes', he replied. A day or two before she had said to him, 'I'm going to have some coffee. You too?' 'How could you say such a terrible thing?' he asked. 'You too you too.' David Hawkes had called and she had asked him, 'Does "you too" mean anything in Chinese?' At first he was nonplussed, but wrote later to say yes, it was a Buddhist word for the road to the other world.

It is impossible to forget the tenderness with which Alison nursed him. She would talk to him and sing to him, or bring books and read to him—the passage about the Bull Mountain[3] and the extra love poem in the paperback edition of the Chinese poems.[4] I have never seen anyone so loving, so singlemindedly and imaginatively devoted.

A week or two after his death she told me that early in the morning of the day he died a marvellous peace and lucidity had come upon him. They had talked of everything and never had he seemed so serene, so happily at peace. This is what everyone ought to feel, I thought, before they die, and is what religious rites are trying to induce artificially for those to whom the blessing is not naturally granted.

The funeral was in Highgate Old Cemetery on a hot, brilliant afternoon. A taxi deposited me at the wrong end of the cemetery at a gate on a wooded hillside. I walked in and found myself in a strange legendary world. Most of the graves were a century old, and no one seemed to have walked up the path for months. On either side were vaults overgrown with weeds and moss, statues twined round with creeper, shattered obelisks, stone archways leading to further avenues of catacombs, with saplings and convolvulus bursting through the cracks. It was very hot and still, like a tropical garden. The path twisted and turned, and I felt I had walked a couple of miles before at last I reached the 'crossroads', like the *carrefour* in the Forest of Brocéliande, with signposts pointing to the Ligne de la Folle Pensée. I turned right, walked what seemed like another mile among the graves, when at last there was Alison's black Morris 1000, a hearse, and a heap of flowers. An undertaker appeared and I asked him to tell me where I could find Dr Waley's funeral. 'I couldn't *tell* you, miss,' he replied, 'but I could direct you.' He took me around several more twists and turns and then suddenly out of the trees appeared a priest, Alison, and a procession of about twenty people. I was too late for the service, but Alison's son John took me to see the grave at the bottom of the valley under a huge sumac tree. It had been a very simple service, and they had read the passage about the Bull Mountain. No one had been buried in the *old* cemetery for years, but the authorities had eventually given this spot under the splendid tree from China where many times Arthur and Alison had brought sandwiches for lunch.

The feeling that Arthur's death had taken us into a world where there moved forces and concatenations bigger than those we encounter in our ordinary existence continued when, a fortnight later, I called at the house in Highgate to see Alison. She took me up to the room where he had died. A great peace filled it and I marvelled at such serenity in the place where such pain had been suffered. 'I have changed nothing', she said. 'But that chair by the window wasn't green, was it?' I asked. 'Oh, that', she replied.'Yes, funny how the creeper has come in.' I looked again. Through the window left open since he died the creeper had burst in like a lion. It had entirely covered the armchair with a thick coat of green leaves. It had flung tendrils across an entire wall. It had seized the long curtain and twined itself tightly round it in a spiral grip from floor to ceiling. It was as though the world of nature had flung itself into the room, and I thought of the swarms of bees which sometimes alight on the graves of saints or the birds which descend at the funerals of great men. That Arthur should have received this oblation seemed entirely fitting.

Dr Waley's Translations

by J. M. Cohen

There are two principal approaches to the translation of poetry: the imitative and the re-creative. Of these the first is the more exacting and the more restrictive, since it sets itself the task of transferring the foreign original into English with the least possible alteration of metre, rhyme scheme, general balance, and order of phrase. Every image must carry over its original value and associations. Such a present-day exponent of this method as Professor Bowra must have always before him an unattainable ideal of perfection wherein all is changed yet nothing is changed; and even such a virtuoso must be happiest when translating from the language with which he is least familiar. For the more intimate his knowledge of the original tongue the more conscious he must be of what he has failed to bring over.

At its best the Bowra method can show some startling successes; in recent times there have been Mr Day Lewis's translation of Valéry's 'Graveyard by the Sea', Mr Spender's rendering of Rilke's 'Orpheus, Euridice, Hermes', Miss Ruth Spiers's versions of Rilke and Mr Vernon Watkins's of Hölderlin; while Professor Bowra has himself published some accomplished pieces from the Russian. But this approach has its weaknesses. Apart from such technical points as the paucity of feminine rhymes in English and their relative abundance in Russian or Spanish; or those jog-trot associations of dactylic metre in English which would render an imitative translation of 'Hermann und Dorothea' absurd, there is, in this approach, one great limitation: that it is only suitable for rendering languages similar to our own in syntax and metrical conventions. Professor Bowra himself exposed the weakness of the imitative approach by remarking once that Dr Arthur Waley's translations from the Chinese were, in form and sound, absolutely different from the originals which had been read to him by a Chinese student. Dr Waley had himself previously answered this objection in the notes on technique in the introduction to his first collection of *A Hundred and Seventy Chinese Poems*. To transmit the 'flat' and 'deflected' tones peculiar to Chinese prosody would, he baldly stated, be impossible.

The second, or re-creative, form of translation requires an interpretative artist who is at the same time both poet and scholar, and this is particularly true if his field lies outside the familiar home farm of the contemporary and the European, in a country where entirely different types of poetic husbandry are practised. All that the translator can hope directly to distil from the Chinese or the Japanese must be, like Dr Sitwell's favourite apparition, something which, at a summons, disappears 'with a curious Perfume and a most melodious twang'. Not only are the verse-forms inimitable, but syntax, imagery, association and the whole cultural background are remote. The re-creative poet's task, therefore, is very different from the exacting work of the imitator. He must clothe this apparition in robes neither curiously archaic nor contemporary and modish, finding equivalents for the untransmittable qualities that distinguish age from age, poet from poet and metre from metre in his originals. His is not the restricted and unattainable ideal of the imitator. Yet it requires nothing less of him than the genius of a creative poet harnessed to a seemingly minor task.

Nothing emphasizes Dr Waley's pre-eminence in this field of re-creation more than the reprinting of his thirty-year-old *Nō Plays of Japan*. The convention of these 'plays' is utterly unfamiliar. The Japanese original is not a play, but a mixed art-form originating in the 15th century and basically mimetic. . . . Dr Waley had often to supplement his text by drawing stage directions, speeches of minor characters, and other material from the *Nō no Shiori*, a technical book of instructions for actors. The plays are highly stylized and draw their plots from songs and tales familiar to their audience and consequently referred to only obliquely in the text. Confronted with this allusiveness and with the impossibility of conveying those details of dress, gesture and the timing of phrase which play so important a part in Nō performances, Dr Waley nevertheless succeeds in presenting something which is both authentic and moving. The final chorus of *The Damask Drum* has all the beauty of a ritual significant yet strange. It speaks of a princess whose aged lover has for long beaten the drum that should summon her, but in vain. Then in despair he has drowned himself and is now wandering in the cold hells of the Lesser and Greater Lotus, still racked by desire for her.

> By the pool's white waters, upon the laurel's bough
> The drum was hung.
> He did not know his hour, but struck and struck
> Till all the will had ebbed from his heart's core;
> Then leapt into the lake and died.
> And while his body rocked
> Like driftwood on the waves,
> His soul, an angry ghost,
> Possessed the lady's wits, haunted her heart with woe. . . .

The plays make use of the Buddhist conception of earth-bound spirits, still attached by their desires to the scene of their worldly lives, to lend distance to the drama, which is generally viewed in retrospect. The chorus of *The Damask Drum* ends with what is almost a generalised statement concerning these unhappy revenants:

> I have learned to know them;
> Such, such are the demons of the World of Night.
> 'O hateful lady, hateful!' he cried, and sank again
> Into the whirlpool of desire.[1]

[1] See p. 268.

Dr Waley in his introduction explains the purpose of the plays' preoccupation with the spirits of the dead:

No does not make a frontal attack on the emotions. It creeps at the subject warily. For the action, in the commonest class of play, does not take place before our eyes, but is lived through again in mimic and recital by the ghost of one of the participants in it. Thus we get no possibility of crude realities; a vision of life indeed, but painted with the colours of memory, longing or regret.

At this point he refers to a paper which he read before the Japan Society in 1919, showing how the theme of *The Duchess of Malfi* would have been treated by a Nō writer.[2] This introduction, though it starts by making rather abrupt demands of the reader, conveys by copious quotations from the Nō writer and critic, Seami, some of the subtleties of presentation which are only implicit in the 'libretto'. The Nō audience is bound to view the movement of a hand or the sweep of a sleeve with that same fine attention which the Japanese give to the arrangement of two or three flowers in a vase: the Nō play has that same classical economy of material. It is short and devoid of elaboration, yet rich in such lyrical moments as the lines spoken by the chorus for Komachi's ghost, possessed by the spirit of her lover whom in life she deserted:

> The cup she held at the feast
> Like gentle moonlight dropped its glint on her sleeve.
> O how fell she from splendour,
> How came the white of winter
> To crown her head?

But these versions of the Nō plays, lovely though they are, do not display Dr Waley at the height of his poetic powers. Chinese poetry, relying on meticulous description and spare imagery, must state in words all that the Japanese actor may convey by costume, music and mime. The contrast between the Chinese and the Japanese conventions is as sharp as that between Crabbe's exactness of phrase and the overtones of Yeats's *Plays for Dancers*. This contrast the translator admirably conveys, though it is the

[2] See pp. 309-13.

same poetic technique that he applies to both. His metrical practice, so he states, is based on G. M. Hopkins's theories of 'sprung rhythm'.[3] But in no sense does he owe any debt to the Jesuit father's practice. The mingled Buddhism and Taoism that inspire the great Chinese poets of the 8th century are entirely undramatic; they instil no sense of sin, prompt no forensic dispute between the godlike and the human in the poet's heart. They ask of the religious man only an exact admission of his state. This he must view as objectively and clearly as he views the landscape outside his door, or the road along which a vanished friend fails to return. Dr Waley uses 'sprung rhythm', therefore, in a far less emotionally congested way than did the discoverer of that medium. To him it is as natural a measure as blank verse, and one that has the advantage of being free from 19th-century associations. In adopting it he made much the same decision as did Mr Robert Graves, at roughly the same time, by his use of Skelton's metres, or Dr Sitwell in turning to popular song, nursery rhyme, and even sometimes to Skelton also, to rescue her from the associative and over-worked iambic norm. Dr Waley's 'sprung rhythms' have the virtue of freshness, and of a conversational ease which aptly renders the very restrained and direct emotion of such a reflective writer as Po Chü-i. A short piece from his biography of that poet will convey its quality:

There is one that I love in a far, far land;
There is something that harrows me, tied in the depths of my heart.
So far is the land that I cannot visit him;
I can only gaze in longing, day on day,
So deep the sorrow that it cannot be torn away;
Never a night but I brood on it, hour by hour.
And on such a night as this, when the lamp grows dim,
Lying alone, waiting for dawn to break
In the autumn sky, with the tempest at its height,
If I do not learn what the fasting Dhutas preach,
How shall I banish the thoughts that rise from the past?

[3] See p. 158.

For Buddhism admits of no tragedy. Man's circumstances are the fruit of his deeds, in this or previous lives. Po Chü-i may regret that he cannot learn the Indian ascetic's lesson of the need to abandon desire if he would avoid pain; he may not be able to banish the thoughts that rise from the past; yet neither can he blame, as a Western poet might, the injustice of the gods for robbing him of his friend. But Po Chü-i is not always reflective and elegiac. He is capable of such a satire on militarism as 'The Old Man with the Broken Arm',[4] which is the more pointed for the smoothness of its narration, and of such tenderness as the poem written in his old age 'Going to the Mountains with a little Dancing Girl'.[5]

But there are more dramatic Chinese poems than Po Chü-i's: the great *fu* or odes for recitation written in the last centuries B.C. and in the first of the Christian era. These Dr Waley renders with equal or greater mastery. There is 'The Nightmare',[6] for instance, for which he makes use of the *Piers Plowman* metre, and the poem of the Wangsun, that 'crafty creature, mean of size', the counterpart of Mr Robert Graves's rumbustious monsters. Perhaps it was not until his 1923 volume, *The Temple*, in which he began to translate these *fu*, that Dr Waley displayed his full powers. Yet that 'Great Summons', to a dead or sick man to return to the pleasures of this world, published four years before, showed the sweep and variety of which he was capable when dealing with poems of greater breadth than those of the 8th-century elegists.[7] Nothing in modern English poetry makes a more immediate impact than the opening of his translation from that ode . . . in its revised form published in *Chinese Poems*, 1946. Yet a later passage in the poem demonstrates even better the translator's mastery of the rich texture:

> Peacocks shall fill your gardens; you shall rear
> The roc and phoenix, and red jungle-fowl,
> Whose cry at dawn assembles river storks
> To join the play of cranes and ibises;

[4] See p. 192.   [5] See p. 204.   [6] See p. 182.   [7] See p. 165.

34

Where the wild swan all day
Pursues the glint of idle kingfishers.
O Soul come back to watch the birds in flight.

But even more magnificent than 'The Great Summons' are two poems from *The Temple*, 'Poverty'[8] and 'The Bones of Chuang Tzu'[9]—the great Taoist philosopher of whom Dr Waley has written in his *Three Ways of Thought in Ancient China*. This is of all Dr Waley's translations the one from which it is most difficult to quote, for part of its magic lies in the variations of pace which he has introduced into it. Yet perhaps it is at the moment when the poet questions those bones which he found lying by the wayside that poet and translator alike touch one of those moments when poetry transcends itself and tips over into parable. 'Dead man, how was it?' he asks.

Fled you with your friend from famine and for the last grains
Gambled and lost? Was this earth your tomb,
Or did floods carry you from afar? Were you mighty, were you wise,
Were you foolish and poor? A warrior, or a girl?
Then a wonder came; for out of the silence a voice—
Thin echo only, in no substance was the Spirit seen—
Mysteriously answered, saying, 'I was a man of Sung,
Of the clan of Chuang; Chou was my name.
Beyond the climes of common thought
My reason soared, yet could I not save myself;
For at the last, when the long charter of my years was told,
I, too, for all my magic, by Age was brought
To the Black Hill of Death.
Wherefore, O Master, do you question me?'

What claims can one make for a poet who writes with such splendour, and yet has published hardly a handful of poems that are not translations? As a technician, of course, he equals Dr Sitwell in the subtlety of his texture and the apparent effortlessness of his effects. As an interpreter of Chinese and Japanese civilization he displays an exact and clear scholarship. On reading his intro-

[8] See p. 171.   [9] See p. 178.

ductions one realizes the labours for exact equivalence that go to his renderings; every metrical variation in the original has been given its counterpart in the translation. Yet his *Chinese Poems* are of another quality than the late R. A. Nicholson's translation of the Persian *Mathnawi*, for which claims of this sort can be made. It is rather by reverting to a pre-romantic definition of poetry that we can best assess the true value of Dr Waley's work. Re-creation, as opposed to imitative translation, played a very large part in the development of English poetry right up to the age of sensibility; Chaucer's *Troilus and Criseyde* owes a great deal to Boccaccio, Henryson's *Morall Fabillis* are re-created from Aesop, Dunbar's *Lament for the Makaris* is a variation on the traditional theme of 'Ubi sunt'. Again the 16th-century sonneteers shape and reshape the material of Petrarch's sonnets; Crashaw adapts Strada, Cowley perverts Pindar; Pope twists Horace, and Johnson Juvenal—each to his own uses. None of these examples, however, presents a very close parallel to Dr Waley's practice; he is consciously the translator, only half-consciously, perhaps, a poet in his own right. Yet by considering how much that is best in our poetry derives from other poetry rather than from incidents and experiences in the poet's own life one can see better the strength of Dr Waley's claim to be rated with the creative and the profoundly original; and once this claim is conceded it will not be long before his *Chinese Poems* is ranked as one of the half-dozen outstanding books of poetry by authors now living.

Times Literary Supplement
20 October 1950.

Arthur Waley at the British Museum

by Basil Gray

I only got to know Arthur Waley when I entered his old department of Oriental Prints and Drawings as his successor on the 1st January 1930, and therefore at the very moment of his own retirement. Consequently, I cannot write of his time there from personal knowledge. Nevertheless Waley's legacy to my department has been a basic influence in its development. I believe also that the Museum and its tradition of independent scholarship had a formative influence on Waley's work which persisted after he had left its service.

There can surely never have been a museum department like that, whose sole staff was the pair of poets, Laurence Binyon and Arthur Waley. Binyon had joined the Print Room staff of the Museum in 1893 and he too was fortunate to find a man of literary tasts and sympathy as his chief, Sidney Colvin, Keeper of Prints and Drawings from 1884 to 1912. It was for the vacancy caused by his retirement that Waley wished to be a candidate, but his application was overtaken by events. For it was then that Binyon was able to persuade the authorities to set up an Oriental Sub-Department to take charge of the collections of Chinese and Japanese paintings and of Japanese woodcut prints which he had helped Colvin to build up, and to begin to form collections of Persian and Indian drawings and miniatures. In early 1913 Binyon became its first head and in June of that year Waley was appointed as his assistant. There cannot therefore be strict accuracy in the account which he gave of his beginnings in the Museum many years later in the new preface that he wrote for the 1962 edition of his *Chinese Poems*. He there states that it was only to escape from the task imposed upon him by the head of the Print Room, Campbell Dodgson, of counting and sorting a large batch of modern German bookplates printed on very thin paper, which kept sticking together, that he joined the Oriental Sub-Department.[1] The only truth which may lie behind this allegorical story is that the two departments were not then, nor even when I joined seventeen years later, completely separate; and we both used to take our turn in the supervision of the Students' Room, shared by both sections. A search in the accession registers of the Prints and Drawings department showed no entry in Arthur Waley's hand nor any large batch of German woodcuts acquired about that time; but it did show that in that year the Museum acquired the extensive set of proof copies of the woodcuts by the Dalziel brothers in the 1860's as illustrations to the popular magazines and gift books of that period. I can imagine that Waley might have been asked by Dodgson to help count these while on duty in the Students' Room. That he was 'kept in' like a school boy until he had got the total right is a further embroidery which memory supplied from his just recollection of Dodgson's general strictness and Germanic thoroughness. He was indeed accountable to the Trustees for Waley's general conduct, his leave of absence, and so on.

There remains a little mystery about the way in which Waley spent the year from the end of March 1912 until his appointment in June 1913. It seems that the winter of 1912–13 was spent in Germany, for his letter accepting nomination to compete for the vacancy in the Print Room is dated from Dresden in February 1913. But the testimonials which he was required to forward are dated March 1912. They are from Sydney Cockerell, J. T. Sheppard, who had been his tutor at King's, and Oswald Sickert, the brother of the painter and then on the staff of the *Encyclopaedia*

[1] See pp. 132-3.

Britannica. Cockerell judged him 'a man of remarkable intelligence and acumen, very much interested in art and music'. Sheppard wrote of his 'enthusiasm for scholarship, which is rare. . . . His range of interests is wide and his work independent. He has the power of assimilating fresh knowledge and of interesting himself in fresh subjects.' These claims for him were indeed fully justified by the capacity he soon showed for teaching himself Chinese and Japanese. On his application form he claimed that he could already read easily Italian, Dutch, Portuguese, French, German and Spanish and speak the last three fluently. He had some Hebrew and Sanskrit, as well as Greek and Latin, in which he had obtained a I(2) at Cambridge in 1910.

It was, however, Oswald Sickert who knew him best and had suggested to him that he might go into the British Museum service. In his testimonial he wrote that Waley was 'a young man of exceptional intelligence and originality. . . . The quickness of his interest and his capacity for making something of his own out of everything he observes seem to be extraordinary.' Sickert was a friend of Laurence Binyon and it was later he who directed Waley's interest to the Nō drama: his letters to Charles Ricketts, another and closer friend of Binyon's, written from Japan in 1916, were prefixed to Waley's 1921 volume of translations of Nō plays.

In fact Waley set to work to learn Chinese and Japanese simultaneously as soon as he was settled in the Museum. When the war broke out, being medically unfit, he seized the chance for quiet study; and anyone who knew him can testify to his capacity for complete absorption in the work he was doing. He learnt by reading in the best literary texts on which he could lay his hands, and this accounts for the flow of translations from both languages and from very varied works which he began to publish from 1916 onwards. The translations published in the first number of the *Bulletin of the School of Oriental Studies* in 1917 under the title of 'pre-T'ang Poetry' must have been made during the previous years. At the same period Waley started to write short

39

articles for the *Burlington Magazine*, the first of which appeared in January 1917. It describes a version of the very much copied scroll-painting entitled 'Going up the River', and was followed in the June issue by a note on 'The Rarity of Ancient Chinese Paintings', which mainly consists of translation from the 9th-century critic, Chang Yên-yüan. Waley's official work at the Museum at this time consisted in describing the collection of Chinese paintings and in preparing an index of Chinese painters represented in the collection in either original or reproduction. This index was published by the Trustees in 1922 and has been recognised ever since as a useful tool to scholarship. It is upon it that the lists included in Sirén's 'Chinese Painting' are based.

The descriptions of the Museum's Chinese paintings have remained unpublished, except that some part of this material was reused in the volume *An Introduction to Chinese Painting*, published in 1923. They included brief but generally adequate descriptions of all paintings acquired up to 1924, but the major part of the typescript, which has always been available to students of the collection, consists of brief biographies of the painters, with translations from Chinese and Japanese sources. These all represent original research by Waley, but are often only nominally connected with the paintings in the collection. As in all collections formed before 1914, most of the paintings are indifferent works with famous names attached with more or less ultimate relevance to the style represented. Waley obviously took every opportunity he could find for enlivening his task. The greater number of the paintings came from two collections which had been acquired by the Museum *en bloc* before the creation of the Sub-Department, the William Anderson collection formed in Japan in the 1870's and the Olga Julia Wegener collection formed in China and purchased in 1910. Of course there was also the 'Admonitions' scroll, attributed to the early master Ku K'ai-chih, and on this Waley wrote the lengthy excursus which was subsequently printed in *An Introduction to Chinese Painting*. Indeed this book arose out of this part of his official work. For instance, the long iconographic note on Bodhidharma written for the catalogue was also printed in the book. Most of the notes on the Ming artists are brief or even perfunctory, but Wang Hui is the subject of a long account, including a number of extracts from biographies which are not given by Oswald Sirén. Other artists more generally noticed include Yü Chih-ting and Ch'ên Hung-shou, Huang Shên and Kao Ch'i-p'ei. Although the Museum had no original painting by either Wu Li or Lang Shih-ning, there are long accounts of both painters on the strength of some attributions. Longest of all the accounts is that of Yün Shou-p'ing, and this was published in the sole issue of the *Year Book of Oriental Art and Culture* for 1924–25, which he had agreed to edit for Messrs Benn. The curious thing is that this note on Yün Shou-p'ing accompanied the publication of a twelve-fold screen painting on silk, then belonging to Morton H. Sands, who later bequeathed it to the British Museum. It bears the signature of the well-known bird and flower painter, Shên Nan-pin, and the date 1750, which of course Waley must have read, though the section of the screen on which it appears is not reproduced with the article. By some quirk of memory he must have transposed the names of these two very different painters before sitting down to write the article about it. The incident does, however, suggest that Waley's interest in Chinese painting was largely literary, which is borne out by the series of eight articles which he contributed to the *Burlington Magazine* in 1920–21 on 'Chinese Philosophy of Art', which consist almost entirely of translations from the works of Chinese critics. Even when writing about painting his comparisons were apt to be taken from the literary world, Lhermontoff, Stendhal or Julian Huxley. Throughout this period, too, he was of course making some of his best-known translations of Chinese poems.

About 1925 Waley's interest shifted for the time towards Japan. Just as the first volume of *The Tale of Genji* appeared in June of that year, so he turned in his Museum work to describing the collection of Japanese woodcut books, many of which were transferred to the Sub-Department in that year from the Library of the Museum, where they had been under the charge of Dr Lionel Giles, deputy keeper of the Department of Oriental Printed Books and Manuscripts. The collection went back to the 19th century and even earlier, for the nucleus had come from Dr Engelbert Kaempfer who had visited Japan in 1690–93 and whose library and papers had been purchased by Sir Hans Sloane, founder of the Museum. However, the illustrated books now transferred from the Library were mainly from the same source as the large collection of Japanese paintings—from the surgeon, William Anderson, from whom they had been purchased in 1894. In the 1920's some choice colour-printed books were added to the Museum collection from auction sales in Paris, and Arthur Waley went over there once or twice to select them. His type-script catalogue of this collection of about two hundred and fifty books, as it then was, is thorough and methodical, but there was little available in the way of bibliographical information at that time, and the dating of the editions could only be attempted in many cases on the appearance of the paper and inks used, and the advertisements of other books sometimes to be found at the end. Waley showed almost excessive caution in estimating the age of these books but he gathered all the internal evidence for dating and ascription. The catalogue is a great improvement on the printed catalogue entries made by Douglas and published by the Museum Trustees in 1903, but there was little to interest Waley in this work and he must have been glad to finish it and to go on to a far more important and exacting work which was to occupy him for the rest of his time in the Museum service.

This was the cataloguing of the Buddhist paintings brought back from the walled chamber in Ch'ien Fo Tung near the city of Tun-huang, in the extreme west of Kansu province, by Sir Aurel Stein. The whole of this material was brought to London in the first place for conservation and mounting, a process which took many years to complete. Then in 1919 the paintings were divided between the Government of India and the British Museum, which had shared in the expense of Stein's journey to Central Asia in 1906–08. Waley's catalogue covered both parts of the collection, as was right, for the division was made for reasons which had nothing to do with scholarship. He naturally regarded his work primarily as an exercise in iconography, rather than in art history, for his basic tasks were to read and interpret the many incomplete inscriptions on the paintings, and in their light to identify the subjects portrayed. He wrote a short but richly packed introduction in which he explained the background in the Buddhist texts to this iconography, but referred only briefly to the historical setting and to the physical make-up of the paintings. He regarded them as provincial work of little artistic interest other than for the evidence they provide for the study of Buddhist art in the T'ang period. In fact, he was almost exclusively interested in the subject matter of these paintings, once more showing a literary approach to his task. He had just finished it when he retired from the Museum on grounds of ill-health at the end of 1929. He saw the book through the press and it was published in 1931.

What then did Arthur Waley owe to the British Museum? I would suggest that it was for him the ideal milieu in which to pursue his studies, with all the resources of the great library on which to draw, and at a centre of scholarship to which scholars from all over the world naturally came; where, therefore, he could be sure of finding both quiet and stimulating contacts. Moreover he had in Binyon a chief and colleague with whom he could work in harmony, if not exactly in unison. Their approach to Oriental art was very different; but each respected the integrity of the other and could rely on a sympathetic understanding of his aims. No one could have been more aware than Binyon of Waley's gifts and of the value of his contribution to the appreciation of Chinese and Japanese culture through his translations. It was not surprising therefore that, looking back in 1960, Waley should have written of eighteen years in which Binyon 'was an ideal friend and chief'. In his retirement he never moved far from the Museum, and it surely remained for him the centre of his life in Bloomsbury, to which he could cycle to look up a reference or to meet a colleague in less than five minutes. It seems that it was the Museum which first directed him to Oriental studies and many foreigners did not realise that he had left it. I have been aware throughout my career there of Waley's standards of scholarship and of penetration; his influence was critical, concentrated, sharp and quickening. Binyon's was a gentler spirit; from him I learnt above all how to look at and appreciate the painting of Asia; from Waley the many approaches that are needed to penetrate to the basic patterns of Eastern thought and society.

From the Chinese

by David Hawkes

'Another Waley' can be expected almost as regularly as the swallows or the latest effusion of some favourite writer of crime fiction; yet each of the more than two dozen books which he has produced since the end of the First World War has been not a careless pot-boiler but the distillation of profound scholarship and patient research.

Many a younger scholar would feel that to have produced just one of those many books would be sufficient justification for a lifetime devoted to the frustrations and intricacies of sinology. Indeed, many who read his latest book will envy the startling mental vigour which makes him, at seventy-one, as fresh and up-to-date as when, a whole age ago, he represented a junior, exotic branch of the now historical Bloomsbury Group.

This astonishing up-to-dateness must be emphasized. It is a common error to suppose that what is easy and pleasant to read must therefore be shallow and unreliable, and Dr Waley's style, in prose as in verse, has always been limpid and delightful. Moreover, he has, since resigning an Assistantship at the British Museum some thirty years ago, remained a private person. No doubt he has been the better able to concentrate his intellectual powers without the distraction of a career, but, lacking the nimbus of academic authority, he has sometimes been exposed to the patronizing criticisms of scholars immeasurably his inferiors. One must therefore observe that, more than any other sinological scholar in this country, he has from first to last remained in the van of current research. To give only two instances: *Zen Buddhism and Its Relation to Art*,[1] published in 1922,

[1] See pp. 314–23.

mentions the use made of Japanese works published in 1920, while his latest work on the Tun-huang literature draws extensively on the most recent Chinese researches on the subject.

Dr Waley's achievements have been not only in sinology but in the field of Japanese literature as well. However, it is as a translator of Chinese poetry that he is justly most famous, and it was no doubt in recognition of this fact that he was awarded the Queen's Medal for Poetry in 1953. A biographer attempting, as biographers are wont, to detect some scheme in the catalogue of his publications would observe that all the books on Chinese art were published between 1922 and 1931, that the translations from Japanese were all published between 1919 and 1935, and that 1934–39 were devoted exclusively to Ancient China and 1956–58 to the 19th century, but the translations from Chinese poetry, beginning in 1918 with the publication of *A Hundred and Seventy Chinese Poems* and continuing at intervals, reveal a lifelong preoccupation with poetry that would wreck any such attempt at systematization.

The translator of Chinese poetry is in a far worse plight than, say, the translator from French. French is a language not so impossibly dissimilar from our own that we cannot achieve fairly similar effects with verse. We use rhyme in much the same way, for instance, and we say things, on average, in about the same number of syllables. Most Chinese verse has only a few syllables —very often five—to the line, representing at least five *words* of English and generally more. It always employs rhyme—usually one rhyme to the whole poem, unless the poem is very long. It is therefore totally impossible to do for Chinese verse what the clever translator from French so often can: use an English verse-form which, though not identical, is a 'correct' equivalent.

> Au milieu de la guerre, en un sie sans foy . . .
>
> In midst of wars, a world of faithless men . . .

No amount of human wit and invention can render the following into a corresponding ten syllables of English verse:

wan huo shu sheng man ch'ien yai ch'iu feng kao

A myriad valleys full of the soughing of treetops
A thousand heights round which the wind of autumn
   whistles shrill.

—except, of course, by writing nonsense verse:

Much-vale trees-sound full Lot-cliffs fall-wind high.

Dr Waley's solution of this problem is by now so familiar and
so much imitated (often very badly) that one frequently meets
people who are under the impression that Chinese poetry in the
original is itself written in a sort of rhymeless *vers libre*. Sir Alan
Herbert's parodies of Chinese verse which appeared some years
ago in *Punch* no doubt owed something to this impression. But
an earlier generation of translators invariably used rhymed verse.
Indeed, it would never have occurred to them to do otherwise.

> A petal falls!—the spring begins to fail,
> And my heart saddens with the growing gale.
> Come then, ere autumn spoils bestrew the ground
> Do not forget to pass the wine-cup round.

The above quatrain by H. A. Giles shows some of the limitations of this kind of translation. Dr Waley himself published a
solitary example of rhymed verse translation in the introduction
to *The Temple and Other Poems* (1923). It is so good that one wishes
he had attempted more in this genre, and . . . [it shows] . . . that
his rejection of rhyme was by no means due to any inability to
employ it gracefully. . . .

Dr Waley has, at one time and another, written a good deal
about his method of translation. The fullest and also the most
recent exposition is in an article in the *Atlantic Monthly* published
in November 1958. . . . A somewhat similar statement . . .
appears at the beginning of *A Hundred and Seventy Chinese Poems*
(1918),[2] and a glance at the translations contained in that book
shows that the 'sprung rhythm' method was already, at that early
date, well developed:

[2] See pp. 131–7 and 152–64.

> A géntle wínd fáns the cálm níght
> A bríght móon shínes on the hígh tówer. . . .

Used without printed accents (and Dr Waley's translations never have them) 'sprung rhythm' has, in common with certain other kinds of verse, one serious drawback. The stress is ambiguous. For instance, there is nothing to indicate that the two lines cited above should not be read as an anapaestic jingle after the manner of the 'War Song of the Saracens' or 'John Wellington Wells':

> **A** géntle wind fáns the calm níght
> **A** bríght moon shines ón the high tówer.

It is Dr Waley's misfortune as well as his good fortune to be a great scholar; for he is read and criticized by many scholars, foreign as well as English, to whom the subtleties which cause him to sit 'hundred of times . . . for hours in front of texts the meaning of which I understood perfectly, and yet have been unable to see how they ought to be put into English . . .'[3] might just as well not have been—who would, in fact, commend him more if he used the sort of Internationalese often favoured by scholars nowadays.

Dr Waley seems early to have realized that translation of exotic texts is not enough if the reader has no mental framework to place them in. Hence were produced several delightful books in which he employed the arts of the historian and the biographer to convey to the western reader something of the milieu in which these poems were written.

The 'literary biography', in which the subject's different works are each sampled in quotation as their turn comes to be mentioned in the life, is common enough in this country. But Dr Waley's biographies of Chinese poets—*The Life and Times of Po Chü-i* (1949), *The Poetry and Career of Li Po* (1950), and *Yuan Mei* (1956) —though they appear to be structurally identical with, for example, a book like Mr Blunden's *Shelley*, nevertheless differ in that the biographical facts about the Chinese poets had mostly,

[3] See p. 158.

for want of other sources, to be reconstructed from the poems themselves.

If the many poems translated in these books seem often a trifle thin and unmemorable, this is probably not the translator's fault. Occasional verse, of which the Chinese wrote far too much —at least, they preserved too much—is often of greatest value to the biographer when it is least inspiring as literature.

The blending of narrative with translation in order to paint a portrait of a person or an age is a technique which Dr Waley learnt to deploy with great skill and felicity. Both *The Real Tripitaka* (1952) and *The Opium War through Chinese Eyes* (1958) really belong to this genre, although the translations contained in them are for the most part not poetry but prose.

The biggest work of translation which Dr Waley ever undertook—and some will think the greatest in a less literal sense—was his translation in six bulky volumes of the enormous 10th-century Japanese novel, *The Tale of Genji* (1925–33). It must have come as a revelation to many people that a work challenging comparison with Proust in its subtle treatment of time and of mental association, and displaying a quite 'modern' development of character, should have appeared some six centuries before the first crude beginnings of the novel in Europe. The sheer application required to translate a work of this size at all (and medieval Japanese is an extremely difficult language to translate from) is staggering. But to have translated with delicacy and tact, and sustained these qualities throughout the book's whole great length, so that the novel emerged in English dress as the great and important work of art it is—this was a work of genius.

Something of the weariness of a work of this magnitude comes through in a remark made in *The Real Tripitaka*, where Dr Waley is writing of another great translator, the 7th-century Chinese monk Hsüan-tsang, who brought back the Buddhist Idealist writings from India. Describing how the aged Hsüan-tsang, worn out by his labours, wearily declined to undertake the translation of the forty-nine Ratnakūta texts, he says, 'I remember my own feelings when having completed the six volumes of *The Tale of Genji* I was asked to set to work upon *The Dream of the Red Chamber*, a book of almost equal length'.

The delightful *Pillow-Book of Sei Shōnagon* (1928) and *The Lady Who Loved Insects* (1929) were presumably by-products of this Japanese period. Some Waley connoisseurs prefer the *Pillow-Book* to all his other works. Certainly it deserves to be far more widely read. The sensitive, witty lady who wrote it must be accounted one of the world's most gifted diarists. *Monkey* (1942), the much-abridged translation of a 16th-century Chinese novel, is also a favourite. It is the only Chinese novel he ever attempted and increases one's regret that he never felt able to attack *The Dream of the Red Chamber*, the one really great Chinese novel, which two competent translations published during the past few years have still not quite brought to life for the English reader.

If Dr Waley is known to the general reader chiefly as the translator of Chinese poetry or of the exquisite *Tale of Genji*, most scholars would probably feel that his greatest contribution has been in the books, mostly published between 1934 and 1939, in which the thought, manners and institutions of Ancient China were for the first time vividly represented for the English reader: *The Way and Its Power* (1934), *The Book of Songs* (1937), *The Analects of Confucius* (1938), *Three Ways of Thought in Ancient China* (1939), *The Nine Songs* (1955).

Until less than half a century ago the accepted picture of Ancient China was as remote from reality as Archbishop Ussher's view of world history. The new picture which has emerged during the past thirty or forty years has been filled in bit by bit by the labours of the archaeologist, the palaeographer, the etymologist, the textual critic, and a host of others. It may be said that in the books just mentioned Dr Waley merely coordinated the results of all these findings and presented them in a delectable synthesis. In fact, though, Dr Waley brought to this study a wide reading in anthropology and the literatures of many lands (a glance at the footnotes of *The Book of Songs* shows something of this range of interests), which enabled him to place Ancient China in a wider context, so that it seems no longer the culture of a forgotten moon-world, but a part of our own heritage as fellow-men.

From all this it must seem obvious that Dr Waley's work cannot have been achieved merely by artistic sensibility and an assemblage of various skills, but must have been animated by some underlying principle or philosophy. To call this principle humanism is true but insufficient. It is a particular kind of humanism, which refuses to be misled by cant about literary history and social evolution—which insists on approaching any society or any work or art, whatever its time and place, with equal seriousness and alertness. This intensity of approach, if one may call it that, means that the occasional modern parallel—for example, the comparison of 3rd-century totalitarianism in *Three Ways of Thought in Ancient China*[4]—seems not, as this kind of thing so often does in the case of other translators and popularizers, a cheap and shallow artifice but a poignant and illuminating truth about human behaviour. . . .

Times Literary Supplement
3 March 1961.

[4] See p. 353.

In Your Distant Street Few Drums Were Heard

by Donald Keene

My first encounters with Arthur Waley could hardly have been described as auspicious. I learned in January of 1949 that he was to deliver a lecture in Cambridge and wrote inviting him to tea. Waley responded with a postcard explaining that he had another engagement, but suggesting I introduce myself at the lecture. That afternoon I waited impatiently for my meeting with the great scholar, who for me was more of a legend than reality. I had never seen a photograph of Waley, and the one thing I thought I knew about him, apart from his books, proved to be incorrect: people in America had informed me that he worked at the British Museum though, I discovered, this had not been true for many years. I had no introduction to Waley, and I cannot now imagine what gave me the courage to invite him to tea. Perhaps I decided that the rules of decorum could be suspended in the case of an idol. Through several frustrating years as a graduate student the example of Waley's achievements, more than anything else, had sustained me in my resolution to study Chinese and Japanese literature, and when I decided in 1948 to go to England the pleasure of meeting Waley had certainly been in my mind.

And now it was about to happen. No doubt it was to help the time pass that I tuned in on the broadcast from Germany of an opera by Wagner. Hardly had Wotan and Fricka started to scream at one another than there was a knock at the door and, in answer to my shout, a total stranger entered. I jumped up in surprise, wondering who this might be. 'I am Dr Waley', the visitor said.

In my confusion I hastily turned off the radio and stammered something about having been studying. Waley with a few words arranged a meeting for the following day. Some time later I learned from a friend that Waley had expressed his amazement that anyone could possibly study Japanese while listening to American jazz played full blast. I had no way to explain that the loud noises had been Wagner, not jazz, and that (despite my hasty improvisation) I had not really been studying. I was despondent, sure that Waley would refuse to take seriously anyone with such coarse and incomprehensible habits of study. Only much later did it occur to me that perhaps my best qualification for being accepted as an acquaintance by this great collector of eccentrics was as the strange American who could not study except to the violent throb of jazz.

The lecture that night was a reading of Waley's translations from the Ainu epic, *Kutune Shirka*. I knew nothing about the Ainu except for their reputation of being exceedingly hairy, and it was a revelation to hear their delicate poetry read in Waley's rather high-pitched but precisely intoned voice. Occasionally he interposed a comment, as after he read the passage:

> The fencing done long ago
> Standing so crooked;
> The new fencing
> So high and straight.
> The old fencing like a black cloud,
> The new fencing like a white cloud.
> They stretched around the castle
> Like a great mass of cloud—
> So pleasant, so lovely!

With a smile Waley said the Ainu had certainly done something for fences. After the lecture, inevitably, there were silly questions, including one from myself, asking Dr Waley if *Kutune Shirka* did not remind him of Maeterlinck. I was desperately eager to make an impression, and as desperately aware of my failure.

The Ainu poetry was the third revelation of a literature I owed to Waley. My first acquaintance with his work occurred when I was sixteen and, mainly out of curiosity, purchased a volume of *More Translations from the Chinese*, then being remaindered by a Times Square bookshop for nineteen cents. I knew not a word of Chinese when I bought the book, but my copy (which I still have) is marked not only with the usual underlinings but with strings of crudely written Chinese characters laboriously copied a year or two later, after I had begun the study of Chinese under Waley's influence.

The second revelation had come with *The Tale of Genji*, purchased under almost identical circumstances. The great sympathy I felt for China during the war with Japan had made me reluctant even to consider that the Japanese might also have a culture, but the inducement of the price at which the book was remaindered overcame my prejudices. Again I was overwhelmed. When I entered the U.S. Navy Language School in 1942 to study Japanese, I would have much preferred to be studying Chinese, but I had at least the consolation that one day I should be able to read *The Tale of Genji* in the original.

Like other devoted readers of Waley's translations, I was convinced, though I had scarcely compared any of them with the originals, that they were entirely faithful. Acquaintances who knew the Far East had told me that despite Waley's refusal to visit that part of the world he had been uncannily accurate in evoking its atmosphere. But delighted as I was with every word of Waley, I longed to read the originals, feeling somewhat contradictorily that they must be even superior to the best trans- lation. While in Hawaii in 1943 on duty with the Navy I per- suaded the professor of Japanese at the University to offer a special seminar on *The Tale of Genji*, and I spent my day off each week preparing for the class. I confess that the original text was so difficult, so far beyond my capacities, that I derived extremely little pleasure from it. I turned back to Waley with increasing wonder.

When I decided in 1946, after leaving the Navy, to pursue my studies of Chinese and Japanese literature at Columbia, my inspiration, of course, was Waley. I hoped that like him I would be able to work in both languages, but gradually I came to realize that I was unequal to this task. It was not merely that I found it difficult to gain an adequate command of two entirely different and equally perplexing languages, but a matter of temperament. I was interested and often deeply moved by most Japanese literature, but for reasons that I cannot analyse remained insensitive (or was even hostile) to much Chinese literature, excepting always the poetry. Reading *The Tale of Genji* was nightmarishly difficult, but eventually I could sense the beauty that had attracted Waley; when it came to *The Dream of the Red Chamber*, however, a reading of the first ten or so chapters in the original left me with a distaste for the book I have never over-come. This, of course, is indicative of my limitations; more important, it demonstrates Waley's incredible catholicity of tastes. Certainly he had his likes and dislikes—in Japanese literature, for example, he seemed never to have cared much for the *haiku* or the later drama—but probably never again will there be an orientalist who undertakes translations of such different works as *The Tale of Genji* and *The Analects*, *The Pillow-Book*, and *Travels of an Alchemist*, *The Nō Plays* and *Monkey*. I confess I have never been able to read through *Monkey*, though many people enjoy it most of Waley's works; this inability led me to the reluctant conclusion that I could not fruitfully continue my studies of Chinese. The most I could aspire to was to become half of Waley.

As a scholar of Japanese, I have sometimes persuaded myself that Waley preferred Japanese literature to Chinese. Once he told me that *The Pillow-Book* was his own favourite of his works, and even his taste in Chinese poetry (for Po Chü-i rather than Li Po or Tu Fu) corresponded with Japanese rather than Chinese preferences. Certainly in his early career, as he himself said, he sometimes used Japanese instead of Chinese meanings for characters in his translations of Chinese poetry. ('They fought south of the castle' became 'They fought south of the ramparts' in later editions, when Waley realized his mistake.) But it would be false to suggest that Waley in fact preferred Japanese literature. He was capable of unlimited enthusiasm for any artistic work of excellence, to such a degree that he would undertake to learn a new and difficult language like Ainu solely for the pleasure of reading the literature and communicating his pleasure in matchless translations.

For me, as for all others interested in translating either Chinese or Japanese literature, Waley was our only predecessor. It is amusing now to read correspondence exchanged between him and Herbert Giles in 1920, when Giles took the younger man to task with avuncular authority for his departures from the originals.[1] I cannot imagine anyone reading Giles' translations today except as a curiosity or a horrible example of the follies committed in the name of rhyme. Giles was by no means incompetent in Chinese, however, and he could sometimes catch Waley in a mistranslation. But this was hardly surprising. When Waley first began his translation of *The Tale of Genji*, for example, there were no modern annotated editions of the kind that now abound. He relied mainly on the 18th-century commentaries of Motoori, generally available only in smudgy woodblock editions. Not until the Fifth Part of the translation was he able to benefit by the scholarship of Kaneko's edition. Even beginners today, if they are armed with the products of the modern Japanese editors, which explain in straightforward contemporary Japanese the meaning of the maddeningly ambiguous originals, can point out with an air of superiority Waley's lapses from accuracy. Waley was aware in later years of such mistakes, and sometimes condemned passages of his own translations for being too free (like

[1] See p. 300, note 1.

Murasaki's celebrated discussion of the novel in the Tamakazura chapter of *The Tale of Genji*). But these blemishes, though they have been given more than enough publicity, are not only pardonable, but essentially do not affect the value of his work. Waley brought new life to masterpieces of Chinese and Japanese literature by transmuting them into an incredibly sensitive and supple English. The beauty of Waley's language is too well known to need discussion here, but perhaps his greatest achievement was to establish the tone most appropriate to each of the works he translated, whether Chinese songs of the 3rd century BC or Japanese prose of the 11th century. *The Tale of Genji* could have been translated into a style reminiscent of *Le Morte d'Arthur*, or into the 19th-century Gothic favoured by Waley's predecessors in almost all their translations from classical literature. For that matter, a new translation of *The Tale of Genji* might be attempted today into contemporary English or American idiom emphasizing, for example, the guts and sweat of the characters, or into a neutral mid-Atlantic style that belongs to no time or place. But Waley's choice of tone, whether for Sei Shōnagon or Yüan Mei, was invariably definitive. Whatever new translations scholars may produce in the future, hoping to improve on the accuracy of Waley's versions, they are unlikely to alter his tone. Both in Chinese and Japanese literatures he established such strong traditions that it is only fair to say that we all belong to the School of Waley. This does not necessarily mean that we cannot go beyond his work. Ivan Morris's complete translation of *The Pillow Book of Sei Shōnagon* is unquestionably an advance on Waley's partial version. But the voice that Morris uses is Waley's. Anyone who imagines that an original text can itself dictate the appropriate tone or voice is urged to consult Beaujard's accurate and incredibly boring French translation.

The freedom of Waley's translations has often aroused controversy. From his first exchanges with Giles, Waley defended the free translation as necessary in transmitting the poetic quality of a work, an aspect as important as the surface meaning of the words. He described to me once how he had translated *The Tale of Genji*. He would read a passage over until he understood its meaning; then, without looking back at the passage, he wrote out an English assimilation. He would later consult the original again. If the content of the translation was the same, he would let it pass, even if some words had been added or deleted. Such a method could be extremely irresponsible if adopted by a less gifted translator, but Waley's extraordinary knowledge of every period of Chinese and Japanese made it possible for him to comprehend instinctively even passages of the utmost obscurity. He was capable of writing short scholarly articles on grammatical particles, but they did not absorb him nearly so much as his larger-scaled works, intended for the general public, which by their nature were bound to contain errors. Sometimes Waley revised translations made at an earlier time, but when in 1958 he reconsidered in an essay on translation a section of his *Tale of Genji*, he felt he would not wish to alter it because it still conveyed to him the mood of the original.[2]

Waley's translations always combined intuitive interpretation with his scholarly knowledge of the original works. Again and again this combination enabled him to guess what had gone wrong in a text that was obviously corrupt. Professor Gustav Haloun, to whom Waley dedicated his *Book of Songs*, was a textual scholar of the most rigorous principles, but he considered Waley's emendations to be those of a genius, not to be measured by normal academic standards. Waley nevertheless sometimes made mistakes not only on the meaning of phrases but of interpretation, as he himself admitted after reading Sam Houston Brock's translation of *Sotoba Komachi*, the Nō play he had translated thirty years before. Waley found that his version was 'hopelessly overladen and wordy and that it tried in a quite unwarrantable way to improve on the original'.[3]

Waley's attitude towards his successors was always friendly,

[2] See p. 154.   [3] See p. 155.

though sometimes I got the impression he felt we had arrived on the scene a little too late, and he had already gathered all the plums. He once mentioned in conversation that although he had continued to read Nō plays in the decades following the publication of his translations, he never regretted his selection. This was discouraging to a young translator who hoped to find some gem that had escaped Waley's earlier notice. Waley was handicapped when translating the Nō plays by the lack of annotated editions explaining the obscure, cryptic references that stud almost every line. He had no guide even to the plays most esteemed by Japanese audiences over the centuries. This meant, however, that his choices were fresh and entirely personal. We of a later generation of translators, with ready access to editions of the Nō plays copiously annotated by excellent scholars, cannot help being influenced by their preferences. The mistakes Waley made because he was insufficiently aided by modern textual criticism were compensated for by his unorthodox and often brilliantly successful discoveries of works the Japanese themselves had ignored.

I got to know Waley well in the months and years following my initial debacle in Cambridge, and we often spoke together long hours, beginning in the early afternoon and continuing until it was too dark to see each other. (I never experienced any of the difficulty in conversing with him mentioned by some. An eminent publisher once complained to me that although he had known Waley for thirty years he had never had a civil word from him!) Our conversations covered many subjects, but we spoke most often of orientalism. He flattered me by asking my interpretation of characters that meant absolutely nothing to me, or by assuming my knowledge was as diverse as his own. I enjoyed it even when for some reason I was left alone in his room and I could examine his books—the well-worn edition of the *Tripitaka*, the many volumes on art, anthropology and history of parts of the world he never touched on in his writings. I wish I had kept a diary recording the substance of our conversations, but it never occurred to me I could forget a word.

On occasion Waley could be devastating. When I showed him my translation of a Chinese play he returned it with nothing more than the query, 'Have you ever written any poetry of your own?' Or again, when, having been thoroughly disappointed by the meagre sales and lack of interest in my first book, I expressed the hope that my second book might be better received, Waley thought for a moment and said, 'Of course I don't know how other people will find it, but I liked it rather better than your first'. This was hardly the reassurance I needed. But Waley's refusal to indulge in flattery made his praise for my *Anthology of Japanese Literature*, which I dedicated to him, all the more precious.

Waley was always ready to meet younger scholars. His letters are dotted with references to visitors—an American studying the Chinese theatre, a Japanese novelist, a Swiss translator. If Waley did not suffer fools gladly, he was a warm and courteous host to anyone who interested him. His sharpest criticism was reserved not for the mistakes of the young and inexperienced but for the tediousness of the old and distinguished. His letters make frequent mentions of the 'gruelling' dinners he had to attend and of his dread of forthcoming occasions: 'I am very well, but my spirits weighed down by the approach of the King's annual Feast, which I have cut so often that I felt I must face it this year.' At such occasions his neighbours at dinner, accustomed to the banalities that pass for conversation, rarely appreciated having Waley beside them. Once, as he told me, he was seated next to an eminent mathematician and made a remark about the similarity in the use of numbers by the Romans and Chinese. The mathematician, horrified by what he took for shop talk, turned ostentatiously to his neighbour on the other side and began a more normal conversation, on the drain pipes in the Old Court that needed repairing.

The last letter I had from Waley reached me in Japan in November 1961. It was typed: 'Thank you for so many things—

your letter, the Hanako article which was just what I wanted some one to write and finally the Chikamatsu book. The latter we are reading aloud and I think you have done them perfectly. My hand is still useless for writing, Beryl is very ill with chorea and in a state painful to suffer and of course also painful to witness. In addition I hear I must turn out of my flat. The landlord is the University of London of which I regard myself as an ornament. But a last appeal for grace was not even answered. Work at present is out of the question. I read a great deal out loud to Beryl, as for example Lord Birkenhead's Life of that monster Lord Cherwell, Isaac Disraeli's *Curiosities of Literature*—a marvellous book, Harold Acton's second volume on the Bourbons at Naples, the autobiography of George Sand, the Life of Tolstoy by his son. Nothing Oriental.'

Of course, Waley's praise for my translation gave me great pleasure. No praise could have meant more. But the series of disasters described in the letter dismayed me so much that I felt I must see Waley, to offer what comfort I could. I arrived in England in February 1962 and went directly to Gordon Square. The day was dark and the cold penetrating. I climbed the familiar stairs, marvelling as always that a man of Waley's age could still manage them. He met me with no special display of emotion, but suggested we go at once to see Miss de Zoete. He warned me, 'Don't ask her any questions. She understands everything and will try to answer. Just kiss her and say you're glad to see her.' But when I sat before Miss de Zoete, who was terribly afflicted, the sight was so heartrending that it was quite impossible for me to kiss her. I sat there stunned, conscious only of her suffering and of the infinite tenderness that had made Waley resolve not to send her to a hospital, where ignorant nurses would surely make her last days even less bearable.

We left and went down into the kitchen, where we sat in gloomy silence. I asked whether it was true that he had given up orientalism, and he said it was, both because of the injury to his hand that made writing impossible and because he felt that the subjects he could write about now no longer interested him. He said he planned to spend his remaining years refreshing his knowledge of European literature. I asked if he would not reconsider, and offered to become his amanuensis, but Waley shook off the suggestion. He got up to prepare lunch and warmed a tin of steak and kidneys. I wanted badly to say something of comfort but could think of nothing.

This was the last time I saw Waley, and although I wrote him several times I had no answers. It was a terrible blow not to have seen him again, and it is sad that my last glimpse of him must have been at his deepest point of depression. But to hear his voice speaking again, always graceful and with infinite shadings and accents, I need only open his books.

The Silences of
Arthur Waley

by Naomi Lewis

I knew, or met, at different degrees of distance, several Arthur Waleys, the nearest being always the most remote. As many have done, and will continue to do, I came upon *A Hundred and Seventy Chinese Poems* when I was twelve or so. Something in their manner (as I see it now) affected me very deeply—the end-stopped travelling lines, so precise in word and statement, yet with a measureless content of distance and of time. Thereafter, with a persistence lasting through years, I read whatever I could find of his writing. I also recall giving *Monkey* as a wedding gift to a friend; it seemed a perfect choice. Though the time was in the unluxurious early 1940s, when even books were scarce, this action, like many others of my youth, has baffled me again and again over two decades. Yet, reading it once more the other day, I can see an aptness after all in that unique, profound, hilarious allegory.

When I saw Arthur Waley for the first time, at a friend's house in the early 1950s, he could well have been the sage of my early imaginings—a man with the mask of a noble, kingly bird, but somehow grey and withdrawn. He followed the conversation, observing or tasting it, but taking no part that I can recall. Later, I came to realize that he was not only the sparest of talkers, but a man of many kinds of silence. It is said of Coleridge, that master-talker, that he could hold his listeners spellbound for hours, but afterwards, few could ever remember what they had really heard. The Waleyan silence had the reverse effect. Wit, story, pointed commentary, gnomic profundity—had one only imagined these?

Presently (though I never lost my feelings of shyness, even of awe) I was to meet him quite often, with Alison—chiefly, then, in a kind of attic studio at the top of an old house in Bloomsbury. There were windows at both ends of the very long room and the south one looked out, by an odd chance, on to the leafy crown of an oriental tree, known (I think) as the Tree of Heaven. The happiest occasions were in his latest years when he and Alison had moved to their beautiful Highgate house with its transforming view over London—one of those dense, panoramic, almost floating views in which spires and trees and evening lights resume a forgotten domination.

Even then, so much of his life was rooted still in Bloomsbury —The British Museum, the University, the bookshops, and other such haunts. Coming from my own home in Red Lion Square, I would sometimes meet Arthur Waley as a neighbour. The most frequent place was that east–west Bloomsbury thoroughfare, Theobalds Road. This contains, besides the south edge of Gray's Inn, an excellent public library and the homely local branches of several banks. Moving to bank or library I would many a time encounter Arthur Waley on just such an errand—probably wearing a favourite, much-worn dark-red pullover, flapping rain-coat with bulging pockets, and carrying a very old shopping bag. His mouth was grave, but his eyes were full of friendliness— conspiratorial is the nearest word I can find. What did we say? Did he 'clear up points about the Eighteen Kinds of Nothing, the stored Consciousness and the like', for the sake of discussing which themes the great Hsiao Yü held up Tripitaka's request for a passport? More likely he offered an item of news about garden or book or the day's events. But it had, always, the Waleyan air of moment. The fact was that he did not, and could not, use idle words. Every utterance appeared fine, essential, selected to the least syllable.

1.
A Victorian tea party. Arthur Waley's parents: his father, David Schloss, in Panama hat, his mother, Rachel, facing the camera

2. *Arthur Waley, aged eight*

There is a passage in one of his books that suggests to me something of his conversational manner.

Under his feet there sprang up at once a lotus made of stone. No sooner did he stand upon it than it vanished and reappeared a few feet ahead of him. In this way, from stepping stone to stepping stone, he walked dry-footed to the base of the magic mountain.

Yes, the text does go on to say that the sides were steep to climb. But (if we read further still) 'the traveller does reach the mountain top', and then 'vast spaces opened all around him, coloured by the mountain's golden glint'.

Arthur Waley's reading aloud of his own poetry had the same curious effect of absolute probing selection. How to describe it? His voice was extremely quiet, though every syllable was audible: the total effect was at once under-emphasised yet piercing. The sentence endings—these were usually the same as the line endings—were always absolute stops, as if to cut off the outward echo or reverberation. The echo of the thought remained.

In the last years at Highgate he was neither grey nor withdrawn. There were even parties held in the house and garden, and at such times he would come and go among his friends with a very pleased and dreamlike smile. I can see him sitting in an alcove, gravely beatific, surrounded by young and older guests, like a noble senior spirit of the Ludlow woods, offering—not at all without guile—a triumphant return invitation to Comus. I remember also that Harriet Cohen [the noted British pianist] was, amusedly, part of this unintentional *tableau*. The two had much in common: beauty, a sense of grief travelled through, and an esoteric knowledge of music that made their exchanges far above the heads of most other listeners.

The summer that shone on the last part of his life did not fail him on the day of his funeral in the Old Highgate cemetery—an enchanting, rustic ground where, I am told, only the distinguished and the pauper are now allowed to lie—if a space remains at all even for these. Here, on a hot June morning, friends came, losing their way among the grassy tree-hung wandering paths, full of wild flowers that one does not expect to see in a city, passing the tombs of Mrs Henry Wood and the Duke of St Albans and that large and puzzling one that is supposed to contain the Dickens children. The setting and the occasion gave to some of the younger stragglers a temporary Blake-like air. The Bull Mountain passage from Mencius was read; the light chirping of birds did not run counter to the text. Again, by the strangest chance, the place found for him in this crowded ground (after, I am told, much doubtful searching of the records) was overhung by another of those eastern trees, another Tree of Heaven.

This may have seemed the last of Arthur Waley's silences. But its content, for those who find his work, is not likely to cease reverberating.

The Genius of Arthur Waley

by Ivan Morris

When Arthur Waley's first translations of Chinese poems were privately printed in 1916, the literatures of China and Japan were the preserve of specialists and of dabblers in quaint exotica. Now, half a century later, they have become part of the main stream of intelligent reading in the West, so that a knowledge of classical Chinese poetry and of works like *The Tale of Genji* and the Nō plays are as essential to any broad, humanistic education as Homer and Virgil. Without Waley's books it is unlikely that the classics of the Far East would have become such an important part of our heritage. In France, for example, despite a long tradition of Oriental studies and many scholarly translations, *The Tale of Genji* is hardly known except to the occasional *japonologue*; and few educated Frenchmen have read the poems of Po Chü-i or heard of Yüan Mei.

Arthur Waley's writing swept away a mass of entrenched misconceptions and led to a new era in Western understanding of Chinese poetry. The seminal importance of his 'Notes on Chinese Prosody'[1] was recognized by Lytton Strachey in a letter from Tidmarsh dated 7 July 1918:

Dear Waley

I've read the brochure on Chinese Prosody with great interest. Thank you so much for sending it.

The vistas of folly and ignorance you open up are alarming. Do *none* of

[1] See pp. 284–94.

these pundits know what they're talking about? I wish you would write a book on Chinese Literature. It's badly wanted.

I should like to know more about the allusiveness of that poetry, which we're always being told about. Perhaps they've got that too all wrong—the soft-heads. But I daresay there's a substratum of truth in it. Another brochure, please.

Yours,
Lytton.

Waley pioneered knowledge in the West about many subjects other than Oriental literature. His long paper on Zen Buddhism, for example, was published in 1922, at least five years before the first of Dr Suzuki's writings appeared in English. Based entirely on Chinese and Japanese sources, it must be one of the earliest treatments of Zen in any Western language.[2]

Arthur Waley's ability to understand Far Eastern culture and to make it important for readers in the West was due to a rare concatenation of talents. First, he was a meticulous and erudite scholar. His education at Rugby and at King's College, where he was one of the talented group of men who studied at Cambridge shortly before the First World War, gave him a thorough training in the classics, a training that can be of the greatest use to the Orientalist but which is becoming increasingly rare among younger specialists in the field. When asked a few years ago how he had become so proficient in Chinese without any help from a teacher, he said that anyone with a good classical education could learn Chinese by himself without difficulty.[3] Waley's vast learning added a valuable dimension to his understanding of Chinese and Japanese culture, enabling him to discern the type of analogies and contrasts that are not encouraged by the more rigid specialization now in vogue.

To each of the multifarious subjects he studied his approach was balanced and completely honest. He always insisted on reading all the available material before he formed his own

---

[2] See pp. 314–23 for a brief extract from this paper.
[3] Letter from Mrs Enid Candlin, 14 February 1968.

conclusions and started to write. When he was working on his book about the Opium War, a student from Cambridge mentioned an article about Gutzlaff, the Prussian buccaneer missionary, that had appeared in a 19th-century Edinburgh magazine. 'The look of amazement on his face was one that I never saw again. By sheer luck I had found something in the Cambridge University Library unavailable to him in the British Museum.'[4]

Waley's scholarship was profound and his range of knowledge incredibly wide; yet he eschewed pedantry, academic conceit, and the temptation to impress readers by a display of superior erudition. Though never 'writing down' or popularizing, he kept his scholarly works as simple and direct as possible, allowing no barriers to separate him from the general reader to whom they were mainly directed; and his discussions of even the most recondite topics are vivified by delightful flashes of wit. From all his books and articles it is clear that scholarship to Arthur Waley was no tedious duty, but a continual fascination. As Professor Enoki has written, 'Waley was forever enjoying himself in the rich garden of Chinese and Japanese culture.'[5] He plucked only the flowers that delighted him and truly appealed to his taste; and so in all his scholarly works it was virtually impossible for him to be boring.

Secondly, he was a remarkable linguist. Apart from knowing the common European languages, he had a complete command of written Chinese and Japanese, two of the hardest languages in the world, and as unlike each other as they are from English; he could read Mongol, Ainu, and Sanskrit; he was conversant with the intricacies of Talmudic literature. Like Sir George Sansom, the other great English interpreter of Japanese culture, Waley was an autodidact in Oriental languages. To teach oneself Chinese or Japanese is no mean feat even with today's plethora of dictionaries, grammars, teaching aids, and language records.

[4] Letter from Dr Edward LeFevour, 23 February 1968.
[5] Enoki Kazuo, 'Uērē to Tōyōgaku', *Kokusai Bunka* 147, September 1966, p. 27.

69

Half a century ago it was a fantastic achievement. Yet within a few years, while working as an Assistant Keeper in the British Museum, Waley had mastered both Chinese and Japanese so efficiently that already by 1919, when he was thirty, he had published five volumes of translated poems, four from classical Chinese and one from classical Japanese. In his Introduction to *Japanese Poetry* (1919) he points out that the poems can be rightly enjoyed only in the original; then he reassuringly adds, '... since the classical language has an easy grammar and limited vocabulary, a few months should suffice for the mastering of it'. Unfortunately students of classical Japanese will find that this statement applies exclusively to its author.

Despite his gift for languages Waley never made any serious effort to learn spoken Chinese or Japanese, and when he met visitors from the Far East he often had to communicate with them by writing Chinese characters on slips of paper. The current pedagogic theory that it is impossible to read a language properly without 'oral and aural comprehension' hardly fits Arthur Waley, who was virtually inarticulate in Chinese and Japanese. I think this may have been part of his refusal to scatter his energies. Waley's interest in the Far East was focused on its classical cultures, and a knowledge of the modern spoken languages seemed largely irrelevant. Dr Yashiro Yukio, the eminent Japanese art historian, who knew Waley since 1921, has written,

At this time [1921] he used to walk about with the *Kogetsu-shō* commentary of the *Genji Monogatari* which he kept bringing out and reading whenever he had the time. Now and again he would ask me questions which I sometimes found difficult to answer. Waley was the type of man who never discussed what he was doing and, though I was meeting him almost daily, he never once told me he was translating the *Genji Monogatari*. However, I somehow sensed that he was so engaged; but, since Waley was very sensitive about his own privacy, I respected his feelings and never asked him any unnecessary questions.

On Waley's translation of the *Genji Monogatari*, I once read a Japanese newspaper article contributed by a Japanese scholar, who said that Waley no doubt translated the *Genji Monogatari* from a modern Japanese text which, judging from the time when Waley was working on his translation, would be Yosano Akiko's version. However, I knew for a fact that Waley constantly carried around with him the *Kogetsu-shō* and was hard at work reading the *Genji Monogatari* with the *Kogetsu-shō* commentaries. It is of course possible that Waley did also make supplementary use of modern Japanese language versions of the *Genji Monogatari*; but it is typically Japanese to assume that Waley would find a modern Japanese language version of the *Genji Monogatari* easier to understand than the original. The plain fact is that, at that time, Waley did not know modern Japanese very well. He hardly ever spoke Japanese and, on the rare occasions when he did, he simply reeled off a few disjointed Japanese words. The truth is that he even read ancient Japanese literature with great effort, painstakingly and patiently translating word by word, relying on dictionaries and commentaries. Consequently classic versions of the *Genji Monogatari* with their full and detailed annotations and explanations were less difficult for Waley to read than any straightforward version in the modern Japanese language.

I remember one particular incident that illustrates Waley's unfamiliarity with the modern Japanese language. As the clouds of the Second World War gathered, England was placed on a wartime footing and Waley was drafted into that section of the Government Post Office which censored Japanese communications. On receiving this assignment, Waley wrote urgently to me in Japan saying: 'Willy-nilly, I have now been placed in the position of having to read modern Japanese; and I would accordingly like to take advantage of this opportunity to study modern Japanese language and literature. Please, therefore, send me a number of novels currently popular in Japan.' I remember I got together a number of novels by Tanizaki Junichirō and Akutagawa Ryūnosuke, and sent them to him.[6]

As Waley pointed out to me many years ago when I brought up the perennial question of free *versus* literal translations, so much is inevitably lost in translating Oriental literature that one must give a great deal in return. Later I realized that what enabled him to do this was a rare mastery of style and a self-assurance that allowed him, after he had thoroughly understood a Chinese or Japanese text, to recast it entirely in supple, idiomatic, vibrant English, rather than stick to a phrase-by-phrase or sentence-by-sentence rendering, which might convey the surface meaning but would inevitably mar the artistry of the original. Without

[6] Yashiro Yukio, 'Arthur Waley', *Japan Quarterly*, Vol. XIV, 1967, pp. 366–7.

this literary talent all his scholarly and linguistic gifts would never have brought the Far Eastern classics alive in English.

Though he undoubtedly ranks as one of the best English stylists of our time, Waley's own poems and stories are not, in my opinion, outstanding.[7] It was in translation that his literary gifts were fulfilled; and, fortunately for us all, he found his perfect medium in the field of Far Eastern classical literature. When Edith Sitwell writes of Waley's 'miraculous art'[8] she is of course referring to these translations.

The difficulty of putting Chinese and Japanese verse into anything that resembles English poetry can hardly be imagined by anyone who has not attempted it. *Uta* and *haiku*, because of their extreme economy of form and reliance on allusiveness, word plays, and prosodic conventions, are virtually untranslatable, and the effort is usually wasted. *Japanese Poetry*, though useful for the student and the adulator of things Japanese, ranks low among Waley's translations; and his efforts to create English verse out of the hundreds of *uta* in *The Tale of Genji* and *The Pillow Book* are, as a rule, perfunctory. Chinese poems, being less inhibited and convoluted, and written in a language whose sentence order is far closer to English than to Japanese, often lends itself to effective translation—but only when handled by a master. Waley's astonishing achievements with Chinese verse, from *A Hundred and Seventy Chinese Poems* in 1918 until *Yuan Mei* in 1956, were possible because he was a genuinely original modern poet whose renderings are works of English literature in their own right. 'Nobody . . . has ever transformed foreign verse into better English poetry. . . . His supreme gift was fineness of ear,'[9] Raymond Mortimer has written.

A good deal has been said about the influence on Waley's poetry of Pound, Eliot, and especially Gerard Manley Hopkins. I doubt whether it was important. In his reaction against the

[7] Since I include a fair sampling of Waley's original poems and also his most successful story (pp. 379–91), the reader will be able to decide this question for himself.

[8] See letter from Edith Sitwell to Arthur Waley, p. 97.

[9] Raymond Mortimer, 'Arthur Waley', *Sunday Times*, 3 July 1966.

conventions of rhyme and the iambic he belonged to the general trend of post-war poetry; and his discovery of the flexible use of stress in lines of unequal length came before he had ever read Hopkins or heard of 'sprung rhythm'.[10] As Mr Roy Fuller has written,

It is quite clear that Waley's work would have emerged, and in more or less the same form, had Hopkins, Pound, and Eliot never existed. The varying length and accents of his line, its general avoidance of the iambic but occasional delicate lapse into it—such things are of great interest; but the unique clarity and ironic tone are vital too. How far do these come from the original? Waley himself has said that he made his sympathy with Chinese verse appear more close by choosing poems to translate that echoed his own cast of mind.[11]

His success with prose translation is equally impressive, though here the technical difficulties are less obvious. Waley's style, which has been well described as a mixture of fastidiousness and informality—a description, incidentally, that applies to the man himself as well as to his writing—is elegant, limpid, natural; his *Tale of Genji*, as Mortimer says, 'ranks with the most beautiful English prose of our time' and is certainly one of the great monuments in the history of translation. What daunts one most about his prose versions is their seeming effortlessness, the way in which the meaning of the original is conveyed in plain, spontaneous English so that after a few pages one entirely forgets one is reading a translation.

To transmute a classical Oriental text into modern idiomatic English without sacrificing the sense or the beauty of the original is a remarkable creative accomplishment. A fairly literal translation from *The Pillow Book* will be followed by Waley's re-creation:

About the fifth month going to a mountain village is extremely charming. The marsh-water truly looks all over as if it were only very green, but, when [one *or* someone] goes slowly directly across [places] where the surface is

---

[10] Introduction by Arthur Waley to 1962 ed. of *A Hundred and Seventy Chinese Poems* (p. 137); see also Arthur Waley, 'Notes on Translation' (p. 158).

[11] Unpublished article by Mr Roy Fuller; see also 'Arthur Waley in Conversation', pp. 138–51.

casual and where the grass grows in profusion (*or* where the grass casually grows in profusion on the surface), fantastic (?fantastically clear) water underneath, although it is not deep, splashes up as the person walks [which is] very charming. It is (also) regrettable when a branch of a hedge on the side [of the road] catches, entering the compartment of the carriage, and one intends to seize it quickly and break it off but suddenly (*or* by chance) one misses it and passes by. It is (also) charming when the scent of sage-brush that has been crushed by the carriage permeates [the air] close [to where one sits] as the wheel rises up.

In the fifth month I love driving out to some mountain villages. The pools that lie across the road look like patches of green grass; but while the carriage slowly pushes its way right through them, one sees that there is only a scum of some strange, thin weed, with clear, bright water underneath. Though it is quite shallow, great spurts fly up as our horsemen gallop across, making a lovely sight. Then, where the road runs between hedges, a leafy bough will sometimes dart in at the carriage window; but however quickly one snatches at it, one is always too late.

Sometimes a spray of *yomogi* will get caught in the wheel, and for a moment, as the wheel brings it level, a delicious scent hovers at our window.

There are those who complain that Waley's versions are so free that they obscure the character of the original. If he were translating scientific texts or political treatises, such a charge might be justified. But it decidedly does not apply to works like *The Pillow Book*, *The Tale of Genji* or *The Ainu Epic*; for here the main value is literary, and any pedantically 'accurate' translation will vitiate their character in a far more damaging way—by making them unreadable. Waley has also been criticised for trying to improve on his writers, for chivalrously making Lady Murasaki and the others say what they might have wanted to say if only they had enjoyed the full resources of modern English. I do not suggest that these versions are irreproachable, and Waley himself would have been the last to think so.[12] Yet, short of concocting some sort of mock-archaic translationese, how could Waley be expected to convey the characteristics of classical Chinese or Japanese in a language as remote as English? As for the objection that he had made the ideas and sentiments seem

[12] E.g., see p. 155.

more modern than they really are, I can only say that whenever one of Waley's passages has struck me as improbably sophisticated and up to date, a comparison with the original text revealed that he was being scrupulously faithful to the author's meaning.

Combined with Arthur Waley's talents as a scholar, a linguist and a writer was a devotion and commitment to literature that inspired his vast enterprises. Despite his great modesty about his writing he had total confidence in his own literary judgment and, once he had decided that a work was worth undertaking, neither length nor textual difficulties daunted him. Sir Stanley Unwin recalls that he once asked Waley what his next work would be:

He replied that he would like to translate a novel by Lady Murasaki, *The Tale of Genji*, written in the days of King Canute in early Japanese which a modern Japanese could no more read than could the average Englishman read Anglo-Saxon. He added that it was so long—six volumes in the Japanese edition he was reading—that no publisher could be expected to commit himself to its publication in English. 'Is it a really outstanding work?' I enquired. Waley's quiet reply: 'Oh yes, one of the two or three greatest novels ever written', startled me. 'Well then,' I said, 'we must find a way of doing it'; and there and then our plans were laid to carry through the venture on a basis which kept the risk of loss to reasonable dimensions. I had implicit faith in Waley's judgment, but it was not until he delivered the first volume that I realized what a gem he had brought us.

With his refined sensibility and keen aesthetic understanding Waley was a true Heian gentleman—whence, no doubt, his particular sympathy with that magnificent period in Japanese culture. Literature, especially poetry, was central in his life, as it was for men and women of the Heian Court, not as an academic subject but as a vital, inspiring force. Indeed it may have been his passion for the art of poetry that first impelled him to learn Oriental languages. A few years ago when asked how he came to interest himself in Chinese and Japanese literature (a question that all of us who study these subjects have the pleasure of answering at least fifty times a year) he explained that as a young man he had a devouring interest in poetry, an interest which remained unslaked after he had read most of what was available in the West, and it was this that induced him to study Far Eastern languages.[13] Waley's final wish as he lay dying was to hear for the last time some of the works of literature that had been so important to him while he lived: Donne's 'The Ecstasy', George Herbert's 'The Collar', Fêng Mêng-lung's 'Love-Poem', and finally the magnificent passage about Bull Mountain from Mencius, which was read once more during his quiet burial service in Old Highgate Cemetery.[14]

Without Waley's type of sensibility and enthusiasm great translations from the Oriental classics, or indeed from any literature, are impossible. This point is worth remembering when we contemplate today's profusion of language-literature specialists labouring to fulfil elaborate translation programmes that have been compiled by committees of teachers, editors, and bureaucrats. Waley himself detested the institutional approach to literature and scholarship and had grave doubts about the value of such programmes—doubts that were hardly allayed a few years ago when UNESCO asked him in all seriousness whether he would consider doing *The Tale of Genji* as part of their 'Translation of Representative Works' series. A translation for Waley was a creative work of art and could no more be produced to order than an original poem or novel.[15]

Waley's enthusiasm for the works that excited him was supported by an enviable fund of energy. Between 1916 and 1964 he wrote some forty books, more than eighty articles, and about one hundred book reviews, his books alone totalling over nine thousand pages. His extraordinary power of concentration allowed him to pursue his solitary study of Chinese and Japanese grammar through the Zeppelin raids in the First World War and twenty-five years and one war later, to continue writing in London during the height of the Blitz. 'One must not be dis-

[13] Letter from Mr I. Mansk, 18 March 1968.   [14] See pp. 209, 231–2.
[15] 'Notes on Translation', pp. 162–3.

tracted from good work', he once remarked, 'by forces one cannot influence.' While he was at work, all else was eliminated. Once, when a solicitous charwoman asked whether her Hoover was disturbing him, he smilingly replied, 'I *cannot* be disturbed while I am working'.

His enthusiasm did not wane even in his last years, though inevitably the pace became slower. He continued to read voraciously until the very end; and only a few months before he died, when he was already racked with the agonizing illness that killed him, he was planning a major work on the early history of the Southern Zen school, in preparation for which he made detailed notes about the sources of certain ancient Buddhist verses and wrote an article on the 10th-century Zen book, *Tsu-t'ang chi*. It is the existence of people with Waley's brilliance and vigour that make predictions of increased longevity less depressing than they might otherwise be. We are informed that by the end of this century normal life expectancy (in the event that human life continues at all) will have increased to 120. One cannot help wondering what Waley might have done with an extra forty years of productive life. Perhaps his interests would have expanded westward to include India and the Near East. Already in 1953, in order to translate *The Hymn of the Soul*, he had taught himself Syriac; and, if he had lived, he might have achieved for the literatures of many other countries what he did so magnificently for those of China and Japan.

In the breadth of his interests and knowledge Waley was a Renaissance man. During our conversations I never ceased to be amazed and abashed by the scope of his reading, which included not only all the major classics of world literature but a variety of arcana and obscure writings, both Western and Oriental; and he seemed to remember it all. He wore his vast erudition lightly, even casually. I do not think it ever occurred to him how prodigious his reading was; and in his conversation he often paid one the compliment of assuming that one knew as many books as he.

Waley was firmly rooted in the culture of the West; but his familiarity with foreign literatures and ways of thought led to a broad, catholic approach that William Empson stressed some years ago when he wrote, 'A large capacity to accept the assumptions of any world-view, without assuming any merit for our own, is the basic virtue of Waley's mind'.[16]

Apart from his devotion to literature and art, Waley was extremely musical. During the First World War he became a keen amateur flautist. Dr Yashiro describes the first evening he spent with Waley a few years after the war: 'Nights came late on a summer evening in London, After dinner we went up to the roof. Waley brought out a small piccolo, which he began playing. . . . At that time I came to the private conclusion that he was an extremely interesting Western hermit. . . . It was our common love for music that brought us first together.'[17] During the decades that followed he tried to collect as many simple fluting instruments as he could find, and he learned how to play them all. He had a sound technical knowledge of musical theory and derived deep pleasure from performances of both classical and modern music on the BBC Third Programme; frequently he would leave a gathering and hurry home to be in time for a concert. Apart from a deep understanding of classical ballet, he loved the wild enchantment of the flamenco; with his friend, Beryl de Zoete, he also became absorbed in the beautiful rhythms of Indian and Balinese dancing.

Waley was also a discerning critic; he wrote articles on anthropology, art, archaeology, and many other subjects unrelated to Oriental literature. Among the entries in the bibliography by Mr F. A. Johns are a translation from the Apocalypse, a review of a German study of the Royal Prussian Turfan expedition, a version of Hroswitha's Latin text of *Callimachus* (which was performed in the West End in 1920), an article on the verb 'to say' as an auxiliary in Africa and China, a study on

[16] William Empson, 'Waley's Courtesy', *New Statesman*, 13 March 1964.
[17] Yashiro, *op. cit.*, p. 366.

the magic use of phallic representations, and a couple of charming pieces on skiing.[18] Skiing, in fact, was one of his passions, and he was an adept practitioner, characteristically preferring the more deserted slopes. R. C. Trevalyan's *Epistola Ad A. W.*, written in 1932 (a year before the final volume of *The Tale of Genji*) starts by imploring Arthur Waley not to take any unnecessary risks while gliding down the slopes:

> What wise man of his own free will would linger a fog-bound
> Smoke-breathing prisoner vegetant all winter in London?
> How should I then blame you, after afar to some Austrian highland
> Already hence you are flown, duly armed with needful equipment
> For that dangerous art you love? This alone I entreat you:
> Let not a noble lust for glory, or rash emulation
> Urge you on pathless heights to attempt some desperate exploit
> Of foolhardy peril; since were it not well to remember
> How still half untold is Genji's story? And were aught
> Untoward (which heaven forfend) perchance to befall you,
> Who else lives there endowed with grace and mastery of style,
> Or scholarship befitting the interpreter of Murasaki?
> Nay, who else, friend, save you alone is possessed of the magic
> Charm to unlock the remote treasuries wherein the buried wealth
> Of China's lyric art has lain despised and unheeded
> Age upon age by the proud incurious Muse of the Far West?[19]

He was also a keen cyclist (in earlier days, I am told, he could regularly be seen pedalling along the streets of Bloomsbury wearing a crumpled beret which he ceremoniously doffed to ladies whom he recognized); more recently he liked the sensation of travelling at full speed along the new M.1 motorway.

There was, of course, a good deal that did *not* interest him. This included modern politics: while he enjoyed some of the droller aspects of political life, I think that he regarded most politicians as rogues, and rather unattractive ones at that. Though essentially a-political, he was deeply concerned with the indignities that certain régimes inflict on their victims, and, when I

[18] See pp. 350–1.   [19] R. C. Trevalyan, *Rimeless Numbers*, Hogarth Press, 1932.

informed him about the Amnesty movement for helping prisoners of conscience, he was immediately interested and said he would like to give his support. He loathed the hypocrisy and cruelty of Western incursions like the Opium Wars,[20] and on one occasion remarked that anyone who could be indifferent to these attacks on China would also be indifferent to the atrocities of the Nazis.[21]

Since his early years Waley was absorbed in the classical theatre, and he helped to introduce the Nō drama to the West; but he had little patience with most modern plays ('I don't think one need wait any longer', he was overheard saying as he strode out of the theatre after the first act of *Waiting for Godot*[22]); and on the whole he disliked the cinema. He took almost no interest in games; at school he enjoyed cricket, but not so much for its competitive aspect as for the image of white flannel against new-mown grass and for the crisp sound of bat against ball, which remained in his mind as a symbol of the long summer days of childhood.

He had little interest in travel as such, though he did pay several visits to Paris and Venice, and of course to the slopes of Switzerland, Austria, and Norway. The strangest thing about Waley was his failure to visit China and Japan. I asked him about this, but never received a direct answer. Raymond Mortimer is surely right when he says that Waley 'felt so much at home in T'ang China and Heian Japan that he could not face the modern ugliness amid which one has to seek out the many intact remains of beauty'.[23] He carried his own images of China and Japan within himself and had no wish to dilute them by tourism. Students of the Far East who nowadays seem convinced that periodic visits to the 'field' are an essential part of their work might do well to contemplate the example of Arthur Waley, who never journeyed east of Constantinople. He also declined offers to visit the United States. In reply to an invitation from Columbia University a few years

---

[20] See pp. 372–4. [21] LeFevour, *loc. cit.*
[22] Sir Vere Redman, 'Arthur Waley, The Disembodied Man', *Asahi Evening News*, August 1966.
[23] Mortimer, *loc. cit.*

ago he explained that he was 'invincibly set against *déplacements* of any kind'. Yet until the very end he eagerly sought intellectual *déplacements*.

Arthur Waley's reluctance to undertake long journeys confirmed the picture that many people had of him as being a frail, desiccated recluse (a recent article is typically entitled 'Waley, The Hermit Japonologist'), a man so absorbed in his books that he had become cold, supercilious, inaccessible. Anyone who knew Waley well realizes that this picture is totally false. Far from being frail, he enjoyed unusually robust health: he was skiing well into his sixties, and in his seventies could climb the steep stairs of his house with splendid agility. The doctors and nurses who attended him during his last illness were amazed by his vitality and resilience and by his fantastic endurance of pain. Again and again he rallied after they had given up hope, and he remained perfectly lucid, indeed brilliant, throughout most of his ordeal. Towards the end he displayed remarkable courage by gradually reducing the use of pain-killers. 'The pain', he explained, 'is a small price to pay for being myself. Every moment is precious.'

The only important disability from which Waley suffered is not generally known. In 1910 he lost the sight of his left eye and was informed that, unless he took great care, he was almost certain to go totally blind. Far from being cowed by this prediction, he used it to prove that doctors can often be too gloomy. He was unsparing in the use of his good eye; yet towards the end his vision actually improved. 'They were wrong about my sight', he remarked during his last illness. 'They may be wrong about this also.'

The idea that he was a sort of remote hermit is especially misleading. He had a remarkable capacity for friendship and an exquisite sense of fun. Sir Osbert Sitwell has said that, of all the people he has known, Waley probably had the greatest range of friends, 'extending from dons and savants to spiritualists and members of Parliament. . . .'[24]

[24] See p. 101.

He was able to establish warm, natural relations even in the most unpromising conditions. Mr Kudō Shinichirō, now vice-president of the Mainichi newspaper, recalls that he was a correspondent in London when the Second World War broke out. The authorities decreed that all cables to Japan must be submitted for censorship in English translation; subsequently they relented and agreed to recruit a censor who would read messages in romanized Japanese. Mr Kudō and his colleagues were flabbergasted when this censor turned out to be none other than the renowned scholar, Arthur Waley. What amazed them even more was his affable, considerate attitude under trying circumstances. Owing to the time difference, cables to Japan were frequently not filed before two or three o'clock in the morning; yet Waley never showed the slightest annoyance at being kept up so late, and he was always cheerful and polite to the Japanese correspondents who were ruining his nights. On one occasion, when they gave a party in honour of their censor, he twitted them goodnaturedly with their crude journalese. 'Really, gentlemen, you should polish your language a little', he said. 'I am sure that phrases like "it is regarded" (*to mirareru*) and "according to informed circles" (*kansoku-suji ni yoreba*) are not good Japanese. And you, Mr Kudō, won't you do something about your calligraphy?' At Christmas time the correspondents presented Waley with a lacquered Japanese box and were delighted to receive a letter of thanks written in impeccable stanzas of seven-word lines.[25]

Though unworldly and uncynical, he was a keen observer of human foibles and could be wonderfully witty, delighting in bizarre observations and outrageous comments which he would utter in a clear, high-pitched voice. A few years ago, when asked about Mao Tse-tung's poems, he replied that they were 'better than Hitler's pictures and perhaps not quite so good as Winston Churchill's'.

[25] Kudō Shinichirō, 'Kenetsukan Uērē', *Kokusai Bunka* 147, September 1966, p. 13.

Above all, Waley was very human, very kind. As one acquaintance has written, 'What I remember, even now, is his unstudied and courtly kindliness—it seemed to radiate from him, it was "mandarin" in the best sense of the term'.[26] I recall that on the evening of my final oral examination for the Ph.D. degree at the School of Oriental and African Studies, in which Arthur Waley was to be one of the two examiners, I was sitting at home, contemplating my almost certain *débâcle*, when the telephone rang and I heard Waley's voice (my number was not listed and he must have taken considerable trouble to find it): 'You are probably worrying about tomorrow', he said with his usual laconicism. 'You needn't.' After the ordeal was over, he invited me to join him at the café next to the Russell Square underground station. In my nervousness I knocked over my cup of coffee, spilling the scalding liquid over Arthur Waley's lap. The pain must have been considerable and the damage to his suit irreparable; but he laughed it off, adding some erudite comment about procedures in the examination system during the Ming dynasty.

This experience did not deter him from showing similar consideration to another student some ten years later:

The evening of the day on which I had my doctoral oral I was alone in London and very depressed; I telephoned Waley about something else and did not mention my state of mind. Yet he quickly asked me to come to dinner. When I said I didn't think I would, he insisted. During the dinner and after, he made a successful effort on my behalf. I think he was a kind man; one might almost say soft-hearted.[27]

I confess that, for all Waley's warmth and generosity, he struck me as rather intimidating. This was partly due to the prestige he had in my eyes; for it was his books that had first fired me with the ambition to learn Oriental languages, and he was always an awe-inspiring figure for me. There could also be something rather daunting about his manner. On occasion his usual affability would give way to an air of dignified remoteness, which made one feel

[26] ·I. Mansk, *loc. cit.*   [27] LeFevour, *loc. cit.*

(no doubt correctly) that one was wasting his time. I am sure he was unaware of this himself. The forbidding quality one sometimes found in him came not from any belief in his own superiority —he was the last person to think in such terms—but from the sensitive diffidence of a man who was reserved, fastidious, and, in the true sense of the word, refined. 'He emanated an atmosphere of peacefulness which I have never quite encountered with any other man', Sir Vere Redman has written. 'His voice was firm and always audible, but it was quiet and somehow it imposed its quietness. I myself tended to lower my voice in his presence and I noticed that characters even more aggressive and loud-mouthed than I am did the same. We spoke less loudly and, indeed, we just spoke less, because we found ourselves in his presence asking ourselves if we really had anything to say. He, for his part, never spoke unless he had something to say.'[28]

Waley has often been described as an eccentric: but I think this is inaccurate, for eccentricity usually involves some deliberate defiance of convention, whereas Waley was totally unconcerned with creating any impression. What is true—and this may have reinforced the idea that there was a supercilious streak in him—is that he had a genuine horror of the obvious, resulting in a low tolerance for the banalities of speech and behaviour. His manner of expression was sparse and accurate, and he abhorred all forms of gush. Confronted with flippancy, pretentiousness, or false enthusiasm, he would retire instinctively behind a mask of cool, withdrawn calm. Small talk was anathema to him; and often, I think, he literally did not hear boring remarks. When meeting friends and colleagues, he liked to plunge directly into the conversation that interested them without the usual catechism of preliminaries about health and weather. I remember that, when I first visited him at his house in Highgate Village, it was pouring with rain and I had managed to lose my way several times after emerging from the station. Waley, whom I had not seen for over two years, hurried downstairs to open the door and, totally

[28] Redman, loc. cit.

ignoring my mumbled explanations about being late, started in with 'Have you seen the new edition of *Torikaebaya Monogatari*? The gloss has some extraordinary mistakes.' I am told that when visited one summer day by a loquacious Spanish *littérateur* who had wanted to meet him for years, Waley carefully selected a book for him and said, 'Shall we go into the garden and read? I am sure you will enjoy these poems.'

To a quite remarkable extent he managed to keep aloof from what he regarded as the inessentials of life. Despite his many involvements with people, he had no interest in belonging to groups or institutions. He was part of old Bloomsbury and was friendly with T. S. Eliot and Ezra Pound; but he never joined the 'Bloomsbury set' or the Vorticist movement. He received numerous academic distinctions and knew almost every distinguished Oriental scholar of his day; but he never accepted a regular university post, and he eschewed committees, common-room meetings, and all the time-consuming functions of academe. As an Honorary Lecturer he sometimes gave talks at the School of Oriental and African Studies, and he also conducted occasional seminars; but he disliked the idea of being bound to a regular routine of teaching, especially if the same material had to be covered year after year, and when I said that I had accepted such a job at Columbia University, he sympathetically remarked, 'I suppose you had to'. I am told that when Waley was informally asked whether he might accept the Chair in Chinese at Cambridge University vacated by the death of Professor Haloun, his immediate reaction was a murmured 'I would rather be dead'. Though he was created Companion of the British Empire in 1952 and Companion of Honour in 1956, and was a Queen's Medallist for Poetry, he cared nothing for ranks or awards. He was totally unconcerned with where or how he lived materially; his real world was his study and, though he loved beautiful buildings and rooms, he wanted no ostentation or luxury for himself. Peter Quennell has observed that 'Arthur was no dandy'.[29] Nor was he exactly an epicure. Though he enjoyed good food, he was not prepared to spend much time or trouble acquiring it, and his usual diet was austere. Dr Yashiro describes the first meal to which Waley invited him in 1921: 'Dinner consisted of a dish of vegetables which he had himself cooked, a glass of water, and, for each of us, a raw apple which we ate unpeeled. To be frank, I felt distinctly taken aback by the simplicity of the meal.'[30] So little did Waley care for display that he sometimes gave the impression of being in actual want. When Dr Yashiro again visited his friend in London some twenty years later, he was shocked to find him living in somewhat meagre circumstances; on his return to Japan he suggested raising a pension for the man who had done so much to introduce Oriental culture to the West, and was surprised to hear that such a provision was quite unnecessary.

By refusing to distract himself from the main task, by jealously guarding his energies for what really mattered, Waley was able to produce his vast corpus of work. He himself did not think that his writing would have any effect on English poetry; but it is perhaps still too early to be sure.[31] What is certain is that by his translations and biographies Waley made two major Oriental literatures important for the general reader. Here indeed his influence is not limited to the West; for, as Professor Konishi has written, Waley's biographies have opened the eyes of many readers in Japan to the riches of Li Po, Yüan Mei, and other Chinese poets who until then were often mere names in text-books.[32]

Now that he is dead, one wonders whether anyone will be able to carry on his particular type of work in the field of Far Eastern studies. I am inclined to doubt it. Scholarly work in the

[29] See p. 89.
[30] Yashiro, *op. cit.*, p. 366.
[31] See Peter Quennell, *loc. cit.*, for another opinion.
[32] 'The Li Po and the Yüan Mei that I came to know through Waley were not the same as I had known before, but far closer to me and far clearer. . . . He was able to interpret Chinese culture through his own lucid eyes.' Konishi Jinichi, 'Uērē Sutairu', *Kokusai Bunka* 147, September 1966, p. 20.

West has reached the stage of specialisation at which a general 'Orientalist' like Waley is something of an anachronism; and he recognized the fact himself.[33] Besides, Arthur Waley was a genius with a combination of talents that is unlikely to be repeated.

[33] E.g., see pp. 25 and 143.

A Note on Arthur Waley

by Peter Quennell

My friendship with Arthur Waley began in 1919 several years before we met. At school I was an avid student of the weekly book-reviews; and among them I found an enthusiastic account of a small volume entitled *More Translations from the Chinese*, which I promptly ordered and was soon reading. It added a new dimension to my knowledge of poetry; and, by the time I had reached the last page, I felt almost as familiar with Li Po and Po Chü-i as with Shelley, Wordsworth, Keats and Coleridge. Poems that I remember particularly enjoying were 'The Great Summons'[1] and Po Chü-i's 'The Cranes', which I was astonished to learn had been written about twelve centuries later:

> The western wind has blown but a few days;
> Yet the first leaf already flies from the bough.
> On the drying paths I walk in my thin shoes;
> In the first cold I have donned my quilted coat.
> Through shallow ditches the floods are clearing away;
> Through sparse bamboos trickles a slanting light.
> In the early dusk, down an alley of green moss,
> The garden-boy is leading the cranes home.

No doubt what I chiefly admired at the time was the poem's exquisite pictorial charm; but I was not insensitive to the translator's amazingly skilful management of the English language, and to the deftness with which he dropped his epithets each into the right position. The short preface included an illuminating

[1] See p. 165.

reference to Arthur Waley's personal aims. Speaking of his previous book, *A Hundred and Seventy Chinese Poems*, he observed that no reviewer had treated it 'as an experiment in English unrhymed verse, though this was the aspect . . . which most interested the writer'. Even nowadays few critics pay sufficient attention to Waley's gifts as a purely original poet, whose work has had an important effect upon the other poets of his age. In his verse renderings he developed and perfected an extremely successful type of *vers libre*, much more elastic than ordinary rhymed verse, yet equally harmonious and evocative. His use of the form was never loose or slipshod. Waley was above all else a remarkably exacting craftsman.

It was his exacting taste that first impressed me when we eventually met in London during the year 1925 or 1926. On occasions he would criticise my youthful manuscripts, which certainly required criticism; and no one was better at disentangling some strangely confused and overwritten paragraph. 'Don't you think you should say . . . ' he would enquire in that gentle, unemphatic voice of his; and reluctantly I would agree to sacrifice the superfluous fancy that had cost me so much thought and labour.

He changed little. Towards the end of his life, his shoulders grew bowed, and his general appearance somewhat frail and aged. Otherwise he was scarcely distinguishable from the friend who used to sit with me in Gordon Square, often wearing, if the weather were warm, a pair of old white flannel trousers, to which not long ago I found a slightly caustic reference in one of Virginia Woolf's private notebooks. Arthur was no dandy; nor was he at all moved by the appeal of modern luxury and fashion. The flat he then occupied, though not exactly bleak, was very plainly furnished; and I cannot recollect seeing in his dark, low-ceilinged rooms a single precious or attractive object. I visualise English crockery and homely pots of ink, where I had hoped to find a Japanese sword-hilt, a T'ang figurine, or a venerable Han beaker.

Just as he refused to visit the Far East, despite many urgent invitations—presumably because he did not choose to destroy his visionary images of Japan and China—so all the works of art that he required he carried around with him inside his own brain. Real pictures, drawings, or statues would have been so much expensive and unnecessary luggage. For his deep aestheticism was qualified by a strain of natural puritanism, which he may perhaps have inherited from his devout, hard-working Jewish ancestors, whose name his family had discarded at the beginning of the First World War. When a common friend, Cyril Connolly, met him alone on a Mediterranean island and asked Arthur to lunch with him and his wife at a rather luxurious new hotel, he arrived, like Beatrix Potter's Alderman Ptolemy Tortoise, carrying his own luncheon—a rustic salad he had bought in the market-place, stuffed into a large string bag. At a later period, his most dazzling culinary adventure was his introduction by another helpful acquaintance to a popular brand of 'instant coffee'.

All this puzzled, even at times annoyed me; and yet more puzzling and disconcerting was his habitual unwillingness to talk unless he had something that he really wished to say. Our conversations were interrupted by long, curiously unnerving pauses, while he gazed out into the middle distance, following heaven knows what memorable vision, and allowed the current of vulgar daily life to flow unnoticed past his head. When he talked, he spoke quickly and precisely, often accompanying his words with a brilliant disarming smile; then relapsed once more into thoughtful silence.

His voice I have already mentioned—so faint and high, if he were bored or irritated, that it reached an almost supersonic level. It proceeded from a fine austere mask, the face of a sage or saintly eremite who viewed the ordinary modern newspaper-reading public at a carefully maintained distance. But the mask concealed as much as it revealed—not only sensitive feelings and a warmly affectionate nature, but humour, gaiety, sociability, and an unexpected interest in worldly gossip. Throughout his last years, he was always delighted to receive some entertaining piece of London scandal. He stood a little apart from the so-called 'Bloomsbury set'; but he remained extremely knowledgeable about their feuds and loves and marriages—'Frankie's' unhappy passion for X, 'Roger's' attachment to Mrs Y, or 'Clive's' difficult liaison with Mrs Z.

About his personal life he was exceedingly reserved; and he took as a matter of course his own surprising talents. It seemed never to have occurred to him that there was anything odd in reading a Chinese poem before breakfast, and then going off to spend the day on skis, or deciding to master a new and difficult Far-Eastern dialect at the age of nearly seventy. Nor did he parade his erudition. I remember seeing an amateur of Chinese porcelain hand him an ancient wine-bowl, which had a line of poetry written at the bottom, with the request that he would translate the verse. Arthur glanced at the characters, for a moment meditated, then handed it back, announcing quietly: 'What it says is—"We scoop the glittering moonlight in our cups".' He did not comment on the romantic beauty of the phrase, though, as a poet, he must no doubt have felt it, but preserved his usual air of dignified remoteness and scarcely raised his whispering, reedy voice.

During the penultimate stage of our friendship, Arthur Waley became a fairly regular contributor to an historical magazine that I was editing. Between 1951 and 1956, my co-editor and I published six delightful articles, since republished among his collected essays, *The Fall of Lo-Yang*, *A Chinese Poet in Central Asia*, *Anquetil Duperron and Sir William Jones*, *Life under the Han Dynasty*, *The Heavenly Horses of Ferghana* and *Commodore Anson at Canton*. The first subject was especially well-suited to his peculiar blend of wit and learning. Before depicting the collapse and destruction of a great Chinese metropolis at the beginning of the fourth century, he describes, with gently abrasive humour, the mood of philosophic nihilism that then prevailed at the cultured Chinese Court, where thinkers, while the Hunnish armies surrounded their walls, practised an esoteric 'cult of Non-Being' that absolved the truly civilised man from confronting any unpleasant problem or making any violent effort.

Arthur Waley was as much at his ease in prose as he was in modern verse. When I visited Japan, and spent some uncomfortable months teaching English literature at a Tokyo university, my students told me that they much preferred Mr Waley's version of *The Tale of Genji* to Lady Murasaki's obscure and archaic text. Here again, in his rendering of Murasaki, his enchanting sense of fun plays delicately across the narrative; and the same humour also appears in his admirable biography of the 18th-century poet and literary hedonist Yüan Mei. No-one could have been less of a hedonist than the translator himself; but, having a deeply sympathetic turn of mind, he was able to understand and reproduce even emotions that he failed to share. Arthur Waley was not merely a distinguished scholar who happened to become a gifted artist. He was first and foremost a creative artist who amid the laborious data of scholarship unearthed the raw materials that his talent needed.

A Few Waleyesque Remarks

by Walter Simon

Most of the remarks listed below show the touch of 'finality' so characteristic of Arthur Waley's. utterances. One or two others have been included to pay tribute to the amazing discipline he used to impose on himself.

I

Translation figured prominently at one of the Conferences of British Orientalists, conscientiously attended by Waley. Referring to a member of the Conference who was most anxious that translation of Oriental Literature should be discussed at length, Waley remarked to me before the beginning of the Conference, 'Actually he is not so much interested in translation. He is after edification.'

At the meeting itself, mistakes in translating from Chinese were deplored and gone into at some length. Conscious of the difficulty of the language, one member suggested in the discussion that translations of selected passages should be listed in chronological order to illustrate how progress was made step by step in establishing the meaning of the original. This was too much for Waley. 'Would it not be better still to translate it right?' he exclaimed, thereby bringing the discussion to an abrupt end.

II

At a meeting held at University College Waley read out (in his usual extremely masculine way of reciting) part of his translation of the Ainu epic. In the ensuing discussion one member remarked it could clearly be seen how much the Ainus really loved the bear they were going to kill and that they did so with utter reluctance. 'They killed many more Ainus than bears', was Waley's short retort.

III

Once I expressed surprise that certain scholarly matter was treated in a rather amateurish way. 'Yes, I know,' said Waley, 'most of the literature on this subject is written by former officers or civil servants. But as they retire at forty-five and live on until they are ninety, it is still quite a lot.'

IV

'Have you read so and so's lecture?' I called out to him when our ways crossed in the vicinity of the School of Oriental and African Studies. 'Tell me the greatest atrocity', he called back. Moving over to his side, I was able to oblige.

V

The discipline Waley imposed on himself never ceased to astound me. Was it not difficult for him to keep office hours when working in the British Museum, I asked him one day. 'Not in the least', was his prompt reply.

One might have expected him to relax after the enormous output in the mid-thirties. At that time we used to meet for lunch on alternate Saturdays. Waley, suggesting 1:30 as the best time, explained, 'You see, I would like to put in a full morning's work.'

VI

Though not standing a fool gladly, Waley would sit patiently through lectures and discussions which he considered his duty to attend. Expecting him to be thoroughly bored, I suggested that he should skip a lecture or two. He emphatically refused. 'I might bring up a point that has already been discussed at a previous meeting.'

Why did he resign from such and such society. 'They did not want me to go off the Council, so that was the only way', he explained.

Extract from *Some English Eccentrics*

by Edith Sitwell

Mr Waley is unconquerable. I remember, for instance, the day when he was expected for the week-end at my brother Sacheverell's house in the country, and my sister-in-law and I, finding in the library a small and ancient book in an unknown tongue, placed it beside Mr Waley's bed in the hope that he would confess himself defeated. Next morning, Mr Waley looked a little pale; his manner was languid, but as he placed the book on the breakfast table he announced in a faint voice: 'Turkish. 18th century.' The pages were few; and after an interval of respect we enquired: 'What is it about?' Mr Waley, with sudden animation: 'The Cat and the Bat. The Cat sat on the Mat. The Cat ate the Rat.' 'Oh, it is a child's book.' 'One would imagine so. One would *hope* so!' . . .

1950

Letter from Edith Sitwell to Arthur Waley

Renishaw Hall
Renishaw
near Sheffield

My dear Arthur,

I need not say with what excitement and delight I received *Monkey*. Thank you so much. It is wonderful to have it. What a

3. *At Locker's Park Preparatory School. Arthur Waley,*
vice captain of the cricket team, in 1903

4. *Aged seventeen, after his return from a year at Tours to take up his scholarship at King's College, Cambridge*

lovely and strange work it is. The whole time it is like a dream turning real, and like reality turning into a dream. The *sound* is so strange, too, with the occasional quickening of the involvement, like something whirling round, and the occasional chattering noises. Like the old ladies who say, 'I can't think how you *think* of the things', I will say, 'I can't think how you get that exact fusion of meaning and language, the *clearness* of the language (clearness is the only word I can think of, but it does not express quite what I mean: I was trying to say absence of shadow, like the clearness and directness in Monkey's mind) is very beautiful. The very sound makes one see Dear Monkey on his cloud-trapeze. I feel it is a masterpiece of right sound.'

Really, Arthur, more and more—if such a thing were possible—do I feel what a miraculous art you have. I do *not* know of any work which so abolishes the horrors of time and wretched material worries, as these works of yours. To me, 'Hatsuyuki'[1] is the most wonderful abstract beauty I know. Absolutely incredible. I *can't* dream how you do it. That is only an example.

I don't really *know Monkey* yet, of course. But it has given me that sense of inevitability, of excitement with peace, that your work always does give me. One comes back to ordinary life (when one has to) feeling at peace. . . .

Yours ever,
Edith

How strange it is to come back from *Monkey* and realize how hideous people are making the world. Oh how sad it is, when people like you *might* be left in peace to give one beauty and clearness like this!

1942

[1] *The Nō Plays of Japan*, pp. 244–7.

Weston Hall
Towcester
Northamptonshire
11th April 1968

Dear Ivan,

In case my memories—one or two out of many—may be of interest:

The first time I ever stayed in this house, formally invited by Edith, 'Dear Miss Doble', I arrived to find my fellow guests were Willie Walton, Gerald Berners[1] and Arthur Waley. Edith at once put me at my ease by saying, 'I understand that my brother Sachie loves you and so I know I will love you too'. We never 'looked back' on that, in all the years—our friendship grew and intensified from day to month.

But on this occasion I was not quite 19 and alarmed though fascinated by the company. I had been brought up to try and be a social asset so, when Willie Walton said the only way for a musician to make money would be to write a musical comedy, and as Dr Waley seemed to be left out of the conversation I turned to him and said, 'Don't you think this could be fun?' He looked away and just said, 'No' in that remote tone I learned to love as well as to respect.

Two years later, not long before my elder son was born, he and Beryl de Zoete joined us in Rome. My appetite was voracious and it infuriated me that Beryl and Arthur would merely share, *with us*, a dish of spaghetti, not 'Bolognese' because she was a vegetarian. Sachie insisted on my downing large helpings of veal. One day they were all looking for a Bernini tomb, Beryl heading the way into church after church, Arthur absently but almost humbly following. I, by a fine stroke of intuition, was the first to find it: I gave a yell of 'Here it is!' Beryl said that tomb is

---

[1] Sir William Walton, the composer, and Lord Berners, the author, painter, and musician.

98

much later in date and then Arthur just grasped my hand and said 'Let's have a rest'.

I bought a 17th-century screen in Tokyo in 1959. It depicts scenes from the life of Genji (as they nearly all do, I know) but it hangs over my bed and with the greatest affection I constantly remember Arthur looking at it and never pretending that he approved of my purchase.

Yours sincerely

Georgia Sitwell

Extract from *Noble Essences*

by Sir Osbert Sitwell

No more is man to labour for a vision—even if it be only the base vision of great personal wealth—but instead, merely for the day's food: for the new barbarism decrees an equal share of misery, ugliness, hebetude, shame, and ultimately of nihility, for each and all.

To the ant, the individual is the enemy. But it is precisely in individuality that Western Europe has excelled. Not for use of the Occident the schools of poets and painters, almost indistinguishable one from another in style, and continuing for millenniums: our works of art are sharply differentiated and defined. In our countries—the imaginative greatness of which was built, as was that of Greece, from happy and illustrious combinations of sea with land—even this age, which threatens to end so catastrophically, has been endowed with genius in abundance, though Everyman, now so opprobriously termed Little or Common Man, has failed to respect it or to pay attention. Yet, even apart from its productions, the spectacle of genius or of exceptional talent or personality, of lives spent happily or unhappily in the service of an ideal, and of the application of the rare, yet essential, *common sense* of art towards life may possess its own practical, no less than moral or semihistorical, value.

To indicate, in its ordinary yet highest range of poetry, the sort of common sense I strive to indicate, let us consider an anecdote; what might be termed—except that it is true—the Fable of Arthur Waley and the Frog. We must picture that remarkable poet and scholar sitting, very alert under an aloof and impassive manner, at a semiscientific, semipsychic meeting organized by the late Dr Harry Price—another friend of his; for Arthur Waley has perhaps the greatest range of friendship of any person I know, extending from dons and savants to spiritualists and members of Parliament, from his own kind, poets, painters, musicians, to those who practise their obsolete Eskimo tricks in winter on the topmost slopes of mountains. The hall was crowded with an enthusiastic audience. While everywhere Science was engaged in such feats of imaginative charity as cutting off a dog's head, and keeping that part of it alive in a saucer for weeks or even months, the brain still functioning, Superstition, her illegitimate sister, was, to the contrary, here occupied in the more harmless task of trying to make a frog go to sleep or fall into a trance. Up on the platform, a celebrated expert in hypnotism and paranormal manifestations faced a frog, clammily palpitating, which had been carried hither on a tray by an attendant, and then set on a table. The Professor first made a few perfunctory passes over the creature with his hands, in order to lull it, and then continued his work with an air of more busy concentration. The frog perhaps felt dizzy, and closed his eyes. In any case, he appeared soon to become too frightened to stir. The Professor then quickly popped over his motionless victim a tightly fitting bell-glass, and continued to wave his hands soothingly above it. After a time, all movement ceased within the cover, and the learned hypnotist stopped his antics and announced:

'You will observe, ladies and gentlemen, that the frog has now ceased to breathe.'

Everyone seemed immensely impressed by this evidence of the Professor's psychic powers—everyone, that is, except Arthur Waley, who, without anger, but with decision, spoke up, or snapped out rapidly the words:

'Naturally, it can't breathe, poor little beast, when it's under a glass case! You couldn't, could you? If you'd give it some air, it would soon be able to breathe all right!'

This clinical view, so typical of the speaker and of an artist, upset the audience. The initial uneasy silence was later broken by a good deal of hissing directed at the interloper. The Professor, though at first he had seemed rather stunned, soon roused himself and, in his turn, glared down at his challenger. He thus regarded him for several seconds. Then, perhaps at a loss what to reply, he made a slip. In order to show how foolish and unwarrantable the interruption had been, he unwisely lifted the cover. The frog, who could first be seen to breathe deeply, thereupon took a flying leap into the audience, and landed in the lap of an elaborately dressed lady in the second row. The meeting thereupon ended in uproar and confusion. . . .

1950

Extract from *Left Hand, Right Hand!*

by Sir Osbert Sitwell

The other incident took place some time in the insouciant twenties of this century. Our dear friend Arthur Waley was staying with us at Renishaw, and my father very much admired his translations of Chinese poetry. My father's manners were later in period than himself—about the time of Charles II, but with a touch, too, of the Meredithian baronet, Sir Willoughby Patterne or Sir Austin Feverel, clinging to them; or again they might belong to the eighteenth century, as seen through the pale amber spectacles of one of his favourite artists, once so famous and now so greatly neglected, Orchardson. But formal, exquisite, and elaborate though they were, they could scarcely be more beautiful than Arthur Waley's. Upon a Sunday morning, then, my father was walking round the lake which he had caused to be created, regretting that he had not moved the old river bed further back, and thinking out possible fantasies in stone, torrents to fall through the hanging woods above, pavilions upon islands and decorative effects generally (a few years before, he had determined to have all the white cows in the park stencilled with a blue Chinese pattern, but the animals were so obdurate and perverse as in the end to oblige him to abandon the scheme). The lake is shaped like an hourglass or a figure-of-eight, and a bridge spans its waist. On this bridge my father met Arthur Waley advancing towards him. Each took his hat off ceremoniously and said to the other, 'How much I wish we were going in the same direction!' and passed on. Half an hour later they met again at the same place, having pursued their contrary courses as though they were planets whose goings and comings are immutably fixed by the sun, and repeated the salutation. . . .

1940

Reminiscences of
Arthur Waley

by Sacheverell Sitwell

Arthur Waley had the most universal appreciation and intelligence of anyone I have known. It extended to writings in most languages under the sun from Ainu to Portuguese; to music especially; and of course to painting, architecture, and the other arts. But poetry was his especial love, and his genius lay in that field of creation. Also, he was a student of human nature on which he exercised both his affectionate curiosity and sharpened and whittled down his very particular brand of stark and abbreviated humour. My sister used to say that talking to him was like being asked at school to 'state in the fewest possible words your knowledge and opinion of . . .' whatever it may have been.

My memories of him go back to the day I and my brother met him at luncheon at Maresco Pearce's house in Chelsea in May or June of 1917. The war was at its worst: I was nineteen years old and in the army, and I think he had just published his translations of Chinese poems and the Noh plays from the Japanese. I remember the splendid Breton landscape by Gauguin in the house; and I can see Arthur standing in the street outside in the sunlight as we walked away. From that day we saw him continually and he became a dear friend. I do not think he ever changed much physically. His fine intellectual features had always the stamp of youth on them.

Having been ill for five months, been operated on, and still finding it difficult to hold a pen, I hope to be forgiven for assembling other reminiscences in the form of stray memories which will inevitably lack context and coordination. I hope, though, that they will present his unique character, for there will never be another like him. I remember staying at Girgenti in Sicily while he was there, when the almond trees were in blossom—it must have been February—and climbing over the Greek temples in his company. And in about the same year, being in Rome with him and spending a couple of days visiting every building and fountain and tomb by Bernini, and also going to Caprarola and admiring that wonderful terrace with its faun caryatids looking out towards Soracte. It is a beautiful memory of the long distant past—for I think this was in 1926 or 1927. Also, in a different vein, going with him to the theatre to see Fred and Adele Astaire dance the Charleston, and of course meeting him on numberless evenings at the Russian Ballet.

His great learning and his silences intimidated some persons. A woman neighbour of ours was so frightened that she had recurrent nightmares of meeting him. She need not have worried. He was kindness itself beneath that. I remember Mrs Ada Leverson asking him if he liked *The Mikado* (Gilbert and Sullivan). It was unfortunate. Another day, carried away on a wave of nerves, someone asked him if he had read *The Wallet of Kai Lung*. Knowing and loving him as I did, I would sometimes feel shy in his presence and would prattle on about the 17th and 18th centuries, when I felt I should not have embarked on anything subsequent to the 10th century at latest. Luckily there were always Bach and Scarlatti to redeem such trivialities.

How unique and extraordinary he was! He would ask a friend of ours to come to tea 'and bring a book', and they would sit through the summer afternoon in the garden of Gordon Square without speaking a word. At one time there was something in his metabolism which prevented any alcohol going to his head. He had treatment for this, and I remember going with him to a party the first time it took effect. He seemed as insouciant as ever.

How funny it must have been when he was driving back from the country with a woman friend when the car broke down and the garage proprietor would only leave his business and attend to them if Arthur stayed at the petrol pump and served his customers! But, then, we must not forget that other or double side of his life which was his skill at winter sports and love of skiing.

He re-created one of the masterpieces of world literature with his translation of *The Tale of Genji*, and his translations from the Chinese enlarged and added new beauties to poetry. In all humility I can never thank him or Beryl de Zoete enough for being two of the handful of admirers of my own poems. In conclusion I have sometimes wondered what would have happened could he have appeared in person in 10th century Kyoto and met Lady Murasaki. It is of course doubtful if he would ever have been allowed to see her. They might have talked from behind a screen. Visibility, so to speak, was poor compared to that allowed the four foreign princes of the Rose Adagio in that other and equally rarefied world of Tchaikowsky's *Sleeping Beauty*. Certainly, had she been allowed to see him, the good looks and intellectual features of this foreign prince among literati and creators and transmitters of poetry would have appealed to Lady Murasaki. But she would have been disappointed by his handwriting, and this could have impeded their friendship.

Reaching Out

by Michael Sullivan

Forty-five years ago Arthur Waley published his *Introduction to the Study of Chinese Painting*, which, with his catalogue of the Stein paintings in the British Museum and New Delhi,[1] was his major contribution to the study of Chinese art. The *Introduction* was written at a time when knowledge of Chinese painting in the West was in its infancy. It gives a very incomplete picture of the subject; it has been called, not entirely unfairly, anecdotal; and it is poorly illustrated. But I should like to write about it, partly because it is in many ways a brilliant book, but even more because I cannot read it without hearing the voice of Waley himself.

It was commonly said that Waley was not really interested in Chinese paintings at all, but only in their inscriptions; and the story was told that one day, hearing that there was an interesting picture at a London dealer's, he bicycled over from Gordon Square, went in and marched up to the picture, read the inscription, and marched out without a word. More probably one glance had told him that the inscription was the only interesting thing about it. In those days one practically never saw a good Chinese painting in London. Waley had a good eye, and he would certainly have spotted a picture of any quality.

At the time when Roger Fry was still obsessed with Clive Bell's doctrine of significant form, Waley showed him some reproductions of Chinese paintings—I think he said they were Zen—and suggested to him that they could not be understood simply in terms of pure form. Fry said this was impossible. But next

[1] *A Study of Paintings Recovered from Tun-huang by Sir Aurel Stein*, London, 1931.

108

time he saw Waley he admitted that 'there might be something in it'. Certainly in his essay on Chinese art in the book put out by Batsford at the time of the Burlington House Exhibition in 1935–36, Fry has retreated from his extreme position of the 'twenties, and this must have been to some extent due to Waley's influence. Perhaps the traffic wasn't all one way, and Waley could not but have felt the impact of Fry's own enthusiasms. Surely it was under Fry's influence that he ended the Preliminary to his *Introduction* with this sentence: 'Never at any moment', he wrote, 'has so great a formal beauty been achieved in Chinese painting [so far, he adds in a cautious footnote, as it is at present known to us] as is seen in the works of such artists as Piero della Francesca, Chardin, or Cézanne.'

It was to prepare himself to compile the catalogue of the Far Eastern paintings in the British Museum that Waley began to teach himself Chinese and Japanese almost as soon as he joined the staff of the Print Room under Laurence Binyon in 1913; and it was partly, he told me, to avoid having to write it that he finally left the Museum in 1930. He saw that the paintings were nearly all second-rate at best, and an honest assessment of them would only have caused embarrassment. But his years at the Museum were productive in other ways. He published, chiefly in the *Burlington*, more than a dozen articles on Chinese paintings in London and on more general problems, including a series of seven on Chinese aesthetics, the result of his extensive reading in the early literature. As a preparation for the catalogue he never wrote, he published *An Index of Chinese Artists* (1922), and in the following year the *Introduction*. The latter was not the first of its kind. Giles, Hirth, Fenollosa, Petrucci, Fergusson and Laurence Binyon had all written surveys of one sort or another; but none of their books, except possibly Binyon's, is remembered to-day except by specialists, and Binyon not so much because the picture he gave was a true one as because he wrote beautifully about the Southern Sung romantics whom everyone admired.

Of course Waley's book has its limitations. When he wrote it, he had hardly seen a single Chinese painting of any quality. He was never in the Far East, and never saw the important collections then being formed in America, notably at the Freer and the Boston Museum of Fine Arts. Nearly all the material accessible to him came from undistinguished London collections, or from reproductions in Japanese periodicals such as *The Kokka*. Fenollosa and Binyon had been deeply influenced by Japanese connoisseurship. To them the greatest moment in Chinese painting had come in the late 12th and early 13th century, when Ma Yüan and Hsia Kuei were delighting the Sung court in Hangchow with their dreamy landscapes, and Mu-ch'i and Liang K'ai were practising their Zen eccentricities in the Liu-t'ung temple across the lake. A first glance at Waley's book might suggest that he took the same view; for practically the whole of it deals with painting up to the end of Southern Sung, the last seven centuries being summarised in one chapter called 'The Yüan and After'.

But a closer look at the text gives a rather different picture. The revered Ma Yüan and Hsia Kuei he dismisses in little over a page, and of the only two Chinese authors he quotes about them, one is uncomplimentary and the other positively insulting. In the intellectual milieu in which Waley lived it was fashionable to upset traditional views; but more than that, he simply did not find the Southern Sung romantics interesting, partly because their compositions and their sentiments were conventional, partly because they were ignored by Chinese historians and scholars, and there was nothing one could say about them as individuals.

Although Waley lumped all post-Sung painters together in the final chapter, and he ends on a note of pessimism (the Chinese artistic renaissance had then barely begun), nowhere does he suggest, as have some other writers, that the last seven centuries have been a period of long slow decline from the pinnacle of the 12th century. He has some pertinent things to say about the literary men's painting, and was the first Western writer to see the importance of that formidable critic Tung Ch'i-ch'ang, about whom he wrote at length and whose influence he considered to have been disastrous. Today the pendulum has of course swung the other way. The post-1949 discovery of the literary school by Western writers has made Waley's censure seem excessive. If he had seen any of Tung Ch'i-ch'ang's dry, intellectually austere paintings, so like one side of his own character, he might have modified his view of him. For he was by no means hostile to the literary school itself. He ends his last chapter with a moving account of the work of the morose Kung Hsien, whose pictures he knew in Japanese reproductions, and he draws attention to a painting by Wang Yüan-ch'i in the Eumorfopoulos collection, which he found interesting. It was twenty years before any other Western writer, except Sirén, came to share his view. He even finds room—admittedly in the chapter on Zen—for the three great 17th-century individualists, Shih-t'ao, Chu Ta and Shih-ch'i, who were then quite unknown in Europe.

Certainly if Waley had seen more good pictures by the scholarly amateurs of the Ming and Ch'ing he would have revised his opinion of them, and he would have revelled in the later eccentrics. For in his own intellectual circle the idea that literature and the arts were means of communication between members of an élite was taken for granted, and this was precisely the rôle they fulfilled among the Chinese gentry. One can easily imagine what the biographer of Po Chü-i and Yüan Mei would have made of Shen Chou, T'ang Yin, or Shao Mi. But by the time their pictures could, rarely, be seen in England, Waley's attention was directed wholly to literature.

I have written at some length about the *Introduction* for several reasons. Appearing when it did, it was a very original book. Other Western writers had drawn upon Chinese sources before Waley, but he used them much more critically, separating the sense from the nonsense with great skill and wit. In some ways this was just the sort of book that a Chinese scholar might have written. If it is anecdotal, the literature of Chinese painting consists very largely of stories about the personal lives of painters.

Like a Chinese scholar, Waley draws heavily upon the writings of earlier scholars, and is interested above all in ideas and men, treating the work of art not, as the Japanese do, as an almost sacred thing-in-itself, but as the visible extension of a personality or the expression of an idea. The *Introduction* is a triumph of rigorous scholarship and imaginative sympathy.

It is astonishing that Waley's insight into the Chinese attitude to art came entirely from his own reading, and that he was never able to look at Chinese paintings in Chinese company, never passed the hours unrolling scrolls and drinking tea, while the conversation roamed in apparently haphazard fashion over pictures and painters, seals and colophons, and gossip about friends and more trivial matters. But it is all in his book, because Waley was not writing about an alien culture at all. The importance of friends, the rather rarefied standards, the delicate perception, the predominantly literary taste of the Chinese amateur, were all very much part of Waley himself. He had, in many ways, a very Chinese mind. It was also a courageous book to write at that time. Waley says almost nothing that would appeal to readers brought up on Ch'ing porcelain and the writings of Fenollosa and Binyon, and is severe about the only kind of painting they liked. But he was always fearless. He told us how as a boy he used to career across Wimbledon Common on a bicycle towed by a kite, till this dangerous sport was forbidden by his parents; and at the end of his life, he faced with an almost Chinese stoicism the pain of his last months, made the harder to bear by the quite erroneous conviction that grew upon him, from the small sales of his *Ballads and Stories from Tun-huang*, that no one was reading his books any longer, and he was forgotten.

Among memories of him is one of a summer afternoon in Gordon Square with Beryl de Zoete. We sat on the grass, Waley with his arm in a sling. He had come back from a skiing holiday, the floor of his flat was polished like a mirror, and he had slipped and broken his right wrist. Around us the houses were coming down, or being devoured piecemeal by the University: the

Strachey sisters had just had to move from the square to make way for the Computer Centre, and Waley himself was about to leave his own flat, decorated with Vanessa Bell's faded paintings, for Highgate. He talked about how Sydney Cockerell had introduced him to Turner's drawings when he was seventeen, about Roger Fry's lectures and the Omega Workshop, and remarked that Virginia Woolf's life of Fry was a failure because she wasn't interested in painting anyway and didn't understand what he was driving at. 'Virginia' he said 'never should have done it.'

No one who knew him could forget the way he spoke. One remark I particularly treasure. My wife had been ill for a long time, and he often asked about her. I told him that I had been reading his Po Chü-i to her and that she had said that one last line moved her especially, and she thought it better in his English than in the original. 'What Khoan really means', he said, in that high, thin, rather fastidious voice, 'is that I mistranslated it.' The day after Beryl died he came and spent an evening with us. He talked about her for hours, and told us how he had read his Chinese poems to her night after night till, he said, only her eyes showed that she still understood.

To read the *Introduction* again is to hear him talk, to enjoy the intensity of his conversation when his mind was engaged, his abrupt switching-off when it was not. In company his silences could be rather awful, and could overwhelm a group of quite formidable people at the dinner table. But when he talked, the conversation, which he dominated quite unconsciously, roamed over literature and ideas, art and people, in much the same proportion as it does in the *Introduction*, and he expressed himself with the same grace, simplicity and wit. For such an austerely honest man, he was wonderful company.

Letter from Alison Waley to Ivan Morris

Sent

Upper Engadine, Switzerland

3rd March 1967

Dear Ivan Morris,

Herewith, pages. About Arthur.

The circumstances of our first meeting, in the spring of 1929, were bizarre enough, I realized later, to delight him—and our conversation ran thus:

He: What do you want to do?

I: Write short stories.

He: So do I. Do you write poetry?

I: Of course. Everybody does, surely?

He: What sort of poetry do you like?

I: Well . . . it used to be all, or nearly. But now it's spoilt a bit.

He: What DO you mean?

I: Well, I got hold of a book—scarcely even that—called *Poems from the Chinese*. Translations. Part of a series. Published by Benn. I got not only it but all the poets—Binyon, de la Mare, Blunden, everybody—but *The Chinese* is the only one I brought twelve thousand miles. It's somehow made other kinds of poetry just . . . dull.

He: Who's the translator?

I: Waley, I think. Yes, Arthur Waley. Do you know him?

He: Yes.

I: Oh, how lucky you are—you know everyone!

He: I . . . don't know him very well.

And indeed, how true that constantly proved to be.

What a presumption is any assertion in relation to any human being, however loved, however 'known'. Even as I turn my mind towards the task of 'saying', I hear him shuffling his papers with irritation. 'Very well, very well . . . but you're bound to get it all wrong. You *know* that.'

'Yes, I know that.'

And then, in sudden change: 'Anything you say . . . will be right.'

Living with Arthur Waley convinced me of many things, of which perhaps the most interesting, in its way, is that genius is not the 'art of taking pains'.

How one's Victorian elders—mine, as his, and though we were reared a world apart—enjoyed telling us so: a smug complacent dictum calculated, one supposes, to spur growing things to further effort, with no truth in it whatever. For genius, I suspected (for I was, even as a child, one for what is called heredity) and now know, is a matter of genes. The 'genius' is set at birth, or at a point before; and what life does with it—or, for that matter, it with life—is the issue.

Arthur Waley, it was assumed by his family (he being somewhat odd and 'retreated') was a child prodigy; it was decided, in music. This partly, no doubt, because of his faultless and fastidious 'ear', partly (for family findings have often an element of great non-sense) because he had been christened 'Arthur'—after an uncle (who was a minor composer) who disappeared to America (as so often happened) and was 'not spoken of' (again, as so often happened).

What more intriguing knowledge for a highly impressionable child to glean than that he 'took after' the Black Sheep, the Mysterious; more, the 'Unmentionable'. At the end of his life he yet had—and even I had acquired—a soft spot for Uncle Arthur. However, this man who died, it is understood, at thirty or thereabouts had less influence perhaps on the small Arthur than this name—this prince of heroic legend—which he deplored to the end: 'It really is the *worst* name.' For in those turn-of-the-century days this name lit with an incandescent light a fabled country of the mind: a country fraught with challenge, terrors, pitfalls, and betrayals; demanding superhuman qualities of courage, tenacity, and the single heart. (He was, as Fate decreed, to need all three.) And, presenting a reality, as it did, to sensitive children, it was to others an opportunity for childish sadism: for derision, jeers, and the cruel verbal jousting that goes on in every preparatory school.

Arthur—romantic, timid, diffident—went to boarding school 'too early.' This was 'to make a man of him', and because he was his mother's favourite—for Victorian England did not countenance distinctions of the sort. How deep this relationship went may be measured perhaps by the simple fact that, in our re-reading of Proust some months before he died, Arthur suddenly broke down and begged me not to continue.

It would seem that the small boy early learned to make escape from the humdrum and repetitive into a world of fantasy, and the joys and terrors he thus experienced are not for us, nor even for him, to regret. They gave us neither the noble knight nor the recalcitrant musician but one, poet and scholar, who was to throw open to our Western minds a whole new landscape of thinking and behaviour, of fidelity and betrayal, of beauty and perception.

His 'eccentricity', I think, was no more than preoccupation, intellectual or sensual, which would be at all times total. To intrude upon it brought forth either a blank, unseeing gaze or, if one persisted, a remark startling in its simplicity and springing direct from an intricate defence mechanism. So, at a preview of pictures, when a highly important lady approached him with 'And now, Dr Waley, tell us, which are *your* favourites?' the response was an instant nervous cry, pitched on that curious high note which sometimes, but by no means always, was his voice (I dubbed it his ceramic voice): 'I like only the famous ones!'

Time and again such responses, quenching and dire as they were in their effect, were interpreted (quite wrongly, for they sprang from a social shyness that, except among the few, was always with him) as cruel shafts calculated to devastate. Only when he was deeply angry did he 'use' his wit, but then he wielded it with the accuracy—and the detachment—of a headsman. I know there *are* heads worn a little aslant to this day. When any one of these incidents was recalled in his hearing, he was always astonished and hastened to dissociate himself: 'I am sure that is apocryphal', he would murmur.

Am I right in believing he accepted the idea of some kind of Destiny? This is the sort of question that it would have been useless to put to him—indeed, it would have been, like all philosophic inquiries, received with no small degree of impatience, for it falls into a category that requires 'rigid' thinking, and his mental processes were essentially as open and unconfined as the universe.

This fact showed itself also in his feeling about poetry. He had—as I (both being shamelessly romantic)—little use for the cerebral, 'scientific' poets of the thirties and none at all for the wordsmiths. Poetry for him was really a form of music and, commensurately, the 'colour' that music is. To have a perfect phrase bent, as it were crippled, into shape for the purposes of metre or rhyming plan repelled him and it was with difficulty that he could be persuaded to give attention even to the classics for this reason. Shakespeare, on the other hand, with its caesura, was excepted; and the sonnets were always at hand.

He had an 'unlust' for the pretentious and the effortful. It has been said that Edith Sitwell once assured the world that her friend Arthur Waley 'understood' her earlier poems. I think 'understood' would have irritated Arthur as quite irrelevant and indeed untrue if referring to meaning. He 'accepted' them with enormous pleasure for the music that they were. But to him any conscious analysis would have constituted an outrage, like an analysis of the emotion of love.

He delighted in the work of Dylan Thomas (except in those poems where Dylan is experimenting with postures), for here two poets met within the enchantment of the observed world:

each object detailed, outlined with wonder. *Under Milk Wood* was an unwearying feast. Some of his poems, however, simple though they seemed, Arthur pushed aside with 'I like to know what things *mean*. Do you know what this means?'

' "Friend my enemy I call you out. . . ." Yes, indeed.'

'Well, don't bother to tell me—I don't want to know.' Then, 'How can you *prove* he means what you think?'

'I don't want to prove. I know, is enough. And one knows Dylan.'

For himself, he could be persuaded to translate nothing, not one line, that did not excite, grip, and haunt his imagination. How often, even in the last years, he was 'haunted day and night' by the feeling that he must put a story, a poem, or even merely a phrase into his own language, the 'restlessness and fret' never subsiding until this was done. I have known him fly to Paris, to sources surer than were available in England, for the meaning of a single word. Perhaps only so are masterpieces made. And in the February of 1966—the month of the car accident that crumpled his spine (already, as was discovered, affected by cancer of an upper vertebra) and paralyzed him from the breast down— he was working every moment of eight hours a day on something new: each morning researching at the library of the School of Oriental and African Studies. 'It will be as long as *Genji*', he confided, eyes shining.

He could not know, nor could I, how little time lay before him, and he ignored completely his physical predicament. One morning I returned home to find he had instructed the nurse to wheel his bed alongside the table where, still, his papers were spread and he had, with her help, sorted them to some extent. I had said I meant to get a bed-table that would tilt and swing across and could be adjusted to any height. 'Are you sure', he said now, 'that it will be firm enough to hold my typewriter?' I asked him if I should cancel our hotel rooms for April in Rome. 'Wait a little. They may still be useful.'

Most felicitous for him were the simply stated emotions of unsophisticated peoples. These, cut to the bare bone for reticence, deeply fatalistic, were the natural and spontaneous expression of persons who suffered desolation, despair, joy, hope, love to the degree that he himself suffered these. And enchantment would catch at him strangely. Not long before he died he came to me lost in the 'sheer poetry' of a children's jingle:

> The wind, the wind, the wind blows high.
> The snow is falling from the sky.
> Maisie Drummond says she'll die
> For want of the Golden City. . . .

'Perfect, isn't it? Perfect.' For him there was always the Golden City: now real, now vanishing, but more than real at the moment of his death. It was, strangely, as though he had always known it would be so.

In music, indeed, he was lost far, far beyond my reach. I could only race the little car—how often!—back from Box Hill, from Hatfield, Epping Forest, or the West lest we should lose a single note of Bach, Handel, Haydn, of Beethoven, Stravinsky, Fauré. And as we sped, hood down and against the wind, I would sing a melody from one of the sonatas or symphonies or preludes and he would break in with its complex orchestration, whistled exact and clear as a bird.

How often, also, we would race home to watch, from the high windows of the house we found and bought in the same hour, the lights of London break into coloured constellations far below, giving our names to these—Montmartre, the Bay of Naples, Ankara, Excalibur, Sodome et Gomorrhe.

Feeling, himself, as he did so deeply, he had a rare and exquisite awareness of feeling in others. I never knew him to intrude upon another's emotional experience. If he entered a room where one was reading or writing or playing the piano, he would sit quickly down with folded hands until the book was closed, the pen was laid aside, or the last note had died to silence.

Arthur's childhood was of an 'aloneness' not unusual to the second of three brothers—too young to be included in the exploits of the older, too old for the mental or the physical activities of the younger. So, as a youth, he would rove daylong the Ashdown Forest, peopling every glade with the shades of his own imaginings. So, the very small boy, tying his kite to the handlebars of his bicycle, he would hurtle and bound over the spaces of Wimbledon Common at the wind's speed with a daring and a defiance that was later to make him the equal of many a professional on skis.

Once, in 1947, alighting at a tiny Engadine railway platform and wondering bleakly why I had not been met, I lifted my eyes to the shining mountain peak. Far up the snowy slope a black dot moved, zigzagging at speed. Presently discernible—and incredible—it was shooting hedges, leaping roads, springing soundlessly down, direct and swift as a bird, to swing to my side and brake superbly at my feet. I had been met.

Brought up to the turn-of-the-century 'all-knowing' age of science, he was yet the most tolerant, the least cynical and materialistic of men. In the post-war fashionable world of atheism, he had nevertheless inherently within him unfathomable deeps both of reverence and worship. The God, the Truth, wherein he trusted was beauty, and at length love; and for it his every sense was keen and fresh as a child's. Wonder never deserted him. With each thing of loveliness or of interest on which his eye alighted it was as though seen for the first time. 'Wonderful', he would whisper.

And so it was in the hour of dying: his brown gaze, warm, serene, moving slowly from the racing clouds of the bright spring sky to the face of my son standing at the foot of the bed, to the great branch of fifty red roses I had torn from the garden in the darkness of the night that it might arch across the grey-green walls of his room, and again to my eyes beside him on the pillow. Wonderful, it said.

A month later, the crimson petals had scattered over bookcases and floor. The main stem had sprung two new green wands, two feet long and straining toward the window; hair-roots trailed in the water. I took the branch back to the garden, dug a hole, and planted it.

Arthur Waley's tastes were fixed and simple. He disliked behaviours that were studied, manners that were unnatural. Above all things he disliked to be lionised, singled out, or 'contained' within any grouping. Thus, though he was certainly *in* the 'Bloomsbury set', there was a very real sense in which he was not *of* it. No phrase made him more nearly furious than 'your world'. 'My world, my world—what do you mean, *my* world!' he would demand. And indeed, in the sense that a world restricts, behind that battery of defences and barricades where stretched his limitless horizons of feeling and perception, no 'world' was: nor no man was ever less 'contained'.

True it is, essentially, that I knew him 'better' than anyone. But that very 'better' is hard to express—being inner, esoteric, and, as it were, unguessed. Arthur and I had curious relationships, punctuated by partings, woven into our near forty years of knowledge of one another—many of them, I realize only now (and quite unknown to him) arising straight out of *Genji*. But the most precious was that of Postman and Lady Five in 'The Two Lunatics'.[1] 'And the world wonders why *that*'s my favourite story,' he said to me, so short a time before his death. Difficult, indeed.

It is not because I am his wife that I reassert (for others have said it) that this man had genius. Nor because I am one who

[1] See pp. 235–6.

loved him to the near elimination of all else. But because, quite simply, it was so. And of genius, whatever is written must yet fall short in its assessment. For who can measure the immeasurable? And, unless we are in a position to outstrip that shining and most lonely traveller, how shall we look back upon the landmarks of his travel?

'You're bound to get it all wrong.'

'Yes. I know.'

Recollections of a Younger Brother

by Hubert Waley

My earliest recollections of Arthur depict him against the background of Hill House, Wimbledon, after we had left London in 1896.

A still extant photo of the nursery shows a trapeze alongside the usual furniture of the period. The room was also equipped with a very professional-looking carpenter's bench. We had regular lessons in carpentry and no doubt made many suitable articles for presentation in the home. But the only product which I can remember is a remarkable paperweight made by Arthur which occupied a prominent place on our Mother's writing desk till the day of her death. It consisted of strips of lead and red cloth fastened to a block of wood with tin-tacks and brass-headed upholstery nails, and used to remind me, when I was grown up, of some of the exhibits in the Anthropological Gallery of the British Museum.

Arthur was an enthusiastic follower of Volunteer Manœuvres on Wimbledon Common and used to come home with pockets full of brass cartridge cases. He enjoyed the normal out-door occupations of a school-boy, but I think that he already showed signs of a certain quiet tenseness and originality unusual at that age.

I recall that on our arrival at Wimbledon, before our unpacking was complete, our nurse organised tea in the nursery and could find no spoons. Arthur saved the situation by producing a pencil from his pocket and suggesting we might stir our tea with it.

123

Our nurse exclaimed, 'Why, Master Arthur carries a pencil everywhere—I expect he'll be a great author some day!'

After a few terms at day-school it was found that Arthur worried disproportionately about whether he was going to be punctual each morning, so he was sent to a boarding-school at Chilverton Elms, near Dover, for several terms. It was here that his remarkable power of concentrating on his work was first noticed. It must have been soon after this time that he showed an early interest in languages by studying Ogham inscriptions during a family holiday in Wales. He left Rugby a year early and filled in time with a brief stay in Germany and a longer and happier stay in France with a French family at St Germain-en-Laye. During this period he read widely both in German and French, as well as gaining proficiency in conversation in both languages. I recall gratefully the help which Arthur gave me in my own struggles to learn some French. He almost reconciled me to the existence of irregular verbs by pointing out that they sprang, not from the sadistic tendencies of grammarians but from the pertinacity of little groups of conquered people who clung courageously to their mother tongues. As a first reading-book for my studies he chose Maeterlinck's plays, because, as he pointed out, you couldn't conceive works of literature using fewer difficult words or simpler grammatical constructions. I think it possible that these plays gave him an early glimpse of the hypnotic effect obtainable by saying the same thing in the same words twice over. He followed Maeterlinck with Baudelaire, reading aloud to me with evident emotion the poem which compares the clumsy gait of a captive albatross with the majestic sweep of the bird's wings in flight, and then reflects that albatrosses are like poets—capable of rising to great heights but ill-adapted to pedestrian progress. This poem clearly made a strong personal appeal to him.

I think he had an intuition that he was heading for some sort of poetical career and recognised in himself the first stirrings of what used then to be called 'anti-herd' instincts. These individualistic instincts made him resent any worldly-wise advice from well-meaning relatives and he was particularly incensed by a cousin who recommended him to look out, while up at the University, for friends likely to be able to exercise 'influence' on his behalf later on. His attitude to the competitive aspects of commerce and politics was aloof, but he was practical in his personal money affairs and alert to contemporary social problems. I remember his interest in seeing the workings of a Communist state when visiting me in Zagreb in 1953.

Music played an important part in Arthur's life. He was never an expert executant, but for many years was inseparable from a sort of primitive flute, good for rendering folk songs, and later on he acquired a harpsichord on which he picked out 18th-century pieces. The classical composers of the 19th century were antipathetic to him. But he returned from Spain in 1912 with a repertoire of 'Flamenco' music.

Arthur's enthusiasm for visual art certainly began during his early teens and its manifestation which I best recall was brass-rubbing. This hobby fitted in well with his interest in Church Architecture and his fondness for cycling. The stark simplicity of the earlier brasses appealed to him and I remember bringing down some ridicule on my head by looking at an over-elaborate shallow-cut 17th-century brass memorial tablet.

I am inclined to think that scorn for the over-ornate was the key to Arthur's preferences at that time and perhaps long after. Among my lumber I recently came across an old water colour of a modest Regency villa, bought by one of us at the Caledonian Market, Islington. The sight of it recalled a remark which Arthur made at the time. 'That kind of house looks nice simply because the Napoleonic Wars impoverished people so that they couldn't afford to spoil their buildings with ornamentation.'

It was in the autumn of 1910, while he was still uncertain as to whether he should spend a fourth year at Cambridge, that a medical calamity befell him. He almost completely lost the sight of one eye. Conical cornea was diagnosed and he was ordered to give his eyes a complete rest and warned against the danger of his other eye deteriorating also. This danger must have tried his habitual stoicism to the utmost. But when he was with me at Easter, 1911, on a Norwegian skiing holiday he showed very few signs of the depression which he must have felt.

Some of my happiest memories relate to exploring London in Arthur's company. In search of 18th-century houses and Regency Terraces we strolled on Sundays round Highgate and Primrose Hill. More enterprising expeditions took us in an easterly direction, particularly to Lea Bridge, where we hired a boat and plied our oars energetically, looking neither to right nor left, so as to avoid seeing the dead cats and dogs which floated near the banks. A puzzled friend once asked Arthur what attracted him about the river Lea, to which he replied that he admired the abrupt way in which London ended there instead of tailing off into suburbs. The attractions of the Lea River did not divert us entirely from exploring the Thames. The dockyard slums and the flat Tilbury landscape where Lascars could be seen straying hand-in-hand were tinged with romance by our cult of Conrad. Our cult of Henry James also lent interest to our London walks. A girl preacher in Hyde Park used to remind us of James's Verena Tarrant.

Georgian façades in London streets always attracted his favourable attention and he so entirely lost his heart to an architecturally irreproachable hotel in Soho that he booked in for a night there when our home was being decorated. He was fond of recounting afterwards how shocked the proprietor looked when he explained that he was alone and wished to remain so.

Curiously enough I can't remember that we ever went to the theatre together, though it comes back to me that for a short time we affected a facetious habit of lapsing into Irishisms borrowed from Synge's *Playboy of the Western World*. In fact I blush to remember the extent to which our conversation was peppered with literary allusions. George and Weedon Grossmith's Mr

Pooter (*Diary of a Nobody*) was a rather general vogue and Arthur had a particular fondness for phrases culled from Flaubert's *Bouvard et Pécuchet*. Nor were we guiltless of sometimes adopting half-involuntarily the infectious Strachey squeak. We were regular attendants at Collins's Music Hall in Islington. A fragment of a wartime song which we heard there floats into my mind: 'Courage! When we've beaten the German and the Turk we all shall draw their wages while they do the dirty work!' We thought this at any rate an intelligible war aim, however unattainable and unKeynesian.

I cannot recall that we ever visited together London's great picture galleries, but I remember his praising Piero della Francesca. In general he preferred drawings and sketches to large canvases, which tended to incur a charge of pomposity. The economy of line in the British Museum's famous Ku K'ai-chih scroll impressed him deeply. This did not however prevent him from frequently putting forward the view that in common honesty the scroll ought to be returned to the Chinese. It was Arthur who first opened my eyes to the lyrical qualities of Chaplin's films. We saw 'Charlie at the Bank' in a local picture house near Notting Hill Gate. He drew my attention to the poetical quality of love-making from which Chaplin awakes to find himself stroking the head of a mop. This was in 1915.

In 1916 he distributed to a few dozen friends a booklet containing translations of 52 Chinese poems, which he had had privately printed. The printers supplied the copies unbound and Arthur and I joined forces to bind them in bits of rather florid wall-paper.

This was Arthur's first appearance in print as a translator. Thereafter his life was certainly dominated by his oriental studies, pursued first in the Museum, and, after his retirement in 1929, in a succession of homes (if one can call a room in the Russell Hotel a home) all in the neighbourhood of the Museum except his last home in Highgate Village.

His homes were—Cartwright Gardens (1920–23), 36 Gordon

Square (1924–33), Russell Hotel (1933–36), 50 Gordon Square (1936–62), 22 Great James's Street (1962–63), 50 Southwood Lane, Highgate (1963–66).

Arthur had no inclination for country life as a permanency but came often on visits both to his mother's cottage and to our farm-house home at Stebbing. He used to gaze with mild wonder and sympathy at normal domestic routines and was once heard to exclaim 'I hope there is nothing I can do to help!'

Finally I would like to mention the readiness with which he came to the assistance of sufferers under the Nazi regime. The instance which I remember best is his preparing for publication some unfinished work of Professor Henri Maspero, who died in a German concentration camp.

5. *Lone walking tour of Spain, about 1910*

6. *Week-end at Ham Spray, with Lytton Strachey, Carrington and Tiglath. On the left, Paul Hyslop*

Part II: ANTHOLOGY

Introduction to *A Hundred and Seventy Chinese Poems* (1962 edition)

by Arthur Waley

The first thing that strikes me today, in re-reading the *Hundred and Seventy Chinese Poems* (written over forty years ago) is that the original introduction instead of beginning with 'the limitations of Chinese literature' ought to have begun with something about my own limitations. Rather than embark on enormous generalizations about the whole of Chinese literature I ought to have confessed that though during the four years I had been doing Chinese I had read fairly widely, what I had read (in ancient poetry for example) amounted to no more than a few thousand poems out of hundreds of thousands. Indeed my generalizations seem to me now to need so much qualification that I have asked the publishers to let me write a fresh introduction. . . .[1]

As I am often asked what led to my taking up the study of Chinese, I will begin with an account of the strangely accidental way in which this happened. I took Classics at Cambridge and would have liked to become a Don. But in the Tripos I only got a 1.3 and my chance of getting a Fellowship was very remote. I had an uncle who exported things (chiefly pianos, I think) to South America. It was decided that I had better go into his firm

[1] For an extract from the 1918 Introduction, see pp. 295–6. *Ed.*

131

and for that purpose it was essential that I should learn Spanish. I was sent to Seville where for a time I lived in a room looking out on the Giralda. The view was one several times painted by Matisse, who once occupied the same room. I got to know the French painter Bréal, a man of great taste, who lived by painting cynical 'pot-boilers' of local gypsies, for which there was a steady demand in Paris. To him I confided that I did not like the idea of the export business. He said there were other much more civilized forms of business; for example his friend Oswald Sickert, the brother of the famous painter, had recently (with nothing to recommend him save a few stories in the *Yellow Book* and an unpublished novel) become director of the *Encyclopaedia Britannica*, and would certainly be delighted to give me a job. After a year in Spain I returned to England armed with a letter of introduction to Sickert. He was extremely kind and welcoming; but it turned out that he was not a 'director' at all. He had secured, not without difficulty, a very minor post, and was far from being in a position to hand out jobs to other people. He asked if I had ever thought of going into the British Museum. I hadn't, partly because (believe it or not) I had at that time barely heard of the British Museum. Sickert said that there was certainly a vacancy at the Print Room of the Museum. His friend, the poet Laurence Binyon, who was on the staff had just told him so. I asked my father if I might try for the post. He told me he did not think I had any chance. There was a very stiff examination (Sickert had dismissed it as a mere formality) and he also told me that the cleverest young man he knew, Laurie Magnus, had recently sat for it and failed. However there seemed to be no harm in trying, and I passed quite easily.

The head of the Print Room was then that famous connoisseur of German art, Campbell Dodgson. He had a passion for modern German bookplates. He had just purchased a large fresh batch of them and almost my first job at the Print Room was to count and sort them. As they were on very thin paper one side of which was adhesive, they stuck together and each time I counted them the total came out different. It was my half-day, but I was 'kept in' like a boy at school, until late in the afternoon I managed to convince Dodgson that I had counted them right.[2] How was I to escape from that sort of thing? Exporting pianos would have been far preferable. Shortly afterwards I heard that the Print Room was to be split up into European and Oriental sub-departments. Binyon was to be head of the Oriental part and I asked (simply to escape from German bookplates) if I might become his assistant. For eighteen years he was an ideal friend and chief. At that time, apart from a mild interest in Japanese prints, I knew nothing about Oriental art or languages.

I soon found it was very difficult to do the work I was now supposed to do without some knowledge of both Chinese and Japanese. One was, for example, in constant danger of making one artist out of two, or *vice versa*. So I got to work to learn both languages simultaneously. The first Chinese poems I read were those inscribed on paintings, just as my first introduction to *The Tale of Genji* was an extract inscribed on a Japanese print.

That is the story of how I came, quite accidentally, to study Chinese and Japanese. I should like also to tell very briefly the story of how my first book, *A Hundred and Seventy Chinese Poems*, came into existence.

I soon began to feel that I needed guidance. I went to the recently-founded School of Oriental Studies, then in Finsbury Circus, and consulted an old missionary, who was in charge of Chinese studies. He was not at all encouraging. 'You'll find that the Chinese are very weak in that line', he said, referring to poetry. 'They have their ancient *Book of Odes* by Confucius, but that is all.' However, seeing that I did not look convinced, he kindly said I might go up to the Library and see if I could find anything. There was, of course, in those days no catalogue and the books were arranged in a rather haphazard way, but I soon discovered hundreds of volumes of poetry. I began to make rough translations of poems that I thought would go well in

[2] See pp. 37–8.

English, not at all with a view to publication, but because I wanted my friends to share in the pleasure that I was getting from reading Chinese poetry. Among people who were interested by these translations were Roger Fry, Lowes Dickinson, and Logan Pearsall-Smith, the author of *Trivia*. Roger Fry was at that time interested in printing. He thought verse ought to be printed in lines that undulated in a way that reinforced the rhythms, and he asked if I objected to his printing some of my translations in this way, as an experiment. The idea of their being printed at all of course thrilled me, and spell-bound by Roger's enthusiasm (as everyone was) I had not the courage to say (what was in fact the case) that I could see no point at all in the 'undulations'. A meeting of the Omega Workshops was called at which about a dozen people were present. Roger Fry asked each of them in turn how many copies of translations such as mine (irrespective of 'undulation') it would be possible to sell. The highest estimate was twenty. Saxon Turner, of the Treasury, answered inaudibly. He was asked to repeat what he had said and removing his pipe from his mouth, he answered with great firmness and clarity, 'None'. Roger had been collecting estimates (with or without undulation). It was clear that in order to cover costs he must sell at least two hundred copies, so as the result of the meeting he gave up the idea of printing my translations. But I, for the first time in my life, began in consequence of this meeting to have some vague idea about the cost of getting a small work printed. For a few pounds I had about forty short poems printed in a normal way by an ordinary printer, bound the sheets in some spare wall-paper and sent the resulting booklet to a number of friends, as a sort of Christmas card. It had a mixed reception. Professor Bateson, for example, wrote on a postcard: 'I am afraid I can't get much from your translations. I don't need a Chinese poet to tell me that rivers don't turn back in their courses.' He was evidently referring to the couplet:

> The hundred rivers eastward travel to the ocean:
> Never shall they turn back again to the West.

He was a cultivated and benevolent man and must, I think, to write such a postcard, have been very much irritated by the poems.

I had at that time a corporate admiration for the whole Strachey family, and longed for them to be interested in what I did. I was pained, then, when Lytton Strachey wrote ribald parodies of the poems, not intended of course for my eye: but 'Carrington' (the paintress Dora Carrington, who adored Lytton and looked after him for so long) took care that I should see them. I thought them very stupid, and Lytton fell off his pedestal.[3]

In 1917 things took a turn. The School of Oriental Studies began to bring out a *Bulletin* and in the first two numbers I published, as 'papers contributed', most of what afterwards became the *Hundred and Seventy*. Several literary magazines also printed single poems. But the real turning-point was an article in the *Literary Supplement* of November 15, by some one (I was told it was A. Clutton-Brock) who had seen the two *Bulletins*. The article was called 'A New Planet', and the writer of it said: 'It is a strange and wonderful experience to read the translations.' Pearsall-Smith called the attention of Constable's to this article and so the *Hundred and Seventy* came into existence.

The book was not a best-seller in any grandiose sense, but the sales were at any rate sufficient to refute the gloomy predictions of Omega. I think one of the reasons that it remained in fairly steady demand for forty years is that it appeals to people who do not ordinarily read poetry. When in 1940 I was working in a Government office a number of young girl typists and clerks brought me copies of the *Hundred and Seventy* to sign. Several of them said they did not ordinarily read poetry and had, before coming across my book, always supposed that it was something 'special and difficult'. The reason they got on all right with Chinese poetry was, I think, that it mainly deals with the concrete and particular, with things one can touch and see—a beautiful tree or lovely person—and not with abstract conceptions such as

[3] But see letter from Lytton Strachey to Arthur Waley, pp. 67–8. *Ed.*

Beauty and Love. The English upper class, on the other hand, brought up at the universities in a tradition inspired largely by Plato, has reconciled itself to abstractions and even to the belief that the general is, in some mysterious way, truer and nobler than the particular. But ordinary people in England have very little use for abstractions and when poetry, under the influence of the higher education, becomes abstract, it bores them. On the other hand, the view that something essential was lacking in Chinese poetry was expressed in 1919 by my friend E. M. Forster who said, when reviewing one of my books, that Chinese poems were 'lovely' but not 'beautiful'. As he spoke of Beauty having 'her head in the sky', he must, I think, have been expressing a demand for the ideal as opposed to the real.

I have sometimes seen it said that my translations have had a considerable effect on English poetry. Concrete examples were never cited and I myself am unable to supply any. This view, however, was evidently held by Edward Shanks, the poet and critic, for when someone tried to introduce us at a party he turned away saying: 'That man has done more harm to English poetry than anyone else.' The statement was so unexpected and seemed to me so astonishing that I was quite dumbfounded and by the time I 'came to', Shanks had disappeared, so that I was not able to ask him to explain. I suppose he meant that I had encouraged poets to abandon traditional metres and, in particular, not to use rhyme. It seems therefore that at this point it would be a good thing to explain briefly how my translations of Chinese poetry are intended to work metrically and in what relation they stand to traditional English metre.

Most of the poems are, in the original, in lines consisting of five one-syllable words, with a pause after the first two. If one translates literally one generally gets a line with five stresses and (as many English words have several syllables) a number of unaccented syllables. I do not, as ordinary verse does, make it a general rule that stressed syllables have to be separated by unstressed ones. For example I can write: 'In dárk wóods a lonely cuckoo sings.' This of course puts a lot of emphasis on the stressed words and one has to be sure that the sense and also the vowel quality of the words are capable of carrying so much emphasis. Normally not more than two unstressed syllables come between stresses. Stresses not separated by unstressed syllables (like the dárk wóods in the line quoted above) must occur sufficiently frequently to give the verse its general character and movement; but they need not necessarily occur in each line. It is in fact a form of Sprung Rhythm, as Gerard Manley Hopkins used the term. It is true that in translating the lyric parts of Japanese Nō plays some years later I was as regards diction a good deal influenced by Hopkins. But I had invented the sort of Sprung Rhythm that I used in translating Chinese poetry several years before the poems of Hopkins were printed, so that (contrary to what some critics have suggested) Hopkins had no influence on the metric of my translations from Chinese.

Chinese poetry rhymes. At the time when these translations first appeared (1917) rhyme was considered the hall-mark of poetry, and there are still people who consider that a translator of poetry who does not use rhyme has not done his job. But rhymes are so scarce in English (as compared with Chinese) that a rhymed translation can only be a paraphrase and is apt to fall back on feeble padding. On the whole however people are used nowadays to poetry that does not rhyme or only uses rhyme as an occasional ornament, and I think lack of rhyme will not be generally felt as an obstacle.

1960

Arthur Waley in Conversation

BBC interview[1] with Roy Fuller (1963)

Fuller: Mr Waley, what I should like to talk most about are
your translations from Oriental languages, particularly
the Chinese. And I want to talk about them as English
poetry more than as translations. For it seems to me
that, although they've been famous for over forty years,
they've been neglected as English verse and as part of
the revolution in English verse against iambic Tenny-
sonian verse which took place just before the First
World War. I know you have complained that your
translations were not considered experiments in English
verse. Have you felt that happened all the time?

Waley: If it has happened, it's only natural, because the number
of people that are at all interested in the technique of
poetry is very small. Much larger is the number of
people who enjoy poetry, which is more to the point. . . .

Fuller: I think you had a small book of translations from the
Chinese published in 1916.

Waley: I started at a very early age indeed. I suppose it was
about '99.

Fuller: As early as that?

Waley: I remember, I wrote a poem whose first line was 'Long
lines of banners, horses, men, move across the plain'—
that was all meant to be one line. I was at a school with

[1] Produced by Mrs Helen Rapp. *Ed.*

Scott-Moncrieff, the translator of Proust, who was then eleven, I think. And he got hold of it and told me it wasn't poetry because in poetry all the lines must have ten syllables. I was completely floored by that. I went home and there was a lot of poetry in my father's library. It took me about a half an hour before I found one line with ten syllables; they all seemed to have eight. I confronted Scott-Moncrieff with this and he was very hurt and said his father was a well-known literary man and must be right. But I think the line I quoted to you contains some of the accents—some on neighbouring syllables and so on.

Fuller: Yes, but when you came to rationalise this method of writing verse, did you find any conscious literary antecedents?

Waley: I don't think so exactly. When I began translating I noticed that I had rules, that I said to myself, 'No, that doesn't scan, that's not right, and so on'. After a time I tried to discover what those rules were, and then followed them consciously for the next forty years or so.

Fuller: All the same, round about that time there were quite a few others, I won't say writing the same kind of verse, but also reacting against iambic verse, against strict metre.

Waley: Yes, but they were mostly writing prose chopped up into lengths, weren't they? I mean they weren't writing anything that sang at all, or was intended to, or that was metrical. I don't mean that they're necessarily the worse for that, because even Whitman is really prose printed differently, and I adore Whitman.

Fuller: I know that you had poems in the *Little Review* in 1917. Now that was very much an organ of the Pound–Eliot movement, wasn't it? Did you feel yourself a part of that?

Waley: Well, I suppose it was because Pound thought I'd fit in that he asked me to send poems. They'd been published in the *Bulletin of the School of Oriental Studies*. And Pound was a very great friend of the Director of that School, Denison Ross.

Fuller: Oh, I see. That's a most interesting link. The introduction to *A Hundred and Seventy Chinese Poems* published in 1918 contained a quotation from Eliot, which I suppose must have been one of the first quotations by a critic from Eliot. I think you were saying that Chinese poetry doesn't contain many images, nothing resembling Eliot's 'like a patient etherised upon a table'.

Waley: Yes.

Fuller: You must have known Eliot's work very well even then?

Waley: Oh yes, certainly, and I saw quite a lot of him at that time. He still sometimes refers to me as his oldest friend, but somehow we don't meet much nowadays. There used to be a dinner every Monday evening at which Pound and Eliot were both usually present and Ford Maddox Hueffer.

Fuller: Was this in a restaurant?

Waley: Yes, a restaurant in Frith Street. It was purely social and friendly. Poetry and the technique of poetry were talked about a good deal. But it was very unpretentious. It was the nicest thing of that kind I've ever been associated with.

Fuller: Who was the ruling spirit? Pound?

Waley: Pound, yes. Very much laying down the law.

Fuller: Did he lay down the law to you about your own translations?

Waley: No. He gave me advice. I don't think I agreed with it, but what he said about poetry and this business of making poetry is much the best that I've ever heard said in the course of my life.

Fuller: I always feel that there's a sort of Chinese flavour about a lot of Eliot's poetry of that period—the end-stopped line, which is very characteristic of that period of Eliot's verse, and which is a Chinese characteristic, isn't it?

Waley: Yes, quite. But I think the influence is all through Pound, certainly not through me.

Fuller: Of course, one of Pound's tenets at that time was that English literature is nourished by translation and that the great ages of English literature are great ages of translation.

Waley: Yes, I remember him saying that.

Fuller: Of course, there were other revolutionary poetic worlds contemporaneous with the Eliot–Pound world. At that time you worked in Bloomsbury. Did you live there?

Waley: I lived mostly in Notting Hill Gate. Part of the time in Gravesend.

Fuller: Was the Eliot–Pound world linked, for example, with the Sitwell world?

Waley: Very little, except perhaps, in a rather shadowy way, through Wyndham Lewis. Of course, Wyndham Lewis painted the celebrated picture of Edith Sitwell and they saw quite a lot of one another for a time.

Fuller: Did you feel that their particular kind of revolution had some influence on you? Or was it something you merely observed?

Waley: I wasn't conscious of the influence, but I wonder if one generally is conscious of such things.

Fuller: When did the Eliot–Pound dinners end?

Waley: They ended whenever it was that Pound went and lived in Paris. I suppose it would be about 1921.

Fuller: And you didn't go on seeing Eliot?

Waley: Oh, I've always seen Eliot intermittently, but in recent years not so often as I used to. We used to lunch together once a week, in addition to the dinners. I'm very fond of him.

Fuller: When did you feel that his poetic revolution had become the establishment, that he'd begun to be accepted?

Waley: Did many people imitate him at all or become exact followers of his? I always thought that the people who wrote in freer verse were more influenced by American things than by Eliot himself.

Fuller: The American business is interesting, isn't it? I mean, there you were with these two Americans. Did you feel their Americanness at the time? Was Eliot very American in those early days?

Waley: He was very Boston, I think.

Fuller: That is not really American.

Waley: Pound was much more of the soil.

Fuller: You were then working at the British Museum, weren't you?

Waley: Yes.

Fuller: Did you feel that it wasn't giving you enough time for your work of translation, or did you manage to carry it on fairly well?

Waley: No, I wanted more time. And I began to feel that I could earn enough money to be able safely to give up the Museum.

Fuller: You'd already done the bulk of the translations that now appear in the volume *Chinese Poems*, had you?

Waley: Yes.

Fuller: What had still to come were these lives of poets with the poems embedded in them. Did you feel at first that you were more strictly bound by the original? Do you feel you've got freer as the years have passed?

Waley: Well, it's gone up and down. There are certain kinds of things I translate rather freely like the Japanese Nō plays, which are not literal translations at all. And other things are very close to the originals.

Fuller: What about the reception of your translations in the Oriental countries? Has there been any reaction there?

Waley: In Japan a great deal. Not in China, I think. But they get rather cross in China at one translating their own poems and think that, if anybody does it, it ought to be themselves.

Fuller: This combination of being a scholar and a poet is extremely rare. One wishes that it happened more often.

Waley: I think it can only happen when scholarship is in a rather rudimentary state as it was as regards Chinese in the days when I started. As it becomes more and more academically minute, the more difficult it is to combine the two roles. There weren't the same standards about having looked at every single edition and being familiar with every commentary, and all that sort of thing.

Fuller: Yes.

Waley: I couldn't now do work which would satisfy the young Americans.

Fuller: Well, the young Americans have bedevilled all sorts of things. May I ask you, Mr Waley, what is your current work?

Waley: I'm making another omnibus, and for that purpose I'm translating considerable parts of the book called *The Secret History of the Mongols*, which I've always been very fond of.

Fuller: Is that in verse?

Waley: No. It's rather a complicated matter because it has a Mongol original, which is really only intelligible through the Chinese paraphrase. And the Mongol original has quite a lot in what it evidently thinks is verse, which the Chinese ignored. . . .

Fuller: I wonder if we could quote a poem for the style, just to have it before us? I'm thinking of a poem like 'Business Men'.

BUSINESS MEN[2]

Business men boast of their skill and cunning
But in philosophy they are like little children.

[2] By Ch'ên Tzǔ-ang (656–98). *Ed.*

Bragging to each other of successful depredations
They neglect to consider the ultimate fate of the body.
What should they know of the Master of Dark Truth
Who saw the wide world in a jade cup,
By illumined conception got clear of Heaven and Earth,
On the chariot of Mutation entered the Gate of Immutability?

Fuller: I know in one place you said that the metre you
developed from a very early age was based on sprung
rhythm. But of course that was rationalising after the
event, because Hopkins's poems, which were also based
on sprung rhythm, weren't published until 1918, which
was long after your own translations began to appear.
Did you know Hopkins's work before it was published
in the collected Bridges edition?

Waley: Well, it so happens I did. Quite considerably before,
because Roger Fry, who was one of my greatest friends,
was related to Bridges's wife and I think it was she who
lent these things which were in the custody of Bridges,
long before they were published, and Roger Fry used to
read them out loud to us.

Fuller: Did they confirm your method, or did they throw any
seeds of fresh development?

Waley: They had a lot of influence on the way that I translated
the Nō plays. I don't think they had any influence on
the translations from Chinese.

Fuller: I mean, as far as the actual texture and sound and rhythm
of the verse are concerned, there's nothing in your
Chinese translations like Hopkins. But it was one of the
things that was happening round about the First World
War. Pound's translations from the Chinese were
published in book form in 1915. Had they appeared in
periodicals before?

Waley: I rather think so. Anyway I saw them in Pound's rooms
long before they were published.

Fuller: Had they an influence on you?

Waley: I don't think so, I think we differed very much. Pound objected to my retaining the length of line of the original, and kept on screaming, 'Break it up—break it up'.

Fuller: I wonder if I'm right in saying it was through the original Chinese lines that you arrived at the idea of a sprung rhythm line with a varying number of beats.

Waley: Yes, it was because my translation of the Chinese tended to come out something like that and only wanted a little manipulation.

Fuller: I think poets who feel the iambic line is something they ought to escape from often have trouble in avoiding writing iambic lines.

Waley: Well, I haven't in all my translations avoided using the iambic line, particularly in those very long poems called *fu*. I've used it quite a lot. But when I'm writing in the other way, it's just in my head, I don't have to think about it. I never remember making an alteration to avoid an iambic line.

Fuller: If an iambic line comes, you let it stay.

Waley: The other way round. I have experimented with translating bits of Wordsworth out of iambic.

Fuller: That sounds a fascinating exercise.

Waley: A great improvement, I assure you.

Fuller: I'm sure it is. A good deal that's wrong with Wordsworth is the Miltonic iambic line. I wonder if you will read a poem which I think illustrates this loose way of writing. (Of course I'm not using the word 'loose' pejoratively.) It's the 9th-century poem called 'The Chrysanthemums in the Eastern Garden'.

THE CHRYSANTHEMUMS IN THE EASTERN GARDEN[3]

The days of my youth left me long ago;
And now in their turn dwindle my years of prime.

---

[3] By Po Chü-i (772–846). *Ed.*

With what thoughts of sadness and loneliness
I walk again in this cold, deserted place!
In the midst of the garden long I stand alone;
The sunshine, faint; the wind and dew chill.
The autumn lettuce is tangled and turned to seed;
The fair trees are blighted and withered away.
All that is left are a few chrysanthemum-flowers
That have newly opened beneath the wattled fence.
I had brought wine and meant to fill my cup,
When the sight of these made me stay my hand.
    I remember, when I was young,
How quickly my mood changed from sad to gay.
If I saw wine, no matter at what season,
Before I drank it, my heart was already glad.
    But now that age comes
A moment of joy is harder and harder to get.
And always I fear that when I am quite old
The strongest liquor will leave me comfortless.
Therefore I ask you, late chrysanthemum-flower,
At this sad season why do you bloom alone?
Though well I know that it was not for my sake,
Taught by you, for a while I will smooth my frown.

Fuller: You've said somewhere that your poems have got to be read aloud to yield their proper rhythmic effect, haven't you?

Waley: I don't remember saying that, but I'll take your word for it.

Fuller: Well, I'd like to go on illustrating this business of beats in the line by having some poems from Yüan Mei read which I think are interesting metrically, as well as being splendid poems. Could we hear the poem he wrote on his fiftieth birthday, which is five-beat.

ON HIS FIFTIETH BIRTHDAY[4]

The third month came, and I was far from home
When suddenly my fifth decade leapt upon me.

[4] By Yüan Mei (1716–98). *Ed.*

I woke at dawn and remembered it was my birthday—
Sitting alone beside a solitary sail.
My first successes came when I was very young;
I got into the habit of thinking I had plenty of time.
Whenever I met an old person of fifty
I felt 'fifty' to be something that did not concern me—
From which I as yet was infinitely far away,
Separated from it by a thick wad of years.
Yet now suddenly I myself have reached it.
With such terrible speed do years go by.
My early friends, who went into Government posts,
Have all by now done things to be proud of;
There were some who had to wait for their success;
But in middle-age they feel they have met their due.
As for me, what else have I to show
For the years that have passed, save temples streaked with grey?
My Court head-dress has fallen into a parlous state;
All my projects have led to utter rout.
I can look forward to little coming in;
What I saved in the past is now all spent.
Someone found out and started to congratulate me;
I stopped my ears and would not listen to the end. . . .
How I envy Fen, Prince of Ying,
The day of whose birth no one could ever discover!
For the present I am happy to wield a feather fan
While I cross the river, singing the song A-t'ung.
To drink my health there are no companions or guests;
To row me on, plenty of hands at the oars.
Wave on wave the grey waters flow;
Gust on gust, the breeze from the distant hills.
There is no one to point at the misty waves and say,
'Out in the offing is an old man of fifty'.

Fuller: Now Yüan Mei's 'New Year's Eve, 1774'.
Waley: This one is seven-beat—one, two, three, four/five, six,
            seven. The cesura comes only after the four.
Fuller: I think this management of the long line is something

you've done most successfully. Awfully difficult to do. Can we have that?

NEW YEAR'S EVE, 1774

On this night year after year I have listened eagerly,
Never missing a single sound of the crackers till dawn came.
But this year on New Year's Eve I cannot bring myself to listen,
Knowing that when the cock crows I shall enter my sixtieth year.
The mighty din of the celebrations has already died away;
If a little time is left, it is only a last scrap.
But the cock, as though feeling for my plight, is slow to open its mouth,
And I that write this am still a man of fifty-nine!

Fuller: We talked about Ezra Pound. Perhaps the most celebrated poem in *Cathay* was the paraphrase he made of
the poem of Li Po which he called 'Exile's Letter'.
You've also translated that poem, haven't you?

Waley: Yes.

Fuller: I think the comparison is interesting. Pound's translation,
of course, I've always known and admired; but when
one comes to read yours, it seems to me that the feeling
that one is getting a more accurate translation adds a
great deal, and certain parts of the Pound poem that I
for one have never really quite understood become
clear. Do you feel that a greater accuracy of translation
does do something to a version of a foreign original?

Waley: Well, of course, it may have just the opposite effect. It
depends. I think Pound often improved the things that
he translated. I wouldn't wish Pound's translations to be
any other way. The chief thing that strikes me is that
he didn't understand what kind of civilisation it was at
all. He'd got it into his head that it was like the Anglo-
Saxon one. And then he'd use a word like 'heaven' for
a word which in the original is the name of an office in
an elaborate bureaucracy.

Fuller: Well, of course one doesn't always want everything

148

translated into terms that one can understand. . . . One wants to feel that there is something in the original which was peculiar to its time and its author. I wonder if we could hear this part of the poem.

from EXILE'S LETTER[5]

When at last far on into the winter I got to the Northern City
It moved me to see how eagerly you did me the honours of your home,
How little you cared for the cost.
Amber cups and fine foods on dishes of green jade—
I ate and drank my fill and had no thought of return.
Sometimes we went out towards the western corner of the City—
To where grey waters flow round the shrine of Chin.
We launched our boat and sported on the stream, to the sound of flageolet and drum.
The little waves were like dragon-scales and the sedge-leaves were pale green.
When it was our mood we took girls with us and gave ourselves to the moments that passed,
Forgetting how soon they would be over—gone like willow-down, like snow.
Rouged faces, flushed with drink, looked well in the sunset.
Clear water, a hundred feet deep, mirrored the faces of the singers—
Singing-girls delicate and graceful in the light of the young moon.
And the girls sang again and again to make the gauze dresses dance,
The clear wind blew the songs away into the sky,
Music winged the air, twisting round the clouds as they passed.
Never again shall the joy of those days come back to us.
I went west to offer up my ballad of Tall Willows,
But got no promotion at the Palace and white-headed returned to the eastern hills.
Once only since then did we meet south of the bridge over the Wei,
To part again north of the Terrace of Tso.
And should you ask how many were my regrets at parting—
They fell upon me thick as the flowers that fall at Spring's end.
But I cannot tell you all—could not even if I went on thinking for ever,

[5] By Li Po (?701–?762). See also pp. 186–7. *Ed.*

So I will call in the boy and make him kneel here and tie this up
And send it to you, a remembrance from a thousand miles away.[6]

Fuller: I wonder how far your great work of translation has
            fulfilled your own poetic talents. I gather that you

[6] As an example of a 'free' translation here is Pound's version of the same passage:

And I was still going, late in the year,
        in the cutting wind from the North,
And thinking how little you cared for the cost,
        and you caring enough to pay it.
And what a reception:
Red jade cups, food well set on a blue jewelled table,
And I was drunk, and had no thought of returning.
And you would walk out with me to the western corner of the castle,
To the dynastic temple, with water about it clear as blue jade,
With boats floating, and the sound of mouth-organs and drums,
With ripples like dragon-scales, going grass green on the water,
Pleasure lasting, with courtezans, going and coming without hindrance,
With the willow flakes falling like snow,
And the vermilioned girls getting drunk about sunset,
And the water a hundred feet deep reflecting green eyebrows
—Eyebrows painted green are a fine sight in young moonlight,
Gracefully painted—
And the girls singing back at each other,
Dancing in transparent brocade,
And the wind lifting the song, and interrupting it,
Tossing it up under the clouds.
        And all this comes to an end.
        And is not again to be met with.
I went up to the court for examination,
Tried Layu's luck, offered the Choyo song,
And got no promotion,
        and went back to the East Mountains
        white-headed.
And once again, later, we met at the South bridgehead.
And then the crowd broke up, you went north to San palace,
And if you ask how I regret that parting:
        It is like the flowers falling at Spring's end
        Confused, whirled in a tangle.
What is the use of talking, and there is no end of talking,
There is no end of things in the heart.

I call in the boy,
Have him sit on his knees here
        To seal this,
And send it a thousand miles, thinking.

Ed.

started by thinking of yourself as a poet at a very early age.

Waley: Well, I really thought of myself as writing stories. A great deal of my youth was occupied in writing stories. I did also write poems very early, but I didn't attach much importance to them.

Fuller: But, looking back, do you feel that in a rather strange way it has fulfilled a poetic talent?

Waley: Yes, it has. It has given me the kind of poetic activities that I wanted.

Fuller: It's remarkable to me that you were able to find in Chinese poetry qualities which are obviously native to yourself. The irony, the relative avoidance of metaphor, the non-romanticism behind most of the poems—all this you've obviously found congenial.

Waley: Yes. Only, you see, I chose the Chinese poems I translated out of thousands and thousands of others, so that naturally makes the approximation still closer.

Fuller: This non-romantic, ironic spirit of Chinese poetry—does it continue to the present day? The most modern poems we've been discussing were 18th-century poems. Does your interest extend to more recent Chinese poetry?

Waley: I'm not well up in it, I confess. I don't very much like poems that are written to order. Perhaps it's my ignorance. I don't really pretend to know. The extent of Chinese poetry is so great that one can't be familiar with it all, and I do find I like the earlier periods better.

Notes on Translation (1958)

by Arthur Waley

I shall begin by saying something that seems obvious, but that cannot really be so obvious or it would not be so often ignored and even contradicted. Different kinds of translation are needed for different purposes. If one is translating a legal document all one needs to do is to convey the meaning; but if one is translating literature one has to convey feeling as well as grammatical sense. The author puts his feelings—exasperation, pity, delight—into the original. They are there in his rhythm, his emphasis, his exact choice of words, and if the translator does not *feel* while he reads, and simply gives a series of rhythmless dictionary meanings, he may think he is being 'faithful', but in fact he is totally misrepresenting the original.

Almost at the end of the *Bhagavad Gita* there is a passage of great power and beauty in which, instructed by the God, the warrior Arjuna at last overcomes all his scruples. There is a war on, he is a soldier and must fight even though the enemy are his friends and kinsmen. This is what various standard translations make him say:

(1) O Unfallen One! By your favour has my ignorance been destroyed, and I have gained memory (of my duties); I am (now) free from doubt; I shall now do (fight) as told by you!

(2) Destroyed is my delusion; through Thy grace, O Achutya, knowledge is gained by me. I stand forth free from doubt. I will act according to Thy word.

(3) My bewilderment has vanished away; I have gotten remembrance by Thy Grace, O Never-Falling. I stand free from doubt. I will do Thy word.

(4) My bewilderment is destroyed; I have gained memory through thy favour, O stable one. I am established; my doubt is gone; I will do thy word.

In addition to being totally without rhythm No. 1 has the disadvantage of a pointless inversion of word order and of quite unnecessary explanations in brackets. If any reader has got as far as this in the poem and yet still needs to be told what it is that Arjuna now remembers and what it is that he proposes to do, he must be so exceptionally inattentive as not to be worth catering for. No. 2 is better; but as the title Achutya will convey nothing to the mind of the reader, it seems better to translate it, as the other three translators have done. And is there any point in trying to preserve, as all the translators do, the Sanskrit idiom 'get memory' for 'to remember'. In No. 3 the rhythm would be better without the 'away' after 'vanished', and 'away' adds nothing to the sense. But I think No. 3 (by Professor Barnett) is the best of the four. No. 4 is spoiled by 'I am established', which, though a correct etymological gloss on the original, is not a possible way of saying 'I have taken my stand'—that is to say, 'I am resolved'.

I suggest something of this kind:

> You, god imperishable,
> Have broken my illusion;
> By your grace I have remembered.
> I take my stand, I doubt no longer.
> I will do your bidding.

I don't pretend that this is more than a pale echo of the original; but I think it has a shade more force and rhythm than the four other versions. No doubt all four translators were aware that they were tackling the finest moment of a fine poem, but this feeling does not seem to me to come through in their translations.

There are indeed in anything one translates certain key passages or lines about which one feels from the start that it is going to be of vital importance to get them exactly right. No makeshift or approximation will do. Such a passage comes at the end of the chapter 'Ukifune' in *The Tale of Genji*. Ukifune, unable to decide between her two lovers, has made up her mind to throw herself into the river. Her maid Ukon pesters her with good advice.

Literally translated the passage runs: 'Ukon, space-nearly lying, that doing: "Thus only when one thinks about things, because the soul of the person who thinks about things goes astray there are indeed likely to be frightening dreams. Having decided one way or the other, oh that you may somehow get on!" So she sighed. [Ukifune] pressing the soft clothes against her face, lay; that indeed.' The dream referred to is evidently (as commentators have recognized) the dream 'too terrible to mention' which Ukifune's mother had had the night before. I translated the passage: 'Ukon now came to sit with her for a little. "When a person goes on tormenting herself as you are doing, we all know what happens: the soul gets loose from the body and goes wandering about by itself. That's why your mother has been having these bad dreams. There's nothing to worry about. Just make up your mind one way or the other, and it will be all right. At least I hope so," she said with a sigh.

'Ukifune lay with the soft bed clothes pressed tight against her face.'

Ukon, of course, is not a peasant. But she is on an infinitely lower rung of the social scale than Ukifune, and this (though I have not attempted to bring it out in my literal translation) is expressed in the verb forms that she uses. One must make her talk as a maid might conceivably talk to a mistress, but remember that she is the daughter of Ukifune's old nurse and is an intimate as well as a servant. Then one must make it clear that she is being aggravating and that it is just this continual flow of well-meant and quite useless advice that is driving Ukifune to desperation. Have I elaborated too much, to the point of spoiling the poignancy of the passage? I don't think so; looking at it some twenty-five years later I do not want to alter it, and even feel that if Ukon had been speaking English, this is more or less what she would have said.

There is not any other translation of the passage with which I can compare mine. If there were, I might suddenly feel that I did, after all, make rather a mess of it. In saying this I have in mind a passage in the Nō play *Sotoba Komachi*:

> Oh how fell she from splendour,
> How came the white of winter
> To crown her head?
> Where are gone the lovely locks, double-twined,
> The coils of jet?
> Lank wisps, scant curls wither now
> On wilted flesh,
> And twin-arches, moth-brows, tinge no more
> With the hue of far hills.

That was the way I translated it in 1921, and it is not bad verse. But I must confess that when recently I read Sam Houston Brock's translation of *Sotoba Komachi* in Donald Keene's anthology, I was rather shaken. His translation of this passage is:

> How was ever such loveliness lost?
> When did she change?
> Her hair a tangle of frosted grass
> Where the black curls lay in her neck
> And the colour lost from the twin arched peaks
> Of her brow.

I felt at once that my translation was hopelessly overladen and wordy and that it tried in a quite unwarrantable way to improve upon the original. Not that I am altogether satisfied with Mr Brock's. If mine is too poetical, his I think is a shade too prosy, and nothing will convince me that 'Of her brow' makes a very good line of verse.

There is a wonderful passage in the Chinese novel *Monkey* where Tripitaka after his Illumination sees his discarded earthly body drifting downstream: 'Tripitaka stared at it in consternation. Monkey laughed. "Don't be frightened, Master," he said, "that's you." And Pigsy said, "It's you, it's you". Sandy clapped his hands.

"It's you, it's you", he cried. The ferryman too joined in the chorus. "There *you* go", he cried. "My best congratulations." In her paraphrase of the book (1930) Helen Hayes says, 'A dead body drifted by them, and the Master saw it with fear. But the Monkey, ever before him, said: "Master, do not be alarmed. It is none other than your own!" The Pilot also rejoiced as he turned to say, "This body was your own! May you know joy!"'

Vital (in the original) is the repetition of the two simple words *shih ni*, 'It's you', and if one gets bored with the repetition and represents the words as only having been spoken by two people, it seems to me that one spoils the whole passage. The second thing to note is that when the ferryman says 'My best congratulations' (*k'o ho*) he is using the ordinary everyday formula of congratulation that one would use if one met an official who had had a rise, and that it is with whimsical intention that it is applied to Tripitaka's advance from ordinary human status to Buddhahood. Helen Hayes's 'May you know joy!' so far from being a banal formula (which is what is required) is something that no one has ever said to anybody.

This brings us to the question of voices. When translating prose dialogue one ought to make the characters say things that people talking English could conceivably say. One ought to hear them talking, just as a novelist hears his characters talk. That sounds obvious and undeniable. But it does not seem to be the principle upon which translators, whether from Far Eastern or European languages, generally work.

Take for example Beatrice Lane's translation of the Nō play *Tsuchigumo*. A concubine called Kochō (Butterfly) is made to say 'Bearing medicine given by the doctor, I, Kochō, have come. Pray tell him so.' Can you hear anyone saying that? A literal translation would be 'Please tell his Honour that Butterfly has come with some medicine for him from the Chief Physician'.

One does not have to be a literary genius in order to avoid translator's pidgin of the kind I have just quoted. One simply has to develop the habit of hearing voices talk. The reader who cannot consult the original will of course tend to think that 'queer' English is the result of a praiseworthy fidelity to the author's idiom and may have a comforting sense that he is getting right inside the author's mind. I have even been told that translations which read well cannot possibly give a true idea of the original. But as a matter of fact when, as in the case quoted above, one compares bits of queer translation with the text, one generally finds that the oddity is completely arbitrary and represents no native idiom at all. People, in fact, who write very well when expressing their own ideas tend (unless they have been to some extent schooled in translation) to lose all power of normal expression when faced with a foreign text. I once edited a volume in which a number of archaeologists, all of them excellent writers when expressing their own ideas, undertook to translate articles by German colleagues. The matter of the articles was purely technical and concrete; the translators knew exactly what had to be said. But one and all they were unable to produce anything but the most abject translator's pidgin. The sight of German sentences put them completely out of their stride.

I have used the expression 'schooled in translation' because I believe that even if it is a question of translating literature (and not merely technical information) there is a lot that could be learned. It is not, after all, as though a translator has to be or even had better be a creative genius. His role is rather like that of the executant in music, as contrasted with the composer. He must start with a certain degree of sensibility to words and rhythm. But I am sure that this sensibility could be enormously stimulated and increased, just as musical sensibility obviously can be.

A French scholar (whom I greatly admire) wrote recently with regard to translators: 'Qu'ils s'effacent derrière les textes et ceux-ci, s'ils ont été vraiment compris, parleront d'eux-mêmes.' Except in the rather rare case of plain concrete statements such as 'The cat chases the mouse', there are seldom sentences that have exact word-for-word equivalents in another language. It becomes a question of choosing between various approximations. One can't, for example, say in English 'Let them efface themselves behind the texts'. One has to say something like, 'They should efface themselves, leaving it to the texts to speak', and so on. I have always found that it was I, not the texts, that had to do the talking. Hundreds of times I have sat for hours in front of texts the meaning of which I understood perfectly, and yet been unable to see how they ought to be put into English in such a way as to re-embody not merely a series of correct dictionary meanings, but also the emphasis, the tone, the eloquence of the original.

'Toute recherche esthétique', the French scholar continues, 'va contre la bonne foi du traducteur.' I would rather say that the true work of the translator begins with 'recherche esthétique'. What comes before that—knowledge of the foreign language—is of course essential as a foundation, but it is a matter of linguistics and has nothing to do with the art that I am discussing. There do of course exist texts in which only logical meaning, and not feeling, is expressed. But particularly in the Far East they are exceedingly rare. The appeal, even in philosophical texts, has always been to emotion rather than to logic.

When I had been translating Chinese poetry for about six years, guided metrically by instinct alone, I discovered that I had been unconsciously obeying a certain rule.[1] This was: to have one stress to each Chinese syllable. The stressed syllables could come side by side, as in

On the hígh hílls nó creature stírs

or they could be separated by anything up to three unstressed syllables, as in

I have stíll to travel in my sólitary bóat.

This gave something which Gerard Manley Hopkins (whom I had not then read) called, I think, 'sprung rhythm'. I did not use rhyme because I found that to do so carries one too far away from the original. But exactly what sounds one uses at the end of a line

[1] See pp. 136–7. *Ed.*

is as important if one is not rhyming as it is if one is using rhyme, and a proper rhythmical relation between the lines is as important in free verse as it is in standard, traditional meters. It is true, however, that the tangles into which rhymers get themselves are sometimes almost incredible. A translator who shall be nameless has the two lines:

> This little grandchild, five years short of twelve,
> As yet can neither spin nor deeply delve.

Believe it or not, all that the original says is

> The little children cannot yet help with the ploughing or weaving.

At the same time, though he has made such a mess here, I don't question that the translator was right in using rhyme, because all his experience and practice had been in writing rhymed poetry. The translator must use the tools that he knows best how to handle. And this reflection reminds me at once of what Lin Shu, the great early 19th-century translator of European fiction into Chinese, said when he was asked why he translated Dickens into ancient Chinese instead of into modern colloquial. His reply was: 'Because ancient Chinese is what I am good at.'

There are indeed so many lessons about translation to be learned from the story of this extraordinary man that I want to devote quite a bit of space to him. Let me introduce him to you by quoting from the preface to his translation of *The Old Curiosity Shop*:

I once went into retreat, shutting myself up in one room for weeks on end. All day the people of the house passed to and fro outside, and although I could not see them I was soon able to distinguish their footsteps and know infallibly who was passing my door.

I have a number of friends who from time to time bring me Western books. I cannot read any Western language, but these friends translate them aloud to me and I have come to be able to distinguish between the different styles of writing as surely as I recognized the footsteps of the people in my house.

Lin Shu (1852–1924) was already famous as a writer of essays and criticism in a terse, clear, and vigorous style of literary

Chinese when, more or less accidentally, his career as a translator began. In 1893 a young friend called Wang Tzu-jen, who had just returned from studying in France, brought him a copy of Dumas's novel *La Dame aux Camélias* and translated it to him viva voce, in ordinary Chinese colloquial. Lin Shu began turning this translation into literary Chinese. It was rather an odd thing to do because, although short stories were sometimes written in literary Chinese, no Chinese novel had ever been in anything but colloquial. The translation was published, and was an immense success.

During the next twenty-five years he published about 160 translations. Wang Tzu-jen, to whom he was deeply devoted, was never again available as a collaborator, and seems to have died rather young. But two of Wang's nephews knew French and collaborated in various works. One of them, twenty years later, helped Lin Shu to translate Bernardin de Saint-Pierre's *Paul et Virginie*. During the twenty-five years or so when he was translating he used at least sixteen different collaborators. Most of them were gifted and highly educated young men who had been sent abroad to study practical subjects, such as naval engineering. They soon became engrossed in their careers, diplomatic or governmental, and it was natural that they were not available as collaborators in translation for very long.

There were, of course, great disadvantages in Lin Shu's method of work. Knowing no foreign language he was, as he more or less confesses in his analogy about footsteps, rather in the position of a blind man at a picture gallery, whose friends are able to tell him everything about the pictures except what they actually look like. Naturally the method led to numerous small mistakes, and he continually received lists of errata from readers all over China. What made him so remarkable as a translator was the immense force and vivacity of his style and the intensity with which he *felt* the stories that were communicated to him. 'People in a book', he writes in the preface to Charlotte Yonge's *The Eagle and the Dove*, 'at once become my nearest and dearest relations. When

7. *Pause between ski-runs, Austria*

8. *Summertime in Switzerland, with Beryl de Zoete, early twenties*

they are in difficulties I fall into despair; when they are successful, I am triumphant. I am no longer a human being, but a puppet whom the author dangles on his strings.'

He worked with immense rapidity. In 1907 alone he published translations of Scott's *The Talisman* and *The Betrothed*, Dickens's *The Old Curiosity Shop* and *Nicholas Nickleby*, Washington Irving's *Sketch Book*, Arthur Morrison's *The Hole in the Wall*, and a number of stories by Conan Doyle and other popular writers.

It is perhaps by his translation of Dickens that he is best known. He translated all the principal Dickens novels, and I have compared a number of passages with the original. To put Dickens into classical Chinese would on the face of it seem to be a grotesque undertaking. But the results are not at all grotesque. Dickens, inevitably, becomes a rather different and to my mind a better writer. All the overelaboration, the overstatement and uncurbed garrulity disappear. The humour is there, but is transmuted by a precise, economical style; every point that Dickens spoils by uncontrolled exuberance, Lin Shu makes quietly and efficiently.

You may question at this point whether it is right to call him a translator at all. But at any rate in the case of the Dickens novels it would be misleading, I think, to use such terms as 'paraphrase' or 'adaptation'. In any case he was the transmitter, on the grandest possible scale, of European fiction to China, and through him Chinese fiction (which had been tied down to ancient storyteller's conventions that no longer fitted what the contemporary novelist wanted to say) was revitalized when it was at its last gasp. I have spoken of the lessons that can be drawn from Lin Shu's achievement. First, then, what matters most is that the translator, whether working at first or at second-hand, should be someone who delights in handling words. As another example of what a difference this makes I would cite the *Four Cautionary Tales* by Harold Acton and Lee Yi-hsieh, who worked together in much the same way as Lin Shu worked with his collaborators.

Whether the translator's style is contemporary or archaic does not matter. Some writers have been brought up on the Bible and handle a Biblical style with vigour and ease. I would cite as an instance Gordon Luce's *The Glass Palace Chronicle of the Kings of Burma*. There is all the difference in the world between the deliberate, consistent archaism of this translation and the pointless occasional Biblicisms (such as 'these twain' for 'these two') of unskillful translators.

The second point concerns the selection of books to translate. About 1910 the novelist and translator Tseng P'u called on Lin Shu at Peking and explained to him that all he was doing was to add to the already vast number of T'ang stories a whole series of new T'ang stories that differed from their predecessors only in the fact that their material was taken from foreign sources. Such a procedure, said Tseng P'u, could have no influence on the future course of Chinese literature. He advised him, among other things, to draw up a list of masterpieces, arranged according to period, country, and literary school, and then work through it in an orderly and systematic way. Lin Shu explained that as he knew no foreign language he was not in a position to draw up such a list, and that he saw no alternative to his present method. The books that his friends brought him were all well-known works, and there would be no point in translating them in a prearranged order.

If Tseng P'u had known anything about Lin Shu's temperament (and it does not appear that he had ever met him before) he would have known how inconceivable it was that Lin should ever work to schedule. Moreover, though Lin Shu translated chiefly because he liked translating and did not, so far as I know, ever aim consciously at 'influencing the future course of Chinese literature', the effect of his prodigious life-work was in fact to revolutionize Chinese fiction.

As to the desirability of programmes and schedules, the question is one which has again come conspicuously to the fore. As part of a new pre-occupation with cultural propaganda, various government-sponsored organizations are busy drawing up lists of works that ought to be translated. Young men with linguistic knowledge but often without any literary gifts are roped in to translate, without any particular enthusiasm, works whose only claim to attention is that they have got into an officially compiled list of 'masterpieces'. I have a feeling that this system is not going to work very well. What matters is that a translator should have been excited by the work he translates, should be haunted day and night by the feeling that he *must* put it into his own language, and should be in a state of restlessness and fret till he has done so. 'Masterpieces' were not always masterpieces and may at any minute cease to be so. Many of them owe their place on the list to all sorts of extrinsic and relatively ephemeral causes. Even so comparatively short a time ago as my own childhood a poem the title of which I pronounced 'Cassaby Anchor' was a 'masterpiece', and I had to learn it by heart. Perhaps one day it will come into its own again; but meanwhile let the translator read widely and choose the things that excite him and that he itches to put into English. If they are not scheduled as 'masterpieces' today, very likely they will be tomorrow. The Japanese pin their faith to translation by committee. Twenty people (with one exception all Japanese) seem to have taken part in the translation of the *Manyōshū* (the earliest Japanese anthology) published in 1940. The results were excellent, but this was due, I am sure, to the fact that the one Westerner concerned was Ralph Hodgson, and it seems clear that he was, in the final stage of the work, given a free hand. The next number in the series was *Japanese Noh Drama* (1954). Here eighteen people seem to have been involved; but it is clear that no Western poet took the bit between his teeth as I believe Ralph Hodgson to have done in the previous case. The result was that the lyric parts of the plays are simply prose, arbitrarily printed as though it were verse, as in the lines

> In recent years
> I have lived a country life.

The Japanese committee finds it 'regrettable' that Japanese literature has hitherto been chiefly translated by foreigners. I believe, on the contrary, that it is almost always better for the translator to be writing in his own language. It is in the highest degree improbable that a writer will command all the resources of a foreign language even as regards vocabulary, and when it comes to rhythm he is almost certain to be completely floored.

These scattered notes on translation deal principally with the Far East, because that is where my own experience lies. But almost all that I have said would apply equally to translation from European languages. I am afraid I may be felt to have taken rather an Only Tailor in the Street line. I have found fault with a good many other people's translations and in some cases have implied that I preferred my own. But I think it is natural that anyone should prefer his own translations. After all, he has made them to the measure of his own tastes and sensibilities, and it is as natural that he should prefer them to other people's as it is that he should prefer to walk in his own shoes.

The Great Summons

Invocation to the soul of a dead or sick man.

Traditionally attributed to Chü Yüan

(3rd or 2nd century BC)

Green Spring receiveth
The vacant earth;
The white sun shineth;
Spring wind provoketh
To burst and burgeon
Each sprout and flower.
The dark ice melts and moves; hide not, my soul!
O Soul, come back again! O do not stray!

O Soul, come back again and go not east or west, or north or south!
For to the East a mighty water drowneth
  Earth's other shore;
Tossed on its waves and heaving with its tides
  The hornless Dragon of the Ocean rideth;
Clouds gather low and fogs enfold the sea
  And gleaming ice drifts past.
O Soul, go not to the East,
To the silent Valley of Sunrise!

O Soul, go not to the South
Where mile on mile the earth is burnt away
And poisonous serpents slither through the flames,

Where on precipitous paths or in deep woods
Tigers and leopards prowl,
And water-scorpions wait;
Where the king-python rears his giant head.
O Soul, go not to the South
Where the three-footed tortoise spits disease!

O Soul, go not to the West
Where level wastes of sand stretch on and on;
And demons rage, swine-headed, hairy-skinned,
With bulging eyes;
Who in wild laughter gnash projecting fangs.
O Soul, go not to the West
Where many perils wait!

O Soul, go not to the North,
To the Lame Dragon's frozen peaks;
Where trees and grasses dare not grow;
Where the river runs too wide to cross
And too deep to plumb,
And the sky is white with snow
And the cold cuts and kills.
O Soul, seek not to fill
The treacherous voids of the North

O Soul, come back to idleness and peace.
In quietude enjoy
The lands of Ching and Ch'u.
There work your will and follow your desire
Till sorrow is forgot,
And carelessness shall bring you length of days.
O Soul, come back to joys beyond all telling!

Where thirty cubits high at harvest-time
The corn is stacked;
Where pies are cooked of millet and water-grain,
Guests watch the steaming bowls
And sniff the pungency of peppered herbs.

The cunning cook adds slices of bird-flesh,
Pigeon and yellow-heron and black-crane.
They taste the badger-stew.
O Soul, come back to feed on foods you love!

Next are brought
Fresh turtle, and sweet chicken cooked in cheese
Pressed by the men of Ch'u.
And pickled sucking-pig
And flesh of whelps floating in liver-sauce
With salad of minced radishes in brine;
All served with that hot spice of southernwood
The land of Wu supplies.
O Soul, come back to choose the meats you love!

Roasted daw, steamed mallard and grilled quail—
On every fowl they fare.
Boiled perch and sparrow broth—in each preserved
The separate flavour that is most its own.
O Soul, come back to where such dainties wait!

The four strong liquors are warming at the fire
So that they grate not on the drinker's throat.
How fragrant rise their fumes, how cool their taste!
Such drink is not for louts or serving-men!
And wise distillers from the land of Wu
Blend unfermented spirit with white yeast
And brew the *li* of Ch'u.
O Soul, come back and let your tremblings cease!

Reed-organs from the lands of Tai and Ch'in
And Wei and Chêng
Gladden the feasters, and old songs are sung:
The 'Rider's Song' that once
Fu-hsi, the ancient monarch made;
And the shrill songs of Ch'u.
Then after prelude from the pipes of Chao
The ballad-singer's voice rises alone.
O Soul, come back to the hollow mulberry-tree![1]

[1] The lute.

Eight and eight the dancers sway,
Weaving their steps to the poet's voice
Who speaks his odes and rhapsodies;
They tap their bells and beat their chimes
Rigidly, lest harp and flute
Should mar the measure.
Then rival singers of the Four Domains
Compete in melody, till not a tune
Is left unsung that human voice could sing.
O Soul, come back and listen to their songs!

Then women enter whose red lips and dazzling teeth
Seduce the eye;
But meek and virtuous, trained in every art,
Fit sharers of play-time,
So soft their flesh and delicate their bones.
O Soul, come back and let them ease your woe!

Then enter other ladies with laughing lips
And sidelong glances under moth eyebrows,
Whose cheeks are fresh and red;
Ladies both great of heart and long of limb,
Whose beauty by sobriety is matched.
Well-padded cheeks and ears with curving rim,
High-arching eyebrows, as with compass drawn,
Great hearts and loving gestures—all are there;
Small waists and necks as slender as the clasp
Of courtiers' buckles.
O Soul, come back to those whose tenderness
Drives angry thoughts away!

Last enter those
Whose every action is contrived to please;
Black-painted eyebrows and white-powdered cheeks.
They reek with scent; with their long sleeves they brush
The faces of the feasters whom they pass,
Or pluck the coats of those who will not stay.
O Soul, come back to pleasures of the night!

.   .   .   .

A summer-house with spacious rooms
And a high hall with beams stained red;
A little closet in the southern wing
Reached by a private stair.
And round the house a covered way should run
Where horses might be trained.

And sometimes riding, sometimes going afoot
You shall explore, O Soul, the parks of spring;
Your jewelled axles gleaming in the sun
And yoke inlaid with gold;
Or amid orchises and sandal-trees
Shall walk in the dark woods.
O Soul, come back and live for these delights!

Peacocks shall fill your gardens; you shall rear
The rock and phoenix, and red jungle-fowl,
Whose cry at dawn assembles river storks
To join the play of cranes and ibises;
Where the wild-swan all day
Pursues the glint of idle kingfishers.
O Soul, come back to watch the birds in flight!

He who has found such manifold delights
Shall feel his cheeks aglow
And the blood-spirit dancing through his limbs.
Stay with me, Soul, and share
The span of days that happiness will bring;
See sons and grandsons serving at the Court
Ennobled and enriched.
O Soul, come back and bring prosperity
To house and stock!

The roads that lead to Ch'u
Shall teem with travellers as thick as clouds,
A thousand miles away.
For the Five Orders of Nobility
Shall summon sages to assist the King
And with godlike discrimination choose

The wise in council; by their aid to probe
The hidden discontents of humble men
And help the lonely poor.
O Soul, come back and end what we began!

Fields, villages and lanes
Shall throng with happy men;
Good rule protect the people and make known
The King's benevolence to all the land;
Stern discipline prepare
Their natures for the soft caress of Art.
O Soul, come back to where the good are praised!

Like the sun shining over the four seas
Shall be the reputation of our King;
His deeds, matched only in Heaven, shall repair
The wrongs endured by every tribe of men—
Northward to Yu and southward to Annam,
To the Sheep's-Gut Mountain and the Eastern Seas.
O Soul, come back to where the wise are sought!

.   .   .   .

Behold the glorious virtues of our King
Triumphant, terrible;
Behold with solemn faces in the Hall
The three Grand Ministers walk up and down—
None chosen for the post save landed-lords
Or, in default, Knights of the Nine Degrees.
Clout and pin-hole are marked, already is hung
The shooting-target, where with bow in hand
And arrows under arm
Each archer does obeisance to each,
Willing to yield his rights of precedence.
O Soul, come back to where men honour still
The name of the Three Kings.[2] [3]

1919

[2] Yü, T'ang and Wên, the three just rulers of antiquity.
[3] For Professor Giles's criticism of this translation and for Arthur Waley's reply, see pp. 301–2. *Ed.*

Poverty

by Yang Hsiung (52 BC–AD 18)

I, Yang Tzŭ, hid from life—
Fled from the common world to a lonely place,
Where to the right a great wilderness touched me,
And on the left my neighbour was the Hill of Sung.
Beggars whose tenements
Lie wall to wall, though they be tattered and poor,
Rough-used, despised and scorned, are yet in companies
And sociable clans conjoined. But I, for solitude
Too sorrowful, faltered at heart and cried aloud,
'O Poverty, come hither and talk with me!
For should I be flung
To the utmost frontiers of space,
To the tenantless margins of the world,
Yet wouldst thou be with me;
Thy henchman am I, O Poverty,
And thy harsh penalties, my pay.
Not in childhood only, in infancy
When laughing I would build
Castles of soil or sand, wast thou
My more than neighbour, for thy roof
Touched mine, and our two homes were one;
But in manhood also weighed I with the great
Lighter, because of thee,
Than fluff or feather; more frail my fortunes
Than gossamer, who to the State submitting
Great worth, found small employ;
Withdrawing, heard no blame.'

Then many years I wandered as a stranger
With these thoughts in my heart:
'Others wear broidered coats; my homespun is not whole.

Others eat millet and rice, I boil the fennel-leaf.
No toy nor treasure is mine,
Nor aught to make me glad.
The swallows by my father's house
Play on; but I abroad the world
Sell my day-labour, pawn my coat for bread.
Servant of many masters,
Hand-chafed I dig, heel-blistered hoe,
Bare-backed to the wind and rain.
And that all this befell me,
That friends and favourites forsook me,
That up the hill of State so laboured was my climb,
Who should bear blame? Who but thou, O Poverty,
Was cause of all my woe?

'I fled thee high and far, but thou across the hills of heaven
Like a hawk didst follow me.
I fled thee among the rocks, in caverns of stone I hid;
But thou up those huge steeps
Didst follow me.
I fled thee to the ocean, sailed that cypress ship
Across the storm, but thou,
Whether on wave-crest or in the hollows of the sea,
Didst ever follow me.
'And if I move, you too are stirring;
If I lie down, you are at rest.
Have you no other friend in all the world?
What would you seek of me?
Go, Poverty! and pester me no more.'

Then said Poverty: 'So be it, my master;
For 'tis plain that should I stay
You will not cease to slander and defame me.
But listen, I too have a heart that is full
And a tale that must be told.

'My father's father long, long ago
Was illustrious in the land; of virtue so excellent
That by the King's throne in council he stood,

Admonishing the rulers how to make statutes and laws.
Of earth were the stairs, roofed over with thatch,
Not carved nor hung.
But when the world in latter days
Was given over to folly, fell about in darkness,
Then gluttons gathered together,
Sought wealth and found it,
Despised my grand-dad, they were so insolent and proud;
Built arbours of onyx, terraces of jade,
And huge halls to dwell in; lapped lakes of wine.
On a broth of swans they fed,
And held no Audience at their court.
Thrice daily would they look into their souls and cry,
"Our hearts are free from sin",
And they that dwelt in the Palace of the King
Had great substance, and their guerdon was gold
Stacked high as the hills.
Your small woes you remember;
But my blest deeds you have forgot.
Did I not teach you
By gradual usage, indifferent to endure
Summer's heat and winter's cold?
(And that which neither heat nor cold can touch—
Is it not eternal as the Gods?)

'I, Poverty,
Turned from you the envy of the covetous, taught you to fear
Neither Chieh the Tyrant nor the Robber Chih.
Others, my master,
Quake behind bolt and bar, while you alone
Live open to the world.
Others by care
And pitiful apprehension are cast down,
While you are gay and free.'
Thus spoke Poverty, and when her speech was ended,
Stern of countenance and with dilated eye,
She gathered up the folds of her garment and rose from where she sat,
Passed down the stairway and left my house.

'Farewell,' said Poverty, 'for now I leave you.
To that hill I take my way
Where sheltering, the Lord of Kuchu's sons
Have learnt to ply my trade.'
Then I, Yang Tzŭ, left the mat where I lay
And cried: 'O Poverty, let my crooked words
Be as unspoken; forget that I have wronged thee.
I have heard truth, O Poverty, and received it.
Live with me always, for of your company
I shall not weary till I die.'
Then Poverty came back and dwelt with me,
Nor since has left my side.

1923

Fighting South of the Ramparts

Anonymous (1ST century AD)

They fought south of the ramparts,
   They died north of the wall.
   They died in the moors and were not buried.
Their flesh was the food of crows.
'Tell the crows we are not afraid;
We have died in the moors and cannot be buried.
Crows, how can our bodies escape you?'
The waters flowed deep
And the rushes in the pool were dark.
The riders fought and were slain;
Their horses wander neighing.
By the bridge there was a house.[1]
Was it south, was it north?
The harvest was never gathered.
How can we give you your offerings?
You served your Prince faithfully,
Though all in vain.
I think of you, faithful soldiers;
Your service shall not be forgotten.
For in the morning you went out to battle
And at night you did not return.

1917

---

[1] There is no trace of it left. This passage describes the havoc of war. The harvest has not been gathered: therefore corn-offerings cannot be made to the spirits of the dead.

The Dancers of Huai-nan

by Chang Hêng (78–139)

(A Fragment)

I saw them dancing at Huai-nan and made this poem of praise:

The instruments of music are made ready,
Strong wine is in our cups;
Flute-songs flutter and a din of magic drums.
Sound scatters like foam, surges free as a flood. . . .
And now when the drinkers were all drunken,
And the sun had fallen to the west,
Up rose the fair ones to the dance.
Well painted and apparelled,
In veils of soft gossamer
All wound and meshed;
And ribbons they unravelled,
And scarfs to bind about their heads.
The wielder of the little stick
Whispers them to their places, and the steady drums
Draw them through the mazes of the dance.
They have raised their long sleeves, they have covered their eyes;
Slowly their shrill voices
Swell the steady song.
And the song said:
As a frightened bird whose love
Has wandered away from the nest,
I flutter my desolate wings.
For the wind blows back to my home,
And I long for my father's house.

Subtly from slender hips they swing,
Swaying, slanting delicately up and down.
And like the crimson mallow's flower

Glows their beauty, shedding flames afar.
They lift languid glances,
Peep distrustfully, till of a sudden
Ablaze with liquid light
Their soft eyes kindle. So dance to dance
Endlessly they weave, break off and dance again.
Now flutter their cuffs like a great bird in flight.
Now toss their long white sleeves like whirling snow.
So the hours go by, till now at last
The powder has blown from their cheeks, the black from their brows,
Flustered now are the fair faces, pins of pearl
Torn away, tangled the black tresses.
With combs they catch and gather in
The straying locks, put on the gossamer gown
That trailing winds about them, and in unison
Of body, song and dress, obedient
Each shadows each, as they glide softly to and fro.

1923

The Bones of Chuang Tzu [1][2]

by Chang Hêng

I, Chang P'ing-Tzu, had traversed the Nine Wilds and seen their
    wonders,
In the eight continents beheld the ways of Man,
The Sun's procession, the orbit of the Stars,
The surging of the dragon, the soaring of the phoenix in his flight.
In the red desert to the south I sweltered,
And northward waded through the wintry burghs of Yu.
Through the Valley of Darkness to the west I wandered,
And eastward travelled to the Sun's extreme abode,
The stooping Mulberry Tree.

So the seasons sped; weak autumn languished,
A small wind woke the cold.

And now with rearing of rein-horse,
Plunging of the tracer, round I fetched
My high-roofed chariot to westward.
Along the dykes we loitered, past many meadows,
And far away among the dunes and hills.
Suddenly I looked and by the roadside
I saw a man's bones lying in the squelchy earth,
Black rime-frost over him; and I in sorrow spoke
And asked him, saying, 'Dead man, how was it?
Fled you with your friend from famine and for the last grains
Gambled and lost? Was this earth your tomb,
Or did floods carry you from afar? Were you mighty, were you wise,
Were you foolish and poor? A warrior, or a girl?'
Then a wonder came; for out of the silence a voice—

[1] The great Taoist philosopher; see my *Three Ways of Thought in Ancient China*.

[2] In an article, 'Life Under the Han Dynasty . . .' (1953) Waley wrote that this is 'to
my mind the finest of all long Chinese poems'. *Ed.*

Thin echo only, in no substance was the Spirit seen—
Mysteriously answered, saying, 'I was a man of Sung,
Of the clan of Chuang; Chou was my name.
Beyond the climes of common thought
My reason soared, yet could I not save myself;
For at the last, when the long charter of my years was told,
I too, for all my magic, by Age was brought
To the Black Hill of Death.
Wherefore, O Master, do you question me?'
Then I answered:
'Let me plead for you upon the Five Hill-tops,
Let me pray for you to the Gods of Heaven and the Gods of Earth,
That your white bones may arise,
And your limbs be joined anew.
The God of the North shall give me back your ears;
I will scour the Southland for your eyes;
From the sunrise will I wrest your feet;
The West shall yield your heart.
I will set each several organ in its throne;
Each subtle sense will I restore.
Would you not have it so?'
The dead man answered me:
'O Friend, how strange and unacceptable your words!
In death I rest and am at peace; in life, I toiled and strove.
Is the hardness of the winter stream
Better than the melting of spring?
All pride that the body knew,
Was it not lighter than dust?
What Ch'ao and Hsü despised,
What Po-ch'eng fled,
Shall I desire, whom death
Already has hidden in the Eternal Way—
Where Li Chu cannot see me,
Nor Tzŭ Yeh hear me,
Where neither Yao nor Shun can praise me,
Nor the tyrants Chieh and Hsin condemn me,
Nor wolf nor tiger harm me,
Lance prick me nor sword wound me?

Of the Primal Spirit is my substance; I am a wave
In the river of Darkness and Light.
The Maker of All Things is my Father and Mother,
Heaven is my bed and earth my cushion,
The thunder and lightning are my drum and fan,
The sun and moon my candle and my torch,
The Milky Way my moat, the stars my jewels.
With Nature am I conjoined;
I have no passion, no desire.
Wash me and I shall be no whiter,
Foul me and I shall yet be clean.
I come not, yet am here;
Hasten not, yet am swift.'
The voice stopped, there was silence.
A ghostly light
Faded and expired.
I gazed upon the dead, stared in sorrow and compassion.
Then I called upon my servant that was with me
To tie his silken scarf about those bones
And wrap them in a cloak of sombre dust;
While I, as offering to the soul of this dead man,
Poured my hot tears upon the margin of the road.

1923

The Lychee Tree

by Wang I (*c.* 120)

Sombre as the heavens when morning clouds arise,
Bushy as a great broom held across the sky,
Vast as the spaces of a lofty house,
Deep fretted as a line of stony hills.
Long branches twining,
Green leaves clustering,
And all a-glimmer like a mist that lightly lies
Across the morning sun;
All spangled, darted with fire like a sky
Of populous stars.
Shell like a fisherman's red net;
Fruit white and lustrous as a pearl, . . .
Lambent as the jewel of Ho, more strange
Than the saffron-stone of Wu.
Now sigh we at the beauty of its show.
Now triumph in its taste.
Sweet juices lie in the mouth;
Soft scents invade the mind.
All flavours here are joined, yet none is master;
A hundred diverse tastes
Blend in such harmony no man can say
That one outstrips the rest. Sovereign of sweets,
Peerless, pre-eminent fruit, who dwellest apart
In noble solitude!

1923

The Nightmare

by Wang Yen-shou (*c.* 130)

One night, about the time I came of age, I dreamt that demon creatures fought with me while I slept. . . . When I woke I told this vision in verse, that the dreamers of posterity might use my poem as a spell to drive off evil dreams. And so often has it proved its worth that I dare not any longer hide it from the world. The words are these:

Once, as in the darkness I lay asleep by night,
Strange things suddenly saw I in my dream;
All my dream was of monsters that came about me while I slept,
Devils and demons, four-horned, serpent-necked,
Fishes with bird-tails, three-legged bogies
From six eyes staring; dragons hideous,
Yet three-part human.
On rushed the foul flocks, grisly legions,
Stood round me, stretched out their arms,
Danced their hands about me, and sought to snatch me from my bed.
Then cried I (and in my dream
My voice was thick with anger and my words all awry):
'Ill-spawned elves, how dare you
Beset with your dire shapes Creation's cleanest,
Shapeliest creature, Man?' Then straightway I struck out,
Flashed my fists like lightning among them, thumped like thunder,
Here slit Jack-o'-Lantern,
Here smashed fierce Hog-face,
Battered wights and goblins,
Smote venturous vampires, pounded in the dust
Imps, gnomes and lobs,
Kobolds and kelpies;
Swiped bulge-eyed bogies, oafs and elves;
Clove Tough-head's triple skull, threw down

Clutching Night-hag, flogged the gawky Ear-wig Fiend
That floundered toward me on its tail.

I struck at staring eyes,
Stamped on upturned faces; through close ranks
Of hoofs I cut my way, buried my fingers deep
In half-formed flesh;
Ghouls tore at my touch; I slit sharp noses,
Trod on red tongues, seized shaggy manes,
Shook bald-heads by the beard.
Then was a scuffling. Arms and legs together
Chasing, crashing and sliding; a helter-skelter
Of feet lost and found in the tugging and toppling,
Cuffing, cudgelling, frenzied flogging. . . .

So fought I, till terror and dismay
Shook those foul flocks; panic spread like a flame
Down mutinous ranks; they stand, they falter,
Those ghastly legions; but fleeing, suddenly turn
Glazed eyes upon me, to see how now I fare.
At last, to end their treachery
Again I rushed upon them, braved their slaver and snares,
Stood on a high place, and lashed down among them,
Shrieking and cursing as my blows crashed.
Then three by three and four by four
One after another hop-a-trot they fled.
Bellowing and bawling till the air was full of their breath—
Grumbling and snarling,
Those vanquished ogres, demons discomfited,
Some that would fain have run
Lolling and lurching, some that for cramped limbs
Could not stir from where they stood. Some over belly-wounds
Bent double; some in agony gasping and groaning.
Suddenly the clouds broke and (I knew not why)
A thin light filtered the darkness; then, while again
I sighed in wonder that those disastrous creatures,
Dire monstrosities, should dare assail
A clean and comely man, . . . there sounded in my ears

A twittering and crowing. And outdoors it was light.
The noisy cock, mindful that dawn was in the sky,
Had crowed his warning, and the startled ghosts,
Because they heard dawn heralded, had fled
In terror and tribulation from the rising day.

1923

Sailing Homeward

by Chan Fang-shêng (4th century)

Cliffs that rise a thousand feet
    Without a break,
    Lake that stretches a hundred miles
Without a wave,
Sands that are white through all the year,
Without a stain,
Pine-tree woods, winter and summer
Ever-green,
Streams that for ever flow and flow
Without a pause,
Trees that for twenty thousand years
Your vows have kept,
You have suddenly healed the pain of a traveller's heart,
And moved his brush to write a new song.

1918

Ballad from Tun-huang

Anonymous (?7th century)

Such pure moon-white waxen blossoms
Piercing the rich dark leafy green,
Bursting open to smile into the sunlight
They bathe the air in sensuous scent.

Just as those gleaming blooms break out
My thoughts of you traverse the dark ravines,
Just as their scent enchants your senses
I would that my love could soothe your soul.

1960

Self-abandonment

by Li Po (?701–?762)

I sat drinking and did not notice the dusk,
Till falling petals filled the folds of my dress.
Drunken I rose and walked to the moonlit stream;
The birds were gone, and men also few.

1919

Exile's Letter (c. 748)

by Li Po

The best account of Li Po's early life and its pleasures is contained in the famous poem brilliantly paraphrased by Ezra Pound in *Cathay*, under the title *Exile's Letter*. It was written round about 748 and is addressed to a certain Commissary Yüan, of whom nothing further is known.[1]

Do you remember how once at Lo-yang
Tung Tsao-ch'iu built us a wine-tower south of the T'ien-ching Bridge?
With yellow gold and tallies of white jade we bought songs and
    laughter
And we were drunk month after month, scorning princes and rulers.
Among us were the wisest and bravest within the Four Seas, with
    thoughts high as the clouds.
(But with you above all my heart was at no cross-purpose.)
Going round mountains, skirting lakes was as nothing to them,
All their feelings, all their thoughts were ours to share; they held
    nothing back.
Then I went off to Huai-nan to pluck my laurel-branch[2]
And you stayed north of the Lo, sighing over your memories and
    dreams.
But we could not long bear the separation—were soon together again
    exploring the Fairy Castle.[3]
We followed the thirty-six banks of the twisting stream
And all the way the waters were bright with a thousand flowers.
We passed through a myriad valleys
And in each heard the voice of wind among the pines.
At last, on a silver saddle with tassels of gold that reached to the ground
The Governor of Han-tung came out to meet us,

[1] See also the passage from this poem quoted on pp. 149–50. *Ed.*
[2] i.e., to get married.
[3] Name of a mountain near Han-tung.

And the Holy Man of Tzu-yang[4] summoned us, blowing on his jade
   reed-pipe,
And when we came to him he made for us unearthly music, high up
   in the tower that he had built—
A hubbub of sound, as when the phoenix cries to its mate.
And the Governor of Han-tung, because his long sleeves would not
   keep still when the flutes called to him
Rose and did a drunken dance.
Then he brought his embroidered coat and covered me with it
And I slept with my head on his lap.
At that feast our spirits had soared to the Nine Heavens,
But by evening we had scattered like stars or rain,
Away over the hills and rivers to the frontiers of Ch'u.
I went back to my old mountain-nest
And you too went home, crossing the bridge over the Wei.

1950

[4] The Taoist Hu Tzu-yang, fourteenth Patriarch of the Shang-ch'ing School. He
died in or soon after 742, and his grave-inscription was composed by Li Po, at the request
of the Buddhist monk Chêng-ch'ien.

Fighting South of the Ramparts[1] (c. 750)

by Li Po

Last year we were fighting at the source of the Sang-kan;[2]
    This year we are fighting on the Onion River[3] road.
    We have washed our swords in the surf of Parthian seas;
We have pastured our horses among the snows of the T'ien Shan,
The King's armies have grown grey and old
Fighting ten thousand leagues away from home.
The Huns have no trade but cattle and carnage;
They have no fields or ploughlands,
But only wastes where white bones lie among yellow sands.
Where the House of Ch'in built the great wall that was to keep away
    the Tartars.
There, in its turn, the House of Han lit beacons of war.
The beacons are always alight, fighting and marching never stop.
Men die in the field, slashing sword to sword;
The horses of the conquered neigh piteously to Heaven.
Crows and hawks peck for human guts,
Carry them in their beaks and hang them on the branches of withered
    trees.
Captains and soldiers are smeared on the bushes and grass;
The General schemed in vain.
Know therefore that the sword is a cursed thing
Which the wise man uses only if he must.[4]

[1] Cf. p. 175. *Ed.*
[2] Runs west to east through northern Shansi and Hopei, north of the Great Wall.
[3] The Kashgar-darya, in Turkestan.
[4] Quotation from the *Tao-t'e Ching.*

The Pitcher

by Yüan Chên (779–831)

I dreamt I climbed to a high, high plain;
And on the plain I found a deep well.
My throat was dry with climbing and I longed to drink,
And my eyes were eager to look into the cool shaft.
I walked round it, I looked right down;
I saw my image mirrored on the face of the pool.
An earthen pitcher was sinking into the black depths;
There was no rope to pull it to the well-head.
I was strangely troubled lest the pitcher should be lost,
And started wildly running to look for help.
From village to village I scoured that high plain;
The men were gone; fierce dogs snarled.
I came back and walked weeping round the well;
Faster and faster the blinding tears flowed—
Till my own sobbing suddenly woke me up;
My room was silent, no one in the house stirred.
The flame of my candle flickered with a green smoke;
The tears I had shed glittered in the candle-light.
A bell sounded; I knew it was the midnight-chime;
I sat up in bed and tried to arrange my thoughts:
The plain in my dream was the graveyard at Ch'ang-an,
Those hundred acres of untilled land.
The soil heavy and the mounds heaped high;
And the dead below them laid in deep troughs.
Deep are the troughs, yet sometimes dead men
Find their way to the world above the grave.
And to-night my love who died long ago
Came into my dream as the pitcher sunk in the well.
That was why the tears suddenly streamed from my eyes,
Streamed from my eyes and fell on the collar of my dress.

1919

Four Poems by Han-shan ('Cold Mountain') (8th-9th centuries)

The Chinese poet Han-shan lived in the 8th and 9th centuries. He and his brothers worked a farm that they had inherited; but he fell out with them, parted from his wife and family, and wandered from place to place, reading many books and looking in vain for a patron. He finally settled as a recluse on the Cold Mountain (Han-shan) and is always known as 'Han-shan'. This retreat was about twenty-five miles from T'ien-t'ai, famous for its many monasteries, both Buddhist and Taoist, which Han-shan visited from time to time. In one poem he speaks of himself as being over a hundred. This may be an exaggeration; but it is certain that he lived to a great age.

In his poems the Cold Mountain is often the name of a state of mind rather than of a locality. It is on this conception, as well as on that of the 'hidden treasure', the Buddha who is to be sought not somewhere outside us, but 'at home' in the heart, that the mysticism of the poems is based.

The poems, of which just over three hundred survive, have no titles.

I.

I make my way up the Cold Mountain path;
The way up seems never to end.
The valley so long and the ground so stony;
The stream so broad and the brush so tangled and thick.
The moss is slippery, rain or no rain;
The pine-trees sing even when no wind blows.
Who can bring himself to transcend the bonds of the world
And sit with me among the white clouds?

2.

I went off quietly to visit a wise monk,
Where misty mountains rose in myriad piles.
The Master himself showed me my way back,
Pointing to where the moon, that round lamp, hung.

3.

A place to prize is this Cold Mountain,
Whose white clouds for ever idle on their own,
Where the cry of monkeys spreads among the paths,
Where the tiger's roar transcends the world of men.
Walking alone I step from stone to stone,
Singing to myself I clutch at the creepers for support.
The wind in the pine-trees makes its shrill note;
The chatter of the birds mingles its harmony.

4.

Since first I meant to explore the eastern cliff
And have not done so, countless years have passed.
Yesterday I pulled myself up by the creepers,
But half way, was baffled by storm and fog.
The cleft so narrow that my clothing got caught fast;
The moss so sticky that I could not free my shoes.
So I stopped here under this red cinnamon,
To sleep for a while on a pillow of white clouds.

1954

The Old Man with the Broken Arm (c. 809)

(A Satire on Militarism)

by Po Chü-i (772–846)

At Hsin-fêng an old man—four-score and eight;
The hair on his head and the hair of his eyebrows—white as the new snow.
Leaning on the shoulders of his great-grandchildren, he walks in front of the Inn;
With his left arm he leans on their shoulders; his right arm is broken.
I asked the old man how many years had passed since he broke his arm;
I also asked the cause of the injury, how and why it happened?
The old man said he was born and reared in the District of Hsin-fêng;
At the time of his birth—a wise reign; no wars or discords.
'Often I listened in the Pear-Tree Garden to the sound of flute and song;
Naught I knew of banner and lance; nothing of arrow or bow.
Then came the wars of T'ien-pao[1] and the great levy of men;
Of three men in each house—one man was taken.
And those to whom the lot fell, where were they taken to?
Five months' journey, a thousand miles—away to Yün-nan.
We heard it said that in Yün-nan there flows the Lu River;
As the flowers fall from the pepper-trees, poisonous vapours rise.
When the great army waded across, the water seethed like a cauldron;
When barely ten had entered the water, two or three were dead.
To the north of my village, to the south of my village the sound of weeping and wailing,
Children parting from fathers and mothers; husbands parting from wives.
Everyone says that in expeditions against the Man tribes

[1] AD 742–55.

192

Of a million men who are sent out, not one returns.
 I, that am old, was then twenty-four;
My name and fore-name were written down in the rolls of the Board
 of War.
In the depth of the night not daring to let anyone know
I secretly took a huge stone and dashed it against my arm.
For drawing the bow and waving the banner now wholly unfit
I knew henceforward I should not be sent to fight in Yün-nan.
Bones broken and sinews wounded could not fail to hurt;
My plan was to be rejected and sent back to my home.
My arm—broken ever since; it was sixty years ago.
One limb, although destroyed—whole body safe!
But even now on winter nights when the wind and rain blow
From evening on till day's dawn I cannot sleep for pain.
 Not sleeping for pain
 Is a small thing to bear,
Compared with the joy of being alive when all the rest are dead.
For otherwise, years ago, at the ford of Lu River
My body would have died and my soul hovered by the bones that
 no one gathered.
A ghost, I'd have wandered in Yün-nan, always looking for home.
Over the graves of ten thousand soldiers, mournfully hovering.'
 So the old man spoke,
 And I bid you listen to his words.
 Have you not heard
That the Prime Minister of K'ai-yüan,[2] His Excellency Sung,[3]
Did not reward frontier exploits, lest a spirit of aggression should
 prevail?
 And have you not heard
That the Prime Minister of T'ien-Pao, Yang Kuo-chung,[4]
Desiring to win imperial favour, started a frontier war,
But long before he could win the war, people had lost their temper?
Ask the man with the broken arm in the village of Hsin-fêng.

1917

713–42.
[3] Sung Ying; died 737.
[4] Cousin of the notorious mistress of Ming-huang, Yang Kuei-fei.

On Board Ship: Reading Yüan Chên's Poems (c. 815)

by Po Chü-i

I take your poems in my hand and read them beside the candle;
The poems are finished, the candle is low, dawn not yet come.
My eyes smart; I put out the lamp and go on sitting in the dark,
Listening to waves that, driven by the wind, strike the prow of the ship.

1917

Dreaming that I Went with Li and Yü to Visit Yüan Chên (c. 816)

(Written in Exile)

by Po Chü-i

At night I dreamt I was back in Ch'ang-an;
I saw again the faces of old friends.
And in my dreams, under an April sky,
They led me by the hand to wander in the spring winds.
Together we came to the ward of Peace and Quiet;
We stopped our horses at the gate of Yüan Chên.
Yüan Chên was sitting all alone;
When he saw me coming, a smile came to his face.
He pointed back at the flowers in the western court;
Then opened wine in the northern summer-house.
He seemed to be saying that neither of us had changed;
He seemed to be regretting that joy will not stay;
That our souls had met only for a little while,
To part again with hardly time for greeting.
I woke up and thought him still at my side;
I put out my hand; there was nothing there at all.

1919

Madly Singing in the Mountains (c. 816)

by Po Chü-i

There is no one among men that has not a special failing:
And my failing consists in writing verses.
I have broken away from the thousand ties of life:
But this infirmity still remains behind.
Each time that I look at a fine landscape:
Each time that I meet a loved friend,
I raise my voice and recite a stanza of poetry
And am glad as though a God had crossed my path.
Ever since the day I was banished to Hsün-yang
Half my time I have lived among the hills.
And often, when I have finished a new poem,
Alone I climb the road to the Eastern Rock.
I lean my body on the banks of white stone:
I pull down with my hands a green cassia branch.
My mad singing startles the valleys and hills:
The apes and birds all come to peep.
Fearing to become a laughing-stock to the world,
I choose a place that is unfrequented by men.

1917

Children (c. 820)

by Po Chü-i

My nephew, who is six years old, is called 'Tortoise',
My daughter of three—little 'Summer Dress'.
One is beginning to learn to joke and talk;
The other can already recite poems and songs.
At morning they play clinging about my feet;
At night they sleep pillowed against my dress.
Why, children, did you reach the world so late,
Coming to me just when my years are spent?
Young things draw our feelings to them;
Old people easily give their hearts.
The sweetest vintage at last turns sour;
The full moon in the end begins to wane.
And so with men the bonds of love and affection
Soon may change to a load of sorrow and care.
But all the world is bound by love's ties;
Why did I think that I alone should escape?

1918

197

The Hat Given to the Poet by Li Chien (c. 821)

by Po Chü-i

Long ago a white-haired gentleman
  You made the present of a black gauze hat.
  The gauze hat still sits on my head;
But you already are gone to the Nether Springs.
The thing is old, but still fit to wear;
The man is gone and will never be seen again.
Out on the hill the moon is shining to-night
And the trees on your tomb are swayed by the autumn wind.

1918

After Getting Drunk, Becoming Sober in the Night (c. 824)

by Po Chü-i

Our party scattered at yellow dusk and I came home to bed;
I woke at midnight and went for a walk, leaning heavily on a
friend.
As I lay on my pillow my vinous complexion, soothed by sleep, grew
sober;
In front of the tower the ocean moon, accompanying the tide, had risen.
The swallows, about to return to the beams, went back to roost again;
The candle at my window, just going out, suddenly revived its light.
All the time till dawn came, still my thoughts were muddled;
And in my ears something sounded like the music of flutes and strings.

1917

On Being Sixty (831)

by Po Chü-i

Between thirty and forty one is distracted by the Five Lusts;
Between seventy and eighty one is prey to a hundred diseases.
But from fifty to sixty one is free from all ills;
Calm and still—the heart enjoys rest.
I have put behind me Love and Greed, I have done with Profit and
    Fame;
I am still short of illness and decay, and far from decrepit age.
Strength of limb I still possess to seek the rivers and hills;
Still my heart has spirit enough to listen to flutes and strings.
At leisure I open new wine and taste several cups;
Drunken I recall old poems and chant a stray verse.
To Tun-shih and Mêng-tê[1] I offer this advice:
Do not complain of three-score, 'the time of obedient ears'.[2]

1917

[1] Ts'ui Ch'ün and Liu Yü-hsi, who were the same age as Po Chü-i.
[2] Confucius said that not till sixty did 'his ears obey him'.

On His Baldness (832)

by Po Chü-i

At dawn I sighed to see my hairs fall;
   At dusk I sighed to see my hairs fall.
   For I dreaded the time when the last lock should go . . .
They are all gone and I do not mind at all!
I have done with that cumbrous washing and getting dry;
My tiresome comb for ever is laid aside.
Best of all, when the weather is hot and wet,
To have no top-knot weighing down on one's head!
I put aside my messy cloth wrap;
I have got rid of my dusty tasselled fringe.
In a silver jar I have stored a cold stream,
On my bald pate I trickle a ladle full.
Like one baptized with the Water of Buddha's Law,
I sit and receive this cool, cleansing joy.
Now I know why the priest who seeks Repose
Frees his heart by first shaving his head.

1919

A Mad Poem Addressed to my Nephews and Nieces (835)

by Po Chü-i

The World cheats those who cannot read;
I, happily, have mastered script and pen.
The World cheats those who hold no office;
I am blessed with high official rank.
Often the old have much sickness and pain;
With me, luckily, there is not much wrong.
People when they are old are often burdened with ties;
But I have finished with marriage and giving in marriage.
No changes happen to jar the quiet of my mind;
No business comes to impair the vigour of my limbs.
Hence it is that now for ten years
Body and soul have rested in hermit peace.
And all the more, in the last lingering years
What I shall need are very few things.
A single rug to warm me through the winter;
One meal to last me the whole day.
It does not matter that my house is rather small;
One cannot sleep in more than one room!
It does not matter that I have not many horses;
One cannot ride on two horses at once!
As fortunate as me among the people of the world
Possibly one would find seven out of ten.
As contented as me among a hundred men
Look as you may, you will not find one.
In the affairs of others even fools are wise;
In their own business even sages err.
To no one else would I dare to speak my heart,
So my wild words are addressed to my nephews and nieces.

1919

Old Age (835)

(Addressed to Liu Yü-hsi, who was born in the same year)

by Po Chü-i

We are growing old together, you and I,
Let us ask ourselves, what is age like?
The dull eye is closed ere night comes;
The idle head, still uncombed at noon.
Propped on a staff, sometimes a walk abroad;
Or all day sitting with closed doors.
One dares not look in the mirror's polished face;
One cannot read small-letter books.
Deeper and deeper, one's love of old friends;
Fewer and fewer, one's dealings with young men.
One thing only, the pleasure of idle talk,
Is great as ever, when you and I meet.

1919

Going to the Mountains with a Little Dancing Girl, Aged Fifteen (c. 837)

(Written when the poet was about sixty-five)

by Po Chü-i

Two top-knots not yet plaited into one.
Of thirty years—just beyond half.
You who are really a lady of silks and satins
Are now become my hill and stream companion!
At the spring fountains together we splash and play;
On the lovely trees together we climb and sport.

. . . .

Her cheeks grow rosy, as she quickens her sleeve-dancing:
Her brows grow sad, as she slows her song's tune.
Don't go singing the Song of the Willow Branches,[1]
When there's no one here with a heart for you to break!

1917

[1] A plaintive love-song, to which Po Chü-i had himself written words.

On Hearing Someone Sing a Poem by Yüan Chên (c. 840)

(Written long after Chên's death)

by Po Chü-i

No new poems his brush will trace;
　Even his fame is dead.
　His old poems are deep in dust
　　At the bottom of boxes and cupboards.
Once lately, when someone was singing,
　Suddenly I heard a verse—
Before I had time to catch the words
　A pain had stabbed my heart.

1917

A Dream of Mountaineering (842)

(Written when he was seventy)

by Po Chü-i

At night, in my dream, I stoutly climbed a mountain
Going out alone with my staff of holly-wood.
A thousand crags, a hundred hundred valleys—
In my dream-journey none were unexplored
And all the while my feet never grew tired
And my step was as strong as in my young days.
Can it be that when the mind travels backward
The body also returns to its old state?
And can it be, as between body and soul,
That the body may languish, while the soul is still strong?
Soul and body—both are vanities;
Dreaming and waking—both alike unreal.
In the day my feet are palsied and tottering;
In the night my steps go striding over the hills.
As day and night are divided in equal parts—
Between the two, I *get* as much as I *lose*.

1917

Lao Tzŭ (c. 846)

by Po Chü-i

'Those who speak know nothing;
    Those who know are silent.'
    Those words, I am told,
Were spoken by Lao-tzŭ.
If we are to believe that Lao-tzŭ
    Was himself one who knew,
How comes it that he wrote a book
    Of five thousand words?

1918

Last Poem (846)

by Po Chü-i

. . . .

They have put my bed beside the unpainted screen;
    They have shifted my stove in front of the blue curtain.
    I listen to my grandchildren reading me a book;
I watch the servants heating up my soup.
With rapid pencil I answer the poems of friends,
I feel in my pockets and pull out medicine-money.
When this superintendence of trifling affairs is done,
I lie back on my pillows and sleep with my face to the South.

1917

Immeasurable Pain

by Li Hou-chu, last Emperor of the Southern T'ang Dynasty (*c.* 975)

Immeasurable pain!
My dreaming soul last night was king again.
As in past days
I wandered through the Palace of Delight,
And in my dream
Down grassy garden-ways
Glided my chariot, smoother than a summer stream;
There was moonlight,
The trees were blossoming,
And a faint wind softened the air of night,
For it was spring.

1923

Love Poem

by Fêng Mêng-lung (*c.* 1590–1646)

Don't set sail!
The wind is rising and the weather none too good.
Far better come back to my house.
If there is anything you want, just tell me.
If you are cold, my body is warm.
Let us be happy together this one night.
Tomorrow the wind will have dropped;
Then you can go, and I shan't worry about you.

1961

The Little Cart

by Ch'ên Tzŭ-lung (*c.* 1608–1647)

The little cart jolting and banging through the yellow haze of
    dusk;
    The man pushing behind, the woman pulling in front.
They have left the city and do not know where to go.
'Green, green, those elm-tree leaves; *they* will cure my hunger,
If only we could find some quiet place and sup on them together.'

The wind has flattened the yellow mother-wort;
Above it in the distance they see the walls of a house.
'*There* surely must be people living who'll give you something to eat.'
They tap at the door, but no one comes; they look in, but the kitchen
    is empty.
They stand hesitating in the lonely road and their tears fall like rain.

1918

Extracts from *Yuan Mei*
(1716–1798)

Late in the year [1794] Yuan Mei wrote a poem called 'My brush does not grow old':

Writing poems is like the blossoming of flowers;
If there is too much blossom the flowers are generally small;
And all the more, with a man nearing eighty,
Whose powers of invention have long withered away.
Yet all the same, people wanting poems
Continue to clamour for them all day long.
They know that the silkworm, till the moment of its death,
Never ceases to put out fresh threads.
I do my best to turn out something for them,
Though secretly ashamed to show such poor stuff.
Yet oddly enough my good friends that come
All accord in praising what I produce.
I am not the least shaken in my own belief;
But all the same I keep a copy in my drawer.
Can it be that though my body sinks to decay
My writing brush alone is still young?

On the second day of the third month, 1795, he celebrated his eightieth (or, as we in the West should say, seventy-ninth) birthday. He received over three thousand poems and letters of congratulation. From these he chose about two hundred and printed them in a separate little volume. Manchu princes and grandees, generals, leading statesmen, famous scholars and fellow-poets were all represented. Hardly a single famous name of the period, except that of the Emperor Ch'ien Lung himself, is missing. Partly in order to escape from personal congratulations at Nanking he arranged for the marriage of his son Yuan Ch'ih to take place on his birthday and went with him to fetch the bride from Ningpo. She was the daughter of his old friend Shen Jung-ch'ang, a member of one of the foremost Ningpo families, but himself rather unsuccessful in his public career. The girl, Ch'üan-pao ('Complete treasure'), had learnt, from a cousin who lived in the house, how to write poetry, which Yuan's son had never been able to do. 'It looks', writes Yuan Mei, 'as though the family art of poetry will have to descend in the female line.' Near Ningpo he visited the shrine of his 'fifth generation ancestor' Yuan Huai-pin and saw there tablets recording his own election to the Han-lin Academy and his brother Yuan Shu's success in taking the Third Degree. These had presumably been sent by the family, but Yuan Mei himself had never been there before. At Ningpo too he visited the T'ien-i Ko, the most famous private library in Chinese history, founded by Fan Ch'in (1506–85) in the middle of the 16th century. In 1773 the head of the family had sent all the rarer books to Peking, to be copied in connection with Ch'ien Lung's great Imperial Library scheme. It is evident that, contrary to what some accounts suggest, the originals had not been returned to their owner at the time of Yuan's visit. 'The cases are there, but the jewels have departed', he writes, with the note: 'The Sung dynasty printed books and the rare manuscripts that were in the boxes have all disappeared.' Another member of the Fan family, however, still had a collection of about a thousand letters, dating from the Ming dynasty. 'Here', he writes, 'I had better luck, and was even allowed to scribble two or three lines in the margin of one of the letters.' The letter in question was one by Yang Ssu-ch'ang, who in 1641 starved himself to death, after failing to defeat the rebel Chang Hsien-chung.

His travels this spring (1795) were greatly aided by the kindness of Ch'i-feng-e (1746–1806), who lent him a comfortable boat and put several of his own servants at his disposal. 'In all the eighty years of my life', he says in his letter of thanks, 'I have never been the recipient of such limitless generosity and kindness.'

Ch'i-feng-e was an 'honorary Manchu' of Korean origin. In 1796 he got into trouble for failing to investigate properly a falsification of accounts by the Imperial Textile Factory. For a while he had charge of the Yuan-ming-yuan palace near Peking, but was later banished to Turkestan.

On returning from his travels in the summer of 1795, Yuan wrote a number of poems about old age:

Now that I am old I get up very early
And feel like God creating a new world.
I come and go, meeting no one on the way;
Wherever I look, no kitchen-smoke rises.
I want to wash, but the water has not been heated;
I want to drink, but no tea has been made.
My boys and girls are behind closed doors;
My man-servants and maid-servants are all fast asleep.
At first I am cross and feel inclined to shout;
But all of a sudden remember my young days—
How I too in those early morning hours
Lay snoring, and hated to leave my bed.

I find myself going in a certain direction
And am quite sure that I had some plan in my mind.
But by the time I have got half-way
I cannot remember what I wanted to do.
Or again I call out for a servant to come
Evidently meaning to give him some instruction.
By the time he arrives I forget that I have called
And ask instead what he is doing here. . . .
If I step into the garden, a servant rushes to hold me;
If I climb the stairs, the whole household panics.
Whatever I do, someone is sorry for me;
That is what makes being old detestable!

When I was young and had no money to spend
I had a passionate longing for expensive things.
I was always envying people for their fur coats,
For the wonderful things they got to eat and drink.
I dreamt of these things, but none of them came my way,

And in the end I became very depressed.
Nowadays, I have got quite smart clothes,
But am old and ugly, and they do not suit me at all.
All the choicest foods are on my table;
But I only manage to eat a few scraps.
I feel inclined to say to my Creator
'Let me live my days on earth again,
But this time be rich when I am young;
To be poor when one is old does not matter at all.'

On the eighteenth day of the tenth month he fell ill:

If one falls ill, it does not mean one is dying;
But when one is old, anything may happen.
They have sent for a whole series of doctors and healers;
My children sat with me till the third watch.
But an old tree withstands wind and frost;
An idle cloud lightly stays or goes.
This winter cricket's wings must both be there,
Or it would not be able still to fashion its songs.

In the winter he recommended Liu Chih-p'eng to Ts'eng Yü (1760–1831), Transport Commissioner at Yangchow. Ts'eng was a poet and patron of literature. He seems to have got on well with Liu and to have given him a small job of some kind. Some time during 1794 Liu had 'moved to the Southern Garden'. This was an area to the south-west of Soochow where there had once been a famous garden. He may have needed a salary in order to keep the place up.

Yuan Mei had now so far recovered as to go and dine with Ch'en Feng-tzu (1726–99), the Financial Commissioner of Nanking. The food and wine were both excellent, and he got very drunk, a thing which in his whole life had rarely happened to him. Towards the end of the year he wrote:

Everything else in life is easy to break with;
Only my books are hard to leave behind.
I want to go through them all again,
But the days hurry by, and there is not time.

If I start on the Classics I shall never get to history;
If I read philosophy, literature goes by the board.
I look back at the time when I purchased them—
Thousands of dollars, I never worried about the price.
If passages were missing, the pains I took to supply them,
And to fill out sets that were incomplete!
Of the finest texts many are copied by hand;
The toil of which fell to my office clerks.
Day and night I lived with them in intimacy.
I numbered their volumes and marked them with yellow and red.
How many branches of wax-candle light,
How many drops of weary heart's blood!
My sons and grandsons know nothing of this;
Perhaps the book-worms could tell their own tale.
Today I have had a great tidy-up,
And feel I have done everything I was born to do. . . .
It is good to know that the people in the books
Are waiting lined up in the Land of the Dead.
In a little while I shall meet them face to face
And never again need to look at what they wrote!

In 1796 came a horrified letter from an old friend called Chu
Kuei (1731–1806) saying that he had come across an edition of
Yuan's later poems in which his companion on the 1782–86
excursions was mentioned by 'name and surname'. 'I picked up a
writing brush', says Chu Kuei, 'and crossed out the name, thinking
I should ill requite your friendship for me if I did not take steps
to cover up your offence'. 'Is it an offence to make excursions?',
asked Yuan Mei in his reply. 'Or if the offence consisted in a
teacher going with a pupil, what about the excursion to the Rain
Altars that Confucius made with his disciple Fan Ch'ih? Or if it
is wrong for an old man to go about with young ones, how was
it that Confucius went jaunting not with staid contemporaries,
but with "newly-capped youths"? Or is it that you have some
personal objection to Liu? You live six thousand leagues away.
You have never seen him or heard him speak, you do not even
know where he lives or what he does, and yet you have so violent

a feeling against him that you take up your brush and cross out his name. . . . If people hear of it, they will be bound to think that Liu has committed some enormity so frightful that no right-minded gentleman could allow his name to remain on the pages of my book. What do you take him for? Let me tell you he is a descendant of the great Liu Tsung-chou, behaves in an exemplary way to his parents and friends, and is an accomplished writer both of prose and verse. It is true that he is good-looking, and it may have been a great mistake on his part not to have arranged with the Maker of Things, at the time of his birth, to give him an ugly face. By not doing so he no doubt brought upon himself a lot of subsequent criticism. But it appears that such things lie in the hands of the goddess Nü Kua, who moulds her clay as she pleases, and Liu's wishes were not consulted. I have five or six other disciples at the Sui-yuan who happen also to be very good-looking. If they hear of this they will all be wondering whether they too are not in danger.'

Chu Kuei was President of the Board of War and, during part of this year (1796), was Governor-General of Kwantung and Kwangsi, with his headquarters at Canton. It was no doubt here that he heard accounts of Liu's goings-on there in 1784. . . .

This year Yuan Mei was away at Yangchow and Soochow most of the time. He was finding strangely enough that in his old age his sight had improved, and that he no longer needed his spectacles:

Who is it that, now I am old, has given me new eyes?
I have lately stopped wearing my goggles, and see better than before.
You and I have grown old together; you have stood me in good stead,
'Lending me light' for thirty years. But now it is time to part.
Just as my spring is drawing to its close the ice at last has melted;
Almost at dawn the moon of my days has suddenly doubled its light.
From now onward the bridge of my nose and my ears on each side
Will be free from your irksome tugging and dangling for all the rest
    of my days.

He suffered at this time from sleeplessness:

Since I grew old and my soul decayed, all night I cannot sleep,
While mark by mark the float sinks till it touches the Fifth Watch.
Oh that someone would take me by the hand and lead me to the
　　Land of Sleep;
Gladly would I give a year of life as barter for a single dream!

The 'float' of course refers to the water-clock. Another poem
of this period refers to the belief that the 'widower-fish' (a kind
of pike) cannot close its eyes:

Now that I am old I am frightened of the night, for it seems longer
　　than a year;
I might as well be a widower-fish, so little do I sleep.
I watch as eagerly for day as a candidate watches for the lists;
Not till the first salvo of dawn does my torment draw to its close.

But he was still very active. He records that in this year (1796)
he acquired five lady pupils, and towards the close of the year
he was finishing his Cookery Book (*Shih Tan*, 'The Menu'):
'in the intervals of writing poetry I compose my Cookery Book'.
It seems, however, that the Cookery Book, perhaps in an incomplete form, had been circulating in manuscript for some years
before this. For many years past he had been in the habit, whenever
he particularly enjoyed a dish at a friend's house, of sending round
his cook to take a lesson in making this dish. The composing of the
cookery book consisted largely in arranging these recipes in
systematic order, and writing a few pages of general introduction.
In his exhortations and warnings, at the beginning, he is evidently
hard put to it to think of anything to say. One does not need a
major poet to tell one that the cook must keep his hands clean
and not let ashes fall into the food, or that the ingredients must
be fresh and in good condition. One is reminded, in reading him,
of the BBC auntie who tells us that bacon tastes nicer when it
is not green.

Westerners who have heard of Yuan Mei generally associate
his name with the cookery book, owing to the fact that Professor
Giles translated some passages from it in his *History of Chinese*

Literature and elsewhere. It was also translated into French by a writer using the pseudonym Panking, in 1924. Here are a few extracts from it:

A good cook cannot with the utmost application produce more than four successful dishes in one day, and even then it is hard for him to give proper attention to every detail; and he certainly won't get through unless everything is in its right place and he is on his feet the whole time. It is no use to give him a lot of assistants; each of them will have his own ideas, and there will be no proper discipline. The more help he gets, the worse the results will be. I once dined with a merchant. There were three successive sets of dishes and sixteen different sweets. Altogether, more than forty kinds of food were served. My host regarded the dinner as an enormous success. But when I got home I was so hungry that I ordered a bowl of plain rice-gruel. From this it may be imagined how little there was, despite this profusion of dishes, that was at all fit to eat.

I always say that chicken, pork, fish and duck are the original geniuses of the board, each with a flavour of its own, each with its distinctive style; whereas sea-slug and swallows-nest (despite their costliness) are commonplace fellows, with no character—in fact, mere hangers-on. I was once asked to a party given by a certain Governor, who gave us plain boiled swallows-nest, served in enormous vases, like flower-pots. It had no taste at all. The other guests were obsequious in their praise of it. But I said: 'We are here to eat swallows-nest, not to take delivery of it wholesale.' If our host's object was simply to impress, it would have been better to put a hundred pearls into each bowl. Then we should have known that the meal had cost him tens of thousands, without the unpleasantness of being expected to eat what was uneatable.

When I was at Peking there was a certain gentleman who was very fond of inviting guests, but the food was not at all good. One day a guest said to him, 'Do you count me as a good friend?' 'Certainly I do', said the host. The guest then knelt in front of him, saying, 'If you are indeed my friend, I have a request to make to you, and I shall not rise from my knees till it is granted'. 'What is your request?', asked the astonished host. 'That you will promise', said the guest, 'that in future when you ask people to dinner, you will not ask me.'

Governor Yang's Western Ocean (i.e. *European*) *Wafer.*
Take the white of an egg and some flour-powder and mix them into a paste. Make a pair of metal shears with at their ends two plates the shape of the wafer, about the size of a small dish. There should be less than a tenth of an inch

between the two surfaces when the scissors close. Heat on a fierce fire. All that is needed is your paste, your scissors and the fire. In a moment the wafer will be finished, white as snow and lustrous as glazed paper. On top, add a powdering of frosted sugar and pine-kernels.

In the year *ping-hsu* (1766) I stayed at Li-shui with Mr Yeh, and he gave me 'black groats' (*wu-fan*) wine to drink. When I had consumed sixteen cups those present began to be rather concerned, and advised me to stop. I was already reeling, but could not bring myself to keep my hands off it.

It is black in colour; the taste very sweet and fresh. But its excellence is really beyond anything that can be put into words. I was told that at Li-shui when a girl is born they always make a jar of this wine, using high quality dark cooked-millet. They do not open it till the girl's wedding day, so that it is drunk at the earliest fifteen or sixteen years after it is made. When the jar is opened, half has evaporated. What remains is so thick that it is like glue in the mouth and its perfume is so strong that it can be smelt even outside the room.

(By the late summer of 1797 the cookery book had already been printed.)

Early in 1797 he had a bad relapse which he attributed to having been given *shen-ch'i* (apparently a kind of ginseng). After a month a friend recommended sulphur. Yuan's family were aghast, as sulphur was considered to be a very violent and dangerous drug. But three doses of it completely undid the evil effects of the *shen-ch'i*. Another friend wrote urging him to give up taking medicines altogether.

In his weak state he found that reading his own poems was the employment that suited him best:

What is the thing best suited for someone who is lying ill?
To open a book is about as much as I have strength to do.
To delight my ears I may casually listen to a bird outside the window,
But for pleasure of the mind I nowadays read only my own poems.
The far-off doings of all my life lie there, one upon another;
Ten thousand leagues, from place to place, I follow my journey's
    course.
I have read through six thousand three hundred poems;
It is almost as though those spring dreams were mine to live again.

The Chinese believe, as we do, that to be born under the planet Jove gives one a laughing, 'jovial' nature. One of Yuan Mei's disciples (Li Hsien-ch'iao) even suggests that Yuan was the Spirit of the Planet Jupiter, lodging for a while on earth as a 'hero of the comic'. His laughter still resounded through the house in the days of his last illness:

The east wind again has brought the splendour of spring flowers;
The willows gradually turn more green, the grass gradually sprouts.
When I look into the stream I must not repine at the snow on my two
    brows;
How few people have lived to see the flowers of four reigns!
Every moment I am now given comes as a gift from Heaven;
There is no limit to the glorious things that happen in the spring.
If you want to call, you need only pause outside the hedge and listen;
The place from which most laughter comes is certain to be my house!

But he was not always in the mood for laughing:

The first sign of farewell to life
Is the turning inside out of all one's tastes.
The great drinker stops caring for wine,
The traveller wants only to be left where he is.
My life-long passion was my love of company,
And the more my visitors talked, the better I liked them.
But ever since my illness came upon me
At the first word I at once stop up my ears.
And worse still, when my wife or children come
I cannot bring myself even to wave a hand.
I know that this is a very bad sign;
My old body has almost done its task.
But strangely enough I go through my old books
With as great delight as I did in former days.
And ill though I am still write poems,
Chanting them aloud till the night is far spent.
Shall it be 'push the door' or 'knock at the door'?
I weigh each word, each line from beginning to end.
I see to it that every phrase is alive;

I do not accept a single dead word.
Perhaps the fact that this habit has not left me
Shows that I still have a little longer to live.

The 'push' *versus* 'knock' is an allusion, and a very apt one, to the 9th-century poet Chia Tao who was encountered in the streets of the Capital 'pushing' and 'knocking' in the air with his hands, in an effort to decide which word he ought to use in a poem he was composing.

It was a cold summer:

There is no mistaking that the surface of the pond is covered with
lotus leaves;
Mid-summer has just been feted, yet the air has an autumn chill,
Heaven, deciding that an old invalid should look like an old invalid
Is forcing him in the sixth month still to be wrapped in furs.

A letter came from Liu Chih-p'eng enclosing a medical prescription and asking for details about Yuan Mei's health. This is the last we hear of him; he was now no longer a dashing young man-about-town, but a middle-aged minor official (perhaps about 37 at this time), and judging from the poems by him that Yuan Mei includes in his collection of poems by friends, much sobered down.

This year there was an 'intercalary' sixth month—an extra month put in . . . to keep the solar and lunar years in step. On the fifteenth of this extra month Yuan Mei drew up the document that is generally called his Will. It contains, in fact, instructions for the immediate transference of most of his property, during his lifetime, to his nephew and son; and also further instructions that were to take effect when he died. He gives a general account of his career in order to explain how it is that, having started with nothing, he is now able to leave to his heirs no less than thirty thousand ounces of silver (about £10,000 at the then current rate of exchange), 'a sum far beyond what in early days I ever expected, and sufficient to keep both of you in comfort'. Then after speaking of his pictures, curios and so on he says:

I want you two to keep them properly dusted and cleaned and put back in their proper cupboards, so that when people call they may see them looking just as they did in my lifetime. If that can be kept up for thirty years, I shall rest contented in my grave. Of any longer period it is useless to think. What may have happened by that time neither you nor I can know.

Actually the house and its treasures remained virtually intact till 1853, when the whole area was laid waste by the T'ai-p'ing revolutionaries. After directions about the care of family graves, he goes on:

My prose works, works in parallelistic style (*wai-chi*), poems, letters, poetry talks and essays on the classics, the poems by my three sisters, the collection of poems by friends, the ghost stories and cookery-book—of all these the blocks are here and you must take care of them and jointly arrange for their printing and sale.

As regards notices of my death, you are to manage them between you. I would rather you sent out too few than too many. Those intended for people of high rank or position should be on light pink paper and the announcement should be in small letters. Uncoloured paper must not be used. For distribution to ordinary people, small, antique slips are the really refined thing. The sending out of large sheets of paper is a vulgarity.

At Nanking it has become customary for placards to be published, just like those by which pedlars announce their wares, inviting all men of substance and position to attend at the ritual lamentations. This is a bad custom, and I hereby forbid you to do anything of the kind. It will be quite enough if three or four people with whom I was on intimate terms get together and mourn for a couple of days. There is no need to compose an account of my life for this occasion; for there already exists Academician Wu's notice, a copy of which should be given to each of the mourners. . . . You can see what is to be spent on my burial by referring to the bills for your grandparent's interment. You are to share the expenses, which should not come to more than fifty ounces of silver. I should not like more to be spent than I spent on my parents. The only monument (on the path to the tomb) is to be a slab bearing the inscription:

'Tomb of Yuan, of the Sui-yuan, Ch'ing dynasty. For a thousand autumns and ten thousand generations there will certainly be those who appreciate me.'

It should here be mentioned that the inscription on the tomb itself was a short factual account of his life written by his friend

Yao Nai. The Will continues:

There is something I particularly want to enjoin upon you both. A-t'ung (his nephew and heir) is apt to be impatient. With him it is a case of tiger's head and snake's tail; he begins things, but leaves them unfinished. A-ch'ih (his own son) is apt to be timid, and this makes him stand-offish and cold. It is best that they should both realize their shortcomings, against the time when there is no one to help them. . . .

As for recitation of Scriptures, chanting of liturgies and entertainment of monks on the seventh days—these are things that I have always detested. You may tell your sisters to come and make an offering to me, in which case I shall certainly accept it; or to come once and wail; at which I shall be deeply moved. But if monks come to the door, at the first sound of their wooden clappers, my divine soul will stop up its ears and run away, which I am sure you would not like.

In a codicil, after some further directions about the disposition of his main property, he says:

If there is any money left over, I wish it to be used in giving mementos to my daughters and their sons and nephews and, outside the family, to long-standing disciples, trusted servants, to the local beadle and his assistants. . . . As I have said, all my works have already been printed. The only exception is the *Sui Pi* (scholastic jottings) in 30 chapters. I was thinking of getting it printed when my great sickness suddenly came, and I did no more about it. I hope that one day you two, when you have nothing better to do, will arrange together to get it printed, and then fix a price for it and publish it. By doing so you ought to make some profit.

After drawing up this document he went to Yangchow to see a doctor. The new treatment seemed at first to be a great success:

I know that my old wife must be worrying about me
And hastily scribble a few lines of news.
Wanting to please her, I cannot resist the temptation
To make things out even better than they are. . . .

The improvement lasted till the twentieth of the ninth month:

The same illness has been with me for over a year;
It has shifted its ground, but I did not weed it out.
Like a bird in the air, I have risen to sink again;
Like the fish in the pool, I come only to go.

I seem to be in port, only to find myself at sea;
The chariot moves, but at once the steeds are unyoked.
'God's children' indeed! It is He who is the child,
And we mortals the toys with which He plays.

He died on the seventeenth of the eleventh month; January 3, 1798, according to the Western calendar.

The account I have given of Yuan Mei consists so largely of quotations from his works, both in prose and verse, as almost to be an anthology. It is certainly far from being what is called a 'critical biography'. Still less is it a Life and Times; and indeed he was, during all but a few years in his career, so completely sequestered from the political events of the day that it would be profitless to discuss him in connection with them. The only aspect of Manchu policy that touched him closely was the Literary Inquisition, and to this I have paid a good deal of attention. In many ways his outlook was typical of his time. His anti-puritanism, his scepticism about many supposedly ancient texts, his dislike of Neo-Confucian metaphysics, his view that women had a right to be educated, were attitudes that were characteristic of the period. Even the ultra-conservative Shen Te-ch'ien, who disagreed with so many of Yuan Mei's opinions, appears to have shared his view about female education; for he too accepted lady-pupils. The one respect (apart from his genius as a writer) in which Yuan Mei seems to have been unique was his persistence, despite the advice of many friends, in publishing writings of a sort that other authors suppressed. It was thought clownish and undignified to print humorous poems, and improper to print references to concubines, young actors, and so on. But in Yuan Mei's view it is the highest duty of a poet to preserve the truth (*ts'un ch'i chen*), to show all things, himself included, as they really are. Added to this was a sense of loyalty to those whom he loved. Why hush up the fact that Liu, whose society had added so greatly to his happiness, went with him on his travels, merely because the world regarded Liu as a disreputable character? Would it have been human, I think he felt, to write epitaphs about a host of

9. *Italy, late twenties*

10.
Listening to Edith
Sitwell at an
historic poetry
reading at Aeolian
Hall. Left to right:
Arthur Waley,
Princess Elizabeth,
Osbert Sitwell,
Queen Elizabeth,
Princess Margaret,
Walter de la Mare

indifferent acquaintances, and none, for example, about Miss Fang, the concubine who served him devotedly for twenty-four years? Yet for writings of this kind he was bitterly criticized. But other reasons were at work. To have hushed up certain aspects of his life might have seemed to imply that he was ashamed of them; and he was not. He lived in strict accord with principles which, though like other philosophies they may have been adopted to justify his behaviour, seemed to him valid and respectable. Finally, there was undoubtedly a streak of impishness, even of impudence in him, which made him enjoy shocking people.

When one turns to the question of his art as a writer and its actual value, I find the subject a very difficult one. In my view the value of literature depends neither on content nor on form, but on the relation between the two. To discuss this relation I must obviously be able to quote in the original, which is not here possible. To deal with the relation between Yuan's content and a translated form would be quite irrelevant.

Despite their imperfections my translations have in the past done something towards inspiring a number of people with the idea that, for lovers of poetry, Chinese is a language worth learning. I hope that this book may serve the same purpose and in particular do something to dispel the common idea that all good Chinese poetry belongs to a remote antiquity.

1956

Chuang Tzu on Death (early 3rd century BC)

Extract from *Three Ways of Thought in Ancient China*

When Chuang Tzu's wife died, Hui Tzu[1] came to the house to join in the rites of mourning. To his surprise he found Chuang Tzu sitting with an inverted bowl on his knees, drumming upon it and singing a song.[2] 'After all,' said Hui Tzu, 'she lived with you, brought up your children, grew old along with you. That you should not mourn for her is bad enough; but to let your friends find you drumming and singing—that is going too far!' 'You misjudge me', said Chuang Tzu. 'When she died, I was in despair, as any man well might be. But soon, pondering on what had happened, I told myself that in death no strange new fate befalls us. In the beginning we lack not life only, but form. Not form only, but spirit. We are blended in the one great featureless indistinguishable mass. Then a time came when the mass evolved spirit, spirit evolved form, form evolved life. And now life in its turn has evolved death. For not nature only but man's being has its seasons, its sequence of spring and autumn, summer and winter. If some one is tired and has gone to lie down, we do not pursue him with shouting and bawling. She whom I have lost has lain down to sleep for a while in the Great Inner Room. To break in upon her rest with

[1] Famous logician and friendly opponent of Chuang Tzu. *Ed.*
[2] Both his attitude and his occupation were the reverse of what the rites of mourning demand.

the noise of lamentation would but show that I knew nothing of nature's Sovereign Law. That is why I ceased to mourn.'

Chuang Tzu's attitude towards death, exemplified again and again in the book, is but part of a general attitude towards the universal laws of nature, which is one not merely of resignation nor even of acquiescence, but a lyrical, almost ecstatic acceptance, which has inspired some of the most moving passages in Taoist literature. I have here collected one or two further passages about death.

When Chuang Tzu was going to Ch'u he saw by the roadside a skull, clean and bare, but with every bone in its place. Touching it gently with his chariot-whip he bent over it and asked it saying, 'Sir, was it some insatiable ambition that drove you to transgress the law and brought you to this? Was it the fall of a kingdom, the blow of an executioner's axe that brought you to this? Or had you done some shameful deed and could not face the reproaches of father and mother, of wife and child, and so were brought to this? Was it hunger and cold that brought you to this, or was it that the springs and autumns of your span had in their due course carried you to this?'

Having thus addressed the skull, he put it under his head as a pillow and went to sleep. At midnight the skull appeared to him in a dream and said to him, 'All that you said to me—your glib, commonplace chatter—is just what I should expect from a live man, showing as it does in every phrase a mind hampered by trammels from which we dead are entirely free. Would you like to hear a word or two about the dead?'

'I certainly should', said Chuang Tzu.

'Among the dead', said the skull, 'none is king, none is subject, there is no division of the seasons; for us the whole world is spring, the whole world is autumn. No monarch on his throne has joy greater than ours.'

Chuang Tzu did not believe this. 'Suppose', he said, 'I could get the Clerk of Destinies to make your frame anew, to clothe your bones once more with flesh and skin, send you back to father and mother, wife and child, friends and home, I do not think you would refuse.'

A deep frown furrowed the skeleton's brow. 'How can you imagine', it asked, 'that I would cast away joy greater than that of a king upon his throne, only to go back again to the toils of the living world?'

Tzu-lai fell ill. He was already at the last gasp; his wife and children stood weeping and wailing round his bed. 'Pst,' said Tzu-li, who had come to call, 'stand back! A great Change is at work; let us not disturb it.' Then, leaning against the door, he said to Tzu-lai, 'Mighty are the works of the Changer! What is he about to make of you, to what use will he put you? Perhaps a rat's liver, perhaps a beetle's claw!' 'A child', said Tzu-lai, 'at its parents' bidding must go north and south, east or west; how much the more when those parents of all Nature, the great powers Yin and Yang, command him, must he needs go where they will. They have asked me to die, and if I do not obey them, shall I not rank as an unmanageable child? I can make no complaint against them. These great forces housed me in my bodily frame, spent me in youth's toil, gave me repose when I was old, will give me rest at my death. Why should the powers that have done so much for me in life, do less for me in death?

'If the bronze in the founder's crucible were suddenly to jump up and say, "I don't want to be a tripod, a plough-share or a bell. I must be the sword *Without Flaw*," the caster would think it was indeed unmannerly metal that had got into his stock.

'In this life I have had the luck to be fashioned in human form. But were I now to say to the Great Transformer, "I refuse to let anything be made out of me but a man", he would think that it was indeed an unmannerly being who had come into his hands.'

How do I know that wanting to be alive is not a great mistake? How do I know that hating to die is not like thinking one has lost one's way, when all the time one is on the path that leads to home? Li Chi was the daughter of the frontier guardsman at Ai. When first she was captured and carried away to Chin, she wept till her dress was soaked with tears. But when she came to the king's palace, sat with him on his couch and shared with him the dainties of the royal board, she began to wonder why she had wept. How do I know that the dead do not wonder why they should ever have prayed for long life? It is said that those who dream of drinking wine will weep when day comes; and that those who dream of weeping will next day go hunting. But while a man is dreaming, he does not know that he is dreaming; nor can he interpret a dream till the dream is done. It is only when he wakes, that he knows it was a dream. Not till the Great Wakening can he know that all this was one Great Dream. . . .

Once Chuang Chou[1] dreamt that he was a butterfly. He did not know that he had ever been anything but a butterfly and was content to hover from flower to flower. Suddenly he woke and found to his astonishment that he was Chuang Chou. But it was hard to be sure whether he really was Chou and had only dreamt that he was a butterfly, or was really a butterfly, and was only dreaming that he was Chou.

1939

[1] i.e., Chuang Tzu.

Mencius on Human Nature (early 3rd century BC)

Extract from *Three Ways of Thought in Ancient China*

THE BETTER FEELINGS

The whole teaching of Mencius centres round the word Goodness (*jên*). Different schools of Confucianism meant different things by this term. But to Mencius, Goodness meant compassion; it meant not being able to bear that others should suffer. It meant a feeling of responsibility for the sufferings of others, such as was felt by the legendary Yü, subduer of the primeval Flood: 'If anyone were drowned, Yü felt as though it were he himself that had drowned him.' Or such as was felt (so it was said) in ancient times by the counsellor I Yin to whom if he knew that a single man or woman anywhere under Heaven were not enjoying the benefits of wise rule, 'it was as though he had pushed them into a ditch with his own hand; so heavy was the responsibility that he put upon himself for everything that happened under Heaven'.

According to Mencius, feelings such as this are not produced by education. They are the natural birthright of everyone, they are his 'good capacity', his 'good knowledge', his 'good feelings', and the problem of education is not how to get them, but how to keep them. 'He who lets these feelings go and does not know how to recover them is to be pitied indeed! If anyone has a chicken or dog that has strayed, he takes steps to recover them; but people are content to let their good feelings go and make no effort to find them again. Yet what else is education but the recovery of good feelings that have strayed away?' How these feelings are lost, how they are rubbed away by the rough contacts of daily life, is described by Mencius in the allegory of the Bull Mountain:

The Bull Mountain was once covered with lovely trees. But it is near the capital of a great State. People came with their axes and choppers; they cut the woods down, and the mountain has lost its beauty. Yet even so, the day air and the night air came to it, rain and dew moistened it till here and there fresh sprouts began to grow. But soon cattle and sheep came along and browsed on them, and in the end the mountain became gaunt and bare, as it is now. And seeing it thus gaunt and bare people imagine that it was woodless from the start. Now just as the natural state of the mountain was quite different from what now appears, so too in every man (little though they may be apparent) there assuredly were once feelings of decency and kindness; and if these good feelings are no longer there, it is that they have been tampered with, hewn down with axe and bill. As each day dawns they are assailed anew. What chance then has our nature, any more than that mountain, of keeping its beauty? To us, too, comes the air of day, the air of night. Just at dawn, indeed, we have for a moment and in a certain degree a mood in which our promptings and aversions come near to being such as are proper to men. But something is sure to happen before the morning is over, by which these better feelings are ruffled or destroyed. And in the end, when they have been ruffled again and again, the night air is no longer able to preserve them, and soon our feelings are as near as may be to those of beasts and birds; so that anyone might make the same mistake about us as about the mountain, and think that there was never any good in us from the very start. Yet assuredly our present state of feeling is not what we begin with. Truly,

'If rightly tended, no creature but thrives;
If left untended, no creature but pines away.'

Confucius said:

> 'Hold fast to it and you can keep it,
> Let go, and it will stray.
> For its comings and goings it has no time nor tide;
> None knows where it will bide.'

Surely it was of the feelings[1] that he was speaking.

[1] The innate good feelings.

The Dancing Horses (c. 850)

by Chêng Ch'u-hui

The Emperor Hsüan Tsung once had a hundred horses taught to dance. They were divided into two troupes, the Dancers of the Left and the Dancers of the Right, and were given ranks, such as Imperial Pet, Household Favourite and the like. From time to time particularly fine horses would be sent as tribute from abroad; and these too the Emperor sent to be trained with the rest, so that the splendid creatures might display their utmost prowess. The cloths they wore were delicately embroidered, their bridles were of silver and gold, their manes were plaited with pearls and jade. The suite to which they danced was called the Tune of the Tilted Cup, and consisted of more than twenty movements. Every gesture that they made—even the tossing of their heads and the lashing of their tails—was in perfect time with the music. The Emperor also built a wooden platform three storeys high. The grooms rode the horses up an incline to the topmost storey, where they whirled round and round at dazzling speed. Or again, a strong man would hold up a divan on his outstretched hands and one of the horses would dance upon it. At these performances the musicians were divided into four bands, stationed to the left and right, in front and behind. They were all dressed in light yellow shirts and wore belts studded with carved jade, and only young men of exceptional beauty were chosen for the task. As part of the celebrations on the Emperor's birthday there was always a special performance by the dancing horses, held below the Tower of Strenuous Rule.

Then came the revolution[1] of An Lu-shan. The Emperor took

[1] AD 755.

refuge in Szechwan, and the dancing horses, no longer an Imperial troupe, fell into various private hands. An Lu-shan had often seen them at Court and greatly admired them. So it came about that several of them were brought to him at his headquarters in Fan-yang and were purchased by him. After An Lu-shan's fall they fell into the hands of General T'ien Ch'êng-ssu[2] who, knowing nothing of their history, put them in the outer stables along with the ordinary war-horses. One day there was a banquet in the barracks. A military band played, and when the horses heard the music they began to dance. They danced and danced and could not stop. The grooms thought they were bewitched and hit out at them with their brooms. The horses thought they were being beaten for not keeping proper time to the music, and struggled all the more desperately to follow every cadence and phrase. At last the official in charge of the stables went to General T'ien and reported that there was something wrong with the horses. 'Thrash them as hard as you can', said the General. So the better they danced the more pitilessly they were thrashed, till they fell down dead on the stable floor.

There were some who knew that these were dancing horses; but General T'ien was a man of violent temper, and they dared not speak.

1946

[2] AD 704–78.

234

The Two Lunatics (c. 860)

by Tuan Ch'eng-shih

At the beginning of the Yüan Ho period (806–20) there lived in the I-ning Ward at the Capital a mad woman whom everyone knew as Lady Five. She always spent the night under the wall of Princess Yung-mu's Gardens. It happened at this time that the Imperial Envoy Ju was sent on a mission to Nanking. In this city there was a madman who was known to everyone as the Postman. Sometimes he sang, sometimes he wailed, and again and again even his wildest ravings turned out to be true prophecies. In hot weather Postman wore a padded winter coat, but did not sweat a drop; in winter he went almost bare, but his hands were never chapped nor his feet numbed.

When the envoy was riding out of Nanking, Postman suddenly ran up to his horse and shouted to him to stop. 'I have a sister, Lady Five, at the Capital', he said. 'Here is a little letter for her. Be sure to see she gets it.' The envoy had heard about Postman and to humour him said he would be glad to deliver the letter. Postman then fished out a small packet from among the folds of his dress and stuffed it into the top of the envoy's riding-boot, saying: 'Tell Lady Five I am all right and shall soon be coming home.'

When the envoy got to the Capital and was riding up the Ch'ang-lo Embankment he found Lady Five waiting for him. She ran up to his horse and smiled at him saying: 'My brother has given Your Worship a letter for me. Pray deliver it.' It was some while before he remembered what she was talking about. Then suddenly he recollected Postman's request and told his servant to take the packet out of his boot and give it to her. Lady Five undid the wrapping and found that it contained some odd bits of clothing. She put them round her and danced. Then she went back to her place under the wall, and died that same night. The people of the district collected money to bury her. Next year someone came from the south and said Postman had died on the same night as Lady Five.[1]

1947

[1] That is the end of the story. Of course they were not really brother and sister, but only, as it were, colleagues in madness.

Nineteen Japanese Poems

1. Your girl of the East,
   Who is standing in the courtyard
   Drying the hemp she has cut
   And thinking of you all the while,
   Do not, oh do not forget!

   Anonymous (8th century)

2. The hawk that to my cry
   Answered so ill
   They tell me (but is it true?)
   Sits quietly on another's hand.

   Anonymous (10th century)

3. I am like a pool
   That thick weeds have covered;
   What lies deepest in my heart
   There is none can know.

   Anonymous (10th century)

4. If there is but a seed
   On the face of the rock
   A pine will grow;
   And shall not love worth calling love
   Find always a way to meet?

   Anonymous (10th century)

5. Being in doubt
   Whether you would come to me
   Or I go to you,
   I went to bed without shutting
   My plank door of pine-wood.

   Anonymous (10th century)

237

6. Like a wave that when the keen wind blows
   Dashes itself against the rocks—
   It is my own heart only
   That I shatter in the torments of love.

   (*Anonymous* 10th century)

7. Dream, oh dream
   Lead me not to a meeting
   With the man I love,
   Lest afterwards, on waking,
   I should feel too lonely.

   Anonymous (10th century)

8. 'She loves him dearly
   And they often meet.'
   Those few words, false though they are,
   How sweet to overhear!

   Nakahara Akitsune (11th century)

9. Call me thief if you will,
   What better name for me?
   Who in the darkness of the night
   Crept in to steal your heart.

   Anonymous (11th century)

10. Under Mimoro mountain
    In the valley spring has begun.
    Already the water under the snow
    Is knocking against the rocks.

    Minamoto no Kiminobu (*c.* 1090)

11. Like the mountain torrent
    That where the stream runs so swift
    Is severed by a rock,
    Though now divided
    We shall meet again, I think.

    Emperor Toba (12th century)

12. The ghosts of the faithful do not
    Scatter like the white clouds in the sky,
    But in the hall of the lord they served
    Hang like unlettered banners.

    Anonymous (*c.* 1865)

13. With buried face I sit in the yellow dusk.
The prison slaves have not yet lit the lamp.
Gusts of cold wind gnaw my bones;
The clothes on my back are frozen stiff as ice.

Murai Masa (c. 1865

14. By the samisen's sound
Alone they live
At night, these ancient
Streets of the river mouth
Down which I lose my way.

Maeda Yūgure (1883–1951)

Folk-Songs

15. You say I have locked
My heart against you.
But locks can turn, and the key
Lies in your own heart.

16. There was such darkness in my heart
When I came home without seeing you
That though the moon shone bright
I could not see my way.

Lullaby

17. Asleep, is he, or not asleep!
When I asked the pillow
The pillow said,
'Asleep' it said.

18. 'How long these autumn nights are!'
That is what people always say.
But the night I slept with you,
How short it was!

19. Last night I waited in vain;
This morning you turn up.
From what secret tryst
Are you on your way home?

Mainly 1953

239

Extract from *The Pillow-Book of Sei Shōnagon*

(late 10th century)

The character of Shōnagon appears in her book as a series of contradictions. She is desperately anxious not merely to be liked, but to occupy the foremost place in the affections of all whom she knows. Yet her behaviour, as she herself records it, seems consistently calculated to inspire fear rather than affection. Again, she seems at some moments wholly sceptical, at others profoundly religious; now unusually tender-hearted, now egotistical and cold. Yet all this does not imply that her character was in reality complicated to an unusual degree, but comes from the fact that she reveals herself to us entirely and, as it were, from every facet, whereas most writers of diaries and the like, however little conscious intention they may have of publishing their confessions, instinctively present themselves always in the same light. Her detachment about herself is paralleled by a curious aloofness from all the associated emotions of a scene, so that she can describe a sick-bed as though it were a sunset, without the slightest attempt to arouse pity, or for that matter the least fear of provoking disgust.

Perhaps the strongest impression we get is of her extreme fastidiousness and irritability, which must have made her a formidable companion. She probably got on better with the Empress than with anyone else because her reverence for the Imperial Family compelled her in the August Presence to keep her nerves in check.

As a writer she is incomparably the best poet of her time, a fact which is apparent only in her prose and not at all in the conventional *uta* for which she is also famous. Passages such as that about the stormy lake or the few lines about crossing a moonlit river show a beauty of phrasing that Murasaki, a much more deliberate writer, certainly never surpassed. As for Shōnagon's anecdotes, their vivacity is apparent even in translation. Neither in them nor in her more lyrical passages is there any hint of a search for literary effect. She gives back in her pages, with apparently as little effort of her own as a gong that sounds when it is struck, the whole warmth and glitter of the life that surrounded her; and the delicate precision of her perceptions makes diarists such as Lady Anne Clifford (whose name occurs to me at random) seem mere purblind Hottentots.

This gift manifests itself incidentally in her extraordinary power of conveying character. Yukinari, Masahiro and Narimasa, despite their uniform absurdity, live with extraordinary distinctness; as does the Empress herself, the only other woman whom the authoress allows to figure in her pages.

Her style is very much less 'architected' than Murasaki's; but there are moments when she begins building up a huge network of dependent clauses in a manner extremely close to *Genji*, and often one feels that the earlier book leads us, so to speak, to the brink of the other. This fits in with the presumed dates. *Genji* was probably begun in 1001, when Murasaki lost her husband, and the *Pillow-Book* seems, with the possible exception of two or three entries, to have been written before the twelfth month of 1000, when the Empress Sadako died.

Shōnagon has often been spoken of as learned. Our only source of information on the subject is her own book. In it she shows signs of having read the *Mêng-ch'iu*, a collection of edifying Chinese anecdotes, much studied by Japanese children from the 9th to the 19th century. She knows too some poems by Po Chü-i (the easiest of Chinese writers) and refers once to the Analects of Confucius. In Japanese literature she knows the usual round of poems from the *Kokinshū* and *Gosenshū*. To speak, as

European writers have done, of her vast acquaintance with Chinese literature, is an anachronism; for in her time only fragments of this literature had reached Japan. The great poets of the 8th century, for example, were entirely unknown. But the term 'learned' is in any case a relative one. A modern lady-in-waiting who had read a little Greek (or even only a little Gilbert Murray) would certainly pass as learned in her own circle; while at Girton no one would be impressed. And it is likely enough that the attainments by which Shōnagon dazzled the Palace would at the Fujiwara Academy have passed quite unnoticed.

It is, in fact, her extreme readiness of wit rather than her erudition that makes Shōnagon remarkable. I have not been able in my extracts to do her full justice in this respect, because in order to appreciate her allusions and repartees one must be in a position to grasp them immediately. Wit, more often than not, evaporates in the process of explanation.

But the brilliance of an allusion such as that to the Analects may perhaps be vaguely surmised. That anyone possessed of such a gift should enjoy using it seems natural enough. Almost every anecdote in her book centres round some clever repartee or happy quotation of her own. For this she has been reproached, and Murasaki has made her colleague's *shitari-gao* ('have done it!' look, i.e. air of self-satisfaction) proverbial. In life Shōnagon may indeed have been as insupportable as Murasaki evidently found her; but in the *Pillow-Book* her famous *shitari-gao* makes no disagreeable effect. We feel that Shōnagon displays her agile wits with the same delight as an athlete takes in running or leaping.

The Japanese excelled at portraiture. But the portraits that survive are those of statesmen and priests. The 'Yoritomo', by Takanobu (the obstinate-looking man in black triangular garments squatting with a white tablet hugged to his breast[1]), and the Shōichi Kokushi (that old one-eyed priest spread out over a great armchair), by Chō Densu, are among the greatest products of Japanese art. But I recollect no portraits of women till a much

[1] There is a good copy of this at the British Museum.

later date. Murasaki and Shōnagon we know only as posterity imagined them—that is to say, as conventional Court beauties of the Heian period. One does not, however, in reading the *Pillow-Book*, get the impression of a woman in whose life her own appearance figured in any very important way. Had she, on the other hand, been downright ugly, it would have been impossible to secure her a post as lady-in-waiting. We may suppose then that her looks were moderate. We certainly cannot accept the argument of M. Revon: 'Si elle n'avait pas été distinguée de sa personne elle n'aurait pas raillé comme elle fait, les types vulgaires' —reasoning which shows a fortunate unfamiliarity with the conversation of plain women. But we have no reason to doubt that Shōnagon had many lovers. Stress is usually laid on her affairs with Tadanobu, to which, however, she devotes only some few, rather insipid pages. I imagine that her real lovers were for the most part people of her own rank; whereas Tadanobu, rather circuitously (it was owing to his sister's marriage with the Empress's brother) soon became a *pezzo grosso*. But in the 'eighties of the 10th century he was well within Shōnagon's reach, and if they were ever lovers, it may have been before her arrival at Court.

Here is the longest passage which deals with their relationship:

Tadanobu, having heard and believed some absurd rumour about me, began saying the most violent things—for example, that I wasn't fit to be called a human being at all and he couldn't imagine how he had been so foolish as to treat me like one. I was told that he was saying horrible things about me even in the Imperial apartments. I felt uncomfortable about it, but I only said, laughing: 'If these reports are true, then that's what I'm like and there is nothing more to be done. But if they are not true, he will eventually find out that he has been deceived. Let us leave it at that. . . .' Henceforward, if he passed through the Black Door room and heard my voice from behind the screens he would bury his face in his sleeve, as though the merest glimpse of me would disgust him. I did not attempt to explain matters, but got in the habit of always looking in some other direction.

Two months later matters had advanced some way towards a reconciliation, for Shōnagon writes:

He sent for me to come out to him, and (though I did not respond) we met later by accident. 'Darling,' he said, 'why have we given up being lovers? You know now that I have stopped believing those stories about you. I cannot conceive what is the obstacle. Are two people who have been friends for so many years really to drift apart in this way? As it is, my duties bring me constantly in and out of their Majesties' apartments. But if that were to stop, our friendship would simply vanish, with nothing to show for all that has taken place between us.' 'I have no objection to our coming together again', I said. 'In fact, there is only one thing I should be sorry for. If we were seeing one another in the way you mean, I should certainly stop praising you[1]—as I constantly do at present—in her Majesty's hearing, with all the other gentle-women sitting by. You won't, I am sure, misunderstand me. One is embarrassed under such circumstances, something inside one sticks and one remains tongue-tied.' He laughed. 'Am I then never to be praised except by people who know nothing about me?' he asked. 'You may be certain', I said, 'that if we become good friends again I shall never praise you. I cannot bear people, men or women, who are prejudiced in favour of someone they are intimate with or get into a rage if the mildest criticism of someone they are fond of is made in their presence.' 'Oh, I can trust you not to do that!' he exclaimed.

1928

[1] The intimacy would, of course, be secret. Shōnagon's embarrassment would proceed solely from her own conscience.

Extract from *The Wreath of Cloud* (Part III of *The Tale of Genji*)

Autumn had now come, and with it a bitterly cold wind—the 'first wind' whose chill breath 'only a lover's cloak can nullify'. [Genji] made great efforts to keep away from the Western Wing, but all to no purpose; and soon, on the pretext of music-lessons or what not, he was spending the greater part of every day at Tamakatsura's side.

One evening when the moon was some five or six days old he came suddenly to her room. The weather was chilly and overcast, and the wind rustled with a melancholy note through the reeds outside the window. She sat with her head resting against her zithern. To-night too, as on so many previous occasions, he would make his timorous advances, and at the end of it all be just where he started. So Genji grumbled to himself, and continued to behave in a somewhat plaintive and peevish manner during his whole visit. It was however already very late when the fear of giving offence in other quarters[1] drove him from the room. Just as he was leaving he noticed that the flares outside her window were burning very low, and sending for one of his men, he had them kindled anew; but this time at a little distance from the house, under a strangely leaning spindle-tree which spread its branches in the form of a broad canopy, near to the banks of a deep, chilly stream. The thin flares of split pine-wood were placed at wide intervals, casting pale shadows that flickered remotely upon the walls of the unlighted room where she and

---

[1] His wife, Lady Murasaki. *Ed.*

Genji sat. He caught a glimpse of her hand, showing frail and ghostly against the dark background of her hair. Her face, suddenly illumined by the cold glare of the distant torches, wore an uneasy and distrustful air. He had risen to go, but still lingered. 'You should tell your people never to let the flares go out', he said. 'Even in summer, except when there is a moon, it is not wise to leave the garden unlighted. And in Autumn . . . I shall feel very uneasy if you do not promise to remember about this. "Did but the torches flickering at your door burn brightly as the fire within my breast, you should not want for light!" ' And he reminded her of the old song in which the lover asks: 'How long, like the smouldering watch-fire at the gate, must my desire burn only with an inward flame?'

'Would that, like the smoke of the watch-fires that mounts and vanishes at random in the empty sky, the smouldering flame of passion could burn itself away!' So she recited adding: 'I do not know what has come over you. Please leave me at once or people will think. . . .' 'As you wish', he answered, and was stepping into the courtyard, when he heard a sound of music in the wing occupied by the Lady from the Village of Falling Flowers. Some one seemed to be playing the flute to the accompaniment of a Chinese zithern. No doubt Yūgiri[2] was giving a small party. The flute-player could be none other than Tō no Chūjō's son Kashiwagi; for who else at Court performed with such marvellous delicacy and finish? How pleasant would be the effect, thought Genji, if they would consent to come and give a serenade by the stream-side, in the subdued light of those flickering torches! 'I long to join you,' he wrote, 'but, could you see the pale, watery shadows that the watch-flares are casting here in the garden of the western wing, you would know why I am slow to come. . . .' He sent this note to Yūgiri, and presently three figures appeared out of the darkness. 'I should not have sent for you', he called to them, 'had you not played "The Wind's voice tells me. . . ." It is a tune that I can never resist.'

[2] Genji's son. *Ed.*

So saying he brought out his own zithern. When he had played for a while, Yūgiri began to improvise on his flute in the Banshiki mode.[3] Kashiwagi attempted to join in, but his thoughts were evidently employed elsewhere,[4] for again and again he entered at the wrong beat. 'Too late', cried Genji, and at last Kōbai was obliged to keep his brother in measure by humming the air in a low monotone like the chirping of a meditative grasshopper. Genji made them go through the piece twice, and then handed his zithern to Kashiwagi. It was some while since he had heard the boy play and he now observed with delight that his talent was not by any means confined to wind-instruments. 'You could have given me no greater pleasure', he said, when the piece was over. 'Your father is reckoned a fine performer on the zithern; but you have certainly more than overtaken him. . . . By the way, I should have cautioned you that there is some one seated just within who can probably hear all that is going on out in this portico. So to-night there had better not be too much drinking. Do not be offended, for I was really thinking more of myself than of you. Now that I am getting on in years I find wine far more dangerous than I used to. I am apt to say the most indiscreet things. . . .'.

Tamakatsura did, as a matter of fact, overhear every word of this, as indeed she was intended to, and was thankful that he at any rate saw the necessity of keeping himself in hand. The near presence of the two visitors could not fail to interest her extremely, if for no other reason than merely because they were, after all, though themselves entirely unaware of the fact, so very closely related to her,[5] and for long past she had surreptitiously collected all possible information concerning their characters and pursuits. Kashiwagi was, as to her distress she had frequently ascertained, very deeply in love with her. Again and again during the course of the evening, he was on the verge of collapsing altogether; but never was the state of agitation through which he was passing for a moment reflected in his playing.

1927

[3] Corresponding roughly with the white notes from D to D.
[4] He was in love with Tamakatsura.
[5] Kashiwagi and Kōbai were her half-brothers. *Ed.*

The Lady Who Loved Insects

(Anonymous 12th-century fragment)

Next door to the lady who loved butterflies was the house of a certain Provincial Inspector. He had an only daughter, to whose upbringing he and his wife devoted endless care. She was a strange girl, and used to say: 'Why do people make so much fuss about butterflies and never give a thought to the creatures out of which butterflies grow? It is the Natural Form of things that is always the most important.' She collected all kinds of reptiles and insects such as most people are frightened to touch, and watched them day by day to see what they would turn into, keeping them in various sorts of little boxes and cages. Among all these creatures her favourite was the common caterpillar. Hour after hour, her hair pushed back from her eyes, she would sit gazing at the furry black form that nestled in the palm of her hand. She found that other girls were frightened of these pets, and her only companions were a number of rather rough little boys, who were not in the least afraid. She got them to carry about the insect-boxes, find out the names of the insects or, if this could not be done, help her to give them new names. She hated anything that was not natural. Consequently she would not pluck a single hair from her eyebrows nor would she blacken her teeth, saying it was a dirty and disagreeable custom. So morning, noon and night she tended her insects, bending over them with a strange, white gleaming-smile.[1] People on the whole were frightened of her and kept away; the few who ventured to approach her came back with the strangest reports. If anyone showed the

[1] Because of her unblackened teeth.

slightest distaste for her pets, she would ask him indignantly how he could give way to so silly and vulgar a prejudice, and as she said this she would stare at the visitor under her black, bushy eyebrows in a way that made him feel extremely uncomfortable.

Her parents thought all this very peculiar and would much rather she had been more like other children; but they saw it was no use arguing with her. She for her part took immense trouble in explaining her ideas, but this only resulted in making them feel that she was much cleverer than they. 'No doubt', they would say, 'all you tell us is quite true, and so far as we are concerned you may do as you please. But people as a rule only make pets of charming and pretty things. If it gets about that you keep hairy caterpillars you will be thought a disgusting girl and no one will want to know you.' 'I do not mind what they think', she answered. 'I want to enquire into everything that exists and find out how it began. Nothing else interests me. And it is very silly of them to dislike caterpillars, all of which will soon turn into lovely butterflies.' Then she again explained to them carefully how the cocoon, which is like the thick winter clothes that human beings wear, wraps up the caterpillar till its wings have grown and it is ready to be a butterfly. Then it suddenly waves its white sleeves and flits away. . . .

This was no doubt quite accurate, and they could think of nothing to say in reply; but all the same her views on such matters made them feel very uncomfortable. She would never sit in the same room with her elders, quoting in self-defence the proverb, 'Ghosts and girls are best unseen'; and the above attempt to bring her parents to reason was made through a chink in the half-raised blinds of the living-room. Hearing of such conversations as this, the young people of the district were amazed at the profundity of her researches. 'But what things for a girl to play with!' they said. 'She must be an oddity indeed. Let us go and call upon the girl who loves butterflies.'

Hearing some of the unflattering comparisons that were

being made between herself and the butterfly lady, she rejoined: 'I do not see anything very admirable in making a fuss over butterflies. Even those young men must know by now that the prettiest butterflies are but the sheddings of creatures like my hairy caterpillars, who discard them as a snake drops its skin. And caterpillars are much friendlier playthings. For if you catch hold of a butterfly it frees itself as soon as it can, leaving its golden powder on your hand, and this powder is very dangerous, often causing fevers and agues. Fancy trying to make pets of butterflies! It is horrible to think of.'

To the little boys who formed her retinue she would give pretty things such as she knew they wanted, and in return they would give her all kinds of terrifying insects. She said the caterpillars would be unhappy if there were no creatures with them to admire their glossy coats, and she therefore collected a number of snails, and also of grass-crickets whose ferocious and incessant cries seemed to suggest that they were at war with one another, thus recalling to her mind the line, 'For the ground between a snail's horns what use to fight?'[2] She said she was tired of ordinary boys' names and called her servitors by insect-names, such as Kerao (mole-cricket boy), Inago-maro (locust-man), Amabiko (centipede), and the like. All this was thought very queer and stupid.

Among those who had heard gossip about the girl and her odd pets was a certain young man of good family who vowed that, fond of strange creatures though she might be, he would undertake to give her a fright. So saying he made a marvellously life-like snake with joints that moved and putting it into a scaly bag sent it to her with the poem: 'Creeping and crawling I shall sneak my way to your side, for my persistence[3] is tireless as my body is long.' The servant who brought the bag had no idea what it contained. 'I wonder what can be in it', he said, as he untied the string. 'Certainly something remarkably heavy!'

[2] From one of five drinking-songs written by the Chinese poet Po Chü-i about 829.
[3] 'Persistence' is 'length of heart' (*kokoro-nagasa*) in Japanese.

The bag was opened and to the horror of everyone present a snake protruded its head. But the lady was not at all put out, and having repeated several times the prayer *Namu Amida Butsu* she said, 'Do not be frightened! Remember that any one of you may have been a snake in his former existence. Look at the kindly expression of his face and how he is making himself tremble all down his back. Could anything be clearer than that he is signalling to you not to be afraid? I am amazed that anyone should not understand him.' So she muttered to herself, and drew the bag towards her. But all the same it seemed as though even she were a little bit afraid, for now she hovered near the creature and now fluttered away again, like a moth at the candle, crooning to it all the while in a low insect-voice.

Seeing several of the servants rush out of her room tumbling over one another and screaming with laughter the lady's father asked them what had happened, and at the mention of a snake exclaimed in great consternation, 'A nice trick to play upon a young woman! I cannot understand anyone doing such a dastardly thing. A fine pack of rascals you are, to run off like this and leave her with a dangerous viper in the room.' So saying he seized his sword and brandishing it over his head rushed to his daughter's side. But the moment he saw the snake a doubt crossed his mind and examining it attentively he discovered it was only an extremely well-made toy. Picking it up he said, 'I remember now that I have heard people say how clever the fellow is at making things of this sort. You must be sure to write at once and thank him for his kindness.' When it was known that the snake was only a toy the people who had run away from it declared the joke to be a very silly one. But the lady agreed that it would be rude not to reply and taking a stout, sensible-looking sheet of paper she wrote the following poem, not in *hiragana*, which she never used, but in *katakana*:[4] 'If indeed we are fated to meet, not here will it be, but in Paradise, thou crafty image of a snake.'

[4] A square, inelegant but eminently 'sensible' form of syllabary, now used for telegrams, etc.

And at the side was written: 'In the Garden of Blessings you must plant your seed.'[5]

It happened that a certain Captain of Horse saw this letter and being much struck with it he determined to obtain an interview with the writer. Choosing a time when he knew her father to be busy elsewhere, he posted himself at a wattled gate on the women's side of the house and peeped in. Several little boys were poking about among some very dull-looking bushes and shrubs. Presently one of them called out, 'Just look at these bushes! They're simply covered with creatures. It's the best place we have ever found.' And going to the window he pulled the blind. 'Do look at them', he said again. 'You can see them from the window. Aren't they the loveliest caterpillars you ever saw?' 'Yes, they're not at all bad', said a voice from within. 'You may bring them in here if you like.' 'I've nothing to put them in', said the boy. 'You must look at them where they are.' Presently the blind was pulled right aside and a girl appeared at the window, craning out towards the nearest boughs of the shrubbery. She had pulled her mantle over her head, but her hair hung loose beneath it, and very lovely hair it was too, but rather untidy-looking, and the Captain thought it must be a long time since she had combed it. Her thick, very dark eyebrows gave her face a rather forbidding air. Her other features were by no means bad. But when she smiled her white teeth gleamed and flashed in a manner that rather disgusted him, for there was something wild and barbaric about it.

'What a sad case!' thought the Captain. 'If only she took an ordinary amount of trouble with herself she really would not be bad-looking.' Even as she was he did not find her altogether unattractive; for there was about her a strange kind of vehemence, a liveliness of expression, a brilliance of complexion and colouring that could not fail to make some impression on him. With her clothes in themselves there was nothing wrong. She wore a robe

---

[5] The snake must by good behaviour get itself reborn in some more dignified incarnation.

of soft, glossy silk, with a spinner's jacket, and white trousers. In order to get a good view of the caterpillars she leant right out of the window, crying, 'Aren't they clever! They've come here in order to be out of the sun. Boy, you might just bring me that one there. I should like to have a better look at him. Be sure not to let him fall.' Upon which the boy at once bumped into something and the caterpillar fell with a thud upon the ground. She then handed him a white fan with some Chinese characters written upon it in black ink, saying, 'Pick him up quickly and carry him in on this'.

It was only now that she caught sight of the Captain, who was still loitering at the wicker gate. To see anyone there was a considerable surprise, for the young men of the neighbourhood had long ago decided that she was what they called 'a disastrous character', and it was seldom indeed that anyone came that way. The little boy, too, had become aware of the visitor's presence and cried out in astonishment, 'Look, there's a gentleman standing at the wicker gate. I can't make out what he is doing. He seems to be staring at us.' One of the maids now came along and began to scold her. 'Fie upon you,' she said, 'I shall go straight to your father and tell him you're busy with your nasty insects again, and leaning right out of the window where anyone can see you.' But the girl continued to fiddle about with the hairy caterpillars on the bushes near the window. The maid, who had a horror of such creatures, was far too frightened to come any closer, but called again, 'Madam, go in this instant. You can be seen!' 'Well, what if I can be seen? I am not doing anything to be ashamed of.' 'I'm not joking, I assure you,' said the maid indignantly. 'There's a fine gentleman standing right there at the gate. Go away from the window at once!' 'Kerao,' said the girl at last, 'just go to the gate and see if there is still someone there.' He ran a little distance towards the gate and presently called out, 'It's quite true, there is somebody'. Upon which she gathered several caterpillars in her sleeve and stepped back into the interior of the house.

For a moment he saw her at full length. She was rather tall. Her hair floated out behind her as she moved. It was very thick, but the ends were somewhat wispy, no doubt through lack of trimming. But with a little more looking after it would have made (he thought) a fine crop of hair. Certainly she was no great beauty, but if she dressed and behaved like other people she would, he was sure, be capable of cutting quite a decent figure in Society. What a pity it was! Where had she picked up the distressing opinions that forced her to make such a melancholy spectacle of herself?

He felt that he must at any rate let her know that he had seen her; and using the juice of a flower-stem as ink he wrote the following poem on a piece of thickly folded paper: 'Forgive me that at your wicker gate so long I stand. But from the Caterpillar's bushy brows I cannot take my eyes.' He tapped with his fan, and at once one of the little boys ran out to ask what he wanted. 'Take this to your mistress', he said. But it was intercepted by the maid, to whom the little boy explained that the poem came from the fine gentleman who had been standing about near the gate. 'Woe upon us all,' cried the maid, 'this is the handwriting of Captain So-and-So, that is in the Horse Guard. And to think that he has been watching you mess about with your nauseous worms!' And she went on for some time lamenting over the girl's deplorable oddity. At last the insect-lover could bear it no longer and said, 'If you looked a little more below the surface of things you would not mind so much what other people thought about you. The world in which we live has no reality, it is a mirage, a dream. Suppose someone is offended by what we do or, for the matter of that, is pleased by it, does his opinion make any difference to us in the end? Before long both he and we shall no longer even appear to exist.'

Several of the younger servants had by now gathered round. They found her argument hard to answer, but secretly felt that this was a very dismal view of life. It was not thought likely that she would send an answer. But the Captain was still waiting at the gate and the little boys, who had now all been called back into the house, said the gentleman was looking very unhappy; upon which everyone urged her to write something, and very reluctantly she sent the poem, 'By this you may know the strangeness of my mood. Had you not *kawamushi*[6] called me, I would not have replied.' To which he answered, 'In all the world, I fear, exists no man so delicate that to the hair-tips of a caterpillar's brow he could attune his life'. Then he went back laughing to his home.

What happened next will be found in the second chapter![7]

1929

[6] Hairy caterpillar.
[7] No second chapter exists.

The Owl Speaks:
An Ainu Story

Author and date unknown)

'In old days, when I spoke, it was like a voice echoing through a hollow bow-handle, a handle of rolled cherry-bark. But now I am feeble and old. Is there no one I can send, no bold and clever speaker, who will carry my complaints to the Country of Heaven?' So I said, tapping on the lid of my iron-wood locker; and suddenly a voice at my door said, 'Who bolder, who cleverer a speaker than I? You will not find a better messenger.' And when I looked, it was the young crow. I brought him into my house, and began at once, tapping all the while on the lid of my iron-wood locker, to instruct him about my complaints, so that he might go as my messenger to the Country of Heaven. For three days I instructed him about my complaints, dividing them into three headings; but while I was still speaking I suddenly noticed that the young crow, sitting behind the fire guard, had fallen asleep. At this I fell into a great rage, and setting upon the young crow I beat him to death with my wings. Then, while I tapped the iron-wood lid of my locker, I said again, 'Who will be my messenger and carry my complaints to the Country of Heaven?'

Suddenly a voice at my door said, 'I am a bold and clever speaker. What better messenger could you find?' And when I looked, I saw it was the mountain jay. I brought him in, and while I tapped upon the lid of my iron-wood locker I instructed him about my complaints, arranging them under four principal headings, and continuing for four days. But the jay fell fast

11. *In Christmas snow with Hylo-dog, Alison Grant Robinson, later Alison Waley, 1947*

12. 'Schnee ist faul'; *a fall of soft snow covers the ski-slope in Norway*

asleep, sitting behind the fire guard. When I saw this I was in a great rage, and advancing upon him I beat the jay to death with my wings.

Then, tapping all the while on the iron-wood lid of my locker, 'I want a messenger,' I said, 'a bold and clever speaker to carry my complaints to the Country of Heaven'. Someone entered very quietly and politely, and when I looked, there I saw the young water-ousel in his god-like beauty, sitting on the seat at the left. Then tapping on the lid of my iron-wood locker, I began all night and all day to instruct him about the terms of my complaint. And when I looked at the ousel he showed no sign of wearying. Day and night he listened, for six whole nights and days. When at last I stopped speaking, he flew straight out of the window and up to the Country of Heaven. What I had told him to say was to this effect: There is a famine among the people of the world and they are at the point of death. And what is the reason? The gods in the Country of Heaven that have charge of deer, the gods that have charge of fish, have agreed together to send no more deer, to send no more fish. These gods no longer pay any heed at all to the prayers of the people, and when men go to the mountain they find no deer, and when men go fishing they get no fish. I am heart-rent to see this, and that is why I have sent a messenger to the god of deer and the god of fish.

Some days afterwards, I heard a faint noise in the sky, and when I looked, there was the ousel, more lovely than before, full of dignity and grace, returned from the Country of Heaven to tell me how he had delivered my complaint. 'The reason', he said, 'why the god of deer and the god of fish in the Country of Heaven are sending no deer and no fish is that when men took deer they beat them over the head with a stick, flayed them, and without more ado threw the head away into the woods; and when they caught fish, they hit them over the head with a piece of rotten wood. The deer, weeping bitterly, went to the god of deer, and the fish with the rotten stick in their mouths went to the god of fish. These two gods, very angry, took counsel together and agreed to send no more deer and no more fish. But if men would promise to treat the deer they take with courtesy, and the fish they catch with courtesy, the gods will send them deer and fish.'

When I heard what the god of deer and the god of fish had said, I praised the young ousel and thanked him. 'It is true enough', I said to myself. 'Men have treated the deer and the fish very scurvily.' So I visited men in their dreams when they were asleep, and taught them never again to do such things. Then they saw that it was bad to do as they had done, and ever afterwards they made all the gear with which they caught fish delicately. They decked out the heads of the deer daintily and made offerings before them. Henceforward the fish came happy and proud to the god of fish, with things lovely as prayer-sticks in their mouths; and the deer came happy, on the completing of their monthly shift, to make report to the god of deer. The gods of deer and fish were pleased, and sent plenty of fish, plenty of deer, so that now men had no more troubles, never felt the pinch of hunger, and I am happy about them in my mind. I am old and feeble, and for a long while I have been wanting to go away from here to the Country of Heaven. But I have always been afraid that there might be another famine among the people whom I protect, and so I stayed here. Yet now I feel that there is nothing to worry about; I am going to leave the bravest and strongest men to take my place and protect the people, and am going away to the Country of Heaven.

So spoke the old god, the god that guarded the land, and flew away to the Country of Heaven.

1946

The Little Wolf:
An Ainu Fable

(Author and date unknown)

One day for lack of anything better to do I went for a walk on the seashore. There I met a lad, and when he went to the lower river, I went down to the lower river, and when he went to the upper river, I went to the upper river and stood in his path. So we went six times down and six times up. The lad showed his ill nature in his face and said, 'Little fellow, wicked little fellow, I challenge you. Tell me the old name of this headland and the name it is called by today.' I laughed and said, 'That is a thing everyone knows. In old days mighty gods lived here, and it was called the Cape of the Gods. But now that times are bad and only men live here, it is called the Cape of Offerings.' 'Well then, little fellow,' said he, 'you shall tell me what this river used to be called, and what it is called now.' 'That's a thing everyone knows', I said. 'In the great age it was called the River that Flows Fast. But in these bad days, it is called the River that Flows Slowly.' 'Well, since you know that,' he said, 'you shall tell me who I really am and who you really are.' 'Surely,' I said, 'that's a thing everyone knows. Long ago the God Okikirmui when he went to the mountain built a hunting-lodge, with a fire-guard of hazel-wood. The heat of the fire dried it through and through. When Okikirmui put his feet on one end, the other tilted up. Okikirmui became angry with it, and threw it into the river. It floated away and away till it came to the sea. The other gods saw it drifting about this way and that in the waves, and thought it a pity that a thing made by Okikirmui should be wasted and float about in the sea till it was rotten. So they turned it into a fish, and called it the Fire-guard fish. This fish knew nothing of what it really was, and disguised as a human being loafed about just as you are doing. In fact, you are that fish.' The lad looked cross, very cross, and said, 'You, what about you? You, young fellow, are the wolf's little son.' And so saying he dived into the water. When I looked after him, all I saw was a red fish, lashing its tail and making straight out to sea.

This was the story the young wolf-god told.

1946

Aya No Tsuzumi (The Damask Drum)

Attributed to Seami (1363–1444) but perhaps earlier

PERSONS

A COURTIER   AN OLD GARDENER

THE PRINCESS

COURTIER.

I am a courtier at the Palace of Kinomaru in the country of Chikuzen. You must know that in this place there is a famous pond called the Laurel Pond, where the royal ones often take their walks; so it happened that one day the old man who sweeps the garden here caught sight of the Princess. And from that time he has loved her with a love that gives his heart no rest.

Some one told her of this, and she said, 'Love's equal realm knows no divisions',[1] and in her pity she said, 'By that pond there stands a laurel-tree, and on its branches there hangs a drum. Let him beat the drum, and if the sound is heard in the Palace, he shall see my face again.'

I must tell him of this.

Listen, old Gardener! The worshipful lady has heard of your love and sends you this message: 'Go and beat the drum that hangs on the tree by the pond, and if the sound is heard in the Palace, you shall see my face again.' Go quickly now and beat the drum!

[1] A 12th-century folk-song (*Ryōjin Hisshō*, p. 126), speaks of 'The Way of Love which knows no castes of "high" and "low".'

GARDENER.

With trembling I receive her words. I will go and beat the drum.

COURTIER.

Look, here is the drum she spoke of. Make haste and beat it! (*He leaves the* GARDENER *standing by the tree and seats himself at the foot of the 'Waki's pillar'.*)

GARDENER.

They talk of the moon-tree, the laurel that grows in the Garden of the Moon. . . . But for me there is but one true tree, this laurel by the lake. Oh, may the drum that hangs on its branches give forth a mighty note, a music to bind up my bursting heart.

Listen! the evening bell to help me chimes;
But then tolls in
A heavy tale of day linked on to day,

CHORUS (*speaking for the* GARDENER).

And hope stretched out from dusk to dusk.
But now, a watchman of the hours, I beat
The longed-for stroke.

GARDENER.

I was old, I shunned the daylight,
I was gaunt as an aged crane;
And upon all that misery
Suddenly a sorrow was heaped,
The new sorrow of love.
The days had left their marks,
Coming and coming, like waves that beat on a sandy shore. . . .

CHORUS.

Oh, with a thunder of white waves
The echo of the drum shall roll.

GARDENER.

The after-world draws near me,
Yet even now I wake not
From this autumn of love that closes
In sadness the sequence of my years.

CHORUS.

And slow as the autumn dew
Tears gather in my eyes, to fall
Scattered like dewdrops from a shaken flower
On my coarse-woven dress.
See here the marks, imprint of tangled love,
That all the world will read.

GARDENER.

I said 'I will forget',

CHORUS.

And got worse torment so
Than by remembrance. But all in this world
Is as the horse of the aged man of the land of Sai;[2]
And as a white colt flashes
Past a gap in the hedge, even so our days pass.[3]
And though the time be come,
Yet can none know the road that he at last must tread,
Goal of his dewdrop-life.
All this I knew; yet knowing,
Was blind with folly.

GARDENER.

'Wake, wake', he cries—

[2] A story from *Huai-nan Tzŭ*. What looks like disaster turns out to be good fortune and *vice versa*. The horse broke away and was lost. A revolution occurred during which the Government seized all horses. When the revolution was over the man of Sai's horse was rediscovered. If he had not lost it the Government would have taken it.

[3] This simile, which passed into a proverb in China and Japan, occurs first in *Chuang Tzŭ*, chap. xxii.

CHORUS.
  The watchman of the hours—
  'Wake from the sleep of dawn!'
  And batters on the drum.
  For if its sound be heard, soon shall he see
  Her face, the damask of her dress. . . .
  Aye, damask! He does not know
  That on a damask drum he beats,
  Beats with all the strength of his hands, his aged hands,
  But hears no sound.
  'Am I grown deaf?' he cries, and listens, listens:
  Rain on the windows, lapping of waves on the pool—
  Both these he hears, and silent only
  The drum, strange damask drum.
  Oh, will it never sound?
  I thought to beat the sorrow from my heart,
  Wake music in a damask drum; an echo of love
  From the voiceless fabric of pride!

GARDENER.
  Longed for as the moon that hides
  In the obstinate clouds of a rainy night
  Is the sound of the watchman's drum,
  To roll the darkness from my heart.

CHORUS.
  I beat the drum. The days pass and the hours.
  It was yesterday, and it is to-day.

GARDENER.
  But she for whom I wait

CHORUS.
  Comes not even in dream. At dawn and dusk

GARDENER.

No drum sounds.

CHORUS.

She has not come. Is it not sung that those
Whom love has joined
Not even the God of Thunder can divide?
Of lovers, I alone
Am guideless, comfortless.
Then weary of himself and calling her to witness of his woe,
'Why should I endure', he cried,
'Such life as this?' and in the waters of the pond
He cast himself and died.

(GARDENER *leaves the stage.*)

Enter the PRINCESS.

COURTIER.

I would speak with you, madam.

The drum made no sound, and the aged Gardener in despair
has flung himself into the pond by the laurel-tree, and died.
The soul of such a one may cling to you and do you injury. Go
out and look upon him.

PRINCESS (*speaking wildly, already possessed by the* GARDENER'S
angry ghost, which speaks through her).

Listen, people, listen!
In the noise of the beating waves
I hear the rolling of a drum.
Oh, joyful sound, oh joyful!
The music of a drum.

COURTIER.

Strange, strange!
This lady speaks as one
By phantasy possessed.
What is amiss, what ails her?

PRINCESS.
Truly, by phantasy I am possessed.
Can a damask drum give sound?
When I bade him beat what could not ring,
Then tottered first my wits.

COURTIER.
She spoke, and on the face of the evening pool
A wave stirred.

PRINCESS.
And out of the wave

COURTIER.
A voice spoke.

(*The voice of the* GARDENER *is heard; as he gradually advances along the hashigakari it is seen that he wears a 'demon mask', leans on a staff and carries the 'demon mallet' at his girdle.*)

GARDENER'S GHOST.
I was driftwood in the pool, but the waves of bitterness

CHORUS.
Have washed me back to the shore.

GHOST.
Anger clings to my heart,
Clings even now when neither wrath nor weeping
Are aught but folly.

CHORUS.
One thought consumes me,
The anger of lust denied
Covers me like darkness.
I am become a demon dwelling
In the hell of my dark thoughts,
Storm-cloud of my desires.

GHOST.

'Though the waters parch in the fields
Though the brooks run dry,
Never shall the place be shown
Of the spring that feeds my heart.'[4]
So I had resolved. Oh, why so cruelly
Set they me to win
Voice from a voiceless drum,
Spending my heart in vain?
And I spent my heart on the glimpse of a moon that slipped
Through the boughs of an autumn tree.[5]

CHORUS.

This damask drum that hangs on the laurel-tree

GHOST.

Will it sound, will it sound?

(*He seizes the* PRINCESS *and drags her towards the drum.*)

Try! Strike it!

CHORUS.

'Strike!' he cries;
'The quick beat, the battle-charge!
Loud, loud! Strike, strike,' he rails,
And brandishing his demon-stick
Gives her no rest.
'Oh woe!' the lady weeps,
'No sound, no sound. Oh misery!' she wails.
And he, at the mallet stroke, 'Repent, repent!'
Such torments in the world of night
Abōrasetsu, chief of demons, wields,
Who on the Wheel of Fire
Sears sinful flesh and shatters bones to dust.

[4] Adapted from a poem in the *Gosenshū.*
[5] Adapted from a poem in the *Kokinshū.*

Not less her torture now!
'Oh, agony!' she cries, 'What have I done,
By what dire seed this harvest sown?'

GHOST.

Clear stands the cause before you.

CHORUS.

Clear stands the cause before my eyes;
                    I know it now.
By the pool's white waters, upon the laurel's bough
The drum was hung.
He did not know his hour, but struck and struck
Till all the will had ebbed from his heart's core;
Then leapt into the lake and died.
And while his body rocked
Like driftwood on the waves,
His soul, an angry ghost,
Possessed the lady's wits, haunted her heart with woe.
The mallet lashed, as these waves lash the shore,
Lash on the ice of the eastern shore.
The wind passes; the rain falls
On the Red Lotus, the Lesser and the Greater.[6]
The hair stands up on my head.
'The fish that leaps the falls
To a fell snake is turned.'[7]
I have learned to know them;
Such, such are the demons of the World of Night.
'O hateful lady, hateful!' he cried, and sank again
Into the whirlpool of desire.

1921

---

[6] The names of two of the Cold Hells in the Buddhist Inferno.
[7] There is a legend that the fish who succeed in leaping a certain waterfall turn into dragons. So the Gardener's attempt to raise himself to the level of the Princess has changed him into an evil demon.

Kagekiyo

by Seami

PERSONS

A GIRL (Kagekiyo's daughter) HER ATTENDANT
KAGEKIYO THE PASSIONATE A VILLAGER
CHORUS

GIRL and ATTENDANT.
Late dewdrops are our lives that only wait
Till the wind blows, the wind of morning blows.

GIRL.
I am Hitomaru. I live in the valley of Kamegaye. My father
Kagekiyo the Passionate fought for the House of Hei[1] and for
this was hated by the Genji.[2] I am told they have banished him
to Miyazaki in the country of Hyūga, and there in changed
estate he passes the months and years. I must not be downcast
at the toil of the journey;[3] for hardship is the lot of all that
travel on unfamiliar roads, and I must bear it for my father's
sake.

GIRL and ATTENDANT.
Oh double-wet our sleeves
With the tears of troubled dreaming and the dews
That wet our grassy bed.

---

[1] The Tairas.
[2] The Minamotos, who came into power at the end of the 12th century.
[3] The journey to look for her father.

We leave Sagami; who shall point the way
To Tōtōmi, far off not only in name?[4]
Over the sea we row:
And now the eight-fold Spider Bridge we cross
To Mikawa. How long, O City of the Clouds,[5]
Shall we, inured to travel, see you in our dreams?

ATTENDANT.

We have journeyed so fast that I think we must already have
come to Miyazaki in the country of Hyūga. It is here you should
ask for your father.

(*The voice of* KAGEKIYO *is heard from within his hut.*)

KAGEKIYO.
    Behind this gate,
    This pine-wood barricade shut in alone
    I waste the hours and days;
    By me not numbered, since my eyes no longer
    See the clear light of heaven, but in darkness,
    Unending darkness, profitlessly sleep
    In this low room.
    For garment given but one coat to cover
    From winter winds or summer's fire
    This ruin, this anatomy!

CHORUS (*speaking for* KAGEKIYO).
    Oh better had I left the world, to wear
    The black-stained sleeve.
    Who will now pity me, whose withered frame
    Even to myself is hateful?
    Or who shall make a care to search for me
    And carry consolation to my woes?

    [4] Tōtōmi is written with characters meaning 'distant estuary'. The whole passage is
full of double-meanings which cannot be rendered.
    [5] The Capital.

GIRL.

How strange! That hut is so old, I cannot think that anyone can live there. Yet I heard a voice speaking within. Perhaps some beggar lodges there; I will not go nearer. (*She steps back.*)

KAGEKIYO.

    Though my eyes see not autumn
    Yet has the wind brought tiding

GIRL.

    Of one who wanders
    By ways unknown bewildered,
    Finding rest nowhere—

KAGEKIYO.

    For in the Three Worlds of Being
    Nowhere is rest,[6] but only
    In the Void Eternal.
    None is, and none can answer
    Where to thy asking.

ATTENDANT (*going up to* KAGEKIYO'S *hut*).

I have come to your cottage to ask you something.

KAGEKIYO.

What is it you want?

ATTENDANT.

Can you tell me where the exile lives?

KAGEKIYO.

The exile? What exile do you mean? Tell me his name.

ATTENDANT.

We are looking for Kagekiyo the Passionate who fought for the Taira.

---

[6] Quotation from the Parable Chapter of the *Hokkekyō*.

KAGEKIYO.

I have heard of him indeed. But I am blind, and have not seen him. I have heard such sad tales of his plight that I needs must pity him. Go further; ask elsewhere.

ATTENDANT (*to* GIRL, *who has been waiting*).

It does not seem that we shall find him here. Let us go further and ask again. (*They pass on.*)

KAGEKIYO.

Who can it be that is asking for me? What if it should be the child of this blind man? For long ago when I was at Atsuta in Owari I courted a woman and had a child by her. But since the child was a girl, I thought I would get no good of her and left her with the headman of the valley of Kamegaye. But she was not content to stay with her foster-parents and has come all this way to meet her true father.

CHORUS.

To hear a voice,
To hear and not to see!
Oh pity of blind eyes!
I have let her pass by;
I have not told my name;
But it was love that bound me,
Love's rope that held me.

ATTENDANT (*calling into the side-bridge*).

Hie! Is there any villager about?

VILLAGER (*raising the curtain that divides the side-bridge from the stage*).

What do you want with me?

ATTENDANT.

Do you know where the exile lives?

VILLAGER.

The exile? What exile is it you are asking for?

ATTENDANT.

One called Kagekiyo the Passionate who fought for the Taira.

VILLAGER.

Did you not see some one in a thatched hut under the hillside as you came along?

ATTENDANT.

Why, we saw a blind beggar in a thatched hut.

VILLAGER.

That blind beggar is your man. *He* is Kagekiyo.

(*The* GIRL *starts and trembles.*)

But why does your lady tremble when I tell you that he is Kagekiyo? What is amiss with her?

ATTENDANT.

No wonder that you ask. I will tell you at once; this lady is Kagekiyo's daughter. She has borne the toil of this journey because she longed to meet her father face to face. Please take her to him.

VILLAGER.

She is Kagekiyo's daughter? How strange, how strange! But, lady, calm yourself and listen.

Kagekiyo went blind in both his eyes, and finding himself helpless, shaved his head and called himself the beggar of Hyūga. He begs a little from travellers; and we villagers are sorry for him and see to it that he does not starve. Perhaps he would not tell you his name because he was ashamed of what he has become. But if you will come with me I will shout 'Kagekiyo' at him. He will surely answer to his own name. Then you shall go to

him and talk of what you will, old times or now. Please come this
way.

(*They go towards the hut.*)

Hie, Kagekiyo, Kagekiyo! Are you there, Kagekiyo the
Passionate?

KAGEKIYO (*stopping his ears with his hands, irritably*).
Noise, noise!
Silence! I was vexed already. For a while ago there came
travellers from my home! Do you think I let them stay? No, no.
I could not show them my loathsomeness. . . . It was hard to let
them go—not tell them my name!
A thousand rivers of tears soften my sleeve!
A thousand, thousand things I do in dream
And wake to idleness! Oh I am resolved
To be in the world as one who is not in the world.
Let them shout 'Kagekiyo, Kagekiyo':
Need beggars answer?
Moreover, in this land I have a name.

CHORUS.
'In Hyūga sunward-facing
A fit name found I.
Oh call me not by the name
Of old days that have dropped
Like the bow from a stricken hand!
For I whom passion
Had left for ever
At the sound of that wrathful name
Am angry, angry.'

(*While the* CHORUS *speaks his thought* KAGEKIYO *mimes their
words, waving his stick and finally beating it against his thigh
in a crescendo of rage.*)

KAGEKIYO (*suddenly lowering his voice, gently*).
But while I dwell here . . .

CHORUS.
'But while I dwell here
To those that tend me
Should I grow hateful
Then were I truly
A blind man staffless.
Oh forgive
Profitless anger, tongue untended,
A cripple's spleen.'

KAGEKIYO.
For though my eyes be darkened . . .

CHORUS.
'Though my eyes be darkened
Yet, no word spoken,
Men's thoughts I see.
Listen now to the wind
In the woods upon the hill:
Snow is coming, snow!
Oh bitterness to wake
From dreams of flowers unseen!
And on the shore,
Listen, the waves are lapping
Over rough stones to the cliff.
The evening tide is in.

(KAGEKIYO *fumbles for his staff and rises, coming just outside
the hut. The mention of 'waves', 'shore,' 'tide,' has reminded
him of the great shore-battle at Yashima in which the Tairas
triumphed.*)

'I was one of them, of those Tairas. If you will listen, I will tell
you the tale. . . .'

KAGEKIYO (*to the* VILLAGER).

There was a weight on my mind when I spoke to you so harshly. Pray forgive me.

VILLAGER.

No, no! you are always so! I do not heed you. But tell me, did not some one come before, asking for Kagekiyo?

KAGEKIYO.

No—you are the only one who has asked.

VILLAGER.

It is not true. Some one came here saying that she was Kagekiyo's daughter. Why did you not tell her? I was sorry for her and have brought her back with me.

(*To the* GIRL.) Come now, speak with your father.

GIRL (*going to* KAGEKIYO's *side and touching his sleeve*).

It is I who have come to you.
I have come all the long way,
Through rain, wind, frost and dew.
And now—you have not understood; it was all for nothing.
Am I not worth your love? Oh cruel, cruel!
(*She weeps.*)

KAGEKIYO.

All that till now I thought to have concealed
Is known; where can I hide,
I that have no more refuge than the dew
That finds no leaf to lie on?
Should you, oh flower delicately tended,
Call me your father, then would the World know you
A beggar's daughter. Oh think not ill of me
That I did let you pass!
(*He gropes falteringly with his right hand and touches her sleeve.*)

CHORUS.
Oh sad, sad!
He that of old gave welcome
To casual strangers and would raise an angry voice
If any passed his door,
Now from his own child gladly
Would hide his wretchedness.
He that once
Among all that in the warships of Taira
Shoulder to shoulder, knee locked with knee,
Dwelt crowded—
Even Kagekiyo keen
As the clear moonlight—
Was ever called on to captain
The Royal Pinnace.
And though among his men
Many were brave and many of wise counsel,
Yet was he even as the helm of the boat.
And of the many who served him
None cavilled, disputed.
But now
He that of all was envied
Is like Kirin[7] grown old,
By every jade outrun.

VILLAGER (*seeing the* GIRL *standing sadly apart*).
Poor child, come back again.

(*She comes back to her father's side.*)

Listen, Kagekiyo, there is something your daughter wants
of you.

KAGEKIYO.
What is it she wants?

[7] A Chinese Pegasus. The proverb says, 'Even Kirin, when he was old, was outstripped by hacks'. Seami quotes this proverb, *Works*, p. 9.

VILLAGER.

She tells me that she longs to hear the story of your high deeds at Yashima. Could you not tell us the tale?

KAGEKIYO.

That is a strange thing for a girl to ask. Yet since kind love brought her this long, long way to visit me, I cannot but tell her the tale. Promise me that when it is finished you will send her back again to her home.

VILLAGER.

I will. So soon as your tale is finished, I will send her home.

KAGEKIYO.

It was in the third year of Juyei,[8]
At the close of the third month.
We of Heike were in our ships,
The men of Genji on shore.
Two armies spread along the coast
Eager to bid in battle
For final mastery.
Then said Noritsune, Lord of Noto,
'Last year at Muro Hill in the land of Harima,
At Water Island, even at Jackdaw Pass,
We were beaten again and again; outwitted
By Yoshitsune's strategy.
Oh that some plan might be found, some counsel given
For the slaying of Kurō.'[9] So spoke he.
Then thought Kagekiyo in his heart,
'Though he be called "Judge",
Yet is he no god or demon, this Yoshitsune.
An easy task! Oh easy for one that loves not
His own life chiefly!'

---

[8] 'Le vieux guerrier aveugle, assis devant sa cabane d'exilé, mime son dernier combat de gestes incertains et tremblants' (Péri).   [9] Yoshitsune.

278

So he took leave of Noritsune
And landed upon the beach.
The soldiers of Genji
'Death to him, death to him!' cried
As they swept towards him.

CHORUS.
  And when he saw them,
  'What great to-do!' he cried, then waving
  His sword in the evening sunlight
  He fell upon them swiftly.
  They fled before his sword-point,
  They could not withstand him, those soldiers;
  This way, that way, they scuttled wildly, and he cried,
  'They shall not escape me!'

KAGEKIYO (*breaking in excitedly*).
  Cowards, cowards all of you!

CHORUS.
  Cowards, all of you!
  Sight shameful alike for Gen and Hei.
  Then, thinking that to stop one man
  Could not but be easy,
  Sword under arm,
  'I am Kagekiyo,' he cried,
  'Kagekiyo the Passionate, a captain of the soldiers of Hei.'
  And swiftly pursued, with naked hand to grasp
  The helm that Mionoya wore.
  He clutched at the neck-piece,
  Twice and again he clutched, but it slipped from him, slid
      through his fingers.
  Then crying 'He shall not escape me, this foe I have chosen',
  Swooped like a bird, seized upon the helmet,
  'Eya, eya', he cried, tugging,

Till 'Crack'—the neck-piece tore from the helm and was left
    in his hand,
While the master of it, suddenly free, ran till he was come
A good way off, then turning,
'O mighty Kagekiyo, how terrible the strength of your arm!'
And the other called back to him, 'Nay, say rather "How
    strong the shaft
Of Mionoya's neck!" So laughed they across the battle,
And went off each his way.

    (KAGEKIYO, *who has been miming the battle, breaks off abruptly
    and turns to the* VILLAGER. *The* CHORUS *speaks for him.*)

CHORUS.
  'I am old: I have forgotten—things unforgettable!
My thoughts are tangled: I am ashamed.
But little longer shall this world,
This sorrowful world torment me.
The end is near: go to your home;
Pray for my soul departed, child, candle to my darkness,
Bridge to salvation!

    (*He rises to his feet groping with his stick, comes to the* GIRL,
    and gently pushes her before him towards the wing.)

'I stay', he said; and she 'I go'.
The sound of this word
Was all he kept of her,
Nor passed between them
Remembrance other.

                              1921

Myself (1926)

by Akutagawa Ryūnosuke[1] (1892–1927)

When I am insulted, for some reason or other it is always a good while before I am annoyed. But after about an hour I do invariably begin to feel gradually more and more annoyed.

When I saw Rodin's Count Ugoli—or rather, a photograph of the Count Ugoli—certain homosexual passages in my life suddenly came into my mind.

When I look at trees, it seems to me quite unbelievable that I, like any other human being, have a front and back side.

Sometimes I become a tyrant and want to see large numbers of men and women eaten by lions and tigers. But the mere sight of a bit of bloodstained gauze lying on a surgical tray gives me a sudden feeling of physical indisposition.

I sometimes feel about other people that I should be glad if they were dead, and some of the people about whom I have felt this were my nearest relations.

I have no conscience of any kind, not even an artistic conscience; but nerves I have in abundance.

I am entirely devoid of hate, but I make up for this from time to time by outbursts of contempt.

I know by experience that among my own characteristics the one that fills me with the greatest loathing of myself is the fact that I find falseness everywhere. Moreover, I do not, even at the time, get the slightest feeling of satisfaction by these discoveries.

---

[1] Prolific and intensely original short-story writer whose influential career came abruptly to an end when he committed suicide at the age of thirty-five. This fragment (*Boku wa*), written shortly before his death, is one of his few autobiographical writings. *Ed.*

I listen very closely to the way different sorts of people speak. For example, the way the boy from the fishmonger's says *konnichi wa* (good morning). He doesn't end it with a vowel sound, but says something more like *konchiwaas*. I don't know why he puts this unnecessary *s* at the end of the word.

I am not merely one person. I am a son, a landlord, a male, in my view of life a realist, by temperament a romantic, in philosophy a sceptic, and so on. There's nothing particularly inconvenient about this. Yet I am tormented by a perpetual conflict as to which of these is really me.

Whenever I get a letter or anything else from a woman whom I do not know, I cannot help beginning at once to wonder whether she is good-looking.

All words go in pairs that are like the head and tail of a coin. I call so-and-so pretentious; but that does not mean that in the relevant respects he is at all different from me. When I behave in the same way I am only showing a decent amount of self-respect.

When I go to a doctor, I never succeed in telling him anything definite or precise. With the result that I come away feeling that I have simply been shamming.

In proportion as I move away from where I am living, I feel my identity growing dimmer and dimmer. This phenomenon seems to begin as soon as I am about thirty miles from home.

My spiritual life never goes smoothly forward, but progresses in jumps, like a flea.

When I meet anyone I know by sight, I always bow. If he does not notice that I am doing so, I have a feeling of being out of pocket.

A Poem by Kubla Khan

(*Translated in an unpublished letter from Arthur Waley to Sydney Cockerell*)[1]

Department of Prints and Drawings
British Museum
London: W.C.
Sept. 29, 1916

Dear Mr Cockerell,

I have discovered a poem written by Kubla Khan (Coleridge's person) when he was shown the River Picture. In order to understand it, it is necessary to know that Pien City was captured by the Tartars the year after the picture was painted. Kubla came to the throne in 1260. Pien City was captured in 1127.

> 'Under the T'ien-ching Bridge
> The water—swirl, swirl.
> Beyond the willows, the market boats,
> Flanked by the coaches on the tow-path.
> I see before me Pien City
> In the days when all was well;
> And, happy in the spring-time, countless thronging
> Pre-war men!'

Of course, it may not really have been written by Kubla himself. It is very hard to find out exactly what was the culture of these Mongol Emperors. I think it is very moving, whoever wrote it. . . .

We heard from Mrs Gooden this morning that Steve is well but very depressed. He was one of the few people who really believed we were going to break through in twenty-four hours and march to Berlin. So now he can't make out why it hasn't happened.

Yours sincerely,
Arthur D. Waley

[1] I am grateful to B. S. Cron, Esq., for making this letter available. *Ed.*

Notes on Chinese Prosody

Certain elements are found, but in varying degree, in all human speech. Thus it is difficult to conceive of a language in which rhyme, stress-accent, tone-accent would not to some extent occur. In all languages some vowel-sounds are shorter than others, and in certain cases two consecutive words begin with the same sound. If we number these speech-elements we get (1) rhyme, (2) stress-accent, (3) tone-accent, (4) vowel-quantity, (5) alliteration. No doubt other characteristics could be enumerated, but for the purposes of poetry it is these five which have been principally exploited. English poetry has used chiefly (1), (2), and in earlier times (5); it is doubtful whether (3) has played any part, but an unconscious use has probably been made of (4).

Poetry naturally utilizes the most marked and definite characteristics of the language in which it is written. These are used consciously by the poet; but less important elements also play their part, often only in a negative way. Thus the Japanese actually avoid rhyme; the Greeks, while not exploiting it, seem to have tolerated it when it occurred accidentally.

The expedients consciously used by Chinese poetry before the 6th century were rhyme and length of line. A third element, inherent in the language, was not exploited before that date, but must always have been a factor in the euphony of poetry. I refer to tone.

I need not dwell on this feature of the Chinese language, which is familiar, in theory at any rate, to all scholars. When the vowel-sound of a syllable is 'all on one note', that is to say, when the sound neither rises nor sinks during its utterance, the sound is said to be *p'ing*, level or 'natural'. When the sound rises or falls or is suddenly arrested explosively, it is called *tsê*, 'deflected'. There are thus three varieties of the deflected tone, which the Chinese call *shang* 'rising', *ch'ü* 'departing', and *ju*[1] 'entering'. The last occurs in words which formerly ended in a consonant. The *p'ing* tone and the three *tsê* tones make up the 'four tones' of classical Chinese. These should not be confused with the 'four tones' of the Mandarin dialect, in the description of which the old tone-names have been used in a most misleading manner. The so-called lower-level tone of Pekinese (e.g. in such words as *jen* 'man') is not in any sense 'level'; Guernier[2] defines it as 'sharp rising', *aigu montant*.

I shall here notate the 'level' tone as A and the deflected as B. For the moment we need not concern ourselves with further subdivisions.

I have said that until the 6th century tone-arrangement was not an important element in Chinese prosody. It would seem that the early poets were as insensible to tone-effects as the Greeks were to rhymed endings. Just as Sophocles does not reject couplets whose last feet jingle in a manner disagreeable to modern ears, so the early poets of China took the tones 'as they came'. It does not often happen in a Chinese sentence that five deflected or five level tones follow one another. Consequently in poetry we should not expect to find lines in which all the syllables are *tsê* or all *p'ing*. But such lines do occasionally occur. For example, in a poem by Ts'ao Chih (Giles, No. 1994, AD 192–232) there is a line *wo yü ching tz'u ch'ü*, 'I want to end this lay', which consists of five deflected words. It is possible that the poet was aiming at a particular effect, but I am inclined to believe that Ts'ao Chih thought as little about tone as Shakespeare did about 'quantity'.

The tone-consciousness of Chinese poetry was no doubt of gradual growth. The process might be compared to the change

---

[1] Whenever necessary, I have provided romanized transcriptions of the characters included in the original version of this article. *Ed.*

[2] *Notes sur la langue . . . de . . . Pékin*, p. 10 (published in 1912 by the Association Phonétique Internationale).

which took place in Latin poetry when it became quantitative instead of accentual. But the analogy is not complete. Rome imported a foreign prosody, whereas the changes in Chinese poetry were apparently due to the evolution of the language itself. It is not, however, impossible that this evolution was to some extent influenced by foreign contact.

During the time when this transformation of prosody was developing, the northern part of China was under the rule of the Toba Tartars, founders of the Northern Wei dynasty. In 494 they moved their capital from the Shansi frontier to the Lo-yang in Honan; in 534 Western Wei established itself at Ch'ang-an. Under the T'ang dynasty (618–905) these two places, as the Eastern and Western capitals, became of paramount importance, and a dialect moulded by Tartar occupation may well have spread from them to the rest of China.

It is clear that the increased importance of 'tones' in poetry must have corresponded to a marked development of their use in ordinary speech. Such a development is best accounted for by the necessity of distinguishing between monosyllables which, owing to phonological changes, had become homophonous.

Towards the end of the 5th century Shên Yo (AD 441–513), the reputed 'discoverer' of the Four Tones, had already enunciated[3] certain principles with regard to the tone-arrangement of the twenty character quatrain. 'The second character', he says, 'must not be in the same tone as the fifth, nor the fifth in the same tone as the fifteenth.' Neither of these principles was admitted by later practice, but it is possible that Shên Yo has been inaccurately quoted. The point of interest is that he should have formulated such a canon at all.

Increasing attention was paid to tone-arrangement in the next three centuries, but needless to say the poets worked by ear rather than by rule. The effects produced by the interchange of tone were subtle and the possible combinations almost infinite. Although certain forms began to assert themselves as orthodox,

[3] Quoted in P'i Yü Yü Lei.

it was realized that the tones were made for the poet, not the poet for the tones.

If we apply the rigid formulae of the school books to the poetry of Li Po (701–62) or Tu Fu (712–70), we shall find that the critics have labelled certain forms as orthodox, *cheng ko*, in a quite arbitrary way, while denouncing as *niu*, 'contradictory', metres in which many poems of classical celebrity were written.

But it is necessary before going further to distinguish between the 'Modern Style', *chin t'i*, and the 'Old Style' of poetry, *ku shih*. The Chinese say, 'The important element in the "Modern Style" is the arrangement of tones'. But side by side with it existed and still exists the 'Old Style', which 'disregards the tones'.

Yet the distinction is not absolute. I have found poems classified in one anthology as 'old style' and in another as 'irregular modern style'. The difference might be compared to that between a rhymed couplet by Pope and one by William Morris. It is easy to recognize that a distinction exists, but hard to define it precisely. Probably a few stray couplets might be found in Pope which could be mistaken for the work of Morris, and vice versa; nevertheless it would be possible to make certain broad statements (for example, about the relative *speed* of the lines) which would generally turn out to be true.

The relation between the old and new styles of Chinese poetry is equally difficult to define. Attempts to codify too rigidly the laws which the new style follows led in later times to a narrowing of the technical groundwork of poetry; but other causes were at work to which allusion will be made later.

Most European writers on this subject have not realized that a large part of classical poetry was written in the old style. Indeed, since the content of such poems is usually more interesting than that of poems in the more rigid forms, a large proportion of the poems which have been made accessible to European readers are *ku shih*, 'in the old style': e.g. Tu Fu's 'Recruiter',[4]

---

[4] Harvey St Denys, *Poésies des Thangs*, p. 96.

the 'Lute Girl',[5] and the 'Everlasting Wrong'[6] by Po Chü-i, and many of the Li Po poems translated by St Denys and Giles. It is, in fact, chiefly upon his old style poems that the immense fame of Li Po rests. . . .

In dealing with the technique of Chinese poetry most European writers, then, have confined themselves to (a) the Confucian Odes and (b) the New Style.

Schott[7] accepts the Chinese maxim that in the new style one need only worry about the second, fourth, and sixth characters in the line and the rest will look after themselves. But though this motto is a useful rule of thumb for the native, who in practice qualifies it by the application of other laws which seem to him so self-evident that it would be superfluous to state them, for the European it is wholly misleading.

St Denys,[8] having stated some of the general principles of the new style correctly (but giving the erroneous impression that all T'ang poetry was written in this style), illustrates his remarks by a poem which is not a new-style poem at all, but a song, and which disregards the conventions of tone-arrangement. The poem in question is a famous quatrain of Li Po . . . which displays the tone-arrangement AAABA, ABBBA, BABAB, AAABA (the tones are wrongly marked by St Denys); the first, second, and fourth lines rhyme. This formula would be described by the Chinese as 'the *p'ing* rhyme "yang" used three times; tone-arrangement disregarded'.

Harlez[9] follows Schott, and his very brief exposition is misleading, unless qualified by general rules which he does not mention. Mr Charles Budd[10] devotes seven pages to this department of prosody. He tells us (p. 21) that 'the first and last lines (of a quatrain) always agree exactly, tone for tone'. This is true of the commonest form of seven-syllable quatrain, but it is quite

---

[5] Giles, *Chinese Literature*, p. 165. [6] *Loc. cit.*, p. 169.

[7] *Über die Chinesische Verkunst. Abhandl. d. k. Ak. d. Wiss. zu Berlin*, 1857.

[8] *Op. cit.*, introduction.

[9] Bulletin de l'Ac. Roy. de Belgique, sér. III, xxiv, p. 181.

[10] *Chinese Poems*, 1912.

13. *At a Foyles Writers' Luncheon*

14. *At the home of Georgette Boner, Davos, Switzerland*

untrue of the normal five-syllable verse, which is toned as follows:

B or A, B, A, A, B	or A or B, A, A, B, B
A, A, B or A, B, A	B or A, B, B, A, A
A or B, A, A, B, B	B or A, B, A, A, B
B or A, B, B, A, A	A, A, B or A, B, A.

In both of these schemes the second and fourth lines rhyme, and by an absolute law (which was generally applied long before the T'ang dynasty) the unrhymed lines must end in a different tone to the rhymed lines.

In the poem given by Mr Budd as 'a perfect specimen of the four-line stanza'[11] it will be seen that the first and last lines do *not* agree. There are other inconsistencies in Mr Budd's exposition with which I will not deal here.

Kühnert[12] in his treatise on Chinese rhythm devotes a few pages to poetry, taking his examples from vol. v of Zottoli's *Cursus*. He complains that these examples do not conform to the rules given by Zottoli. This is natural, for Zottoli, like most writers on the subject, has tried to state the laws of Chinese prosody with far too great precision. Erring in the same direction Professor Giles tells us, 'For poetical purposes all the characters in the language are ranged under *two* tones, as *flats* and *sharps*. These occupy certain fixed places, just as dactyls and spondees occupy fixed places in the construction of Latin verse. Thus, in a stanza of the ordinary five-character length the following tonal arrangement must appear:

Sharp sharp flat flat sharp
Flat flat sharp sharp flat
Flat flat flat sharp sharp
Sharp sharp sharp flat flat.'[13]

Professor Giles's 'must' is misleading. If it were true, the

[11] *Op. cit.*, p. 22.
[12] *Über d. Rhythmus im Chinesischem, Abhandl. d. k. Akad. . . . zu Wien*, 1896.
[13] *Chinese Poetry*, p. 199.

shackles of metre would be such that a poet could hardly ever say what he wanted to. But this is only one of many forms which are all recognized as orthodox even by Ming pedants and when we come to examine the actual poetry of the 'golden age' (the time of Li Po and Tu Fu) we find that it is far from orthodox. I could point to many stanzas in Professor Giles's own book which do not in any way conform to his scheme.

The general reader wants above all to know how much freedom Chinese prosody gave to the poet, and what was the nature of the restrictions imposed. It will be observed that Professor Giles not only greatly exaggerates the strictness of the system, but also omits to mention that the earlier poems in his book are subject to no such restrictions, and that among the T'ang and later poems many are in the 'old style' which disregards these laws.

RHYME

Professor Giles states both in the *Encyclopaedia Britannica*[14] and in *Chinese Poetry*[15] that the rhymes used by the classical poets of China are those of the Book of Odes. If this were true, the rhyming of the great T'ang poets would be completely artificial, for it is certain that in the course of 2,000 years the pronunciation of the language had changed. The rhyme-system of the Odes has been amply dealt with by Legge;[16] it is utterly different from that of other Chinese poetry, as is recognized by all native writers on the subject.

The system of rhymes used in 'old style poetry', *ku shih*, both in the period from Han till T'ang and afterwards, has been described by a Chinese scholar, Chu Hua (H. Lü-ch'ih), who settled in Japan at the end of the 18th century and became a friend of the Japanese scholars Takemoto Tōtō-an and Rai Sanyō. A book entitled *The System of Rhymes in Old Poetry* was published by Tōtō-an in 1812. In this book the rhymes, in over

[14] 11th ed., vol. vi, p. 223.   [15] p. 199.   [16] *Chinese Classics*, vol. iv.

200-'old-style' poems, are analysed, dating from the Han dynasty till the end of Ming. The inquiry shows that the Old Style recognizes thirty-four rhymes, many of which are mere assonances. Thus, Tu Fu in the 'Recruiter' (see above) makes *ts'un* rhyme with *k'an*. There is no reason to suppose that in the 8th century the two vowel sounds were identical. Again, we find *tung* rhyming with *chiang*, and *yüeh* (in T'ang times still pronounced *yüet*) with *wu* (formerly pronounced *wut*.)

But a stricter rhyme-system is already discernible in the poetry of the 6th century. About this time, or a little later, the Chinese began to use rhyme-categories as a principle of arrangement in works of reference. The *Kuang Yün* (early 7th century?) diction-ary was arranged on this plan, the number of the rhymes being 206. The greatest possible number of distinctions was obviously made in order to facilitate the use of the book as a work of reference. But Chinese prosody never recognized the subtler distinctions, which must have been to some extent arbitrary.

The rhymes used by the T'ang poets and their successors in writing 'new-style' poetry are 106 in number.[17] These are called the *shih yün* or 'rhymes of poetry', and have been used as the basis of arrangement in many famous dictionaries and concordances. The upper and lower level tones are not distinguished, except that of the thirty 'level' rhymes fifteen of the words chosen as heads to the categories are in the upper level and fifteen in the lower level. This is merely for convenience of arrangement; it does not affect the rhymes. . . .

It has been suggested by European writers that in pre-T'ang poetry a word could rhyme with a word in a different tone, provided their endings were otherwise homophonous. This is not so; the four tones are kept rigidly distinct. *Yang* (in the departing tone) and *yang* (in the level tone) would not be con-sidered by the Chinese to be 'the same sound' at all. It should

[17] There was an increasing tendency only to use the *p'ing* rhymes. In later dynasties, when the pronunciation of the language had changed, poets no longer rhymed by *ear*. The burden of knowing by heart the rhymes in the whole 106 categories became intoler-able, and to-day, if the poet avoids *tsê* rhymes, it is partly because he does not know them!

here be noted that though rhyme in English excludes words which are identical in sound, it does not do so in Chinese any more than in French poetry. Thus *made* and *maid* are not used as rhymes in English, but *te*, 'virtue', and *te*, 'to get', do rhyme in Chinese.

RHYME AND TONE-ARRANGEMENT

The 'normal' scheme of five-syllable quatrain which I have given above shows that there are generally only two rhymes in this form of verse. If, however, the first line also rhymes, various other changes take place in the tone-arrangement, which then becomes:

B or A, B, B, A, A	or A, A, B or A, B, A
B, A, A, B, A	B or A, B, B, A, A
A or B, A, A, B, B	B or A, B, A, A, B
B or A, B, B, A, A	B, A, A, B, A.

On the other hand, in the seven-syllable verse the commonest form is with three rhymes, e.g.:

B or A, B, A, A, B, B, A	or A or B, A, A, B, B, A, A
A or B, A, A, B, B, A, A	B or A, B, A, A, B, B, A
A, A, B or A, B, A, A, B	B or A, B, A, A, A, B, B
B or A, B, A, A, B, B, A	A or B, A, A, B, B, A, A.

CAESURA

In the five-syllable line it comes after the second foot,[18] in the shape of a very slight pause, which is nevertheless sufficient to control the grammatical relations of the line. That is to say, two characters which grammatically 'go together' may not be separated by the caesura. Thus, the line *t'an hsi tz'u jen ch'ü* could never mean 'sighing and sobbing about this, the man went away', but must mean 'sighing and sobbing about this man's departure'.

[18] This has been correctly stated by most writers. It must be owing to a misprint that the *Encyclopaedia Britannica* (*loc. cit.*) gives the impression that the caesura is after the third foot.

The caesura in the seven-syllable line comes after the fourth and is much more definite than that of the five-syllable line. . . .

Nevertheless, it is stated that the great Han Yü (768–824) sometimes used lines with the caesura after the third. . . .

There is another element which is characteristic of most Oriental poetry, and which has been adequately described by many European writers. This element is parallelism, e.g.:

As I lay on my pillow my vinous complexion, soothed by sleep, grew sober:
In front of the tower the ocean moon, accompanying the tide, had risen.

(Po Chü-i, Works, vol. xx, f.19.)

Nor will I dwell on the rhetorical construction of the eight-line stanza, i.e. the 'development' of the theme in the successive couplets (for this, too, became subject to fixed laws).

But before closing, I will name a few tests by which the 'new style' may be distinguished from the 'old'.

NEW STYLE

(A) Rhymes, those of the arrangement into 106 categories; rhymes in the *p'ing* (level) tone are preferred.

(B) *P'ing* and *tsê*.

(1) A tendency to antithetical arrangement, especially in the last part of the lines. This is called *hsieh*.

(2) A tendency for the tones to go in pairs, e.g. AABBA or ABBAA, etc., rather than in threes. This arrangement in pairs is called *nien*.

Three like tones only come together when divided by a caesura; e.g. the line BB/AAA would be avoided, but not the line BBAA/ABB.

OLD STYLE

(A) Rhymes. The thirty-four assonances. Rhymes in the 'deflected' tone are used quite as freely as those in the 'level' tone.

(B) Tone-arrangement. The tones were apparently disregarded. Eighteenth-century writers, following Wang Shih-chêng (1634–1711), tried to discover the laws of 'level' and 'deflected' (*p'ing* and *tsê*) in old-style poetry. Their efforts are embodied in Professor Mori's *Koshi Heisoku* (Tōkiō, 1894). But the 'rules' are subject to so many exceptions and modifications that the attempt does not seem very successful. It is better to accept the maxim ' "old poetry" disregards *p'ing* and *tsê*'. Both 'hsieh clauses' and '*nien* clauses' are occasionally found in 'old-style' poems, but so seldom that their occurrence would appear to be accidental.

I have in the foregoing pages treated almost exclusively of *shih* or 'lyrical poetry'. The *tz'ŭ* was a kind of strophic song, depending on an elaborate pattern of tones, in lines of unequal length. It was an invention of the 10th century, but later critics attempted to treat certain T'ang poems as anticipations of *tz'ŭ* by pronouncing 'level' words as 'deflected' and vice versa where the metre required.

Hua fei hua	A flower; not a flower:
Wu fei wu	A mist: not a mist.
Yeh pan lai	At midnight coming.
T'ien ming ch'ü	At day's dawn going.
Lai ju ch'un meng	Coming like a spring dream
Pu to shih	Only for a little while;
Ch'ü szu chao yün	Gone like a morning cloud
Wu mi ch'u	That cannot be recovered.

This poem of Po Chü-i is read as a *tz'u* by the violent expedient of pronouncing *lai* in the third line and *ch'un* in the fifth as 'deflected' words and *ch'ü* in the last line but one as 'level'.

Adequate treatment of the *tz'u* would require a separate article, as would also the *fu* or 'description', a kind of *vers-libre*.

The above remarks on Chinese prosody are necessarily very incomplete, but I hope they may serve to remove certain misapprehensions which have hitherto prevailed.

1918

Love and Friendship in Chinese Poetry

Extract from the Introduction to *A Hundred and Seventy Chinese Poems* (1918 edition)

The most conspicuous feature of European poetry is its pre-occupation with love. This is apparent not only in actual 'love-poems', but in all poetry where the personality of the writer is in any way obtruded. The poet tends to exhibit himself in a *romantic* light; in fact, to recommend himself as a lover.

The Chinese poet has a tendency different but analogous. He recommends himself not as a lover, but as a friend. He poses as a person of infinite leisure (which is what we should most like our friends to possess) and free from worldly ambitions (which constitute the greatest bars to friendship). He would have us think of him as a boon companion, a great drinker of wine, who will not disgrace a social gathering by quitting it sober.

To the European poet the relation between man and woman is a thing of supreme importance and mystery. To the Chinese, it is something commonplace, obvious—a need of the body, not a satisfaction of the *emotions*. These he reserves entirely for friendship.

Accordingly we find that while our poets tend to lay stress on physical courage and other qualities which normal women admire, Po Chü-i is not ashamed to write such a poem as 'Alarm at entering the Gorges'. Our poets imagine themselves very much as Art has portrayed them—bare-headed and wild-eyed, with shirts unbuttoned at the neck as though they feared that a seizure of emotion might at any minute suffocate them. The

Chinese poet introduces himself as a timid recluse, 'Reading the Book of Changes at the Northern Window', playing chess with a Taoist priest, or practising calligraphy with an occasional visitor. If 'With a Portrait of the Author' had been the rule in the Chinese book-market, it is in such occupations as these that he would be shown; a neat and tranquil figure compared with our lurid frontispieces.

It has been the habit of Europe to idealize love at the expense of friendship and so to place too heavy a burden on the relation of man and woman. The Chinese erred in the opposite direction, regarding their wives and concubines simply as instruments of procreation. For sympathy and intellectual companionship they looked only to their friends. But these friends were bound by no such tie as held women to their masters; sooner or later they drifted away to frontier campaigns, remote governorships, or country retirement. It would not be an exaggeration to say that half the poems in the Chinese language are poems of parting or separation.

1918

Notes on the 'Lute-Girl's Song'[1]

This well-known poem by Po Chü-i has been translated by Professor Giles (*Chinese Literature*, p. 165).[2] He has omitted the Preface which explains the circumstances under which the poem was written. In the following pages I shall translate this Preface and shall also venture to criticize a few points in Professor Giles's translation of the poem. He has lately submitted several of my translations to the most searching criticism and will not, I am sure, resent my very tentative emendations.

PREFACE

In the tenth year of Yüan Ho (AD 815), I was banished to the city of Kiukiang with the rank of sub-Prefect. In the autumn of the following year I was seeing off a visitor at the mouth of the P'ên River. The *P'ên Shui* ran into the Yangtze west of Kiukiang. . . . We heard some one playing the lute on board a boat at night. I listened and recognized by a certain bell-like quality in the melody that it was a Ch'ang-an tune (*lit.*, 'that it had a sound of the Capital').

I enquired who the player was and learnt that she had been a dancing-girl at Ch'ang-an and had taken lessons in lute-playing from the masters Mou and Ts'ao. But when she grew old and her beauty faded, she let a merchant take her as his wife.

[1] I retain the title by which the poem is best known to English readers. The 'Song was *made for* not *sung by* the girl.

[2] 'A good translation of this "Lute Song" by the American poet Witter Bynner will be found in *From the Chinese*, an anthology edited by R. C. Trevalyan.' Waley, *The Life and Times of Po Chü-i*, p. 118. For Professor Giles's 1901 translation, see below, pp. 303–5. Ed.

Hearing this, I ordered wine and persuaded her to play several tunes. When she had done playing she fell to telling us regretfully of the joys of her youth, and how she was now cruising about homeless and distressed, among the rivers and lakes.

During the two years which had passed since I fell from office I had always been happy enough. But that night, moved by the girl's story, I suddenly began to feel the sorrows of exile. So I made for her a long-line ballad of 620 words, calling it 'The Lute Song'. [620 is a 'round number'. Each line consists of seven characters, making 616 in all.]

THE POEM

Professor Giles says that 'the "guest" is the poet himself, setting out a second time for his place of banishment, as mentioned above, from a point about half-way thither, where he had been struck down by illness'.

I submit that this account is inconsistent both with the Preface and with the facts of the poet's life as known to us through his poems and through his biographies in the two T'ang Histories.

The poet was banished to Kiukiang at the end of the year AD 814. He did not reach the place till 815 and in 818 was further removed to Chung-chou, high up the river. He never 'set out a second time for his place of banishment'. Nor is the site of this episode 'half-way thither', but quite close to Kiukiang. Finally it is the 'host' not the 'guest' who is the poet himself.

Professor Giles: 'beneath the maple's flower-like leaves, blooming amid autumnal decay.'
Surely 'upon maple-leaves and reed-flowers autumn had wrought her decay'. Professor Giles omits *ti*, 'reed', but perhaps has another text.

Professor Giles: 'lamps trimmed again.'
Literally it must mean 'lamps turned round'. Can this imply trimmed? Some texts read *hsieh*, 'carried', 'brought', which is much easier.

Professor Giles: 'twice or thrice sweeping the strings!'
It should be 'she turned the "pegs" (to tune the instrument) and struck the strings (with her plectrum), playing two or three notes'.

Professor Giles: 'Every note she struck.'
This should be 'with every string muted' . . . (*lit.*, 'covered and pressed down with the hand'); so at least the Japanese commentaries, and the explanation seems reasonable.

Professor Giles: 'Now softly, now slowly, her plectrum sped to and fro.'
Here the use of the hand and the use of the plectrum are both involved: 'Lightly holding (or 'checking' the string with the hand), slowly twisting (the string between finger and thumb); now stroking (the string with the plectrum), now scooping under it.' I am not confident that this suggestion is correct, but it at least represents an attempt to translate the text, which Professor Giles's version, so it seems to me, does not.

Professor Giles: 'So fell the plectrum once more upon the strings with a slash like the rent of silk.'
This again is not even an attempt to translate the text. Surely the sense is: 'When the tune was ended, she withdrew her plectrum, sweeping it (as a painter sweeps his brush) across her breast, and the four strings (played in *arpeggio*) sounded with a slash like the rent of silk.'

Professor Giles: 'My childhood was spent at the capital, in my home near the hills.'
This 'generalization' of special references is perhaps intentional on the translator's part. The Hsia-ma Ling was near the Capital, six *li* south of Wan-nien Hsien. It was originally called Hsia-ma Ling and was the tomb-mound of Tung Chung-shu (*Biog. Dictionary*, 2092).

Professor Giles translates 'mother'. But surely 'aunt' is the only rendering that can be justified.

Professor Giles: 'I live by the marshy river-bank' should be: 'I live near P'ên River.'

Lines 75–6 are omitted by Professor Giles. They run:
'By the spring river on flowery mornings, at night under the autumn moon,
Many times and again I brought wine and drank it all alone.'

Professor Giles: 'Sit down awhile and sing to us yet again.'
But the girl has been playing on the lute, not singing. *T'an i ch'ü* can only mean 'play one tune'.

Professor Giles: 'While I commit thy story to writing.'
This does not bring out the force of *fan*, which ... surely ... means 'translate': 'While I translate your tune into a lute-poem.'

Professor Giles: 'sat down and quickly broke forth into another *song (sic)*, sad and soft, unlike the *song* of just now.' This is hardly translation. It should surely be '... sat down again, set the strings in motion, and the strings [under her plectrum] moved even more swiftly than before'.

Professor Giles does not bring out the adversative force of *chuan* (corresponding to the Japanese *utata* which is written with this character). For '*song* of just now' substitute '*tune* of just now'.

In conclusion, I will add a few remarks concerning Professor Giles's criticism of my translation of the 'Great Summons'.[1]

___

[1] For Waley's translation see pp. 165–7 above. Here is Professor Giles's criticism: 'A version of this difficult rhapsody was published in *The Statesman* of 31st May 1919, as "Translated by Arthur Waley", and reproduced in "More Translations from the Chinese", 1919. It was a bold attempt and as a free, too free paraphrase—without the excuse of rhyme—it would have had a chance of escaping criticism but as a translation, in justice to the poet and to readers who cannot verify from the original text, a good deal of amendment is necessary. Hence the attempt contained in the following pages,

(1) He objects to my calling it a 'translation'. Surely the only other term possible, namely 'paraphrase', has always been used of adaptations which have made much wider departures from the original than I have done. Professor Giles will agree with me that no literal translation of the poem can preserve its character as a *poem*. My object was to do this, and in the introduction to 'More Translations' I called attention to the fact that this book aimed at fuller literary form, which necessarily implies a less literal method. It is unfair to say that I am 'a translator who claims to be strictly literal' simply because *in another book*, I had said that in *it* I had 'aimed at literal translation not paraphrase'.

(2) Professor Giles's translation differs from mine chiefly (a) because he has followed other commentators, (b) because I was trying to turn a Chinese poem into an English one, a process that cannot be achieved merely by tagging rhymes on to the ends of the lines.

To effect this purpose I have (as every translator of poetry must) often translated rather the implied meaning than the actual words. For example, in the first line of the poem . . . the metaphor is that of interchange, of one sentry relieving another— or the like. This is better brought out by my translation 'Green spring receiveth the vacant earth', than by Professor Giles's 'The green spring comes and goes'. It seems to me irrelevant to point out that the words 'vacant earth' do not occur in the original.

(3) I have not sought scientific equivalents to the names of birds, animals, etc. In a translation made as a 'crib' for specialists one can talk of the *jang-ho*, *kao*, *lou*, *kun*, and the like. But in a literary translation one must find equivalents consistent with the elevation of style which poetry demands. If these do not correspond exactly to the Chinese, *tant pis!* I was translating a poem, not a work on natural history.[2]

---

which may in turn be capable of improvement at the hands of students resident in China who can enlist, as I cannot, the services of a well-educated native scholar.' *New China Review*, v. 2, 1920, p. 320. *Ed.*

[2] Similarly, the word 'harp' which Professor Giles will not admit as an equivalent to *se* and *ch'in* may in a non-technical work be used in a much wider sense than he will

(4) The verses which I omitted were cut out intentionally. I felt that in so long a poem they could easily be spared. I ought perhaps to have notified the reader of this, but we have seen above that Professor Giles himself omits a couplet without comment or explanation.

(5) Finally, I think that my critic is guilty of some confusion of thought as to his motives in re-translating the poem. He claims that the work was undertaken 'in justice to the poet and to readers who cannot verify from the original text'. But his paper appears to be addressed throughout to the specialist, who is indeed alone capable of forming a judgment in such matters. The general reader will accept whatever makes good sense and good poetry. That Professor Giles's version makes better sense and better poetry than mine I will allow in two passages only. In stanza thirteen 'skill' for *te* is better than 'virtue'; in stanza fifteen I gladly welcome 'necks like the gazelle' as the true rendering of *ching jo hsien pei*.

My own motive in penning the above notes on Po Chü-i's poem was to show that it is from a very glassy house indeed that my critic has hurled his courteous and learned stones. If further proof be needed, I would ask the reader to compare with the original Professor Giles's translation (*Chinese Literature*, p. 179) of Ssŭ-k'ung T'u's *Shih P'in.*

1920

---

allow. The *kinnōr* of the Hebrews was certainly not a harp in the strict sense of the word, yet both A. V. and R. V. translate *kinnōr* by 'harp'. Moreover the Japanese word *koto* has constantly been translated 'harp' (which sense is given in Brinkley's dictionary), though no one imagines that it resembles the harp of European concert rooms.

Translation of the 'Lute-Girl's Song'

by Herbert Giles

'By night, at the riverside, adieus were spoken: *beneath the maple's flower-like leaves, blooming amid autumnal decay.*[1] Host had dismounted to speed the parting guest, already on board his boat. Then a stirrup-cup went round, but no flute, no guitar, was heard. And so, ere the heart was warmed with wine, came words of cold farewell beneath the bright moon, glittering over the bosom of the broad stream ... when suddenly across the water a lute broke forth into sound. Host forgot to go, guest lingered on, wondering whence the music, and asking who the performer might be. At this, all was hushed, but no answer given. A boat approached, and the musician was invited to join the party. Cups were refilled, *lamps trimmed again*, and preparations for festivity renewed. At length, after much pressing, she came forth, hiding her face behind her lute; and *twice or thrice sweeping the strings*, betrayed emotion ere her song was sung. Then *every note she struck* swelled with pathos deep and strong, as though telling the tale of a wrecked and hopeless life, while with bent head and rapid finger she poured forth her soul in melody. *Now softly, now slowly, her plectrum sped to and fro*; now this air, now that; loudly, with the crash of falling rain; softly, as the murmur of whispered words; now loud and soft together, like the patter of pearls and pearlets dropping upon a marble dish. Or liquid, like the warbling of the mango-bird in

[1] The italicized passages are those discussed by Waley, pp. 298–300 above. *Ed.*

303

the bush; trickling, like the streamlet on its downward course. And then, like the torrent, stilled by the grip of frost, so for a moment was the music lulled, in a passion too deep for sound. Then, as bursts the water from the broken vase, as clash the arms upon the mailed horseman, *so fell the plectrum once more upon the strings with a slash like the rent of silk.*

'Silence on all sides: not a sound stirred the air. The autumn moon shone silver athwart the tide, as with a sigh the musician thrust her plectrum beneath the strings and quietly prepared to take leave. *"My childhood"*, said she, *"was spent at the capital, in my home near the hills.* At thirteen, I learnt the guitar, and my name was enrolled among the *primas* of the day. The *maëstro* himself acknowledged my skill: the most beauteous of women envied my lovely face. The youths of the neighbourhood vied with each other to do me honour: a single song brought me I know not how many costly bales. Golden ornaments and silver pins were smashed, blood-red skirts of silk were stained with wine, in oft-times echoing applause. And so I laughed on from year to year, while the spring breeze and autumn moon swept over my careless head.

' "Then my brother went away to the wars: my *mother* died. Nights passed and mornings came; and with them my beauty began to fade. My doors were no longer thronged; but few cavaliers remained. So I took a husband and became a trader's wife. He was all for gain, and little recked of separation from me. Last month he went off to buy tea, and I remained behind, to wander in my lonely boat on moon-lit nights over the cold wave, thinking of the happy days gone by, my reddened eyes telling of tearful dreams."

'The sweet melody of the lute had already moved my soul to pity, and now these words pierced me to the heart again. "O lady", I cried, "we are companions in misfortune, and need no ceremony to be friends. Last year I quitted the Imperial city, and fever-stricken reached this spot, where in its desolation, from year's end to year's end, no flute or guitar is heard. *I live by the marshy river-bank*, surrounded by yellow reeds and stunted bamboos. Day and night no sounds reach my ears save the blood-stained note of the nightjar, the gibbon's mournful wail. Hill songs I have, and village pipes with their harsh discordant twang. But now that I listen to thy lute's discourse, methinks 'tis the music of the gods. Prithee *sit down awhile and sing to us yet again, while I commit thy story to writing.*"

'Grateful to me (for she had been standing long), the lute-girl *sat down and quickly broke forth into another song, sad and soft, unlike the song of just now.* Then all her hearers melted into tears unrestrained; and none flowed more freely than mine, until my bosom was wet with weeping.'

Leibniz and Fu Hsi

The ordinary numbers with which we are acquainted in arithmetic are expressed by means of multiples of powers of 10: for instance, $4705 = 4 \times 10^3 + 7 \times 10^2 + 0 \times 10 + 5$.

This method of representing numbers is called the denary scale of notation and 10 is said to be the base of the scale. In like manner any other number than 10 may be taken as the base of a scale of notation. If 2 is the base, 'two' will be written 10, 'three' will be written 11, 'four' (i.e. 2^2) will be written 100, and so on.

The mathematician Leibniz (1646–1716), who wrote several essays on the binary scale of notation, saw in it a symbol of 'One God and Nothing else beside', and recommended it on this ground to his patron the Duke of Brunswick-Wolfenbüttel. Through the Catholic missionary Père Bouvet (one of the six 'mathématiciens du Roi' sent by Louis to the court of Peking) Leibniz became acquainted with the diagrams of Fu Hsi (c. 3000 BC), and recognized the fact that the Pa Kuei, or 'Eight Diagrams', were merely the numbers 7 to 0, written in a binary notation. Similarly, that the Sixty-four Diagrams were the numbers 63 to 0 written in the same notation.

The Eight Diagrams, written in Fu Hsi's order, are ☰, ☱, ☲, ☳, ☴, ☵, ☶, ☷. If for the unbroken line we write 1, and for the broken line 0, we get[1] 111, 110, 101, 100, 011, 010, 001, and 000.

This series, translated into the denary (common) scale, becomes 7, 6, 5, 4, 3, 2, 1, 0. The Sixty-four Diagrams (in Fu Hsi's order) will be found to express a similar series. It is curious that although

[1] The diagrams are to be read from the bottom upwards, as in the Book of Changes.

306

this fact about the diagrams was known in the 17th century, no subsequent commentator, either Chinese or European, appears to have mentioned it. In 1728 Père Visdelou, another of the 'six mathematicians' at Peking, and consequently the associate of Bouvet, submitted to the Cardinals of the Congregation de Propaganda Fide a notice of the 'Book of Changes'. He makes no allusion to Leibniz's discovery. Had he explained the mathematical nature of the diagrams, subsequent commentators would have followed suit and the information would have been handed down to Zottoli, Legge, Harlez, etc.

Even Kawakami, in his *History of Mathematics in the Far East*, mentions the Eight Diagrams without noting the only fact about them which could conceivably interest mathematicians. This is probably because the sixty-four chapters of the book are not arranged in Fu Hsi's natural order, but in the 'artificial' order of Wên Wang (1231–1135 BC). This king occupied two years of imprisonment in arranging the diagrams into an order based upon symbolic meanings which he attached to them. But most Chinese editions of the book give Fu Hsi's order in the introductory pages, and explain that this 'natural order' was afterwards altered by Wên Wang. One of the reasons for the change is said to have been that Wên, being in prison, felt that the 'natural order of things' had gone wrong, and that the diagrams must be changed in consequence.

The invention of the diagrams, which (even if we regard Fu Hsi as mythical) appears to have been made in the third millennium BC, was a mathematical discovery of great importance. But we have no evidence that the series was ever used for general purposes of enumeration.

Perhaps the most interesting point is that the diagrams employ the method of 'value by position', which is the distinguishing feature of our 'Arabic' notation. Thus, in the first of the Sixty-four Diagrams the bottom line represents 2 to the fifth power, the next line 2 to the fourth power, and so on; just as in the Arabic number 2533 the left-hand figure represents tens to the third power, the next figure tens to the second power, and so forth.[2]

This method of position was not used in Europe till the 16th century, when we learnt it from the Arabs, who in turn had taken it from the Hindus. It is not thought to have been in use in India before the 6th century AD. It was unknown to the great early civilizations of Egypt and Babylon, but it appears that the Chinese had mastered the theory of it 3000 years before Christ.

Schindler (*Ostasiatische Zeitschrift*, iii, 465) considers the sign ☰, which occurs on an old Chinese bronze, to be an owner's mark. It might be the binary number 1001, i.e. 9 in common notation. Yang Hsiung (53 BC–AD 18) invented a set of 81 diagrams consisting each of four lines of three different kinds. The text of the *Po Ku T'u*, the catalogue of Hui Tsung's bronzes, etc., says that this diagram is like those of Yang. In which case, if $---$ $=$ 0, the number is 28 (expressed in the three-scale); or if $---$ is 2, the number is equivalent to our 52. Obviously these are only two of six possible alternatives.

1921

[2] It is interesting to compare the ancient Mayan system of place notation, which was vigesimal: the bottom line represented 20 to the power of nought (i.e. 1); the first line from the bottom, 20 to the power of 1 (i.e. 20); the second line from the bottom, 20 squared (i.e. 400); etc. The bar had a value of 5 and the dot a value of 1. Thus 465 was written ⋅∶⋅ and 902 ∷ J. E. S. Thompson, *The Rise and Fall of Maya Civilization*, University of Oklahoma Press, 1954. *Ed.*

A Comparison of Nō with Greek Tragedy and Other Forms of Ancient Drama

Extract from the Introduction to *The Nō Plays of Japan*

The reader will naturally look for some comparison of Nō with other forms of ancient drama. The open-air performances of Nō, with their circular auditorium and round stage in the middle, correspond in a general way to the conditions of Greek drama. The *Gaku-ya* or actor's room has its exact counterpart. 'On the side away from the spectators was a wooden building to which the performers could retire to change their costume.'[1] I gather that *all* the actors in Greek tragedy wore masks, which . . . is not true of Nō. Still less does the function of the Nō chorus, who remain seated and motionless throughout the play (except for the raising of their fans when they sing) correspond with that of the 'company of twelve or fifteen persons' who 'stood in the foreground' and danced the choruses of Greek plays.

'Though much is obscure in the matter of Greek music and dancing, this at least is certain, that they were essentially *imitative*'; so Seami, *Yūgaku no michi wa issai monomane ari*—'The arts of music and dancing [the term *yūgaku* comprises both these] consist entirely in imitation.'

The *libretti* of Greek tragedy have won for themselves a separate existence simply as poetic literature. Yet even of them it has been said that 'the words are only part of the poem'. Still

[1] J. T. Sheppard, *Greek Tragedy*, 1911.

less did the words of Nō constitute the whole 'poem', yet if some cataclysm were to sweep away the Nō theatre, I think the plays (as literature) would live.

It is above all in 'architecture', in the relation of parts to the whole that these poems are supreme.[1] The early writers created a 'form' or general pattern which the weakest writing cannot wholly rob of its beauty. The plays are like those carved lamp-bearing angels in the churches at Seville; a type of such beauty was created by a sculptor of the 16th century that even the most degraded modern descendant of these masterpieces retains a certain distinction of form.

First comes the *jidai* or opening-couplet, enigmatic, abrupt. Then in contrast to this vague shadow come the hard outlines of the *waki*'s exposition, the formal naming of himself, his origin and destination. Then, shadowy again, the 'song of travel', in which picture after picture dissolves almost before it is seen.

But all this has been mere introduction—the imagination has been quickened, the attention grasped in preparation for one thing only—the hero's entry. In the 'first chant', in the dialogue which follows, in the successive dances and climax, this absolute mastery of construction is what has most struck me in reading the plays.

Again, Nō does not make a frontal attack on the emotions. It creeps at the subject warily. For the action, in the commonest class of play, does not take place before our eyes, but is lived through again in mimic and recital by the ghost of one of the participants in it. Thus we get no possibility of crude realities; a vision of life indeed, but painted with the colours of memory, longing or regret.

In a paper read before the Japan Society in 1919 I tried to illustrate this point by showing, perhaps in too fragmentary and disjointed a manner, how the theme of Webster's *Duchess of Malfi* would have been treated by a Nō writer. I said then (and the Society kindly allows me to repeat those remarks):

[1] This, too, is the only aspect of them that I can here discuss; no other kind of criticism being possible without quotation of the actual words used by the poet.

The plot of the play is thus summarized by Rupert Brooke in his *John Webster and the Elizabethan Drama*: 'The Duchess of Malfi is a young widow forbidden by her brothers, Ferdinand and the Cardinal, to marry again. They put a creature of theirs, Bosola, into her service as a spy. The Duchess loves and marries Antonio, her steward, and has three children. Bosola ultimately discovers and reports this. Antonio and the Duchess have to fly. The Duchess is captured, imprisoned and mentally tortured and put to death. Ferdinand goes mad. In the last Act he, the Cardinal, Antonio and Bosola are all killed with various confusions and in various horror.'

Just as Webster took his themes from previous works (in this case from Painter's *Palace of Pleasure*), so the Nō plays took theirs from the Romances or *Monogatari*. Let us reconstruct the *Duchess* as a Nō play, using Webster's text as our *Monogatari*.

Great simplification is necessary, for the Nō play corresponds in length to one act of our five act plays, and has no space for divagations. The comic is altogether excluded, being reserved for the *kyōgen* or farces which are played as interludes between the Nō.

The persons need not be more than two—the Pilgrim, who will act the part of *waki*, and the Duchess, who will be *shite* or Protagonist. The chorus takes no part in the action, but speaks for the *shite* while she is miming the more engrossing parts of her role.

The Pilgrim comes on to the stage and first pronounces in his *Jidai* or preliminary couplet, some Buddhist aphorism appropriate to the subject of the play. He then names himself to the audience thus (in prose):

'I am a pilgrim from Rome. I have visited all the other shrines of Italy, but have never been to Loretto. I will journey once to the shrine of Loretto.'

Then follows (in verse) the *Song of Travel* in which the Pilgrim describes the scenes through which he passes on his way to the shrine. While he is kneeling at the shrine, *Shite* (the Protagonist) comes on to the stage. She is a young woman dressed, 'contrary to the Italian fashion', in a loose-bodied gown. She carries in her hand an unripe apricot. She calls to the Pilgrim and engages him in conversation. He asks her if it were not at this shrine that the Duchess of Malfi took refuge. The young woman answers with a kind of eager exaltation, her words gradually rising from prose to poetry. She tells the story of the Duchess's flight, adding certain intimate touches which force the priest to ask abruptly, 'Who is it that is speaking to me?'

And the girl shuddering (for it is hateful to a ghost to name itself) answers: '*Hazukashi ya!* I am the soul of the Duke Ferdinand's sister, she that was once called Duchess of Malfi. Love still ties my soul to the earth. *Toburai tabitamaye!* Pray for me, oh, pray for my release!'

Here closes the first part of the play. In the second the young ghost, her memory quickened by the Pilgrim's prayers (and this is part of the medicine of salvation), endures again the memory of her final hours. She mimes the action of kissing the hand (*vide* Act IV, Scene 1), finds it very cold:

> I fear you are not well after your travel.
> Oh! horrible!
> What witchcraft doth he practise, that he hath left
> A dead man's hand here?

And each successive scene of the torture is so vividly mimed that though it exists only in the Protagonist's brain, it is as real to the audience as if the figure of dead Antonio lay propped upon the stage, or as if the madmen were actually leaping and screaming before them.

Finally she acts the scene of her own execution:

> Heaven-gates are not so highly arched
> As princes' palaces; they that enter there
> Must go upon their knees. (*She kneels.*)
> Come, violent death,
> Serve for mandragora to make me sleep!
> Go tell my brothers, when I am laid out,
> They then may feed in quiet.
> (*She sinks her head and folds her hands.*)

The chorus, taking up the word 'quiet', chant a phrase from the *Hokkekyō*: *Sangai Mu-an*, 'In the Three Worlds there is no quietness or rest'.

But the Pilgrim's prayers have been answered. Her soul has broken its bonds: it is free to depart. The ghost recedes, grows dimmer and dimmer, till at last

> *use-ni-keri*
> *use-ni-keri*

it vanishes from sight.

1921

Extract from 'Zen Buddhism and Its Relation to Art'

from *An Introduction to the Study of Chinese Painting*[1]

The connection between Zen and art is important, not only because of the inspiration which Zen gave to the artist, but also because through Zen was obtained a better understanding of the psychological conditions under which art is produced than has prevailed in any other civilization.

Art was regarded as a kind of Zen, as a delving down into the Buddha that each of us unknowingly carries within him, as Benjamin carried Joseph's cup in his sack. Through Zen we annihilate Time and see the Universe not split up into myriad fragments, but in its primal unity. Unless, says the Zen aesthetician, the artist's work is imbued with his vision of the subjective, non-phenomenal aspect of life, his productions will be mere toys.

I do not mean that in Zen Chinese artists found a short cut to the production of beauty. Zen aims at the annihilation of consciousness, whereas art is produced by an interaction of conscious and unconscious faculties. How far such an interaction can be promoted by the psychic discipline of Zen no layman can judge; moreover, the whole question of the artist's psychology is controversial and obscure.

Perhaps it is not even very important that the artist himself should have a sound aesthetic; but it is of the utmost importance to the artist that the public should have some notion of the conditions under which art can be produced—should have some key to the vagaries of a section of humanity which will in any case always be found troublesome and irritating.

[1] See p. 68. *Ed.*

Such a key Zen supplied, and it is in the language of Zen that, after the 12th century, art is usually discussed in China and Japan.

Zen paintings are of two kinds. (1) Representations of animals, birds, and flowers, in which the artist attempted to identify himself with the object depicted, to externalize its inner Buddha. These were achieved not by study from the life, as the early Sung nature-pieces had been, but by intense and concentrated visualization of the subject to be painted. This mental picture was rapidly transferred to paper before the spell of concentration (*samādhi*) was broken. (2) Illustrations of episodes in the lives of the great Zen teachers. This branch of Zen art was essentially dramatic. It sought to express the characters of the persons involved, subtly to reveal the grandeur of soul which lay hidden behind apparent uncouthness or stupidity. Typical of this kind of paintings are the pictures of 'Tan-hsia Burning the Image'.[2]

One night Tan-hsia, a Zen priest, stayed as a guest at an ordinary Buddhist monastery. There was no firewood in his cell. As the night was cold he went into the chapel, seized a wooden statue of Shākyamuni, and, chopping it up, made himself a comfortable fire. To him the idol of Buddha was a mere block of wood; his indignant hosts took a different view. The controversy is the same as that which occupies the central place in the Nō play *Sotoba Komachi*.

Other common subjects are Bodhidharma with tightly closed lips, as he appeared before the Emperor of China; Bodhidharma crossing the Yangtze on a reed; Hui-k'o, the Second Patriarch, cutting off his own arm in order to persuade Bodhidharma that he was in earnest; Hui-k'o waiting waist-deep in the snow till Bodhidharma deigned to admit him; Tē-shan tearing up his commentary on the *Diamond Sutra*.

THE ZEN PAINTERS

Shih K'o. Before considering the Southern Sung Zen painters I must deal with their rather mysterious forerunner, Shih K'o.

[2] See Kümmel, *Die Kunst Ostasiens*, Pl. 118.

His master is said to have been the late T'ang Buddhist painter, Chang Nan-pên, of whom I have already spoken. Chang flourished[3] c. 874–89; but we do not know his exact dates. He may well have been alive at the beginning of the 10th century. Shih K'o was a native of Ch'ēng-tu, at which town Chang Nan-pên had worked between 881 and 885. He was sharp-tongued and of a satirical turn of mind. If he was out of humour with his customers, however rich and influential they might be, he would make game of them in the pictures which they had ordered. The 16th century writer Tu Mu[4] tells us that in his comic pictures Shih K'o 'drew' only the faces, arms, and feet of his figures; the draperies were indicated by 'rough strokes'.

The Hui Tsung Collection possessed (in the first quarter of the 12th century) twenty-one pieces attributed to him—Taoist subjects, star-divinities, Madame Chung K'uei, and one Lohan. From the pen of Su Tung-p'o's friend Li Ch'ien we have a description of an elaborate mythological picture by Shih K'o, 'The Jade Emperor Holding His Court'[5]: 'Celestial fairies and magical officers, Golden Boys and Jewel Maidens, the Three Marshals, the Great Unity, the Seven Aboriginals, the Four Holy Ones, Rain, Thunder, and Lightning, the presiding spirits of every hill and stream, all powers and dominations whether above the earth or below it—these and no less are seen assembled in the Emperor's Presence. The Jade Emperor himself, great Lord of Heaven, sits with his face to the south, robed in stately apparel....

'It was from Shih K'o's wild mockery of the world in which he lived that his painting derived its masterly freedom; he can break all the rules of his art and yet delight and surprise us. If the types he depicts are sometimes uncouth, odd, or repulsive, this is only that he may display the variety of Nature. In this picture, for example, he has, in order to make game of us, bedecked the persons of some of the water divinities with fish or crabs.

[3] See *Shu Hua P'u*, 48, 8.   [4] Ibid., 12, 10.
[5] Ibid., 82, 20. The Jade Emperor is the paramount Taoist divinity.

'I have seen a painting by Shih K'o of an old man and woman drinking vinegar, their wrinkled noses and wry mouths vividly expressing its sourness. I also remember his "Demons' Hundred Gambols". Chung K'uei and his wife are seated at a table with wine and victuals in front of them. They and their attendants are all marvellously portrayed. In the foreground are groups of big and little demons who are amusing the bridal pair by doing tricks to the accompaniment of music. . . .

'In this picture of the Jade Emperor he did not dare to carry his jesting too far; but he could not resist decking the water-gods with crab-pendants, that he might get at least one smile from posterity.'

Upon Shih K'o's picture of the 'Three Laughers' Su Tung-p'o wrote the following inscription: 'The three of them are laughing in chorus; even their clothes, hats, shoes all have an amused air, The acolyte behind them is beside himself with laughter.'

The 14th century writer Chu Tê-jun[6] praises the 'beautiful and delicate colouring' of Shih K'o's 'Madame Chung K'uei and her Little Sisters' and finds in it an interesting survival of T'ang style. This is presumably the same picture that was in the Hui Tsung Collection. The story of Chung K'uei was as follows: One night the Emperor Ming Huang of the T'ang dynasty dreamt that he saw an imp stealing Yang Kuei-fei's jade flute. Presently a huge figure in a broken Court hat and top-boots came striding in, seized the imp between his finger and thumb, gouged its eyes out, and ate it whole. When the Emperor asked who he was, he answered that he was the spirit of a certain student named Chung K'uei, who in the 7th century, having failed to pass his examinations, dashed out his brains against the steps of the Examination Hall. The Emperor of the day, taking pity on him, ordered him to be given a Court burial. In gratitude for this he had vowed to devote his spirit-life to protecting the Emperors of China from all elves, goblins, and evil influences. Next day Ming Huang described his dream to Wu Tao-tzŭ, who

[6] *Shu Hua P'u*, 82, 20.

thereupon painted the famous picture of Chung K'uei beating a small imp with his stick.[7]

The picture probably suggested the story. It is said that the name Chung K'uei means 'stick' in Shantung dialect, and that Chung K'uei is simply The Man with the Stick. It existed as a personal name from early times, and was apparently used by both men and women.[8]

There arose (probably towards the end of T'ang) the legend of a female Chung K'uei, sometimes treated of as the demon-queller's wife. It seems to be thus that she figures in the picture of the 'Demons' Hundred Gambols' mentioned above. In the picture praised by Chu Tê-jun were represented 'a young bride with four female imps in attendance upon her'. These were presumably her sisters, but the legend of Madame Chung K'uei is hard to disentangle. In any case, both the Chung K'ueis are commonly shown with a retinue of attendant imps. Favourite subjects are 'Chung K'uei's Wedding', 'Chung K'uei Playing the Lute by Moonlight' (by Ma Yüan, for example), and 'Chung K'uei Moving House'. These subjects gave scope for a great deal of *grotesquerie* similar to that of the Arhat pictures by Lu Lêng-ch'ieh.

Shih K'o's pictures in Japan. The Shōhōji, near Kyōto, possesses a pair of paintings[9] inscribed with an inscription to the effect that they were painted in the first year of the period Ch'ien Tên (965 or possibly 919) by Shih K'o of Ssechuan. They were given to this temple by a Court lady in the 17th century; their previous history is quite unknown. The one which represents a man leaning on a tiger is inscribed: *Êrh tsu tiao hsin*, which may mean either 'The Second Patriarch Attuning his Heart', or 'Two Patriarchs Attuning their Hearts'. The difficulty of accepting the first explanation is that the Second Patriarch of the Zen sect is not

---

[7] A copy of it is reproduced in *Kokka*, 30.

[8] It was borne by Yao Hsüan of the N. Wei dynasty (5th century) in conjunction with the name Pi-hsieh, 'Exorcist', and by an aunt of the 5th-century general Tsung Ch'io, famous for his campaigns in Indo-China.

[9] *Kokka*, 95; *Shimbi Taikwan*, III; *Tōyō*, VIII.

particularly associated with the tiger. If we accept the alternative and consider the pictures to represent two unnamed Patriarchs, we are still left in doubt as to which of the Zen Patriarchs can possibly be meant, for clearly the Patriarchs of the Magic Sect cannot come into consideration.

Kokka, 95, identifies the figures with the two Lohan Bhadra and Jivaka. This seems very improbable; and are Lohan ever referred to as Patriarchs (*tsu*)? Were it not for the inscription the figure leaning on the tiger would probably have been taken for Fêng-kan, the frequent companion (particularly in Japanese paintings) of Han-shan and Shih-tê.[10]

It is also true that were it not for the inscription which attributes the pictures to Shih K'o they would certainly have passed as the work of a Southern Sung artist. And it is this fact which gives them their archaeological importance. They seem to prove that we must regard the ink-technique of the 13th-century Zen painters as a revival rather than a discovery.

THE LIU-T'UNG-SSŬ SCHOOL

One institution, about which till recently very little was known, seems to have been an important factor in the propagation of Zen art and ideas. About AD 1215 a Zen priest came from the far south-west of China to Hangchow, the capital, and there refounded a ruined monastery, the Liu T'ung-ssŭ, which stood on the shores of the famous Western Lake. His name was Mu-ch'i. He seems to have been the first to practise in connection with Zen the swift, erratic type of monochrome invented more than two hundred years earlier by Shih K'o. In hurried swirls of ink he sought to record before they faded visions and exaltations produced whether by the frenzy of wine, the stupor of tea, or the vacancy of absorption.

Sometimes his design is tangled and chaotic; sometimes, as in his famous 'Persimmons', passion has congealed into a stupendous

[10] The pictures are accompanied by an inscription by the 19th-century calligraphist Yü Chi. The publication of it might throw light on the subjects of the paintings.

calm. Of his fellow-workers the best known is Lo-chua'ng, a painter of birds and flowers. Liang K'ai, once a fashionable painter, left the Court and with his pupil Li Ch'üeh worked in the manner of Mu-ch'i. Examples of Liang K'ai's work before and after his conversion are still preserved in Japan.

Finally, about the middle of the 14th century, a Japanese priest, Mokuan, came to China and, under circumstances which I have elsewhere[11] described, confusingly became Mu-ch'i II. It may be that it was he who sent back to his own country some of the numerous pictures signed Mu-ch'i which are now in Japan. Which of them are by Mu-ch'i and which by Mokuan is a problem which remains to be solved.

Very little is known of the lives of these 13th-century Zen artists. Numerous works in Japan have been assigned to them. Many of them have been published in Japanese art-journals; others have never been shown except as accessories of the tea-ceremony. The work of critically examining and sifting this material has only just begun. For this reason I have treated them with a brevity which does not at all do justice to their importance.

P'u-ming. In the 14th century Zen did not flourish, giving place in many instances to the Lamaistic Buddhism which was the religion of the Mongols. But some of the earlier Mongol rulers patronized Zen, and 'south of the River', particularly at Soochow, Zen priests carried on the thought and art of their Southern Sung predecessors.

At the Ch'êng-t'ien-ssǔ in Soochow the priest P'u-ming, called Hsüeh-ch'uang ('Snowy Window'), painted ink-orchids. . . . Neither of the two other Mongol dynasty priests of whom I am about to speak was a member of the Zen sect, and one of them ought not perhaps to be classified as a Buddhist at all. But their art was very closely allied to that of their Zen confrères.

P'u-kuang. Of this artist Professor Pelliot writes: 'Il fut au début du XIVe siècle le chef d'une secte religieuse reconnue comme une véritable religion par les souverains mongols, la secte

---

[11] See my *Zen Buddhism*, Luzac, 1922.

15. *Reading in Regent's Park, February 1966*

16. *Arthur Waley died at his home in Highgate Village, 27 June 1966*

des *dhŭta*.'[12] Upon the recommendation of Chao Mêng-fu he was made professor in the Chao-wên College. In 1312 he wrote a preface to the *Sutra of the 42 Articles*.

In mediaeval Japan the *dhŭta* (called *zuta kotsujiki*) were mendicant Buddhist friars; they certainly did not constitute a separate religion. The part they played in China will no doubt be clearer when Professor Pelliot has published his notes on the subject. It is as an artist that P'u-kuang here concerns us. His best-authenticated work is an album of nineteen leaves representing Bodhidharma, P'u-tai, and seventeen Lohan[13]—rapid sketches of astounding dexterity and economy of line. It is not surprising to learn that P'u-kuang was famous chiefly for his calligraphy; his painting, indeed, seems to be a side-product of that art. Here we have the Lohan in their last stage of secularization. Starting as cult-figures, they became in Kuan-hsiu's hands impressive Indian magicians; and in Li Lung-mien's, Chinese sages. P'u-kuang treats them with as little reference to their sacred character as would a Japanese artist in a *surimono*.

He is, in fact, the precursor of *Wên-jên-hua* ('Literary Man's Painting'). His dexterous wayward urbanity belongs to the milieu of the Ming eclectics rather than to the over-gilded setting of the Mongol Court which honoured him.

Po-tzŭ-t'ing. Po-tzŭ-t'ing came from Chia-ting in Ssechuan. At one time he expounded the doctrines of the T'ien-tai Sect at Ch'ih-Ch'êng in Chekiang. 'But by nature he loved the track of waves and journeying of clouds. He begged his way from village to village, saying little to those he met, but mixing that little with strange jests. He loved to paint rocks and irises, and would cover his pictures with poetical inscriptions.'

Zen art was revived at the beginning of the Manchu dynasty by a small group of which the most important was the priest Tao-Chi (born about 1630, died about 1717). This new Zen art was, like that of the 14th century, allied to the Literary style

---

[12] *T'oung-pao*, 1922, p. 351. See also *Bulletin de l'école française d'Extrême-Orient*, III, 315-16; IV, 438. [13] Reproductions in *Kokka*, 333. . . .

(*Wên-jên-hua*), of which the greatest contemporary exponent was Chu Ta,[14] who himself became a priest in 1644. Both men were members of aristocratic Ming families; both sought to drown with painting and religion the shame of the Manchu conquest. 'In their pictures', wrote Chêng Hsieh,[15] rather over-rhetorically, 'the tear-stains outnumber the brush-marks.'

Rather junior to them was K'un-ts'an, a priest in the Bull's Head Temple at Nanking; it was said that, whereas Tao-chi achieved complete 'realization' in his art but not in his religious life, K'un-ts'an 'failed to convey in his painting the full measure of his spiritual illumination'.

In art Tao-chi preached a doctrine of individualism. 'One may imitate the old masters' methods of brushwork, but still one has not painted "their landscape". By all these categories and rules one becomes a slave to the old masters and is reduced to feeding upon scraps from their table. But the whiskers of the Ancients can never sprout upon my cheeks. . . . Once my motto was *My own way*. But now I realize that, after all, there is only one way, and that which I discovered for myself and called my own way was really the way of the Ancients.'[16] The Yu-chêng Shu-chü at Shanghai has published a collection of his landscapes, under the title *Shih-T'ao Shang-jên Shan-shui tês'*.

THE DRAGON

Allied rather to Taoist than to Zen mysticism is the art of dragon-painting, which reached its zenith in the 13th century. The British Museum possesses a dragon-painting in ink with washes of light red. The monster descends across the picture from right to left, hollow-eyed, noseless, with three huge teeth protuding from its lower jaw; the prongs of its beard hang like

[14] Called Pa-ta Shan-jên, 'the Eight-Great Hermit', in allusion to his devotion to the *Sutra on the Eight Great Awakings of Man* (Nanjio's Catalogue, No. 512).
[15] Called 'Plank-bridge', a famous 18th-century poet.
[16] His essay on painting was published in 1728 under the title *K'u Kua Ho-shang Hua Yü Lu*. It was reprinted in 1908.

pink icicles under its chin. From each side of its forehead coiling antennae sprout. Its scaly trunk is wreathed in a swirl of mist and darkness. White clouds of billowy shape hem it in below and above; on the lower cloud is the cursive signature 'So-wêng'. The creator of this dim monster presents that extraordinary combination of Bohemianism and administrative efficiency which so often startles us in reading Chinese biographies. He was Lord Cromer, with a touch of Aubrey Beardsley.

Ch'ên Jung. Ch'ên Jung, called So-wêng, was born at Ch'ang-lo in Fuhkien about 1200. He passed his examinations in 1235 and became clerk to the Imperial Academy. Later he was made Governor of P'u-t'ien in Fuhkien, and rose to a high rank at Court. 'In his early days he was a magistrate in Shansi. Here he built roads and aqueducts, instituted schemes of poor relief, and repaired temples and schools. He showed great forbearance in the discharge of his office; and in his private life, the utmost simplicity. He would often gather round him the scholars of the neighbourhood and discuss with them the obscurities of the Classics. On his holidays he would talk of literature with men of refinement or compose poems in their company. Chia Ssŭ-tao[17] once invited him to serve under his banner; but Jung was drunk when the invitation came and answered flippantly. Ssŭ-tao, who had a great respect for his character, did not take it ill. 'The vigour of his prose and verse won him a great reputation in the era Pao Yu.[18]

'He would make clouds by splashing ink and mists by spitting water. When excited by wine, he would give a great shout, and seizing his cap, use it as a painting-brush, roughly smearing his design. Afterwards he finished the picture with a proper brush. Sometimes it would be a complete dragon; sometimes only an arm or the head was showing; or again there would be nothing but a dim adumbration of undefinable shapes, such as no other mind could have conceived; yet all of marvellous beauty.' . . .

1922

[17] Died 1276.   [18] 1253-59.

A Chinaman's Description of Brighton in 1877

The following description of Brighton was written by Li Shu-ch'ang, secretary to the first Chinese ambassador in London. It is printed in the 11th section of the 'Small Square Cup' geographical miscellany.

PU–LAI–TUN

Pu-lai-tun is a place famous for its beauty. It is in Europe, on the coast of the land of Ying. It lies about 160 leagues south of Lun-tun and can be reached by coach in two hours. The people of the Capital go there for sport or repose. Landwards, a ridge of low hills girds the town, while towards the sea is a deep and rocky cliff that men of taste have hollowed out into a vast chamber, where rare and marvellous fish from every quarter of the world are kept in tanks of glass through which perpetual waters flow. There is, indeed, no ocean-creature that cannot here be viewed.

Here too is a bridge, set upon wooden piers, that goes out several thousand feet into the sea, so built that wanderers, climbing to a height, may lean and gaze afar; and at the end of the bridge there is a music-room.

For the rest, there is short grass along the downs, flat sands along the shore, green windows and gay roofs in the town, and in company with these the sea, a mighty vision, now dark, now dazzling, stretches for ever and ever its vast expanse of grey.

The people of the Capital in their hundreds of thousands live close-packed as the teeth of a comb; their streets and markets intersect, covering each day a huger space, and where there should be a view of dancing waters, only the sails and masts of merchant-ships are seen. Even the lively clatter of hand-weavers and craftsmen is lacking, and all is merged in dusty squalor.

It is then for the quietness and cleanness of this place that each year, when the Hall of Meeting is closed, holiday-makers with one accord come hither to take their rest. Its winds are mild; its weather, clear. At its horizon sky and ocean meet. The fine ladies of the land go walking happy, sleeve to sleeve, in coats and skirts of diverse cut, trailing by like clouds. Sometimes a boat or two will pass, dipping its small oars into the empty darkness of the sea. The rich and powerful drive by in spotless coaches, their fiery horses racing neck to neck, to distant picnics and carousals.

Dusk thickens, the lamps are lit, a row of flames darts up along the shore. The music, played above the waters, is caught up and cast back again by wind and tide, faltering in wafts of dim, mysterious sound, as though it floated from another world.

A month after I reached Lun-tun a well-to-do gentleman named A-shih-pe-li (Ashberry) brought me to the place and I was quick to admire its matchless beauty. Afterwards I returned many times, and each time with equal delight. Since then, years have passed and I have visited famous places in many lands; but never on any day has Pu-lai-tun been absent from my thoughts, such power does this place hold over the affections of all who have beheld it.

The Land of Ying is famous chiefly for her giant strength and vast prosperity, and men have judged her only by the toughness of her ships, the hugeness of her cannons, by her swift progress in the race for gain, and they know that by these she has got her will between the Four Seas. But such people do not know that for sport and recreation, for ease and comfort she has such places as this pleasant town.

In ancient days the philosopher Hsün Tzŭ spoke of the evils which come when lands think only of strength and security. But

Luan Chên, when he appeared before the Baron of Ch'u, spoke first of the right ordering of the multitude and next in praise of leisure. It seems, however, it is strength and security which breed good order and leisure, and by the possession of a Pu-lai-tun a country's might may well be judged.

1923

'The Art of Murasaki'

Extract from the Introduction to *The Sacred Tree*

Most critics have agreed that the book is a remarkable one and that Murasaki is a writer of considerable talent; but few have dealt with the points that seem to me fundamental. No one has discussed, in anything but the most shadowy way, the all-important question of how she has turned to account the particular elements in story-telling which she has chosen to exploit. The work, it is true, is a translation, and this fact prevents discussion of Murasaki as a poet, as an actual handler of words. But it has for long been customary to criticize Russian novels as though Mrs Garnett's translation were the original; nor is there any harm in doing so, provided actual questions of style are set aside.

One reviewer did indeed analyse the nature of Murasaki's achievement to the extent of classifying her as 'psychological' and in this respect he even went so far as to class her with Marcel Proust. Now it is clear that, if we contrast *Genji* with such fiction as does not exploit the ramifications of the human mind at all (the *Arabian Nights* or *Mother Goose*), it appears to be 'psychological'. But if we go on to compare it with Stendhal, with Tolstoy, with Proust, *The Tale of Genji* appears by contrast to possess little more psychological complication than a Grimm's fairy tale.

Yet it does for a very definite reason belong more to the category which includes Proust, than to the category which includes Grimm. Murasaki, like the novelist of to-day, is not principally interested in the events of the story, but rather in the effect which these events may have upon the minds of her characters. Such books as hers it is convenient, I think, to call

327

'novels,' while reserving for other works of fiction the name
'story' or 'romance'. She is 'modern' again owing to the accident
that medieval Buddhism possessed certain psychological conceptions which happen to be current in Europe to-day. The idea
that human personality is built up of different layers which may
act in conflict, that an emotion may exist in the fullest intensity
and yet be unperceived by the person in whom it is at work—
such conceptions were commonplaces in ancient Japan. They
give to Murasaki's work a certain rather fallacious air of modernity. But it is not psychological elements such as these that
Murasaki is principally exploiting. She is, I think, obtaining her
effects by means which are so unfamiliar to European readers
(though they have, in varying degrees, often been exploited in
the West) that while they work as they were intended to do and
produce aesthetic pleasure, the reader is quite unconscious how
this pleasure arose.

What then are the essential characteristics of Murasaki's art?
Foremost, I think, is the way in which she handles the whole
course of narrative as a series of contrasted effects. Examine the
relation of Chapter VIII (*The Feast of the Flowers*) to its environment. The effect of these subtly-chosen successions is more like
that of music (of the movements, say, in a Mozart symphony)
than anything that we are familiar with in European fiction. True,
at the time when the criticisms to which I refer were made only
one volume of the work had been translated; but the quality
which I have mentioned is, I should have supposed, abundantly
illustrated in the first chapters. That to one critic *The Tale of Genji*
should have appeared to be memoirs—a realistic record of
accidental happenings rather than a novel—is to me utterly
incomprehensible. But the first painted *makimonos* that were
brought to Europe created the same impression. They were
regarded merely as a succession of topographical records, joined
together more or less fortuitously; and Murasaki's art obviously
has a close analogy with that of the *makimono*. Then there is her
feeling for shape and tempo. She knows that, not only in the

work as a whole, but in each part of it there is a beginning, a middle and an end, and that each of these divisions has its own character, its appropriate pace and intensity. It is inconceivable, for example, that she should open a book or episode with a highly-coloured and elaborate passage of lyrical description, calculated to crush under its weight all that follows. Another point in which she excels is the actual putting of her characters on to the scene. First their existence is hinted at, our curiosity is aroused, we are given a glimpse; and only after much manoeuvring is the complete entry made. The modern novelist tends to fling his characters on to the canvas without tact or precaution of any kind. That credence, attention even, may be a hard thing to win does not occur to him, for he is corrupted by a race of readers who come to a novel seeking the pleasures of instruction rather than those of art; readers who will forgive every species of clumsiness provided they are shown some stratum of life with which they were not previously familiar.

How finally does Murasaki achieve the extraordinary reality, the almost 'historical' character with which she succeeds in investing her scenes? Many readers have agreed with me in feeling that such episodes as the death of Yūgao, the clash of the coaches at the Kamo festival, the visit of Genji to the mountains, the death of Aoi, become, after one reading, a permanent accession to the world as one knows it, are things which have 'happened' as much as the most vivid piece of personal experience. This sense of reality with which she invests her narrative is not the result of realism in any ordinary sense. It is not the outcome of those clever pieces of small observation by which the modern novelist strives to attain the same effect. Still less is it due to solid character building; for Murasaki's characters are mere embodiments of some dominant characteristic; Genji's father is easy-going; Aoi, proud; Murasaki, long-suffering; Oborozukiyo, light-headed. This sense of reality is due rather, I think, to a narrative gift of a kind that is absolutely extinct in Europe. To analyse such a gift would require pages of quotation. What does it in the last resort consist in, save a pre-eminent capacity for saying the most relevant things in the most effective order? Yet, simple as this sounds, I believe that in it rests, unperceived by the eye of the Western critic, more than half the secret of Murasaki's art. Her construction is in fact classical; elegance, symmetry, restraint—these are the qualities which she can set in the scales against the interesting irregularities of European fiction. That such qualities should not be easily recognized in the West is but natural; for here the novel has always been Gothic through and through.

1926

'Murasaki's Affinities as a Writer'

Extract from the Introduction to *The Bridge of Dreams*

The number and diversity of the authors to whom critics of this translation have compared Murasaki is extraordinary. Proust, Jane Austen, Boccaccio, Shakespeare have in turn been invoked; and strangest of all—Sir John Mallory. Some of the comparisons, such as the last one, seem to me unaccountable. But many are perfectly valid, so long as we restrict them to certain superficial resemblances in method or style; which was, I am sure, the intention of these critics, for no one could wish to suggest that there is any fundamental kinship between, say, Murasaki and Proust. To the Proust resemblance I have myself called attention. It consists in the device of mentioning certain characters in the story long before they actually appear, of making them as it were loom in the distance. Obviously this practice constitutes no very important ingredient in the art of either writer. But it is true in reading *Genji* one constantly comes across parallels and adumbrations of the most diverse description, which gives to the book, and particularly to the earlier volumes, a strange quality of unevenness. At moments, when for example a fresh family of princesses is being introduced, we seem to be listening to a fairy-story. The 'gossamer-fly' passage belongs to the Romantic period. There are more than once scraps of dialogue (for example, that between Niou's and Kaoru's messengers in this volume) which in the original at any rate remind one of Shakespeare; and the scene in which the priests take Ukifune for a monster naturally recalls the discovery of Caliban in *The*

Tempest. But there are touches that connect Murasaki's method with that of the epics; certain obligatory refrains—such as the admiring remarks of the gentlewomen when one of the heroes appears—that are far removed from the sophistication of the Western novel even in its earliest stages. Her book indeed is like those caves, common in a certain part of Spain, in which as one climbs from chamber to chamber the natural formation of the rock seems in succession to assume a semblance to every known form of sculpture—here a figure from Chartres, there a Buddha from Yun-kang, a Persian conqueror, a Byzantine ivory. That such should be the impression that Murasaki's book makes on us remains surprising only if we cling to the false conception of human development as a ladder, to a particular rung of which every civilization must at any moment have attained. On the contrary, a civilization is a mosaic, and it is natural that when we see the stones arranged in a new way, we should feel at first that they do not belong together. Failure to understand this is particularly fatal when we are confronted with an arrangement so very unfamiliar as that presented by the cultures of the Far East. When the French scholar Marcel Granet showed that in certain beliefs and methods of social adjustment the early Chinese resembled modern African peoples, critics charged him with saying that the ancient Chinese were at the same 'stage' as the Basuto. This was of course absurd precisely because there are no 'stages', but simply patterns sometimes fairly similar, sometimes wholly different. What seems to us like an unaccountable patchiness in Murasaki's art simply reflects the pattern of contemporary life and feeling, made up of elements of which some do not occur in Europe till the 20th century, some dropped out centuries ago, while others have not yet figured in our European pattern at all.

1933

The Originality of Japanese Civilization

There exists in Europe a notion that Japanese civilization is purely derivative. The fault is indirectly that of medieval Japanese commentators who, more as a kind of learned game than as a result of any definite conviction, tried to affiliate the whole of Japanese literature to corresponding Chinese works. Thus *The Pillow-Book* of Sei Shōnagon was matched with the *Tsa Tsuan* of the T'ang poet Li Shang-yin, *The Tale of Genji* made a descendant of the Historical Records by Ssu-ma Ch'ien, and for every poet in the *Manyōshū*[1] a Chinese prototype was found.

I do not think that those parallels were meant to be taken very seriously. No one who had read both books could suppose that the spirited *Pillow-Book* was in any sense an imitation of the dull and humdrum *Tsa Tsuan*.

What those scholiasts were seeking to establish was, as I have said, an affiliation—a sort of schematic relationship between the literature of the two countries: and in this attempt they were obviously influenced by the success of Japanese theology in working out a scheme by which each of the Buddhas and Bodhisatvas is shown to manifest himself, disguised but recognizable, in some native divinity of Japan. What, indeed, these critics sought to imply was not definite literary imitation but a sort of spiritual kinship. In recent times this has been misunderstood, and many statements about the influence of Chinese upon native Japanese literature have been repeated by Western writers,

---

[1] The earliest collection of Japanese poetry.

who had no idea that they were subscribing to an obscure form of medieval mysticism.

As regards art, the prejudice is one that the West has arrived at independently. There is among many European collectors a notion that a work of art loses its beauty from the moment that it can be proved to be Japanese, not Chinese.

A lady the other day brought a piece of wood-carving to the British Museum. 'Aren't they wonderful, these old Chinese artists?', and she caressed the wooden figure. Told, however, that as a matter of fact it was Japanese not Chinese, she exclaimed in horror, 'Oh! my husband will be disappointed!' and turned upon the work of the 'wonderful old artist' a look of contempt and disgust.

In these notes I am going to discuss one or two aspects of Japanese originality. In doing so, I do not of course mean to deny the immense influence of China on Japan any more than I would deny the influence of Greece on Rome.

THE EARLY POETRY

It is not possible that the rest of the world will ever realize the importance of Japanese poetry, because of all poetries it is the most completely untranslatable. Its beauty consists in the perfection with which a thought and a body of sound are fitted into a small rigid frame. An *uta* runs into its mould like quicksilver into a groove. In translation, only the thought survives; the poem no longer 'goes', any more than a watch goes if you take its works out of their casing and empty them upon a sheet of paper. In the few examples that I am about to give, the reader must for himself discover the *possibility* of poetry. If he is a poet, this will present no difficulty; just as a watch-maker would see in the scattered springs and wheels the possibility of a watch.

It is in its folk-songs that the *Manyōshū* comes nearest to European poetry and yet at the same time displays its greatest originality. For in their set pieces the Court writers were bent not so much on expressing themselves in poetry, as on showing that what had been done by poets in China could also be done by poets in Japan. Take the following two songs, robbed in English of all their poetry, at least as statements marked by a magnificent simplicity:

> I have got her,
> Have got Yasumiko;
> She who for any man
> Was thought hard to get,
> Yasumiko I have got!

> The men of valour
> Have gone to the great hunt;
> The noble ladies
> Are trailing their red petticoats
> Over the clean sea-beach.

Or this:

> HE. 'Dawn, dawn, dawn!' the crows are calling.
> SHE. Let them cry!
> For round the little tree-tops
> Of yonder mountain
> The night is still.

The following two songs are also from the *Manyōshū*:

> Clear as gleams the road
> That to-day the workmen were digging
> I have heard it at last,
> The tale that of my lady is told!

> My hand that is sore
> With pounding the rice,
> To-night again
> The young lord's son—
> Will he hold it and sigh?

If we seek a parallel to such folk-epigrams as this, wholly devoid of learned or literary influences, it will be in the *coplas* of Southern Spain:

Tu querer es como el toro,	Your love is like the bull,
Donde lo llaman, va;	Where they call him, he goes;
Y el mio como la piedra,	But mine like the stone,
Donde la ponen, s'esta.	Where they put it, it stops.

But whereas a *copla* rises to the height of poetry only in one example out of several thousand, the *uta* produced, in every country from the 7th to the 13th centuries, an ample succession of exquisite verses [like]:

> If but a seed shall fall,
> Even among the waterless stones
> A tree will grow.
> If you love and I love
> Can it be we shall never meet?
>
> *10th century.*

> As stung by tempests
> A wave I have seen
> Dash itself against the rocks,
> So in these bitter hours myself only
> Am by my thoughts destroyed.
>
> *End of 10th century.*[1]

THE NŌ PLAYS

It is as regards the Nō plays (14th and 15th centuries) that the Japanese have been most anxious to acknowledge a debt where none existed. The theory that they were an imitation of the Yüan dynasty drama[2] was not the result of a comparison between the two, for the Chinese plays were written in colloquial, which was not studied in Japan at the time when the theory first arose. It was simply an assumption that, since the theatre flourished in the two countries at about the same time, the Japanese drama

[1] And see pp. 237–8. *Ed.*
[2] China, 13th and 14th centuries.

must necessarily have been modelled on the Chinese. Such an idea could not possibly survive the reading of a single Chinese play. The points of resemblance are negligible, and the whole spirit and quality utterly different. At the most it might possibly be proved that both dramas owe something to a common source —the Buddhist mystery plays which certainly existed in Japan and can be presumed to have existed in early China, though at present we cannot trace them back beyond the 18th century.[3]

FICTION

Even regarding that most supremely original of all Japanese inventions—the discovery of the psychological novel—there has been some tendency to shift the priority to China, a country which did not in fact produce a novel that could possibly be classified till some eight hundred years later. 'Who knows', wrote a German art-critic as recently as 1924, discussing *The Tale of Genji*, *The Pillow-Book*, and other works of the Heian period, 'whether after all it is only the names and background that are Japanese, while everything that is essential in these books was taken direct from China?' The Japanese themselves have never gone so far as to disown *The Tale of Genji* altogether. But there existed in the Middle Ages a school of commentators who are bent on discovering in Murasaki's most natural phrases an influence of Chinese works such as the *Springs and Autumns*, the *Historical Records* (Shih Chi) or that strange little Chinese romance *The Cave of the Amorous Fairies*[4] that loomed so largely in the minds of Japanese scholars, but could in the nature of things have made, with its jejune and stilted preciosity, so little impression on a grandiose work of realism such as *The Tale of Genji*.

Meanwhile, in painting, Japan was producing a secular art that is no less original than her fiction. No better example of this art

[3] A mystery play dealing with the story of Buddha's disciple Maudgalyāyana was still performed during the 19th century in several villages near Wuhu, Anhui Province.
[4] Yu Hsien K'u.

could be taken than the rolls which illustrate *The Tale of Genji* itself. Here are exploited two factors which the Chinese left almost untouched—costume and the interior. Chinese art and literature tend always to illustrate a generalized, theoretical, average life rather than to mirror the oddities of the individual or the extravagances of the moment. The 'Sage under a tree' of Chinese pictures might equally well be Confucius reading the *Book of Changes* or Sun Yat-sen reading the Bible. But the tilted lovers with extravagantly nodding *eboshi* and vast billowing skirts who sprawl motionless in front of some lady's screen or curtain, anchored it seems not so much by devotion as by the giant voluminosity of their own pinions—these are figures of a moment and a place, figures undreamed of by the artists of China, unimaginable, when the moment was over and the place changed, to the sombre Confucianists of Japan.

UKIYO ART AND LITERATURE

As is well known, when Japanese art was first 'discovered' in Europe it was the colour-prints of the 18th and early 19th centuries that chiefly attracted attention, and the existence of the medieval schools of sculpture and painting was for a long time hardly even suspected. These coloured wood-cuts were supposed to represent a sort of plebeian or even proletarian art, and their discovery seemed to substantiate the growing legend that in the Far East every cooly and workman is an aesthete in disguise. In reality the Ukiyoye,[5] as this school of painting is called, was the creation not of peasants or work-people, but of the new intellectual aristocracy that had grown up in Yedo during the peaceful days of the Tokugawa régime—an aristocracy in which birth and profession counted for nothing at all. The greengrocers, fish-mongers, actors, innkeepers who dominate this new society owe their position to wit, accomplishment, or sometimes even to mere eccentricity, but never to inheritance. That culture had

[5] 'Pictures of the fleeting world.'

become the monopoly of the untitled is noted by Ōta Nampo in his *Kana Sesetsu*.[6] Far away, and seeming almost out of sight when we study Ukiyo books and pictures, were the Court and the official world, resolutely faithful to the wildest unreality, debating the hypothetical virtues of purely legendary Chinese prayers, writing (with the aid of the thesaurus and rhyming-dictionary) intricate poems in the style of the T'ang dynasty, painting views of landscapes that they had never seen in a technique laboriously extracted from treatises and copy-books. In contrast to all this, the art of the 'new aristocracy' was essentially an art of actuality and an art purely illustrative. It was, moreover, largely an art of collaboration between poet and painter. This literary side of Ukiyoye has been almost ignored in Europe, and is indeed to a large extent already inaccessible to the Japanese, so momentary and evanescent are the allusions which gave point to the *hokku* and 'mad poems'[7] of the Ukiyo writers. Great pleasure, of course, can be got out of the prints of Harunobu without knowing what is written on them; but the pleasure is as incomplete as that of hearing the music of Petroushka without seeing the ballet.

The minds of daimyos and bureaucrats were directed towards an alien, remote, and unhistorical past. The commoner classes did not look so far afield; but oddly enough they shared with us that feeling for the picturesqueness of the immediate past which has lately been so rampant in our theatres and music-halls. For them the Genroku period—the women with hair tied up in front with little pieces of ribbon and worn at the back rather George Eliot-wise, low over the neck: the men with shaven heads or small round caps like tam-o'-shanters—had the same fragrance as for us the crinoline and ringlets of the Victorian era.

In the above notes I have, as I set out to do, merely illustrated in a summary way a few phases of Japanese originality. Obviously

---

[6] 1824. Yūhōdō Bunko edition, p. 467.

[7] 'Mad' only in that they mirrored contemporary life, instead of hypothecating a fictitious and antique Chinese existence.

a history of Japanese civilization cannot be written in the compass of one short essay. I must not therefore be reproached with the omission of whole spheres—such as sculpture, architecture, calligraphy, the tea-ceremony—about which it would have been possible to write at equal length and possibly—for here I must plead comparative ignorance—with equal enthusiasm.

1929

Did Buddha Die of Eating Pork?

Anyone who is known to take an interest in the history of Buddhism is bound to be asked from time to time whether it is true that Buddha died of eating pork. The idea that he should have done so comes as a surprise to most Europeans; for we are in the habit of regarding vegetarianism as an intrinsic part of Buddhism. Enquirers with an iconoclastic bend of mind are anxious to have it confirmed that Buddha was something quite different from the conventional holy man—something robuster and at the same time less pretentious; while those who have treasured the figure of Gautama the Saint, immune from every worldly appetite or desire, are eager to secure authority for a figurative interpretation of the pork-eating passage.[1]

The ease with which such a question is answered depends on the extent of the informants' researches. Regarding the passage by itself and merely from the point of view of Pali Buddhism, I think anyone not influenced by romantic preconceptions about Buddha's personality must come to the conclusion[2] that the words sūkaramaddava ('pig-soft') are to be taken literally.

So soon however as one studies the question from a wider aspect and, taking into consideration the equally early[3] Chinese Hīnayāna documents, traces the history of the Buddhist attitude towards the eating of meat, the whole question becomes infinitely

[1] Mahāparinibbāna-sutta (Dīghānikāya 16). Translated in Dialogues of the Buddha II, 137.

[2] As recently the editors of the Pali Text Society's dictionary have done.

[3] I know of no reason for regarding the Sanskrit Āgamas (preserved in Chinese) in general as later than the Pali Nikāyas. In some cases they can certainly be shown to be earlier. The same applies to the various Hīnayāna Vinayas (Monastic Rules) preserved in Chinese.

more complicated, and a confident answer far less easy to give.

The story of Buddha's last meal, as told in the *Mahāparinibbānasutta* ('Book of the Great Decease') is well summed up by E. J. Thomas.[4] At Pāvā, Buddha stayed in the mango grove of Cunda the smith. There Cunda provided a meal with excellent food, hard and soft, and a large amount of *sūkaramaddava*. Before the meal Buddha said, 'Serve me, Cunda, with the *sūkaramaddava* that you have prepared, and serve the order with the other hard and soft food'. Cunda did so, and after the meal Buddha told him to throw the remainder of the *sūkaramaddava* into a hole, as he saw no-one in the world who could digest it other than the Tathāgata.[5] The sharp sickness arose, with flow of blood, and violent deadly pains, but Buddha mindful and conscious controlled them . . . and set out for Kusinārā.

The word *sūkaramaddava* occurs nowhere else (except in discussions of this passage) and the *-maddava* part is capable of at least four interpretations. Granting that it comes from the root MRD 'soft', cognate with Latin *mollis*, it is still ambiguous, for it may either mean 'the soft parts of a pig' or 'pig's soft-food' i.e. food eaten by pigs.[6] But it may again come from the same root as our word 'mill' and mean 'pig-pounded', i.e. 'trampled by pigs'. There is yet another similar root meaning 'to be pleased', and as will be seen below one scholar has supposed the existence of a vegetable called 'pig's-delight'.

The question whether Buddha did or did not die of eating pork has naturally presented itself to the lay mind as a theological one. Actually, however, no theological point is involved. Even specialists have very imperfectly realized that till late in the history of Buddhism, the eating of flesh was permitted, except under certain exceptional circumstances. The Buddhist monk must refrain from eating meat if he 'knows, hears or infers' that

[4] *The Life of Buddha* (Kegan Paul, 1927), p. 149.

[5] No feature in the story is stranger than this apparent touch of irony.

[6] If derived from this root *maddava* may be compared etymologically to our word 'mallow', the *soft* plant.

it has been killed specially for him'.[7] The latitude allowed was very great; for example, it was considered wrong for a monk to go to a house and ask for meat, unless he was ill. But he might ask for it if the householder said to him 'Is there anything else you could fancy?'[8]

It was therefore not in the least surprising that in commenting on the Dīgha-nikāya's account of Buddha's last meal, Buddhaghosha (beginning of the 5th century) should have been quite content to take *sūkaramaddava* as meaning pork. But the commentary on the *Udāna*,[9] in dealing with this passage, says: *sūkaramaddava* in the Great Commentary[10] is said to be the flesh of a pig made soft and oily; but some say it was not pig's flesh but the sprout of a plant trodden by pigs; others that it was a mushroom growing in a place trodden by pigs; others again have taken it in the sense of a flavouring substance.

One's first impression on reading these 'vegetarian' explanations is that they are pure sophistry, dating from a time when the idea of Buddha's eating flesh was so unacceptable that the commentators felt obliged at all costs to twist the passage into another meaning.

If no other vegetable names of similar formation existed, it would indeed seem almost certain that the 'mushroom' explanation was a mere flight of fancy. But Neumann[11] has shown that in Narahari's *Rājanighantu*, among the names of medical plants, there occurs a whole series of compound words having 'pig' as their first element; thus *sukara-kanda*, 'pig-bulb': *sūkara-padika*, 'pig's foot', *sūkareshta* ('sought-out by pigs'). On the analogy of the last, Neumann takes *sūkaramaddava* to mean 'pig's delight', and assumes that it is the name of some kind of truffles.

It seems to me that philologically Neumann's view has much

[7] Majjhima Nikāya (*Jīvaka Sutta*) 55. There is, I think, no corresponding *sūtra* in the Chinese *āgamas;* but the same permission is given in the Chinese Hīnayāna Vinayas, e.g. Ssŭ Fên Lü, 58 (Taishō Tripitaka xxii, 998b).

[8] Exposition of the *Mūlasarvāstivādin Vinaya.* Taishō Tripitaka, xxiv, 588.

[9] i, 399; Steinthal's edition of the *Udāna,* p. 81 seq.

[10] Now lost. For this passage, see Edward Thomas, loc. cit.

[11] Preface to the *Majjhima Nikāya,* p. xx.

to be said for it and has not been sufficiently taken into account. It is perfectly conceivable that the commentators who have been suspected of 'explaining away' the expression 'pork' were in reality better informed than Buddhaghosha. Plant names tend to be local and dialectical. It is quite likely that if such an expression as *sūkaramaddava* meant 'truffles' in Maghada, it might, in the more western and southern centres where Pali Buddhism came into existence, have been entirely unknown and consequently misunderstood.

Unfortunately the term, so far as is known, occurs only in this passage and in discussions of it. In Sanskrit no corresponding expression seems to exist at all.

THE CHINESE HĪNAYĀNA DOCUMENTS

The account of Buddha's Decease occurs in the second book of the Dīrghāgama.[12] This version was translated in 412–13 and is there contemporary with Buddhaghosha. It supports the 'vegetarian' theory. Cunda makes 'a separate stew of ears of the sandal-wood tree, which the world esteems as a great dainty'. 'Tree-ear' is still the current Chinese for a fungus growing on a tree. Fragments of the Sanskrit *Dīrghāgama* exist, but unfortunately not his passage. Presumably the Sanskrit phrase in front of the Chinese translator was Candana *ahicchatraka*, *candanachattra* or the like.

There are four other versions of the Hīnayāna Great Decease.

(1) Nanjio 552, translated in 290–306 by Po Fa-tsu.
(2) Nanjio 119, translator unknown.
(3) Nanjio 118, falsely attributed to Fa-hsien.
(4) A long passage[13] in the *Kshuraka-vāstu* of the *Mūla-sarvāstivāda Vinaya* (translated in 710).

In none of these works is the nature of the food offered by Cunda specified.

[12] Taishō Tripitaka, i, 18b.   [13] Ibid., xxiv, 382 seq.

The passage is quoted in the *Milinda Questions* (§ 175); but in a section that is lacking in the Chinese versions.

The idea then that Buddha died of eating pork is wholly absent from the Chinese Canon, and can never have entered the head of any Far Eastern Buddhist till the Pali scriptures began to be studied at the end of the 19th century. There was indeed another occasion[14] when Buddha accepted a similar offering. The householder Ugga brought him some *sūkara-mamsa*. Here again the Chinese Canon fails us, for this *sutta* does not exist in the *Ekottarāgama* or elsewhere. No-one, I think, has ever suggested that *sūkara-mamsa* ('pig's flesh') does not mean pork.

All that has been said so far applies only to the Hīnayāna. From the Mahāyāna standpoint not merely a philological but a moral issue is involved; for as is well known many of the principal Mahāyāna scriptures forbid the eating of flesh altogether.

The earliest work to contain such a prohibition[15] is the *Mahāparinirvana Sūtra*, a Mahāyāna remodelling of the old Sūtra, of the Great Decease. When Fa-hsien visited India early in the 5th century, he found that in the whole of the Middle Country (Madhyadeśa i.e. Magadha and the surrounding parts) 'the people abstain from taking life. They drink no wine nor do they eat onions or garlic ... they do not breed pigs or poultry or sell any animal food'.[16]

Had Fa-hsien enquired what scriptural authority there was for this absolute prohibition of meat, no doubt the *Mahāparinirvāna Sūtra* would have been pointed to. And it is certain that Fa-hsien took a particular interest in this *sūtra*, for he acquired a copy of it

[14] See *Anguttara Nikaya*, Vol. III, 49 (Manāpadāyī).

[15] Fa-hsien's translation (Nanjio, 120), Taishō Tripitaka, xii, 868c. The wording in the Dharmakshema version (Taishō Tripitaka xii, 386b) is identical. The so-called Southern Version (Nanjio 114) is merely a transcript of Nanjio 113 with a division of chapters imitated from Nanjio 118 and a few verbal alterations.

[On peut signaler ici les Sutras de Maitreya résumés par P. Demiéville, BEFEO. 1920, 4, pp. 165–67: 'L'ermite fait vœu de ne jamais manger de viande, ainsi que l'ordonnent les sutras de miséricorde de tous les buddhas ... Ananda fait remarquer combien est "étrange et particulière" cette prescription de s'abstenir de viande.'—Morale bouddhique, 63–4.]

[16] Taishō Tripitaka, i, 859b.

in Pātaliputra, and it was this version that he translated into Chinese in AD 417.

What was the origin of this new view about meat-eating, which seems to have sprung up somewhere about the 3rd century? An explanation that at once occurs to me is as follows: The Gupta kings, who at this period ruled over the Middle Country, though they tolerated Buddhism and sometimes even supported it, were themselves worshippers of Vishnu. Now the Vaishnavite ascetic 'must abstain from animal food of any kind',[17] and it must naturally have occurred to Buddhists to say 'If even the misguided Hindus abstain from meat, how much the less ought we . . .' or something of that kind. Such an hypothesis finds complete confirmation in the Lankāvatāra Sūtra,[18] a work somewhat later than the Mahāparinirvāna: 'If even the infidels in their heretical treatises and the Lokāyatikas in their worldly teachings and those who fall into the error of regarding (the dharmas) either as permanent or as without duration, as existent or as nonexistent, even such people forbid the eating of meat. . . .' Again:[19] 'Even secular magicians abstain from meat, knowing that upon this depends the success of their performance; how much the more must my disciples in pursuit of the Tathāgata's supreme way of spiritual release. . . .' etc.

The Lankāvatāra has indeed a special chapter[20] (Mamsabhakshana) dealing with the prohibition of meat.

To justify this prohibition it refers to five sūtras:[21] the Angulimālā, the Mahāmegha, the Śrīmālā, the Hastikakshya and the Mahāparinirvāna.

The first is a well-known Hīnayāna sutta and in its early form[22]

---

[17] Vishnu Smrti, 51, 72 (Sacred Books of the East, vii, 171).

[18] Bodhiruci's translation. Taishō Tripitaka, xvi, 561a.

[19] Taishō Tripitaka, xvi, 562b.

[20] Gunabhadra's translation (AD 443), Taishō Tripitaka, xvi, 513c.

[21] Gunabhadra's translation (514b) refers to three sūtras: the Hastikakshya, Mahāmegha and Angulimala. Bodhiruci (564b) adds the Mahanirvana, and substitutes the Śrimālā for the Angulimālā.

[22] Majjhima-nikāya 86. Samyuktagāma 1077. Taishō Tripitaka ii, 281.

346

of course contains no such prohibition. It exists however in an expanded Mahāyāna form, and in one passage[23] says that the 'Buddhas do not eat flesh'. The second (translated 414–21) contains only a very indefinite reference[24] to the question. The third contains no reference to the subject at all, and is obviously quoted by mistake for the Angulimāla. The fourth[25] merely says that the efficacy of the spell at the end of the sūtra depends on abstinence from flesh.

It is evident that at the time when the Lankāvatāra was composed, the Mahāparinirvāna was the only scripture that definitely forbade the eating of meat. When therefore the Mahāyāna set itself to produce its own set of monastic rules, it had but the slenderest authority for enforcing complete vegetarianism. And indeed in the Fan-wang Ching,[26] which Far Eastern Buddhists regard as the foundation of their Monastic Rules, flesh-eating does not rank as a major sin, but merely as one of the forty-eight 'light defilements'. It is thus regarded as less serious than, for example, losing one's temper.

But to return to the question of Buddha's last meal—we have seen that philologically there is no reason why sūkaramaddava should not be the name of a root or fungus. And granted that this was the original meaning, it is quite comprehensible that after the centre of Buddhism shifted westward and southward,[27] this original meaning may have been forgotten.

Had Hīnayāna Buddhism viewed the eating of flesh with abhorrence, the expounders of the Sutta would then have found

[23] Ibid., ii, 540.
[24] Ibid., xii, 1099c. [25] Ibid., xvii, 787a. Translated in 424–41.
[26] Ibid., xxiv, 1005b. It purports to be an extract from a long Sanskrit work. But the Chung Ching Mu Lu (Nanjio 1609; compiled in AD 594) dismisses it as a forgery. The Tibetan version, which has no Sanskrit title and merely prefixes a literal rendering of the full Chinese title, is probably translated from the Chinese. It seems likely indeed that the work was originally composed in China some time after 507; for in that year, at a conference convened by the emperor Wu of the Liang dynasty to discuss the question of meat eating, the Fan-wang Ching is not cited among other relevant scriptures. It is interesting that one of the Vinaya authorities who gave evidence at this enquiry confessed that he was not himself a vegetarian (Taishō, lii, 299).
[27] After the persecutions of Pushyamitra (185–148 BC?).

themselves in an embarrassing position. Actually, however, they had (as we have seen) no such prejudice and it was quite easy for them to accept the term *sūkaramaddava* in the sense pork. The 'other commentators', who maintained that a vegetable was meant, were on this hypothesis not dishonest theologians, but merely people who happened to come from some part of India where the term *sūkaramaddava* in a vegetable sense was still current.

I know of no argument that could render such an hypothesis untenable.

The alternative is to suppose that, although no existing Hīnayāna work contains any general prohibition of the eating of meat, the feeling in favour of vegetarianism, then rather generally prevalent in the world,[28] had affected the Hīnayāna as well as the Mahāyāna, with the result that certain commentators were shocked by the idea of Buddha's eating pork, and invented a fanciful interpretation of the passage. The same sentiment, it must be supposed, is responsible for the substitution of fungi for pork in the Chinese version.

I think the second theory involves rather larger unproved assumptions than the first. But, in the existing state of our knowledge, either seems to me to be reasonable. The interest of such an enquiry as the above, despite its negative result, lies in the picture it gives of the method by which Buddhism adapted itself to fresh currents of thought and feeling in a method in complete contrast with that of Christianity. Whenever, under the influence of fresh environment or creative individual thought, the Buddhists were attracted by a new point of view, they felt the necessity of investing this point of view with written authority. Thus, so long as the religion was a living organism, its scriptures continually expanded and the Tripitaka in its Hīnayāna and Mahāyāna forms is in itself a history of Buddhism. Such a method, implying as it does in the faithful a critical capacity so limited that they will be at any moment ready to accept a modern docu-

[28] The Christian gnostics also advocated complete vegetarianism.

ment as the newly-recovered teaching of the Founder, was not possible in the West. Instead, the Christian Church has often been forced to adopt a complicated metaphorical interpretation of its Scriptures, particularly of the Old Testament, but has (since a very early period) scrupulously avoided the policy of expansion and interpolation which produced the riches of the Tripitaka. Thus, whereas in the West it is to the works of theologians that we must turn if we wish to study the successive phases of Christianity, in Buddhism the whole process of growth lies open before us in the scriptures themselves.

The Western method has its advantages. It is easy to regard past theologians as fallible. In Buddhism on the contrary the successive stages of doctrine, often irreconcilable with what went before, are expounded in scriptures which all make equal claim to be the actual words of Buddha. The difficulty was met, inadequately enough, by maintaining that the later scriptures had been mysteriously 'held up' till the world was in a fit state to receive them. In a case such as the one I have been discussing, this type of explanation could not be very convincing, and it is not surprising to find the great Buddhist biographer and compiler Tao-hsüan (596–667), who founded a sect which based its teaching on the *Vinaya*, embarrassed by the fact that in this portion of the scriptures the eating of flesh (regarded by 7th-century Buddhists with horror) was most definitely permitted. Fortunately the difficulty was solved by a vision in which a prophecy[29] was revealed to him, to the effect that in the degenerate days long after Buddha's death there would be monks who finding support in passages of the Hīnayāna scriptures would misinterpret the meaning of the *Vinaya* and pretend that Buddha allowed the monks to eat meat. 'In those days the monks in their temples will slay living creatures, making the places they live in no better than the homes of hunters or butchers.'

1932

[29] *Fa Yüan Chu-lin*, Ch. 94. Taishō Tripitaka lvii, 980c, quoting Tao-hsüan's lost *I-fa Chu-chih Kan-ying Chi*: 'Record of Rewards to those who held fast to the remnants of the Law.'

Waiting for the New

'Wir müssen auf den Neuen warten' ('We must wait for the New'). One might have thought, from the fervour of his tone, that he was speaking of a new Messiah had he not, as he said the words, standing outside the leafy open window, jerked his head towards the green mountains, still striped at the summit with patches of shimmering snow.

Often in winter, after a great snowfall, the skier looks out of his window at night, and seeing a clear sky pictures to himself the virgin, untracked slopes that await him in the morning. And so great is his longing to see spread out below him the unspoiled slopes, to lay the first track, that a whole night, even though spent in unconsciousness, seems an intolerable time to wait. And what of the summer, when he must spend not a few unconscious hours but half a year of long-dayed months waiting for the New?

But the truth is that for the skier time does not count. Waiting is waiting, whether it be for a night or for six months; and inversely the prospect of a ski-run is as exciting, day after day, to the rentier or pensioner who spends Michaelmas to May Day on the snow, as to the breadwinner who snatches a fortnight at Christmas. Each, on waking, thrills at the thought 'to-day I am going to ski'; each has sat for hours in heavy and perhaps wet ski-ing boots, merely to put off the moment when he must confess to himself 'to-day's ski-ing is over'. As for the great wrench, the loosening of the bindings and stepping out of the skis for the last time, the holiday-skier's great pang—the man of leisure will do all in his power to avoid it. He lingers where there are still streaks of white above the tree-line, or near glaciers that can still be skied upon at three in the morning or nine at night; he will not oil his skis or pack them away. The season is not over;

there is a ski meeting on the Glockner in June, at the Jungfrau in July.

Meanwhile thick grass and leisurely buttercups cover the slopes where in winter-time split seconds were disputed. Beyond these slopes were once mountains, cornices, avalanches, blizzards; now there are only dwarfish green hills, tinged here and there with a mist of blue or yellow flowers. And if the gential, the primulus, the soldanella, the snow-anemones in all their glory were suddenly blotted out by a metre of powder snow, no skier, even though he were also a great lover of flowers, would for an instant mourn. It is an obsession, a madness. Can there be any other sport that has such a hold? Does the fisherman lay down his rod with such a pang? This at least the skier has in common with the fisherman, that he is never tired of talking about his sport, never grows weary indeed of going over and over again through all the familiar stages of the same conversation. 'The Telemark turn still has its uses.' 'Funiculars have ruined ski-ing.' 'Steel edges are dangerous for beginners.' And when there is no one to talk to, the skier does runs in his head, holds triumphantly the 'Schuss' he has never quite ventured, changes the snow at will from the pillows and billows of January powder to the day-dream pliancy of 'Firn' or the glinting steel of early-morning glacier snow. Of the New, lying lightly on hummocks of shale and over the brown autumn grass, he banishes all thought. It is far away; not months only, but manifold contingencies—wars, sickness, penury lie between.

1937

Extract from Letter to Beryl de Zoete

Kitzbühel (Austria)
June 1 [1937]

Darling Beasts,

Here I sit in Tiefenbrunner, with Leni informing me so minutely about the moeurs of Kitzbühel that I could compete with the Batesons, save for the stop-watch, and that is an easy thing to borrow here. I think I shall go to Göttingen, Hotel Gebhard, on the 6th. I got yours of May 19 today. I wound up in the Jungfrau gebiet, and down to Brig. One comes into a world very different from the Bernese Oberland, the canton of Wallis, half-Italian, steep mule-paths, women with red handkerchiefs over their heads and full, striped skirts and a dialect to me completely incomprehensible. The full moon over the largest glaciers in Europe! That was a sight never to forget. This morning Fuchs the guide, in summer reader of the electricity metres, came to the Schweizerhof. 'Jetzt ist schluss,' he said; 'warten wir auf den neuen.' He meant, 'the new snow', but from the way he said it he might have been referring to a Messiah. The flowers and streams in Wallis beat even the Trentino. . . . The Schwarzsee was 24 degrees yesterday at 5 p.m., warmer I think than we ever had it. I am writing an essay called 'Waiting for Winter', on the theme of Fuchs's remark. But I myself am waiting for something closer I hope than winter—the advent of Beasts. . . .

Extract from the Epilogue to 'Three Ways of Thought in Ancient China'

The Taoists held that the object of life should be the cultivation of inner powers; the Confucians, that it should be the pursuit of Goodness. The Realists for the most part ignored the individual, and though there are passages that envisage an ultimate peaceful utopia, their general assumption is that the object of any society is to dominate other societies. These views are none of them idiosyncrasies peculiar to ancient China. The first is still widely held in India and by those elsewhere who have been influenced by Indian thought. The second is the view of religious teachers in America and most parts of Europe. The third is held by a number of vigorous and expanding States. All these views are therefore of immediate interest to us, and that is why I have made them the main subject of this book. But the period with which I have dealt was marked by an unparalleled fecundity of ideas; it is indeed known as the time of the Hundred Schools, though the 'hundred' is of course not to be taken as more than a convenient round number. I have made little mention of various schools about which a good deal could be said. For example, the dialecticians only appear incidentally; their works are too technical to be of interest to the general public, and have survived in so corrupt a form that they can only be discussed in connection with highly specialized problems of text criticism and philology. The Cosmologists, who believed in a mysterious parallel between the structure of man and the universe, I have not mentioned at all. Their theories (for example, the equation of colours with points of the compass) perhaps go back to something fundamental, for similar ideas crop up, to all appearances quite independently, in parts of North America and Africa. But in their detailed working out such theories become too mechanical and arbitrary to be of compelling interest.

Some readers may feel that since ideas do not drop ready-made from the sky but are determined (as I would readily admit) by the environment of the thinkers, I ought to have said more about the nature of the society in which these three ways of thought flourished. The ancient Chinese, they will say, were agriculturalists, but not dairymen, drove horses but did not ride them,[1] used oxen to draw carts but not for ploughing,[2] were strongly patrilineal with a tendency to foster the clan and family at the expense of larger groups, were ancestor-worshippers whose whole economy was bound up with the need for obtaining exotic substances used in the cult of the dead; had 'divine kings' who controlled the weather and the crops and a social system which postulated a rigid division between 'gentlemen' and 'common people', and so on. Cannot you tell us how the philosophies that you describe fit into this environment?

If I make no attempt to do so, it is because I believe in division of labour. To deal adequately with the history of thought requires a special training and a suitable temperament. Too many of the existing books about Chinese thought have been the work of writers who reacted as feebly to the thoughts of Mencius and Chuang Tzu as a Hottentot would react to the news that Blue Peter had won the Derby. The task of analysing Chinese institutions, for example, methods of trade, land-tenure, taxation, legal procedure, demands in its turn quite another training and a different temperament. Moreover, the gaps in our knowledge are immense. Even as late as the 3rd century BC China was still divided into at least six independent States. No serious

[1] Till about 300 B C. [2] Till about 200 B C.

354

study has as yet been made as to the ways in which the cultures of these States differed from one another. We know hardly anything about foreign trade, nor do we know when iron was introduced nor what was its quality; we do not know, as far as I can see, even when the cultivation of wet rice came to China.

That is why, being myself a student of thought and literature rather than of institutions or history, I have confined myself in the main to an account of ideas, regarding it as someone else's job to discover how ways of thought were linked to ways of living.

1939

More Than a Revival

For veteran spectators the performance of Massine's *Boutique Fantasque* at Covent Garden was more than a mere revival. It was a light suddenly flashing into the sealed caverns of memory, a conjuration magically resuscitating the throes and exaltations of youth. It was a night when not only did the *Boutique* live again on the stage, but also in the auditorium old attachments were renewed, old associations restored, old sympathies revived. Would this night, wondered the veterans (mustering loyally like Chelsea pensioners on Empire Day) haunt the memory of the young as the night of the original first performance still haunts the old; would they look back on it as the climax of their ballet-experience? I think they will. Massine as the can-can dancer was the Massine of twenty-odd years ago, with perhaps even an added touch of appropriate disreputability, emphasised by Moira Shearer's rendering of her role in the can-can; for unlike her predecessors, who played up to the studied vulgarity of the male role, Miss Shearer, by her delicate and beautiful interpretation of their part, deliberately acted as a foil to her partner.

There has never been a more perfect Snob than Alexis Rassine, and Henry Legerton was a lithe and rhythmical shop-assistant. John Hart was a perhaps too peppery shop-keeper; fierce, but not with the slow, benignant ferocity of Cocchetri. He had every right to a new conception; but there seemed to be no reason for his 'comic charwoman' type of make-up. The lesser parts were all well done, and the general standard of the performance was as high as that of Massine's earlier revival, the *Three Cornered Hat*.

The material with which the *Boutique* is constructed is commonplace, even hackneyed. What makes it so matchless a ballet is its flawless form. There is a perfect progression from the sleepy, casual, early morning opening to the triumphant climax of the can-can and after the temporary diminuendo of the shop-closing, to the riotous ensembles of the finale. All these effects were triumphantly realised on the night of this memorable revival.

1947

Extract from Letter to Beryl de Zoete[1]

. . . I promised to send you copy of this. I am afraid it is not worth sending. But, as Han Yü says, good faith, *hsin*, is so important, I have scribbled it out. It is a perfect night with all the stars spread on a velvet carpet.

[1] In this letter, sent from Switzerland, Waley copies out his review, 'More Than a Revival' and ends with the above. *Ed.*

Blake the Taoist

Some twenty years ago the Chinese poet Hsü Chih-mo took down a book from my shelves and after reading a few lines he exclaimed, 'This man is a Taoist!' The book was the long prophetic poem *Milton*, by William Blake. In his excitement he bent back the pages of the book at the place where he had opened it, and even today the book still opens of itself at the page which made Hsü cry out in astonishment, 'This man is a Taoist!' The words he had read were these: 'There is a place where contrarieties are equally true. This place is called Beulah. It is a pleasant lovely shadow where no dispute can come.' We both thought at once of the second chapter of the Taoist book *Chuang Tzu*, which bears the title *Chi Wu Lun*, rendered in the standard English translation 'Discourse on the Identity of Contraries'. When *Chuang Tzu* was written the old beliefs, centring round sacrifice to the ancestors, were fading away. It was a time of bitter controversy—the so-called 'warring of the Hundred Schools'. Each School sought continually for fresh arguments by which to convert its adversaries, but the adversaries remained unconvinced. From this empty strife the Taoists escaped in vision (*ming*) to the realm of Tao, in which 'Is' and 'Is not', 'So' and 'Not So' are smoothed away. Blake too lived at a time when traditional beliefs and the forms of society from which they sprang were crumbling, and controversy raged. He, too, through imagination, which corresponds to what the Taoists call 'vision', sought a realm 'where no disputes can come'. In the passage of *Milton* that follows the words I have quoted already ('There is a place where contrarieties are equally true') Blake conveys through the simile of a lovely morning, the transcendent bliss of escape from the realm of contradiction:

Thou hearest the nightingale begin the song of spring.
The lark sitting upon his earthy bed, just as the morn
Appears, listens silent; then springing from the waving cornfield, loud
He leads the choir of day: trill, trill, trill, trill,
Mounting upon the wings of light into the great expanse,
Re-echoing against the lovely blue and shining heavenly shell,
His little throat labours with inspiration; every feather
On throat and breast and wings vibrates with the effluence divine.
All Nature listens silent to him, and the awful sun
Stands still upon the mountain looking on this little bird
With eyes of soft humility and wonder, love and awe.
Then loud from their green covert all the birds begin their song;
The thrush, the linnet and the goldfinch, robin and the wren
Awake the sun from his sweet reverie upon the mountain.
The nightingale again assays his song, and through the day
And through the night warbles luxuriant, every bird of song
Attending his loud harmony with admiration and love. . . .
Thou perceivest the flowers put forth their precious odours,
And none can tell how from so small a centre come such sweets,
Forgetting that within that centre Eternity expands
Its ever-during doors . . .
First, e'er the morning breaks, joy opens in the flowery bosoms,
Joy even to tears, which the sun rising dries, first the wild thyme
And meadowsweet, downy and soft waving among the reeds,
Light-springing on the air lead the sweet dance; they wake
The honeysuckle sleeping on the oak, the flaunting beauty
Revels along upon the wind; the whitethorn, lovely may,
Opens her many lovely eyes, listening, the rose still sleeps,
None dare to wake her. Soon she bursts her crimson-curtained bed
And comes forth in the majesty of beauty; every flower,
The pink, the jessamine, the wall-flower, the carnation,
The jonquil, the mild lily opes her heavens, every tree
And flower and herb soon fill the air with an innumerable dance,
Yet all in order sweet and lovely. Men are sick with love.

The Taoists believed that truth could only be seen through
'vision', through what Blake calls Imagination. Their bugbears
were the intellectualists of the day—the logician Hui Tzu and the

eclectic Kung-sun Lung, who claimed to have 'mastered all the philosophies'. 'Abandon learning and there will be no more grieving', says Lao Tzu. Blake had the same distrust of purely intellectual processes and of those who exalted such processes at the expense of Imagination. His particular bugbears were the French philosophers Voltaire and Rousseau:

> Mock on, mock on, Voltaire, Rousseau;
> Mock on, mock on, 'tis all in vain!
> You throw the sand against the wind,
> And the wind throws it back again.
>
> And every sand becomes a gem
> Reflected in the beams divine;
> Blown back they blind the mocking eye,
> But still in Israel's paths they shine.
>
> The atoms of Democritus
> And Newton's particles of light
> Are sands upon the Red Sea shore,
> Where Israel's tents do shine so bright.

'Prisons', says Blake, 'are built with the stones of Law.' Here, too, the Taoists are on his side, for they believed that the legendary sages of antiquity and the Confucians who honoured them had, by the invention of law and morality, destroyed the natural happiness of men, and not only their happiness, but also their 'natural powers' and 'inborn faculties'. The prohibitions and restraints that the moralists imposed created criminality: 'Saintliness and wisdom', says a Taoist writer, 'were the clasp and catch that fastened the prisoner's cangue; goodness and duty were the bolt and eye that fastened his gyves.' The 'Sages and Confucians' of the Taoists are the kings and priests of Blake's poems—sanctimonious busybodies who write 'Thou shalt not!' over the door of Life. Here is Blake's poem called *The Garden of Love*:

> I went to the Garden of Love
> And saw what I never had seen:
> A chapel was built in the midst,
> Where I used to play in the green.

And the gates of this chapel were shut
And 'Thou shalt not' writ over the door;
So I turned to the Garden of Love
That so many sweet flowers bore.

And I saw it was filled with graves
And tombstones, where flowers should be,
And priests in black gowns were walking their rounds
And binding with briars my joys and desires.

The Taoists were fond of paradoxes. 'The greatest traveller does not know where he has got to; the greatest sight-seer does not know what he is looking at', says Lieh Tzu. 'The perfect door has neither bolt nor bar', says Lao Tzu. Blake used the same method, as in his proverbs, 'The road of excess leads to the palace of wisdom'; 'If the fool would persist in his folly he would become wise'. Let me, as I have mentioned Blake's proverbs, quote some more of them to you, for they lead us to the very heart of Blake's philosophy. I will begin with some that deal with Imagination or what the Taoists call Vision (*ming*):

What is now proved was once only imagined.
Eternity is in love with the productions of Time.
One thought fills immensity.
Everything possible to be believed is an image of truth.
No bird soars too high if he soars with his own wings.

And here are some of the ethical as opposed to the metaphysical proverbs:

Exuberance is beauty.
He who desires but acts not breeds pestilence.
You never know what is enough unless you know what is more
than enough.

This doctrine of 'exuberance' is definitely un-Taoist; but in his proverb 'The most sublime act is to set another before you' Blake reminds us of many Taoist maxims about the importance, both for states and individuals, of 'getting behind' and 'getting underneath'.

And finally, here is a prose passage from *The Last Judgment*, written about 1810:

'The Last Judgment is an overwhelming of bad art and science. Mental things alone are real; what is called corporeal, nobody knows of its dwelling-place, it is a fallacy and its existence an imposture. Where is the existence, outside of mind or thought? Where is it but in the mind of a fool? Some people flatter themselves that there will be no Last Judgment and that bad art will be adopted and mixed with good art, that error or experiment will make a part of Truth. . . . I will not flatter them; error is created, Truth is eternal. Error, or creation, will be burnt up and then, and not till then, Truth and Eternity will appear. It is burnt up the moment men cease to behold it. I assert for myself that I do not behold the outward Creation and that to me it is hindrance, not action. It is as dirt upon my feet—no part of me. "What?" it will be questioned, "when the sun rises do you not see a disc of fire somewhat like a guinea?" O no, no, I see an innumerable company of the heavenly host crying, "Holy, holy, holy is the Lord God Almighty". I question not my corporeal or vegetative eye any more than I would question a window concerning a sight. I look through it and not with it.' Is not all this summed up in Chuang Tzu's one saying: 'The eye envies the mind'?

I have said enough to show that Blake's philosophy has very strong affinities with Taoism. Could he, you will ask, have actually been influenced by Taoist texts? The only such text to which he could possibly have had access was the *Tao-te Ching*. A Latin version of this, made by a Portuguese in the second half of the 18th century, was acquired by the Royal Society of London in 1788. It had belonged to Matthew Raper, who was Chief of Council of the East India Company's establishment at Canton from 1777 till 1781. Raper, in turn, acquired it from the Jesuit missionary Joseph de Grammont, who was at Canton from 1785 to 1790. The work of this anonymous Portuguese is far more than a translation. It is a detailed attempt, founded upon the early 17th-century edition of the *Tao-te Ching* called *Lao Tzu I* ('Wings of Lao Tzu'), to interpret the book in terms of Western mysticism. This manuscript would have excited Blake profoundly. But it is doubtful if he knew enough Latin to read it; and if he had read it he would almost certainly have left some record of the fact. But it is not impossible that some knowledge of Lao Tzu's ideas had reached him in an indirect way, through conversation with someone who had read the manuscript. Blake knew several members of the Royal Society, including Joseph Priestley, the discoverer of oxygen. He may well have questioned them about the manuscript, the acquisition of which by the Royal Society was prominently announced in *Philosophical Transactions*, the journal in which the Society published its proceedings.

Thus a Taoist text may have influenced Blake, though this is very uncertain. It is on the other hand quite certain that Blake's works could throw a very important light on Taoist texts. It has often been said that different parts of such works, for example, of *Chuang Tzu*, cannot be by the same hand because they express contradictory ideas. Now Blake's works, about the authenticity of which there is not the slightest doubt, constantly show the most surprising contradictions, both in his use of terms and symbols, and in his ideas. 'Satan', for example, sometimes stands for what Blake regards as good and sometimes for all that is evil. Terms like 'God' and 'Angel' he uses sometimes in their ordinary sense and sometimes in a meaning peculiar to his own system. In short, the study of Blake proves (what we might in any case have suspected) that mystics are not always consistent, and that if in a given work Confucius is sometimes derided and sometimes treated as the fountain of all wisdom, this does not necessarily mean that the book in question is by a number of different hands.

1948

Some Far Eastern Dreams

There have been moments in modern Europe when people have begun to attach importance to their dreams. Some inkling that dreams are symbolic and have a secret (and not always very reputable) meaning leaked through from the works of Freud early in this century and a few earnest people began to take a rather awe-struck interest in their dreams. Later came Dunne's *Experiment with Time*, and the same people began writing down their dreams to see if they would come true—a possibility that does not seem to have interested Dr Freud. But on the whole we have regarded dreams as negligible aberrations of the spirit. In India and the Far East a very different attitude has been taken. True, one of the basic theories about dreams, found alike in India, China and Japan, is that they are due to small physical disorders or discomforts; for example, if one wears one's belt too tight one will dream of snakes, and one Buddhist school put forward the theory that dreams were due to arbitrary combinations of things familiar in waking life. 'When one is awake', says the *Mahavibhasha Sastra*, 'in one place one sees a man and in another one sees horns. In dreams one combines the two things and sees a horned man.' But such ultrarational theories ignored the common folk-belief that dreams were sent by deities or were caused by the spells and drugs of magicians, and most Eastern theories about dreams, while attributing them to various causes, were concerned chiefly with those sent as warnings or encouragements by the gods. These concessions to popular belief were rather like Jung's revision of Freud's dream theory which to the layman appears rather drab and narrow, in its assumption that the dream is solely a product of the individual subconsciousness; whereas Jung's theory that dreams drew also upon a universal store of consciousness opened the door (as his theories have generally done) to traditional beliefs and mythologies.

In China at any rate it was not only men who received warning dreams from kindly spirits. Chang Hua, the famous poet and statesman, who died in AD 300, had a white parrot to which he was extremely devoted. One day when he was standing in the garden he called to it to come out of the house and perch on his hand. 'I had a bad dream last night', said the parrot, 'warning me to stay at home.' Thinking that the parrot had merely overheard something said by a member of the household and was repeating the words without knowing what they meant, he went into the house, stroked its head and carried it out into the garden. It was at once attacked by a hawk. 'Peck its leg', screamed Chang Hua; which the parrot did, and the hawk let go. But it was a very narrow escape.

Dreams, in these stories, not only give warning of what is about to happen in real life; they impinge on reality, sometimes with embarrassing results. About AD 843, a student at the Chinese National College slept late into the morning and dreamt that he was leaning idly against the door-post of the college when he was accosted by a man dressed in yellow and carrying a hold-all. The stranger asked him his name, and when he told it smiled knowingly and said, 'You'll get through your examinations all right next spring'. The student then asked how several of his friends at the college would get on, and the man at once told him which of them would be successful and which of them would fail. 'Won't you come round with me to the pasty-shop in the Ch'ang-hsing Ward?' said the student. He often went there, for it lay only a few minutes' walk to the south of the college. The pasties for which the shop was famous were brought, but they had not been eating long when, in his dream, a dog-fight began just outside the shop, and he woke with a start. He jumped up and called out to his friends that he wanted to tell them a dream. He had hardly begun telling it when the proprietor of the pasty-shop appeared at the door,. 'Are you aware', he said, 'that you and your friend ordered two pounds of pasty and then went off without settling for them?' The student was very upset, for it so happened that at the moment he had run through his allowance, and had not a penny. Accompanied by the proprietor of the shop he went to a pawnbroker's and pawned his coat. Then he followed the shop-keeper back to the pasty-shop, curious to see whether the place where he was alleged to have sat corresponded with his dream. Everything, the stools, the dishes, the chopsticks, were just the same. 'My companion and I', he said to the shop-keeper, 'were only your customers in a dream. You're surely not going to say that we actually consumed your pasties?' 'You ordered them', said the shop-keeper, 'and that is what matters. But come to think of it, I did notice that though you seemed to be eating them, the pasties did not get any smaller. I thought that perhaps you weren't getting on with them because you didn't like garlic. I did put a little in.'

Next spring the student and the three friends whom the stranger had named all took their degrees.

Sometimes one person's dream appears to another as a waking vision, and this is particularly so between people who are very intimate. In about AD 700, the famous Chinese statesman Liu Yu-ch'iu, then still only a small provincial official, was compelled to leave home for a while on an official mission. On his way back he was surprised to hear a noise of singing and loud laughter coming from a Buddhist shrine that stood by the wayside. He peeped through a chink in the wall and saw a number of gay young people picnicking in the courtyard. Among them he was astonished to see his young wife, to whom he was deeply attached, chattering and laughing. Amazed to see her so far from home and in such company and having tugged at the door and found that it was locked he did the first thing that came into his head— picked up a piece of broken tile and threw it over the wall. There was a tremendous crash, followed by a noise of rushing water, and peeping through his hole, he saw that he had hit the big earthenware bowl which the picnickers had brought to do their washing-up in. The people within were fleeing in every direction and had soon all disappeared. He then managed to climb the wall and searched the whole place. Not a soul could he find, though the one door which led into the premises was still locked as before. Utterly bewildered he hurried home. He was told that his wife was in bed. She soon came out to meet him and after a while she said, 'I have just had such an odd dream. I thought I was picnicking with a lot of other young people at a wayside shrine. I had no idea who they were. Suddenly someone threw a tile over the wall. It landed right in the middle of the cups and dishes, causing the wildest confusion, and I woke with a start.'

This became a classic dream-story and there are many later variants of it.

In AD 759 (these strange stories are very punctilious about dates) an official called Hsieh Wei had been lying sick of a fever for many days, tossing sleepless on his bed when he fell at last into a feverish doze. 'What is the use,' he said to himself in his dream, quite forgetting that he was weak and ill, 'what is the use of lying here in this hot bed? Surely it would be better to get up and go into the fresh air.' So he picked up his walking-stick and in his dream set out for a stroll along the river-bank. He came to a deep, clear pool in which the autumn leaves were reflected, and the idea came to him that it would be refreshing to have a bathe. As a boy he had been fond of swimming, but he was now very much out of practice, and seeing the fish glide swiftly past him he said to himself in his dream, 'We men make a very poor show of it, at best. If only I could get a temporary job as a fish and really swim to some effect.' 'You have only to apply for it', said a voice near him. 'Even a permanent job might not be out of the question, but a temporary job can easily be arranged. I'll see about it for you.' Presently a giant with a fish's head appeared, riding on a leviathan, escorted by a band of fish attendants. He took out a scroll and read out the following proclamation:

Though it is fit that denizens of the waves and dwellers on the land above should for the most part go their separate ways, it has been brought to Our notice that the human official Hsieh Wei shows an unusual partiality for the watery element and has applied for permission to serve us. We, the River Lord, in accordance with his desire, do hereby appoint him to the office of Temporary Red Carp in the eastern pool, giving him at the same time the warning, necessary to one embarking on this career, that bait attached to a hook is on no account to be approached.

Glancing at himself while he listened, Hsieh Wei saw that he was already covered with scales.

He was told that he must report every evening at the eastern pool. But apart from that he was free to wander where he pleased, and he made many long excursions up stream and down, explored countless lakes and tributaries, and soon there was no creek or channel where he had not twisted and gambolled to his heart's content. On one of these occasions he could find nothing to eat and feeling very weak and hungry he followed a fishing-boat in the hope of picking up some scrap that the fisherman threw overboard. Coming closer he saw that the fisherman was Chao Kan, whom he knew very well. Presently Chao cast his line, and the bait smelt very good. But he remembered the warning, and reluctantly swam away. Soon, however, his hunger became unendurable and he said to himself, 'After all, although I have taken a temporary job in the fish-world, I did not resign my human post, and Chao Kan, if I tell him who I am, will certainly not dare to kill an official. He will no doubt take me back to my bureau, and all will be well.' So he swallowed the bait and Chao Kan hauled him in. He began to explain matters, but Chao Kan seemed not to be listening and having passed a string through his gills took him ashore and tied him up in a hidden place among the bull-rushes. Presently a servant came, saying that the Senior Clerk was going to entertain some friends and wanted a large carp. 'I have plenty of small ones,' said the fisherman, hoping to sell Hsieh Wei for a higher price in the market, 'but I have not caught any big ones to-day.' 'I know your tricks', said the servant, and beating about among the bull-rushes he soon found a very big fish indeed. 'I am the Registrar Hsieh Wei', the fish

368

explained. 'I have been seconded to a fish-post, but I still hold my rank as a human official and you ought to make your obeisance to me.' But the servant did not seem to hear what he was saying and carried him off to the Government house. Several of his colleagues were sitting near the gate playing draughts. He called out to them, but all they said was, 'That's a fine big fish'. Wang the fish-cook was sent for and taking Hsieh Wei to the kitchen stood over him knife in hand. 'My good Wang,' cried Hsieh, 'I have never employed anyone but you as my fish-cook ever since I came here. Surely you will not be so ungrateful as to kill me.' But Wang seemed unaware that anything had been said. He laid Hsieh's head on the chopper-board and was just bringing down his knife, when Hsieh woke with a start. He was quite cured of his fever, and when his colleagues came to congratulate him, he told them of his dream. To his astonishment he learnt that everything had happened just as he had dreamed it. 'We saw your lips moving', they said, 'but no sound came out, and we had not the faintest idea that the fish was you.' Neither Hsieh nor his colleagues could ever bring themselves to eat carp again.

A very convincing dream is recorded in the diary of the Japanese monk Jōjin who visited China about AD 1070. After crossing the famous Stone Bridge that leads to the T'ien-t'ai Monastery in eastern China, he writes: 'Looking through my Dream Record I see that on the 30th of the 7th month in the fourth year of Kōhyō (1061) I dreamt I was crossing over a great river by a stone bridge. Before I was across, the bridge broke; but someone else got across by stepping along my bed, and eventually got me across in the same way. Even in my dream I felt sure that the bridge was the Stone Bridge at T'ien-t'ai in China, about which it is said that only one who has attained to the Highest Enlightenment can get safely across.

'Now, long afterwards, I was delighted that my dream had come true and that I succeeded in crossing the bridge. I examined its construction carefully, and it corresponded in every way to the bridge in my dream.'

The passage is interesting because it shows that Jōjin (and probably other people too) carried about with him on his travels a record of dreams covering a period of many years.

Dreams can be bought and sold, or stolen. The Japanese Regent Masatoki, who lived in the 12th century, had two daughters, who were step-sisters. The younger dreamt that the sun and moon fell into her lap. 'I must go and ask Masako what this means', she thought. Masako was the name of the elder sister, who was learned in history, mythology and dream-interpretation. 'This would be a strange enough dream for a man to have,' thought the elder sister, 'and it is stranger still that it should come to a woman.' For she knew such a dream meant that the person concerned would become ruler of the land. Being herself of a masterful and ambitious character she determined to get hold of the dream and said deceitfully to the younger sister, 'This is a terribly unlucky dream. You had better get rid of it as quickly as possible.' 'How can one get rid of a dream?' asked the younger sister. 'Sell it!' said Masako. 'But who is there that would buy a bad dream?' 'I will buy it from you', said Masako.

'But, dear sister, how could I bear to escape from misfortune, only to see it descend upon you?'

'That does not happen', said Masako. 'A dream that is bought brings neither fortune nor misfortune.' The price paid was an ancient Chinese mirror. The young sister went back to her room saying, 'It has happened at last. The mirror that I have always wanted is mine.' Only long afterwards when Masako became the virtual ruler of Japan (1220–25) did the young sister realize what she had lost by selling her dream.

It is dangerous to tell one's dream except to an accredited interpreter. Anyone who hears a dream and has a good enough memory to repeat it word for word can rob the dreamer of its benefits. Mabi, the son of a provincial clerk in Japan, at the end of the 7th century, had a strange dream and went to have it interpreted by a woman dream-interpreter. Before he had time to tell it the sons of the Governor arrived with a great troupe of attendants. Mabi was hustled away to a back room and asked to wait till the distinguished client had been attended to. Just to pass the time he put his ear to the key-hole and listened. 'I am afraid your dream won't come up to that young man's', said the interpreter. 'You did not happen to hear any of it?' Mabi then repeated the dream word for word. 'Listen!' said the woman, who had taken a fancy to Mabi. 'As you have repeated the dream without any mistake, it is yours, if you care to have it. It means that you will be a great scholar and will rise to be a Minister of State.' Sure enough Mabi was chosen, from among all the youths of the kingdom, to go and study in China. He remained there for eighteen years and when he came back was made Minister of the Right. He is the great Kibi no Mabi whose name every Japanese schoolchild knows.

Psycho-analytical patients today sometimes claim to have hoaxed their doctor by telling him fictitious dreams. The doctor, not at all put out, explains that bogus dreams are for him quite as interesting as real ones. What the doctor probably does not know is that this view can be traced back to the third century A D, in China. At that time a famous interpreter of dreams called Chou Hsüan was more than once given bogus dreams by people who fondly imagined that they were scoring off him. Seeing that the prediction he based on such dreams always came true a client asked him if it really made any difference whether a dream was real or concocted. 'None at all', he answered. 'For real dreams and false are both alike products of the soul.'

1955

The British Capture of
Ting-hai in July 1840

Extract from *The Opium War Through Chinese Eyes*[1]

Their first objective was to capture Ting-hai, on Chusan Island, at the tip of the southern arm of Hangchow Bay. Lin had, as we have seen, warned the authorities at Hangchow and Ningpo that English warships were at large and might be making for the north. But he does not seem, judging from the following extract, to have given any description of their appearance or to have explained how they could be distinguished from merchant-ships. In general appearance, of course, the difference was not so marked then as it is today. 'Before the war', says an account derived from a Mr Wang, who was sub-Prefect of Ting-hai, 'whenever a foreign ship arrived everyone from the Commandant, the Prefect and sub-Prefect down to chair-carriers and office lacqueys all took bribes from the foreigners and unless satisfied with what they got would not let them trade. At first not more than one or two or at the most three or four ships came. But the greater the number of ships, the greater the amount taken in bribes, so that so far from being apprehensive when more ships came than usual, their one fear was lest the number should decline. . . . One day it was announced . . . that a far larger number of ships had arrived than ever before. At first the officials and their subordinates were rather puzzled. But the explanation soon occurred to them, and they guffawed with joy. Obviously the ships had assembled here because of the cessation of trade at Canton. "Ting-hai", they said,

[1] See p. 80.

"will become a great trading centre, and we shall all make more and more money out of them day by day".'

What actually happened (5 July) can best be read in Lord Jocelyn's *Six Months with the Chinese Expedition* (1841): 'The ships opened their broadsides upon the town, and the crashing of timber, falling houses, and groans of men resounded from the shore. The firing lasted on our side for nine minutes; but even after it had ceased a few shots were still heard from the unscathed junks. . . . We landed on a deserted beach, a few dead bodies, bows and arrows, broken spears and guns remaining the sole occupants of the field.'

Some Western and even some modern Chinese accounts give the impression that Ting-hai surrendered without putting up any resistance. That is quite false; the town rejected a demand for unconditional surrender and when attacked put up such resistance as was possible. But it had not from the first any chance of withstanding the concentrated fire of fifteen warships; as well might one expect Hiroshima to have hit back at its attackers. The military commander, Chang Ch'ao-fa, died of his wounds;[2] the Prefect Yao Huai-hsiang and the Chief Constable Ch'üan Fu committed suicide rather than submit.

Only the town and its immediate neighbourhood were occupied. An eye-witness[3] says of the people there: 'They have in a thousand instances received great injustice at our hands. While we have been issuing proclamations, talking sweet words . . . our soldiers and sailors have been plundering them and forcibly carrying off their poultry and cattle. . . . We are now going to break open all the unoccupied shops and houses and take possession of them for governmental purposes. As they will no longer bring poultry and vegetables to market, we are going to forage the farms. . . . As they will sell us no fish, we are going to take measures to prevent them fishing at all.'

It perhaps is significant that what seems to be the earliest

---

[2] On 2 August, at Ningpo.
[3] Quoted in the *Chinese Repository*, 1840, p. 325.

printed use of the Indian term 'loot' as an adopted English word occurs in reference to Ting-hai: 'Silks, fans, china, little shoes ... the articles of a Chinese lady's toilette—lay tossed in a sad and telltale mêlée; and many of these fairy shoes were appropriated by us as lawful loot.'[4]

With regard to looting, I am concerned in this book with the impact it made on its victims. I by no means wish to imply that the English expedition behaved worse than was or is usual in war, or that the Chinese themselves would have behaved better under similar circumstances. The system of 'security placards', by which households purchased theoretical immunity from plunder by giving up their live-stock gratis, does however seem unusually cold-blooded.

1958

[4] *Six Months with the Chinese Expedition*, p. 61.

Review of *Ivan Morris's The World of the Shining Prince: Court Life in Ancient Japan*

Years ago, when I was bringing out in successive volumes my translation of the 11TH century Japanese novel *The Tale of Genji*, I constantly received letters asking for information about the background of the story. Did the state of society depicted in the book actually exist or was it imaginary? How did Genji get his income? What were the rules about marriage, concubinage and so on? I answered as best I could; but I had not before embarking on the vast task of translating the book (it is twice as long as *War and Peace*) made any preliminary study of what Ivan Morris calls 'the world of the shining prince', and during the ten years during which I was translating I had no time for research into the period. It gave me a sense of guilt to finish the work knowing so little about the age that produced it; but I soon became immersed in Chinese studies, my great hope meanwhile being that someone would write just such a book as Ivan Morris has now produced. Nominally it is a book about the background of *Genji;* but in his generosity the author has made it to some extent a book about the novel itself. . . .

The author makes a valiant attempt to define the difference between religion and superstition. I would prefer simply to say that 'superstition' is any belief that the speaker thinks silly. How subjective the distinction is becomes apparent from the fact that Ivan Morris puts acupuncture and moxa-treatment under the heading 'superstitions'. Of the latter he boldly says that it was 'as painful as it was useless'. There was however quite a cluster of moxa-burners, all of them qualified doctors, in Vienna before the last war and the usefulness of acupuncture is admitted by the French State medical service. So where are you? On the other hand the belief that you have only to utter the formula *Namu Amida Butsu* and you will automatically go to Heaven is classified by Morris as 'religion'. It seems to have a good claim to a place in the chapter on superstitions; a better claim than Chinese herbal medicine, which the author cavalierly dismisses, along with acupuncture and the rest.

What Ivan Morris does not much discuss is the value of *The Tale of Genji* as literature and its place among other great works of fiction. That no doubt is due to the fact that the main subject of his book is the age in which *Genji* was written, rather than the novel itself. In a review of my translation of the first nine chapters, Raymond Mortimer hailed the novel as 'a new planet' and guessed that, when the remainder of the work came out, *The Tale of Genji* would probably prove to be one of the twelve great novels of the world. . . . He accords to Lady Murasaki 'every quality that goes to make a great novelist—imagination, humour, uncommon good sense . . . a command of narrative on a large scale and a sympathetic, observant regard for human character.'

I do not think that the appearance of the subsequent five volumes caused this critic to alter his opinion, and it seemed to be widely shared. I remember only one dissentient voice, that of *The Churchman*, whose reviewer was astonished at my *naïveté* in supposing that the public would tolerate five more volumes of a work so insufferably boring. Translations, not of the original but of my translation, soon appeared in almost every European language. The only translation, apart from mine, to be made from the Japanese has, so far as I know, been that of Professor

Konrad, who translated *Genji* into Russian.[1] . . . He had the strange and misguided notion that an 11th-century Japanese book ought to be translated into 11th-century Russian. It seems unlikely that he found many readers. The same bizarre notion took possession of Monsieur Haguenaur, who is translating *Genji* into medieval French. A Hungarian version (from the English) appeared recently. Thus *Genji*, not a work that one would expect Marxists to encourage, has had a fair innings behind the Iron Curtain. The only great country where *Genji* is virtually unknown (and the exception is a gigantic one) is China, Japan's neighbour. The Chinese have always shown an extraordinary lack of interest in the past of Japan. There are plenty of books from which a Chinese can learn current Japanese colloquial, but not one (so far as I know) from which he can learn ancient Japanese. One would have thought that more linguistic (if not literary) curiosity would have remedied this strange state of affairs. Thus it comes about that the chief Far Eastern nation has ignored what is perhaps the greatest Far Eastern work of literature.

But what about the fate of *Genji* in Japan itself? It is my impression that, apart from selected passages read at school, very few Japanese to-day know the text in the original; 'Most people who read *The Tale of Genji* nowadays', says Ivan Morris, 'use the modern language version by the eminent novelist Tanizaki Junichirō; and some, including as prominent a literary man as Masamune Hakuchō, find Arthur Waley's translation more comprehensible than the original text.' Morris goes on to enumerate a number of characteristics of early Japanese that make for obscurity. About some of these I am sceptical. I doubt whether the absence of any distinction between past and present tense causes much trouble. The whole narration can in any case be assumed to refer to the past. I also do not recollect that failure to distinguish between singular and plural gives serious trouble; in the example given by Morris on p. 282 it is of no consequence

---

[1] A full German translation by Oscar Berl, *Die Geschichte von Princes Genji,* was published in 2 volumes in 1966 by Manesse Verlag. *Ed.*

whether 'person' or 'persons' is meant. I even doubt whether there is much inherent obscurity in the Heian style; Moto-ori, the great 18th-century critic, writes in it with the utmost clarity. What, to my mind, causes the obscurities in *Genji* is the fact that Murasaki, like other great novelists, sometimes writes badly. I cannot accept as good writing any passage that leaves the reader in doubt as to its meaning. Allowance must also be made for textual corruption. A book that circulated in MS for over five hundred years before being printed cannot possibly have reached us just as it left the author's brush.

Morris's third appendix is called 'Is *The Tale of Genji* complete?' This is how the book ends, in all existing MS and printed editions: 'For Kaoru the suspense [of waiting for a word from his mistress who was hiding in a nunnery] had been torturing, and the complete failure of the boy's mission was a heavy disappointment. He did not know what to think. The story that she had become a nun and shut herself off from the world he was not so simple as to believe. If she was indeed living, no doubt some lover had secretly installed her there and was looking her up from time to time, just as he himself, all too infrequently, had visited her at Uji.'

This seems to me a perfect ending. Ivan Morris thinks that the book as we have it is incomplete: 'We are meant to know something more about Kaoru's and Niou's reactions to Ukifune's retirement to a nunnery.' If the book were by Wilkie Collins, I should entirely agree.

1964

'Et pourtant c'est triste quand meurent les empires'

It is wrong to be sad,
   To see the death of an Empire as tragedy, the ruins in rows
   As a hideous disaster, and the enemy for whom are used
So many playful names, as pitiless foes.

You should learn to pass
The church where multitudes were trapped, the gutted shop
Lightly, or with some humorous remark,
Some 'Jerry again!' or 'I'll bet that made them hop!'

It is wrong to doubt
Cheerful assurances about secret weapons and devices
This year, next year, some time; about despair in Rome,
Shortage and soaring prices.

Et pourtant c'est triste—
Those words, I do not know why,
Found in a French book weeks ago still haunt me:
'It is sad when empires die.'

1940

Censorship

(In Chinese Style)

I have been a censor for fifteen months,
The building where I work has four times been bombed.
Glass, boards and paper, each in turn,
Have been blasted from the windows—where windows are left at all.
It is not easy to wash, keep warm and eat;
At times we lack gas, water or light.
The rules for censors are difficult to keep;
In six months there were over a thousand 'stops'.
The Air Raid Bible alters from day to day;
Official orders are not clearly expressed.
One may mention Harrods, but not Derry and Toms;
One may write of mist but may not write of rain.
Japanese scribbled on thin paper
In faint scrawl tires the eyes to read.
In a small room with ten telephones
And a tape-machine concentration is hard.
Yet the Blue Pencil is a mere toy to wield,
There are worse knots than the tangles of Red Tape.
It is not difficult to censor foreign news,
What is hard today is to censor one's own thoughts—
To sit by and see the blind man
On the sightless horse, riding into the bottomless abyss.

Blitz Poem

There are days when, slipping from the clasp
Of memory, each sound and sight
On some blank shoal of inward feeling
Lies new and separate and bright.
It was so today with the voice
Harsh-edged as Andalusian hills
Of the old Gibraltar woman calling back
Her grandchild that was scraping
Splintered glass from window-sills.

No Discharge

I do not believe that Heaven and Hell are in different places,
I do not believe that the utmost anguish of the damned
Could ever damp the bliss of neighbouring Saints.
I do not believe there have ever been complaints
From any of the Twenty Four Elders or Seven Spirits,
About things like the smell of brimstone. 'At first it seems strong'
They confess, 'but one does not notice it for long,
And we keep our incense burning night and day.'
'While for the groaning and gnashing of teeth', the angels say
'What with the noise of golden harps and new song
They scarcely worry us at all.' To a recent guest
Shy at first amid so much goodness, wondering
Whether one can ever really be friends with the Blest,
Gazing down at the unconsumable Phoenix nest,
At the obstinate host whose daily bread is destruction
Yet none can cease to suffer by being destroyed—
To such, a hospitable Elder will often come
Saying, 'Meet me here when it's dark. You have never enjoyed
Beauty on earth such as I will show you tonight—
The fires of Hell reflected in the Glassy Sea.'
The hours of evening pass; his golden crown, a little tight,
Tires him at first, his unaccustomed wings
Bewilder him, his fingers on the golden strings
Find disconcerting music, and his own voice
Startles him with its raptures when he sings.
Darkness drops; he stands by the smiling Elder
Wing to wing. Shall he look up or down?
At the rose-leaf Phantom caught in the glacier of Heaven?
At the scarlet Fury prancing over Hell-town?
'It's wonderful to look at it, isn't it', an Elder once said,
'Surely this alone makes it worth while to be dead!'
So Heaven and Hell live side by side
And such troubles as happen are of the mildest kind.

Now and again the dull, the gentle damned
Stir, and some salvaged Lucifer will try
To organize revolt. Which Heaven does not mind.
What does it mean? A few lost spirits clutching
Charred banners with the motto 'We want wings',
Or 'Harps for Hell', or 'Golden crowns for all'.
The unpresentable, scrap-heap Lucifer flings
A written protest over Heaven's wall.
'They're bound to answer', 'This time they must do something—'
The meek spirits whisper, waiting outside.
Hours go by. Suddenly a terrible light
Flashes over them. Is is some new device
For blistering Hell—for cutting off their retreat?
No! That transcendent whiteness is the Angel of Day
Telling them quietly but firmly to go away.

1941

Song

I had a bicycle called 'Splendid',
A cricket-bat called 'The Rajah',
Eight box-kites and Scotch soldiers
With kilts and red guns.
I had an album of postmarks,
A Longfellow with pictures,
Corduroy trousers that creaked,
A pencil with three colours.

Where do old things go to?
Could a cricket-bat be thrown away?
Where do the years go to?

In the Gallery

Behind iron railings, across a huge cobbled space, umbrellas laboured unevenly, seeming at moments to press so close into the welter of the stone that the eye lost them as it loses a boat at sea. At last, as though struggling shoreward across the long ladder of the surf, they swayed slowly up the dripping steps and at the top suddenly rippled and collapsed, disclosing between the pillars a herd of baffled pilgrims, who before pressing through the narrow doors, now turned for an instant towards the courtyard and the town, as though to drink in a last breath of reality before plunging into an abstract, inanimate world.

It seemed that beyond the massive portico must open out some vast luminous space; but behind the glazed swing-doors the pilgrims came suddenly upon a dark shallow lobby, where a woman in a shawl held her knitting very close to her eyes, while through the thick air, from a doorway at her side, came a smell of cooking and the sound of birds moving in a cage. Now one by one the pilgrims began to filter through a turnstile into the main hall. Some—for the most part the rougher and stronger of them—through sheer timidity did not press hard enough, and, when they faltered, the woman with the shawl pushed them through, like clothes through a creaking mangle.

Two curving staircases with marble balustrades met on a wide empty landing where darkly, with its back to a high window, stood the life-size statue of a man in evening dress, with drooping moustaches and long hair parted at the side. There were medals and orders on his coat, the ribbon and pins that held them were all shown, as were too the watch-chain, the heavy signet and the rings on his right hand. But though these were metal rendered in metal, they were not more real than the undulating silk necktie and the elastic sides of his shoes. His left hand was slipped rather furtively into the trouser pocket, as though he were feeling for a tip.

The long room, from doorway to doorway, was full of travel. Weaving itself into the sound of their own hushed footfall the pilgrims still heard the uneasy rattle of the night train, and into the dark pools on the wall there crept the image of a breakfast-tray, lying on an unmade bed.

And just as their own thought-pictures, now cavernously framed in gold, took on a mirrored gravity and distinctness unknown in the common world, so too during the journey of which this pilgrimage through the gallery was part, their own image of themselves had gradually cleared and crystallized. They saw themselves no longer as dim lay-figures, called to life only by a series of costumes and occupations—not as a succession of personalities—but as one thing always, that travelled and visited and travelled, perpetually filling and unfilling the same bag, perpetually feeling in the same pocket for change and keys.

And yet the pilgrim's personality, now so strangely sharpened and clarified, was largely an affair of chance. A book, a pair of gloves snatched up at the last moment had fixed his picture of himself and coloured the whole journey.

The air was close and difficult to breathe. It was indeed not so much air as a tight, sweet vapour that rose from the thickly waxed floor. In such an atmosphere any movement would have been tiring, and that of walking was doubly so, for the floor was highly polished, slippery as ice, and the pilgrims, not daring to raise their feet, shuffled down the long gallery like flies clawing the glass walls of an air-tight trap. Their movements, in this lethal cage, became dreamier and dreamier, and but for the sounds of the night-journey, a lock that continually strained and rattled, water that sighed in a pipe, a childish ding-dong bell, the last despairing whistle of a distant engine—echoes that like the remnants of a tempest still snapped and fluttered in the ravaged corridors of the brain—they must have fallen asleep.

But suddenly into this inert and desiccated world there burst a sweep of cumbrous activity. Under the high square door and straight down the long room was pushed a lady in an invalid chair. She did not look to right or left but, propped stiffly on a pile of cushions, between which a picture-paper was thrust, her hands folded over the knob of the steering-bar, she gazed intently at the lines on the glassy floor as though all her strength were concentrated on reaching the end of the long gallery.

The two men who pushed the chair bent so low that their faces could not be seen. This attitude gave them an air of extreme solicitude; they seemed to be anxious that the invalid should be spared the effort of raising her voice, should be able at any moment to convey the most faintly whispered complaint or request. The lady's lips, however, though always slightly parted, never moved, and at times it seemed as though the attention of the two men were fixed not so much on the furtherance of her small passing wishes as on the fulfilment of her main desire: to keep a straight and continual course towards the door at the end of the long room; and for this purpose it was necessary that they should attend not so much to her as to their own feet, planting them in an intricate angular pattern, to obtain a steady purchase on the slippery floor.

The travellers had pushed on into the second room, which appeared to be in all respects identical with the first. But one of them after a while stumbled against something that proved to be a long low seat and, to save himself from falling, suddenly sat down. The others quietly ranged themselves by his side. Here for a time, as previously in the dining-car with its access of space and light, stretching their legs and safely testing the glassy composition of the floor, they enjoyed, on this soft yet solid couch, an extraordinary sense of respite and relief. But with a great gold-framed space on the wall in front of them, they could feel themselves, like birds assembled on a telegraph wire, still to be at work, still to be passively obeying the mysterious impulse of their migration.

It had been growing steadily lighter, and now the sun came out, making all at once a complete and convenient looking-glass of the dark rectangle in front of which they sat. One of the pilgrims stepped forward to arrange his tie; but immediately there was a cranking and jarring in a far corner of the room and a slight flapping sound overhead. With one accord a whole series of yellow blinds spread across the glass roof. By the time the pilgrim had raised his hands to his neck the mirror had ceased to exist. The others looked at him apologetically as, still fingering his bow, he gazed with a certain resentment at the scene which, abolishing his own image, had slanted into the golden frame!

Two naked men in plumed helmets were rescuing an empty bird-cage from a ruined church. Towards the flat blue distance a camel, led by chanting angels, carried lashed to its back a marble fountain and a trumpet draped in cloth of gold.

There was a long silence, broken by the sudden wailing of a child. They gave him a disc to play with, a white, numbered disc, such as each of them had exchanged for his dripping encumbrances, while they themselves continued to gaze spell-bound by the inexplicable revelation that confronted them. Often on their journey things no less astonishing—cities of shapeless slag or rivers of fire plucked from a tangle of trucks, wires and magic lights—had flashed on to the screen of their senses in the hurry of the dark; or at dawn, having steamed quietly into a huge station they had jolted out of it again, finally coming to an unexpected standstill close beside an isolated row of shallow houses on the outskirts of the town.

Then their minds, leaving the steamy carriage, had been projected through the sharp stillness of the morning air, under half-pulled blinds, into a dingy bedroom where a headless figure lay across a wooden chair, or a broken saucer moved as though drawn by wire over the space between the stair-rail and the door. But even these dim vistas and hasty prefigurements, compared with what was now before them, had seemed to the pilgrims to

387

be full of scenic purpose. The fountain? The angels? A sort of bewildered discomfort held the travellers rooted to the spot, waiting for the word, the syllable that should release them.

Slowly, as though drawn by the unspoken question, a white-haired pensioner in a peaked cap, guardian of the two long rooms, shuffled to their side. 'Allegorical', he whispered, bending over the row of pilgrims and laying a finger to his forehead, with the gesture of one who has a harmless madman in his care.

'Allegorical.' The word, though it told so little, served nevertheless a kind of mechanical purpose, passing from mouth to mouth with a series of slight shocks which, gathering scope and momentum, ended at last in an uneasy fidgeting with buckles and catches, a restless scraping of feet.

Soon with a last glance at the strange borderland that had detained them so long, the pilgrims pushed out of their siding. At first they moved forward again in a solid mass. But they had lost their real cohesion. Two of them presently, as though all at once endowed with a propulsion of their own, branched off from the crowd, and drifted separately through the grey hush into an avenue of small side rooms, where they met time after time in front of the same row of grubby Dutch carousals, almost colliding, then parting again, with the sharp twist of a gold-fish into whose pool a pebble has been thrown.

Soon there was a greater disruption. The child, whose first and real fear had been so easily distracted, now began to take fright causelessly at every turn. Soon the discs of the whole family were in its possession. With these in its hand, pausing at every few steps to look back, yet mounting with incredible rapidity, it darted up a steep, dark staircase the very existence of which no one else had perceived. The mother panted after it, followed by the whole family; they did not return. The pilgrims were pushing once more straight through the heavy waxen air. Their course was set; it seemed as though nothing could turn them aside. But like a river in whose banks a breach has accidentally been made, one after another they were drawn through the unnoticed gap, till only a thin trickle of them oozed slowly down the centre of the glassy floor.

The rest, re-animated by the diversion, rose wave on wave. They did not feel the exertion. Their feet perhaps were numbed by so much shuffling and sliding. It was as though by magic that they arrived at the doorway of a low upper room.

They gave a deep sigh of relief. Here at last was no shadow-fair, no hall of mysteries. The air lived, the walls spoke, there were attitudes and textures that they knew.

Military men were frequent; here however not bewigged or helmeted, but bald, or with close-cropped, unlegendary hair. There were stolid queens and princesses whose presence could not bewilder or embarrass the humblest visitor, so rustic and unfashionable were the clothes they wore. There was a schoolboy in an Eton collar cutting a silvery cake into which a sprig of holly was thrust. There was a basket of grey kittens and an orchard full of bloom.

The kittens were high on the wall. Wishing to please the child, to whose inconsequence they owed this breath of solidity, this welcome contact with a sharper, more natural world, one of the pilgrims seized it in his arms and held it close to the picture.

With a cry of delight the child stretched out its hand, but its fingers, that expected warm fur, slid along the glass with a faint creaking sound, not unlike the mewing of an offended cat. Hastily, as though it had touched a thorn, the child drew back its hand, and again burst into tears.

Close by there was a narrow staircase, this time a mere turret stair. It was too insignificant to promise anything of value or importance, but it at least afforded a refuge from the child's cries and, by a simple reckoning, gave hope of a scene intensely actual and alive. They climbed the stairway (the less phlegmatic of the pilgrims) round and round, their hands on the rough stone.

But as they passed towards a door, there struck at them, seen only with the corner of the eye, a sudden, amended vision; solid, purposeful, complete. It was as though a hand had shot out of the future and hooked it into their ken. Incredulous, they wheeled round; the marvel on the walls was still there. But no sooner had they halted than a huge bell suddenly moved in the tower. The sound, coming from so close, had no time to poise for its flight, but leapt at them as mere uproar and confusion. It rattled along the walls, shook dust from the floor, bombarded the narrow stair.

And through the midst of all the din there sounded too, from room to room, one after another the voices of the guardians rising with a burst of startled energy, as though a box of tin soldiers had suddenly been woken for their roll-call by an invisible power.

There was a halt and crush at one of the doors. Wave after wave of pilgrims broke against a dark, obstructing mass, which proved to be the invalid lady's wheeled chair. It advanced slowly now, and also rather unsteadily. Her two attendants or companions had pulled the newspaper from under her pillow and holding it between them were reading as they went. As though to make up for having abstracted this much of their attention, they were pressing very hard on the back rail with their outer hands—too heavily indeed, and the front wheel was in the air. The lady still looked straight in front of her, just as at the beginning when everything still lay ahead, and with hands tightly folded over the steering-bar guided her wheel through the air on a rigid and unvarying course. The statue guarded the final stairway with an air of confident reality. His face was towards the street. He seemed even to regard with a certain contempt—the loftily averted gaze and fastidious pose of the right elbow suggested it—the polished stretches, the dim lifeless walls.

The galleries were cleared; emptied of their last human drop. Even the invalid lady and her chair had at the last moment vanished—decently spirited away.

The pilgrims were trooping out of the hall. There was light ahead; they were nearing the end of their tunnel. Decked again in the damp properties with which, like soul and body at the

Judgment, they were at last re-united, they walked slightly sideways, raising their feet high, down the long series of steps, at every step breathing deeply into their stifled lungs the trivial animation of the outer world.

1948–49

Outline Chronology of Arthur Waley's Life

(including publication dates of some of his major works)

19 August 1889 Born in Tunbridge Wells.

1900–1902 Lockers Park preparatory school.

1903–6 Rugby.

1906 Gained classical scholarship at King's College, Cambridge.

1907–10 King's College, Cambridge.

1910 Obtained a First in Part I of the Classical Tripos.

1913 Appointed to the Oriental Sub-Department of Prints and Drawings in the British Museum.

1917 'A Chinese Picture' in *Burlington Magazine* (first published article).

1917 'Pre-T'ang Poetry' in *Bulletin of the School of Oriental Studies* (first published translation).

1918 *A Hundred and Seventy Chinese Poems* (first published book).

1919 *More Translations from the Chinese.*

1919 *Japanese Poetry: The 'Uta'.*

1921 *The Nō Plays of Japan.*

1923 *An Introduction to the Study of Chinese Painting.*

1923 *The Temple and Other Poems.*

1925 *The Tale of Genji* (first of 6 volumes).

1928 *The Pillow-Book of Sei Shōnagon.*

1929	Left the British Museum.
1933	*The Bridge of Dreams* (last of 6 volumes of *The Tale of Genji*).
1934	*The Way and Its Power.*
1937	*The Book of Songs.*
1938	*The Analects of Confucius.*
1939	*Three Ways of Thought in Ancient China.*
1939–45	Worked as censor in the Ministry of Information.
1942	*Monkey.*
1945	Elected Honorary Fellow of King's College, Cambridge.
1948	Appointed Honorary Lecturer in Chinese Poetry at the School of Oriental Studies, London.
1949	*The Life and Times of Po Chü-i.*
1950	*The Poetry and Career of Li Po.*
1952	*The Real Tripitaka and Other Pieces.*
1952	Created Companion of the British Empire.
1953	Awarded Queen's Medal for Poetry.
1955	*The Nine Songs: A Study of Shamanism in Ancient China.*
1956	*Yuan Mei: Eighteenth Century Chinese Poet.*
1956	Created Companion of Honour.
1958	*The Opium War Through Chinese Eyes.*
1959	Awarded the Order of Merit of the Second Treasure by the Japanese Government.
1960	*Ballads and Songs from Tun-Huang: An Anthology.*
1964	*The Secret History of the Mongols and Other Pieces* (last published book).
1966	'Colloquial in the Yu-hsien k'u' in *Bulletin of the School of Oriental Studies* (last published article).
26 May 1966	Married Alison Grant Robinson.
27 June 1966	Died in Highgate Village, London.

Notes on Contributors

CARMEN BLACKER ('Intent of Courtesy', pp. 21–8) became interested in Japanese for no accountable reason while she was still a child. She began to study the language and culture as soon as feasible, and after taking a degree at the School of Oriental Studies in London she went to Japan to study at Keio University, where she remained for nearly two years writing a book on Fukuzawa Yukichi. She is now a lecturer in Japanese at Cambridge University, and engaged in writing a book on shamanism in Japan.

JOHN MICHAEL COHEN ('Dr Waley's Translations', pp. 29–36). Born London 1903, B.A. Cantab. Professional writer and translator. Has translated chiefly from French and Spanish. He did the *Don Quixote*, the Rabelais, the Montaigne, Rousseau's *Confessions* and several other books for the Penguin Classics series, and also a good deal of poetry in a manner that owes much to Waley's example. He contributed a number of Middles, chiefly on poets and poetry, to the *Times Literary Supplement* during the 50's. His particular interest is in the writing of Spanish America. He first read Waley's *A Hundred and Seventy Chinese Poems* at Cambridge and immediately passed them to his Director of Studies, who returned his copy tobacco-thumbed with reading. He used to meet Waley in London, but had not seen him for some years before his death.

ROY FULLER ('Arthur Waley in Conversation', pp. 138–51). English poet and novelist, born in 1912. His *Collected Poems* appeared in 1962 and since then he has published two further books of verse, *Buff* and *New Poems*. He qualified as a solicitor in 1933 and has practised that profession ever since, for the last thirty years as solicitor to a large London building society. In 1968 he was elected to become Professor of Poetry at Oxford.

BASIL GRAY ('Arthur Waley at the British Museum', pp. 37-44) has been Keeper of the Department of Oriental Antiquities at the British Museum since 1946, after having served from 1930-33 in the Sub-Department of Oriental Prints and Drawings as Assistant Keeper and in the Department of Oriental Antiquities, which was formed in 1933, as Assistant Keeper 1933-40 and Deputy Keeper 1940-46. He has published a volume on Japanese screen painting and has also written on Chinese ceramics and painting. He visited China in 1957 at the invitation of the Government of the People's Republic and was able to visit the Tun-huang Caves. In 1960 he visited Japan by invitation of the Japanese Foreign Office. He is a Fellow of the British Academy and was created C.B.E. in 1957.

DAVID HAWKES ('From the Chinese', pp. 45-51). Born 1923. Open Scholarship in Classics, Christ Church 1941. Read Chinese after war (1945-48) under E. R. Hughes. Research Student at National Peking University (old 'Peita') 1948-51 (was 'liberated' by Eighth Route Army). Lecturer in Chinese at Oxford 1953-58. Visiting Lecturer Harvard, Department of Far Eastern Languages, 1958-59. Professor of Chinese at Oxford since 1959. *The Songs of the South* and *A Little Primer of Tu Fu* are his only full-length books.

DONALD KEENE ('In Your Distant Street Few Drums Were Heard', pp. 52-62). Born 1922 in New York. A.B. Columbia (1942), A.M. Columbia (1947), M.A. Cambridge (1948), Ph.D. Columbia (1949). Served in the U.S. Navy 1942-46. Lecturer in Japanese at Cambridge University 1948-53. Studied at Kyoto University 1953-55 and has spent part of each year since then in Japan. Now Professor of Japanese at Columbia University. Publications: about fifteen volumes of original studies of Japanese literature and civilization and translations of Japanese literature, both classical and modern.

NAOMI LEWIS ('The Silences of Arthur Waley', pp. 63-6). Author and critic. Born in Norfolk, lives in Bloomsbury.

IVAN MORRIS ('The Genius of Arthur Waley', pp. 67-87). Born 1925 in London, attended school in Summer Fields, Oxford, and Gordonstoun. Subsequently he went to the United States and began studying Japanese language and culture at Harvard University. After wartime service in the Pacific he received his B.A. degree in 1947. He then returned to England and did graduate work in Japanese literature at the School of Oriental and African Studies. Having received the Ph.D. degree in 1951, he worked in the Japan and Pacific and the Research Departments of the Foreign Office until 1955. He was in Japan from 1955 to 1959, when he returned to England. Subsequently he went to Columbia University to teach Japanese history and language, and he is now Professor of Japanese and Chairman of the Department of East Asian Languages and Cultures. He has written several books on Japanese politics, history, and literature, and has also translated extensively from both classical and modern works. In 1968 he received the degree of D.Lit. from London University.

PETER QUENNELL ('A Note on Arthur Waley', pp. 88–92). Born 1905. Author of *Byron: The Years of Fame, Byron on Italy, Four Portraits, John Ruskin: The Portrait of a Prophet, Hogarth's Progress, The Singular Preference, Shakespeare: The Poet and His Background*, and many others. Edited *The Cornhill* 1944–51; co-editor of *History Today*. Early in the 'thirties spent some time in Tokyo at the Tokyo Bunrika Daigaku as Professor of English Language and Literature. Now lives in London.

WALTER SIMON ('A Few Waleyesque Remarks', pp. 93–5). C.B.E., Dr. Phil., D.Lit., F.B.A., is Professor Emeritus of Chinese in the University of London, where he taught at the School of Oriental and African Studies from 1936 to 1960. His research work is mainly concerned with Chinese and Tibetan linguistics. He also compiled several textbooks on Chinese, including *A Beginner's Chinese-English Dictionary*.

EDITH SITWELL (extract from *Some English Eccentrics* and unpublished letter to Arthur Waley, pp. 96–7). The elder sister of Osbert and Sacheverell Sitwell. She was born in Scarborough on 7 September 1887 and died in London on 9 December 1964. Edith Sitwell will be chiefly remembered for her poems, and in particular for *Façade*, 'an entertainment' with music composed by

William Walton which received its first performance in 1922 in London. She was also the author of a considerable number of books of prose including *The Queens and the Hive*, a long narrative work on Queen Elizabeth I which was published in 1962. She was unmarried and was made a Dame Commander of the British Empire in 1954.

OSBERT SITWELL (extracts from *Noble Essences* and *Left Hand, Right Hand!*, pp. 100–4). 5th Bart., born December 1892, died May 1969. Lived at the Castello di Montegufoni in Tuscany. Brother to Edith and Sacheverell Sitwell; not married. A Trustee of the Tate Gallery, 1951–58. He was the author of almost ninety books on travel, the arts and poetry; he was also a novelist, his *Before the Bombardment* being his favourite novel.

SACHEVERELL SITWELL ('Reminiscences of Arthur Waley', pp. 105–7). The younger brother of Osbert and Edith Sitwell. He is the author of between seventy and eighty books on the arts, and of many books of poems. Georgia Sitwell, who is Canadian-born, was married to him in 1925. They have two sons.

MICHAEL SULLIVAN ('Reaching Out', pp. 108–13), M.A. (Cantab.), Ph.D. (Harvard), Litt.D. (Cantab.). Professor of Oriental Art at Stanford University, California. Formerly Lecturer in Asian Art, University of London. Books include: *Chinese Art in the Twentieth Century; The Birth of Landscape Painting in China; Chinese Ceramics, Bronzes and Jades in the Collection of Sir Alan and Lady Barlow; A Short History of Chinese Art.*

ALISON WALEY (letter to Ivan Morris, pp. 114–22). Born (Alison Grant) New Zealand, 1901. Studied ballet. Came to England in 1928. Married Hugh Ferguson Robinson, 1930; one son, John Grant Robinson. Lived in Spain. Travelled (back and forth to Australia and New Zealand: engaged in free-lance art, literary and broadcasting work). Returned to London in 1942. Directed to photography as wartime occupation. After the war, returned to free-lance work. Married Arthur David Waley, 1966.

HUBERT WALEY ('Recollections of a Younger Brother', pp. 123-8). Arthur Waley's younger brother, retired Technical Director, British Film Institute. Author of *The Revival of Aesthetics*, Hogarth Press, 1926, and (with Dr. D. A. Spencer) *Cinema Today*, O.U.P., 1954.

Sources for the Anthology

PERSONAL

Introduction by Arthur Waley to the 1962 edition of *A Hundred and Seventy Chinese Poems*, Constable, London, 1962, pp. 3–9.

'Arthur Waley in Conversation', unpublished BBC interview with Roy Fuller, produced by Helen Rapp, broadcast in February 1963.

'Notes on Translation' by Arthur Waley, S.H.[1] 181–93; this article was first published in *The Atlantic Monthly*, November 1958.

TRANSLATIONS FROM THE CHINESE

Poetry

'The Great Summons', traditionally attributed to Ch'ü Yüan (3rd or 2nd century BC), C.P. 36–42.

'Poverty' by Yang Hsiung (52 BC–AD 18), C.P. 45–8.

'Fighting South of the Ramparts', anon., 1st century?, C.P. 52.

'The Dancers of Huai-Nan' by Chang Hêng (78–139), C.P. 70–1.

'The Bones of Chuang Tzu' by Chang Hêng (78–139), C.P. 67–70.

'The Lychee Tree' by Wang I (*c.* 120), C.P. 171.

'The Nightmare' by Wang Yen-shou (*c.* 130), C.P. 74–7.

'Sailing Homeward' by Chan Fang-shêng (4th century), C.P. 107.

'Ballad from Tun-Huang', anon., 7th century? Unpublished translation.

'Self-abandonment' by Li Po (?701–762), C.P. 117.

'Exile's Letter' (*c.* 748) by Li Po, L.P. 12–14.

'Fighting South of the Ramparts' (*c.* 750) by Li Po, L.P. 34–5.

'The Pitcher' by Yüan Chên (779–831), C.P. 192.

Four Poems by Han-shan ('Cold Mountain') (8th–9th centuries), *Chinese Poems*, Allen & Unwin, 1961, pp. 105, 107–9; also introductory note from p. 105.

'The Old Man with the Broken Arm' (*c.* 809) by Po Chü-i (772–846), C.P. 129–31.

---

[1] The abbreviations C.P., L.P. Nō, R.T., S.H., T.W., and Y.M. are explained on p. 402.

Prose

TRANSLATIONS FROM THE JAPANESE

19 Japanese poems. Unpublished translations, mostly included in a BBC broadcast in 1953.

Extract from *The Pillow-Book of Sei Shōnagon* (late 10th century), Allen & Unwin, 1928, pp. 148–57.

Extract from *The Wreath of Cloud* (Part III of *The Tale of Genji*) (early 11th century), Allen & Unwin, 1927, pp. 292–5.

'The Lady Who Loved Insects', anon., 12th century fragment. R.T. 217–24.

'The Owl Speaks: An Ainu Story' (author and date unknown), S.H. 211–13.

'The Little Wolf', an Ainu fable (author and date unknown), from W. Sansom, *Choice*, London, 1946, pp. 115–16.

'Aya no Tsuzumi' ('The Damask Drum'), attrib. to Seami (1363–1444), Nō 171–8.

'Kagekiyo' by Seami, Nō 123–33.

'Myself', autobiographical fragment by Akutagawa Ryūnosuke (1892–1927), unpublished (date of translation unknown).

ARTICLES

'A Poem by Kubla Khan', translated in an unpublished letter to Sydney Cockerell, 29 September 1916.

'Notes on Chinese Prosody', *Journal of the Royal Asiatic Society*, 1918, pp. 249–61.

Love and Friendship in Chinese Poetry. Extract from the Introduction to *A Hundred and Seventy Chinese Poems*, Constable, London, 1918, pp. 18–19.

'Notes on the "Lute-Girl's Song"', *The New China Review*, v. 2, 1920, pp. 591–7.

'Leibniz and Fu Hsi', *School of Oriental Studies Bulletin*, v. 2, 1921, pp. 165–7.

A Comparison of Nō with Greek Tragedy and Other Forms of Ancient Drama. Extract from the Introduction to *The Nō Plays of Japan*, Allen & Unwin, 1921, pp. 51–4.

Extract from 'Zen Buddhism and Its Relation to Art', from *An Introduction to the Study of Chinese Painting*, Ernest Benn, London, 1923, pp. 226–34.

'A Chinaman's Description of Brighton in 1877', *New Statesman*, 15 December 1923.

'The Art of Murasaki.' Extract from the Introduction to *The Sacred Tree*, Allen & Unwin, 1926, pp. 30–3.

'Murasaki's Affinities as a Writer.' Extract from the Introduction to *The Bridge of Dreams*, Allen & Unwin, 1933, pp. 22–4.

'The Originality of Japanese Civilization.' Oxford University Press, 1929.

'Did Buddha Die of Eating Pork?' *Mélanges chinois et bouddhiques*, I. Brussels, 1932, pp. 343–52.

'Waiting for the New', *New Statesman*, 10 July 1937, followed by extract from an unpublished letter from Arthur Waley to Beryl de Zoete dated 1 June 1937.

Extract from the Epilogue to *Three Ways of Thought in Ancient China*, T.W. 252–5.

'More Than a Revival', *New Statesman*, 8 March 1947, followed by extract from an unpublished letter from Arthur Waley to Beryl de Zoete (undated).

'Blake the Taoist', BBC broadcast, January 1948, S.H. 169–75.

'Some Far Eastern Dreams', S.H. 67–74.

The British Capture of Ting-hai in July 1840. Extract from *The Opium War Through Chinese Eyes*, Allen & Unwin, 1958, pp. 108–10.

'*The World of the Shining Prince: Court Life in Ancient Japan*, by Ivan Morris', unpublished review, 1964.

FIVE POEMS AND A PARABLE BY ARTHUR WALEY

'Et pourtant c'est triste quand meurent les empires', *New Statesman*, 23 November 1940.

'Censorship', S.H. 316.

'Blitz Poem', S.H. 319.

'No Discharge', S.H. 317–18.

'Song', S.H. 319.

'In the Gallery', S.H. 309–16.

ABBREVIATIONS

C.P.   *Chinese Poems*, 1946.
L.P.   *The Career and Poetry of Li Po*, 1950.
Nō   *The Nō Plays of Japan*, 1921.
R.T.   *The Real Tripitaka and Other Pieces*, 1952.
S.H.   *The Secret History of the Mongols and Other Pieces*, 1963.
T.W.   *Three Ways of Thought in Ancient China*, 1939.
Y.M.   *Yuan Mei*, 1956.
                (All published by George Allen & Unwin Ltd.)

Index of Chinese and Japanese Authors

72 73 74   12 11 10 9 8 7 6 5 4 3 2 1

hARPER ⚜ ꚏORChBOOKS

American Studies: General

HENRY ADAMS Degradation of the Democratic Dogma. ‡ *Introduction by Charles Hirschfeld.* TB/1450

LOUIS D. BRANDEIS: Other People's Money, *and How the Bankers Use It. Ed. with Intro, by Richard M. Abrams* TB/3081

HENRY STEELE COMMAGER, Ed.: The Struggle for Racial Equality TB/1300

CARL N. DEGLER: Out of Our Past: *The Forces that Shaped Modern America* CN/2

CARL N. DEGLER, Ed.: Pivotal Interpretations of American History
Vol. I TB/1240; Vol. II TB/1241

A. S. EISENSTADT, Ed.: The Craft of American History: *Selected Essays*
Vol. I TB/1255; Vol. II TB/1256

LAWRENCE H. FUCHS, Ed.: American Ethnic Politics TB/1368

MARCUS LEE HANSEN: The Atlantic Migration: 1607-1860. *Edited by Arthur M. Schlesinger. Introduction by Oscar Handlin* TB/1052

MARCUS LEE HANSEN: The Immigrant in American History. *Edited with a Foreword by Arthur M. Schlesinger* TB/1120

ROBERT L. HEILBRONER: The Limits of American Capitalism TB/1305

JOHN HIGHAM, Ed.: The Reconstruction of American History TB/1068

ROBERT H. JACKSON: The Supreme Court in the American System of Government TB/1106

JOHN F. KENNEDY: A Nation of Immigrants. *Illus. Revised and Enlarged. Introduction by Robert F. Kennedy* TB/1118

LEONARD W. LEVY, Ed.: American Constitutional Law: *Historical Essays* TB/1285

LEONARD W. LEVY, Ed.: Judicial Review and the Supreme Court TB/1296

LEONARD W. LEVY: The Law of the Commonwealth and Chief Justice Shaw: *The Evolution of American Law, 1830-1860* TB/1309

GORDON K. LEWIS: Puerto Rico: *Freedom and Power in the Caribbean. Abridged edition* TB/1371

HENRY F. MAY: Protestant Churches and Industrial America TB/1334

RICHARD B. MORRIS: Fair Trial: *Fourteen Who Stood Accused, from Anne Hutchinson to Alger Hiss* TB/1335

GUNNAR MYRDAL: An American Dilemma: *The Negro Problem and Modern Democracy. Introduction by the Author.*
Vol. I TB/1443; Vol. II TB/1444

GILBERT OSOFSKY, Ed.: The Burden of Race: *A Documentary History of Negro-White Relations in America* TB/1405

CONYERS READ, Ed.: The Constitution Reconsidered. *Revised Edition. Preface by Richard B. Morris* TB/1384

ARNOLD ROSE: The Negro in America: *The Condensed Version of Gunnar Myrdal's* An American Dilemma. *Second Edition* TB/3048

JOHN E. SMITH: Themes in American Philosophy: *Purpose, Experience and Community* TB/1466

WILLIAM R. TAYLOR: Cavalier and Yankee: *The Old South and American National Character* TB/1474

American Studies: Colonial

BERNARD BAILYN: The New England Merchants in the Seventeenth Century TB/1149

ROBERT E. BROWN: Middle-Class Democracy and Revolution in Massachusetts, 1691–1780. *New Introduction by Author* TB/1413

JOSEPH CHARLES: The Origins of the American Party System TB/1049

HENRY STEELE COMMAGER & ELMO GIORDANETTI, Eds.: Was America a Mistake? *An Eighteenth Century Controversy* TB/1329

WESLEY FRANK CRAVEN: The Colonies in Transition: 1660-1712† TB/3084

CHARLES GIBSON: Spain in America † TB/3077

CHARLES GIBSON, Ed.: The Spanish Tradition in America + HR/1351

LAWRENCE HENRY GIPSON: The Coming of the Revolution: 1763-1775. † *Illus.* TB/3007

JACK P. GREENE, Ed.: Great Britain and the American Colonies: 1606-1763. + *Introduction by the Author* HR/1477

AUBREY C. LAND, Ed.: Bases of the Plantation Society + HR/1429

JOHN LANKFORD, Ed.: Captain John Smith's America: *Selections from his Writings* ‡ TB/3078

LEONARD W. LEVY: Freedom of Speech and Press in Early American History: *Legacy of Suppression* TB/1109

---

† The New American Nation Series, edited by Henry Steele Commager and Richard B. Morris.
‡ American Perspectives series, edited by Bernard Wishy and William E. Leuchtenburg.
a History of Europe series, edited by J. H. Plumb.
§ The Library of Religion and Culture, edited by Benjamin Nelson.
‖ Researches in the Social, Cultural, and Behavioral Sciences, edited by Benjamin Nelson.
Σ Harper Modern Science Series, edited by James A. Newman.
° Not for sale in Canada.
+ Documentary History of the United States series, edited by Richard B. Morris.
# Documentary History of Western Civilization series, edited by Eugene C. Black and Leonard W. Levy.
Λ The Economic History of the United States series, edited by Henry David et al.
¶ European Perspectives series, edited by Eugene C. Black.
** Contemporary Essays series, edited by Leonard W. Levy.
* The Stratum Series, edited by John Hale.

1

PERRY MILLER: Errand Into the Wilderness
TB/1139
PERRY MILLER & T. H. JOHNSON, Eds.: The Puritans: *A Sourcebook of Their Writings*
Vol. I TB/1093; Vol. II TB/1094
EDMUND S. MORGAN: The Puritan Family: *Religion and Domestic Relations in Seventeenth Century New England* TB/1227
RICHARD B. MORRIS: Government and Labor in Early America TB/1244
WALLACE NOTESTEIN: The English People on the Eve of Colonization: 1603-1630. † *Illus.*
TB/3006
FRANCIS PARKMAN: The Seven Years War: *A Narrative Taken from* Montcalm and Wolfe, The Conspiracy of Pontiac, *and* A Half-Century of Conflict. *Edited by John H. McCallum* TB/3083
LOUIS B. WRIGHT: The Cultural Life of the American Colonies: 1607-1763. † *Illus.*
TB/3005
YVES F. ZOLTVANY, Ed.: The French Tradition in America + HR/1425

American Studies: The Revolution to 1860

JOHN R. ALDEN: The American Revolution: 1775-1783. † *Illus.* TB/3011
MAX BELOFF, Ed.: The Debate on the American Revolution, 1761-1783: *A Sourcebook*
TB/1225
RAY A. BILLINGTON: The Far Western Frontier: 1830-1860. † *Illus.* TB/3012
STUART BRUCHEY: The Roots of American Economic Growth, 1607-1861: *An Essay in Social Causation. New Introduction by the Author.*
TB/1350
WHITNEY R. CROSS: The Burned-Over District: *The Social and Intellectual History of Enthusiastic Religion in Western New York, 1800-1850* TB/1242
NOBLE E. CUNNINGHAM, JR., Ed.: The Early Republic, 1789-1828 + HR/1394
GEORGE DANGERFIELD: The Awakening of American Nationalism, 1815-1828. † *Illus.*
TB/3061
CLEMENT EATON: The Freedom-of-Thought Struggle in the Old South. *Revised and Enlarged. Illus.* TB/1150
CLEMENT EATON: The Growth of Southern Civilization, 1790-1860. † *Illus.* TB/3040
ROBERT H. FERRELL, Ed.: Foundations of American Diplomacy, 1775-1872 + HR/1393
LOUIS FILLER: The Crusade against Slavery: 1830-1860. † *Illus.* TB/3029
DAVID H. FISCHER: The Revolution of American Conservatism: *The Federalist Party in the Era of Jeffersonian Democracy* TB/1449
WILLIAM W. FREEHLING, Ed.: The Nullification Era: *A Documentary Record* ‡ TB/3079
WILLIM W. FREEHLING: Prelude to Civil War: *The Nullification Controversy in South Carolina, 1816-1836* TB/1359
PAUL W. GATES: The Farmer's Age: *Agriculture, 1815-1860* Δ TB/1398
FELIX GILBERT: The Beginnings of American Foreign Policy: *To the Farewell Address*
TB/1200
ALEXANDER HAMILTON: The Reports of Alexander Hamilton. ‡ *Edited by Jacob E. Cooke*
TB/3060
THOMAS JEFFERSON: Notes on the State of Virginia. ‡ *Edited by Thomas P. Abernethy*
TB/3052
FORREST MCDONALD, Ed.: Confederation and Constitution, 1781-1789 + HR/1396

BERNARD MAYO: Myths and Men: *Patrick Henry, George Washington, Thomas Jefferson*
TB/1108
JOHN C. MILLER: Alexander Hamilton and the Growth of the New Nation TB/3057
JOHN C. MILLER: The Federalist Era: 1789-1801. † *Illus.* TB/3027
RICHARD B. MORRIS, Ed.: Alexander Hamilton and the Founding of the Nation. *New Introduction by the Editor* TB/1448
RICHARD B. MORRIS: The American Revolution Reconsidered TB/1363
CURTIS P. NETTELS: The Emergence of a National Economy, 1775-1815 Δ TB/1438
DOUGLASS C. NORTH & ROBERT PAUL THOMAS, Eds.: ·*The Growth of the American Economy to 1860* + HR/1352
R. B. NYE: The Cultural Life of the New Nation: 1776-1830. † *Illus.* TB/3026
GILBERT OSOFSKY, Ed.: Puttin' On Ole Massa: *The Slave Narratives of Henry Bibb, William Wells Brown, and Solomon Northup* ‡
TB/1432
JAMES PARTON: The Presidency of Andrew Jackson. *From Volume III of the* Life of Andrew Jackson. *Ed. with Intro. by Robert V. Remini* TB/3080
FRANCIS S. PHILBRICK: The Rise of the West, 1754-1830. † *Illus.* TB/3067
MARSHALL SMELSER: The Democratic Republic, 1801-1815 † TB/1406
TIMOTHY L. SMITH: Revivalism and Social Reform: *American Protestantism on the Eve of the Civil War* TB/1229
JACK M. SOSIN, Ed.: The Opening of the West + HR/1424
GEORGE ROGERS TAYLOR: The Transportation Revolution, 1815-1860 Δ TB/1347
A. F. TYLER: Freedom's Ferment: *Phases of American Social History from the Revolution to the Outbreak of the Civil War. Illus.*
TB/1074
GLYNDON G. VAN DEUSEN: The Jacksonian Era: 1828-1848. † *Illus.* TB/3028
LOUIS B. WRIGHT: Culture on the Moving Frontier TB/1053

American Studies: The Civil War to 1900

W. R. BROCK: An American Crisis: *Congress and Reconstruction, 1865-67* ° TB/1283
T. C. COCHRAN & WILLIAM MILLER: The Age of Enterprise: *A Social History of Industrial America* TB/1054
W. A. DUNNING: Reconstruction, Political and Economic: 1865-1877 TB/1073
HAROLD U. FAULKNER: Politics, Reform and Expansion: 1890-1900. † *Illus.* TB/3020
GEORGE M. FREDRICKSON: The Inner Civil War: *Northern Intellectuals and the Crisis of the Union* TB/1358
JOHN A. GARRATY: The New Commonwealth, 1877-1890 † TB/1410
JOHN A. GARRATY, Ed.: The Transformation of American Society, 1870-1890 + HR/1395
WILLIAM R. HUTCHISON, Ed.: American Protestant Thought: *The Liberal Era* ‡ TB/1385
HELEN HUNT JACKSON: A Century of Dishonor: *The Early Crusade for Indian Reform.* † *Edited by Andrew F. Rolle* TB/3063
ALBERT D. KIRWAN: Revolt of the Rednecks: *Mississippi Politics, 1876-1925* TB/1199
WILLIAM G. MCLOUGHLIN, Ed.: The American Evangelicals, 1800-1900: An Anthology ‡
TB/1382
ARTHUR MANN: Yankee Reforms in the Urban Age: *Social Reform in Boston, 1800-1900*
TB/1247

2

ARNOLD M. PAUL: Conservative Crisis and the Rule of Law: *Attitudes of Bar and Bench, 1887-1895. New Introduction by Author*
TB/1415

JAMES S. PIKE: The Prostrate State: *South Carolina under Negro Government.* ‡ *Intro. by Robert F. Durden* TB/3085

WHITELAW REID: After the War: *A Tour of the Southern States, 1865-1866.* ‡ *Edited by C. Vann Woodward* TB/3066

FRED A. SHANNON: The Farmer's Last Frontier: *....Agriculture, 1860-1897* TB/1348

VERNON LANE WHARTON: The Negro in Mississippi, 1865-1890 TB/1178

American Studies: The Twentieth Century

RICHARD M. ABRAMS, Ed.: The Issues of the Populist and Progressive Eras, 1892-1912 + HR/1428

RAY STANNARD BAKER: Following the Color Line: *American Negro Citizenship in Progressive Era.* ‡ *Edited by Dewey W. Grantham, Jr. Illus.* TB/3053

RANDOLPH S. BOURNE: War and the Intellectuals: *Collected Essays, 1915-1919.* ‡ *Edited by Carl Resek* TB/3043

A. RUSSELL BUCHANAN: The United States and World War II. † *Illus.*
Vol. I TB/3044; Vol. II TB/3045

THOMAS C. COCHRAN: The American Business System: *A Historical Perspective, 1900-1955* TB/1080

FOSTER RHEA DULLES: America's Rise to World Power: 1898-1954. † *Illus.* TB/3021

JEAN-BAPTISTE DUROSELLE: From Wilson to Roosevelt: *Foreign Policy of the United States, 1913-1945. Trans. by Nancy Lyman Roelker* TB/1370

HAROLD U. FAULKNER: The Decline of Laissez Faire, 1897-1917 TB/1397

JOHN D. HICKS: Republican Ascendancy: 1921-1933. † *Illus.* TB/3041

ROBERT HUNTER: Poverty: *Social Conscience in the Progressive Era.* ‡ *Edited by Peter d'A. Jones* TB/3065

WILLIAM E. LEUCHTENBURG: Franklin D. Roosevelt and the New Deal: 1932-1940. † *Illus.* TB/3025

WILLIAM E. LEUCHTENBURG, Ed.: The New Deal: *A Documentary History* + HR/1354

ARTHUR S. LINK: Woodrow Wilson and the Progressive Era: 1910-1917. † *Illus.* TB/3023

BROADUS MITCHELL: Depression Decade: *From New Era through New Deal, 1929-1941* ∆ TB/1439

GEORGE E. MOWRY: The Era of Theodore Roosevelt and the Birth of Modern America: 1900-1912. † *Illus.* TB/3022

WILLIAM PRESTON, JR.: Aliens and Dissenters: *Federal Suppression of Radicals, 1903-1933* TB/1287

WALTER RAUSCHENBUSCH: Christianity and the Social Crisis. ‡ *Edited by Robert D. Cross* TB/3059

GEORGE SOULE: Prosperity Decade: *From War to Depression, 1917-1929* ∆ TB/1349

GEORGE B. TINDALL, Ed.: A Populist Reader: *Selections from the Works of American Populist Leaders* TB/3069

TWELVE SOUTHERNERS: I'll Take My Stand: *The South and the Agrarian Tradition. Intro. by Louis D. Rubin, Jr.; Biographical Essays by Virginia Rock* TB/1072

Art, Art History, Aesthetics

CREIGHTON GILBERT, Ed.: Renaissance Art ** *Illus.* TB/1465

EMILE MALE: The Gothic Image: *Religious Art in France of the Thirteenth Century.* § *190 illus.* TB/344

MILLARD MEISS: Painting in Florence and Siena After the Black Death: *The Arts, Religion and Society in the Mid-Fourteenth Century. 169 illus.* TB/1148

ERWIN PANOFSKY: Renaissance and Renascences in Western Art. *Illus.* TB/1447

ERWIN PANOFSKY: Studies in Iconology: *Humanistic Themes in the Art of the Renaissance. 180 illus.* TB/1077

JEAN SEZNEC: The Survival of the Pagan Gods: *The Mythological Tradition and Its Place in Renaissance Humanism and Art. 108 illus.* TB/2004

OTTO VON SIMSON: The Gothic Cathedral: *Origins of Gothic Architecture and the Medieval Concept of Order. 58 illus.* TB/2018

HEINRICH ZIMMER: Myths and Symbols in Indian Art and Civilization. *70 illus.* TB/2005

Asian Studies

WOLFGANG FRANKE: China and the West: *The Cultural Encounter, 13th to 20th Centuries. Trans. by R. A. Wilson* TB/1326

L. CARRINGTON GOODRICH: A Short History of the Chinese People. *Illus.* TB/3015

DAN N. JACOBS, Ed.: The New Communist Manifesto and Related Documents. *3rd revised edn.* TB/1078

DAN N. JACOBS & HANS H. BAERWALD, Eds.: Chinese Communism: *Selected Documents* TB/3031

BENJAMIN I. SCHWARTZ: Chinese Communism and the Rise of Mao TB/1308

BENJAMIN I. SCHWARTZ: In Search of Wealth and Power: *Yen Fu and the West* TB/1422

Economics & Economic History

C. E. BLACK: The Dynamics of Modernization: *A Study in Comparative History* TB/1321

STUART BRUCHEY: The Roots of American Economic Growth, 1607-1861: *An Essay in Social Causation. New Introduction by the Author.* TB/1350

GILBERT BURCK & EDITORS OF *Fortune:* The Computer Age: *And its Potential for Management* TB/1179

JOHN ELLIOTT CAIRNES: The Slave Power. ‡ *Edited with Introduction by Harold D. Woodman* TB/1433

SHEPARD B. CLOUGH, THOMAS MOODIE & CAROL MOODIE, Eds.: Economic History of Europe: *Twentieth Century* # HR/1388

THOMAS C.COCHRAN: The American Business System: *A Historical Perspective, 1900-1955* TB/1180

ROBERT A. DAHL & CHARLES E. LINDBLOM: Politics, Economics, and Welfare: *Planning and Politico-Economic Systems Resolved into Basic Social Processes* TB/3037

PETER F. DRUCKER: The New Society: *The Anatomy of Industrial Order* TB/1082

HAROLD U. FAULKNER: The Decline of Laissez Faire, 1897-1917 ∆ TB/1397

PAUL W. GATES: The Farmer's Age: *Agriculture, 1815-1860* ∆ TB/1398

WILLIAM GREENLEAF, Ed.: American Economic Development Since 1860 + HR/1353

J. L. & BARBARA HAMMOND: The Rise of Modern Industry. ‖ *Introduction by R. M. Hartwell* TB/1417

4

J. M. HUSSEY: The Byzantine World   TB/1057
ROBERT LATOUCHE: The Birth of Western Economy: *Economic Aspects of the Dark Ages* °   TB/1290
HENRY CHARLES LEA: The Inquisition of the Middle Ages. || *Introduction by Walter Ullmann*   TB/1456
FERDINAND LOT: The End of the Ancient World and the Beginnings of the Middle Ages. *Introduction by Glanville Downey*   TB/1044
H. R. LOYN: The Norman Conquest   TB/1457
ACHILLE LUCHAIRE: Social France at the time of Philip Augustus. *Intro. by John W. Baldwin*   TB/1314
GUIBERT DE NOGENT: Self and Society in Medieval France: *The Memoirs of Guibert de Nogent*. || Edited by John F. Benton TB/1471
MARSILIUS OF PADUA: The Defender of Peace. *The Defensor Pacis. Translated with an Introduction by Alan Gewirth*   TB/1310
CHARLES PETET-DUTAILLIS: The Feudal Monarchy in France and England: *From the Tenth to the Thirteenth Century* °   TB/1165
STEVEN RUNCIMAN: A History of the Crusades Vol. I: *The First Crusade and the Foundation of the Kingdom of Jerusalem. Illus.*   TB/1143
Vol. II: *The Kingdom of Jerusalem and the Frankish East 1100-1187. Illus.*   TB/1243
Vol. III: *The Kingdom of Acre and the Later Crusades. Illus.*   TB/1298
J. M. WALLACE-HADRILL: The Barbarian West: *The Early Middle Ages, A.D. 400-1000*   TB/1061

History: Renaissance & Reformation

JACOB BURCKHARDT: The Civilization of the Renaissance in Italy. *Introduction by Benjamin Nelson and Charles Trinkaus. Illus.* Vol. I TB/40; Vol. II TB/41
JOHN CALVIN & JACOPO SADOLETO: A Reformation Debate. *Edited by John C. Olin*   TB/1239
FEDERICO CHABOD: Machiavelli and the Renaissance   TB/1193
THOMAS CROMWELL: Thomas Cromwell on Church and Commonwealth,: *Selected Letters 1523-1540.* ¶ *Ed. with an Intro. by Arthur J. Slavin*   TB/1462
R. TREVOR DAVIES: The Golden Century of Spain, 1501-1621 °   TB/1194
J. H. ELLIOTT: Europe Divided, 1559-1598 a °   TB/1414
G. R. ELTON: Reformation Europe, 1517-1559 ° a   TB/1270
DESIDERIUS ERASMUS: Christian Humanism and the Reformation: *Selected Writings. Edited and Translated by John C. Olin*   TB/1166
DESIDERIUS ERASMUS: Erasmus and His Age: *Selected Letters. Edited with an Introduction by Hans J. Hillerbrand. Translated by Marcus A. Haworth*   TB/1461
WALLACE K. FERGUSON et al.: Facets of the Renaissance   TB/1098
WALLACE K. FERGUSON et al.: The Renaissance: *Six Essays. Illus.*   TB/1084
FRANCESCO GUICCIARDINI: History of Florence. *Translated with an Introduction and Notes by Mario Domandi*   TB/1470
WERNER L. GUNDERSHEIMER, Ed.: French Humanism, 1470-1600. * *Illus.*   TB/1473
MARIE BOAS HALL, Ed.: Nature and Nature's Laws: *Documents of the Scientific Revolution* #   HR/1420
HANS J. HILLERBRAND, Ed., The Protestant Reformation #   HR/1342
JOHAN HUIZINGA: Erasmus and the Age of Reformation. *Illus.*   TB/19

JOEL HURSTFIELD: The Elizabethan Nation   TB/1312
JOEL HURSTFIELD, Ed.: The Reformation Crisis   TB/1267
PAUL OSKAR KRISTELLER: Renaissance Thought: *The Classic, Scholastic, and Humanist Strains*   TB/1048
PAUL OSKAR KRISTELLER: Renaissance Thought II: *Papers on Humanism and the Arts*   TB/1163
PAUL O. KRISTELLER & PHILIP P. WIENER, Eds.: Renaissance Essays   TB/1392
DAVID LITTLE: Religion, Order and Law: *A Study in Pre-Revolutionary England.* § *Preface by R. Bellah*   TB/1418
NICCOLO MACHIAVELLI: History of Florence and of the Affairs of Italy: *From the Earliest Times to the Death of Lorenzo the Magnificent. Introduction by Felix Gilbert*   TB/1027
ALFRED VON MARTIN: Sociology of the Renaissance. ° *Introduction by W. K. Ferguson*   TB/1099
GARRETT MATTINGLY et al.: Renaissance Profiles. *Edited by J. H. Plumb*   TB/1162
J. E. NEALE: The Age of Catherine de Medici °   TB/1085
J. H. PARRY: The Establishment of the European Hegemony: 1415-1715: *Trade and Exploration in the Age of the Renaissance*   TB/1045
J. H. PARRY, Ed.: The European Reconnaissance: *Selected Documents* #   HR/1345
BUONACCORSO PITTI & GREGORIO DATI: Two Memoirs of Renaissance Florence: *The Diaries of Buonaccorso Pitti and Gregorio Dati. Edited with Intro. by Gene Brucker. Trans. by Julia Martines*   TB/1333
J. H. PLUMB: The Italian Renaissance: *A Concise Survey of Its History and Culture*   TB/1161
A. F. POLLARD: Henry VIII. *Introduction by A. G. Dickens.* °   TB/1249
RICHARD H. POPKIN: The History of Scepticism from Erasmus to Descartes   TB/139
PAOLO ROSSI: Philosophy, Technology, and the Arts, in the Early Modern Era 1400-1700. || *Edited by Benjamin Nelson. Translated by Salvator Attanasio*   TB/1458
FERDINAND SCHEVILL: The Medici. *Illus.* TB/1010
FERDINAND SCHEVILL: Medieval and Renaissance Florence. *Illus.* Vol. I: *Medieval Florence*   TB/1090
Vol. II: *The Coming of Humanism and the Age of the Medici*   TB/1091
R. H. TAWNEY: The Agrarian Problem in the Sixteenth Century. *Intro. by Lawrence Stone*   TB/1315
H. R. TREVOR-ROPER: The European Witch-craze of the Sixteenth and Seventeenth Centuries and Other Essays °   TB/1416
VESPASIANO: Rennaissance Princes, Popes, and XVth Century: *The Vespasiano Memoirs. Introduction by Myron P. Gilmore. Illus.*   TB/1111

History: Modern European

RENE ALBRECHT-CARRIE, Ed.: The Concert of Europe #   HR/1341
MAX BELOFF: The Age of Absolutism, 1660-1815   TB/1062
OTTO VON BISMARCK: Reflections and Reminiscences. *Ed. with Intro. by Theodore S. Hamerow* ¶   TB/1357
EUGENE C. BLACK, Ed.: British Politics in the Nineteenth Century #   HR/1427

5

EUGENE C. BLACK, Ed.: European Political History, 1815-1870: *Aspects of Liberalism* ¶
TB/1331
ASA BRIGGS: The Making of Modern England, 1783-1867: *The Age of Improvement* °
TB/1203
D. W. BROGAN: The Development of Modern France ° Vol. I: *From the Fall of the Empire to the Dreyfus Affair* TB/1184
Vol. II: *The Shadow of War, World War I, Between the Two Wars* TB/1185
ALAN BULLOCK: Hitler, A Study in Tyranny. ° *Revised Edition. Illus.* TB/1123
EDMUND BURKE: On Revolution. *Ed. by Robert A. Smith* TB/1401
E. R. CARR: International Relations Between the Two World Wars. 1919-1939 ° TB/1279
E. H. CARR: The Twenty Years' Crisis, 1919-1939: *An Introduction to the Study of International Relations* ° TB/1122
GORDON A. CRAIG: From Bismarck to Adenauer: *Aspects of German Statecraft. Revised Edition* TB/1171
LESTER G. CROCKER, Ed.: The Age of Enlightenment # HR/1423
DENIS DIDEROT: The Encyclopedia: *Selections. Edited and Translated with Introduction by Stephen Gendzier* TB/1299
JACQUES DROZ: Europe between Revolutions, 1815-1848. ° *a Trans. by Robert Baldick* TB/1346
JOHANN GOTTLIEB FICHTE: Addresses to the German Nation. *Ed. with Intro. by George A. Kelly* ¶ TB/1366
FRANKLIN L. FORD: Robe and Sword: *The Re-Louis XIV* TB/1217
ROBERT & ELBORG FORSTER, Eds.: European Society in the Eighteenth Century # HR/1404
C. C. GILLISPIE: Genesis and Geology: *The Decades before Darwin* § TB/51
ALBERT GOODWIN, Ed.: The European Nobility in the Enghteenth Century TB/1313
ALBERT GOODWIN: The French Revolution
TB/1064
ALBERT GUERARD: France in the Classical Age: *The Life and Death of an Ideal* TB/1183
JOHN B. HALSTED, Ed.: Romanticism # HR/1387
J. H. HEXTER: Reappraisals in History: *New Views on History and Society in Early Modern Europe* ° TB/1100
STANLEY HOFFMANN et al.: In Search of France: *The Economy, Society and Political System In the Twentieth Century* TB/1219
H. STUART HUGHES: The Obstructed Path: *French Social Thought in the Years of Desperation* TB/1451
JOHAN HUIZINGA: Dutch Civilisation in the 17th Century and Other Essays TB/1453
LIONAL KOCHAN: The Struggle for Germany: 1914-45 TB/1304
HANS KOHN: The Mind of Germany: *The Education of a Nation* TB/1204
HANS KOHN, Ed.: The Mind of Modern Russia: *Historical and Political Thought of Russia's Great Age* TB/1065
WALTER LAQUEUR & GEORGE L. MOSSE, Eds.: Education and Social Structure in the 20th Century. ° *Volume 6 of the Journal of Contemporary History* TB/1339
WALTER LAQUEUR & GEORGE L. MOSSE, Ed.: International Fascism, 1920-1945. ° *Volume 1 of the Journal of Contemporary History* TB/1276
WALTER LAQUEUR & GEORGE L. MOSSE, Eds.: Literature and Politics in the 20th Century. ° *Volume 5 of the Journal of Contemporary History.* TB/1328

WALTER LAQUEUR & GEORGE L. MOSSE, Eds.: The New History: *Trends in Historical Research and Writing Since World War II.* ° *Volume 4 of the Journal of Contemporary History* TB/1327
WALTER LAQUEUR & GEORGE L. MOSSE, Eds.: 1914: *The Coming of the First World War.* ° *Volume3 of the Journal of Contemporary History* TB/1306
C. A. MACARTNEY, Ed.: The Habsburg and Hohenzollern Dynasties in the Seventeenth and Eighteenth Centuries # HR/1400
JOHN MCMANNERS: European History, 1789-1914: *Men, Machines and Freedom* HR/1419
PAUL MANTOUX: The Industrial Revolution in the Eighteenth Century: *An Outline of the Beginnings of the Modern Factory System in England* TB/1079
FRANK E. MANUEL: The Prophets of Paris: *Turgot, Condorcet, Saint-Simon, Fourier, and Comte* TB/1218
KINGSLEY MARTIN: French Liberal Thought in the Eighteenth Century: *A Study of Political Ideas from Bayle to Condorcet* TB/1114
NAPOLEON III: Napoleonic Ideas: *Des Idées Napoléoniennes, par le Prince Napoléon-Louis Bonaparte. Ed. by Brison D. Gooch* ¶
TB/1336
FRANZ NEUMANN: Behemoth: *The Structure and Practice of National Socialism, 1933-1944*
TB/1289
DAVID OGG: Europe of the Ancien Régime, 1715-1783 ° *a* TB/1271
GEORGE RUDE: Revolutionary Europe, 1783-1815 ° *a* TB/1272
MASSIMO SALVADORI, Ed.: Modern Socialism #
TB/1374
HUGH SETON-WATSON: Eastern Europe Between the Wars, 1918-1941 TB/1330
DENIS MACK SMITH, Ed.: The Making of Italy, 1796-1870 # HR/1356
ALBERT SOREL: Europe Under the Old Regime. *Translated by Francis H. Herrick* TB/1121
ROLAND N. STROMBERG, Ed.: Realism, Naturalism, and Symbolism: *Modes of Thought and Expression in Europe, 1848-1914 #* HR/1355
A. J. P. TAYLOR: From Napoleon to Lenin: *Historical Essays* ° TB/1268
A. J. P. TAYLOR: The Habsburg Monarchy, 1809-1918: *A History of the Austrian Empire and Austria-Hungary* ° TB/1187
J. M. THOMPSON: European History, 1494-1789
TB/1431
DAVID THOMSON, Ed.: France: Empire and Republic, 1850-1940 # HR/1387
ALEXIS DE TOCQUEVILLE & GUSTAVE DE BEAUMONT: Tocqueville and Beaumont on Social Reform. *Ed. and trans. with Intro. by Seymour Drescher* TB/1343
G. M. TREVELYAN: British History in the Nineteenth Century and After: 1792-1919 °
TB/1251
H. R. TREVOR-ROPER: Historical Essays TB/1269
W. WARREN WAGAR, Ed.: Science, Faith, and MAN: *European Thought Since 1914 #*
HR/1362
MACK WALKER, Ed.: Metternich's Europe, 1813-1848 # HR/1361
ELIZABETH WISKEMANN: Europe of the Dictators, 1919-1945 ° *a* TB/1273
JOHN B. WOLF: France: 1814-1919: *The Rise of a Liberal-Democratic Society* TB/3019

Literature & Literary Criticism

JACQUES BARZUN: The House of Intellect
TB/1051

W. J. BATE: From Classic to Romantic: *Premises of Taste in Eighteenth Century England*
TB/1036

VAN WYCK BROOKS: Van Wyck Brooks: The Early Years: *A Selection from his Works, 1908-1921 Ed. with Intro. by Claire Sprague*
TB/3082

ERNST R. CURTIUS: European Literature and the Latin Middle Ages. *Trans. by Willard Trask*
TB/2015

RICHMOND LATTIMORE, Translator: The Odyssey of Homer
TB/1389

JOHN STUART MILL: On Bentham and Coleridge. *Introduction by F. R. Leavis*
TB/1070

SAMUEL PEPYS: The Diary of Samual Pepys. ° *Edited by O. F. Morshead. 60 illus. by Ernest Shepard*
TB/1007

ROBERT PREYER, Ed.: Victorian Literature **
TB/1302

ALBION W. TOURGEE: A Fool's Errand: *A Novel of the South during Reconstruction. Intro. by George Fredrickson*
TB/3074

BASIL WILEY: Nineteenth Century Studies: *Coleridge to Matthew Arnold °*
TB/1261

RAYMOND WILLIAMS: Culture and Society, 1780-1950 °
TB/1252

Philosophy

HENRI BERGSON: Time and Free Will: *An Essay on the Immediate Data of Consciousness °*
TB/1021

LUDWIG BINSWANGER: Being-in-the-World: *Selected Papers. Trans. with Intro. by Jacob Needleman*
TB/1365

H. J. BLACKHAM: Six Existentialist Thinkers: *Kierkegaard, Nietzsche, Jaspers, Marcel, Heidegger, Sartre °*
TB/1002

J. M. BOCHENSKI: The Methods of Contemporary Thought. *Trans. by Peter Caws* TB/1377

CRANE BRINTON: Nietzsche. *Preface, Bibliography, and Epilogue by the Author* TB/1197

ERNST CASSIRER: Rousseau, Kant and Goethe. *Intro. by Peter Gay*
TB/1092

FREDERICK COPLESTON, S. J.: Medieval Philosophy
TB/376

F. M. CORNFORD: From Religion to Philosophy: *A Study in the Origins of Western Speculation* §
TB/20

WILFRID DESAN: The Tragic Finale: *An Essay on the Philosophy of Jean-Paul Sartre* TB/1030

MARVIN FARBER: The Aims of Phenomenology: *The Motives, Methods, and Impact of Husserl's Thought*
TB/1291

MARVIN FARBER: Basic Issues of Philosophy: *Experience, Reality, and Human Values*
TB/1344

MARVIN FARBER: Phenomenology and Existence: *Towards a Philosophy within Nature* TB/1295

PAUL FRIEDLANDER: Plato: *An Introduction*
TB/2017

MICHAEL GELVEN: A Commentary on Heidegger's "Being and Time"
TB/1464

J. GLENN GRAY: Hegel and Greek Thought
TB/1409

W. K. C. GUTHRIE: The Greek Philosophers: *From Thales to Aristotle °*
TB/1008

G. W. F. HEGEL: On Art, Religion Philosophy: *Introductory Lectures to the Realm of Absolute Spirit. || Edited with an Introduction by J. Glenn Gray*
TB/1463

G. W. F. HEGEL: Phenomenology of Mind. ° || *Introduction by George Lichtheim* TB/1303

MARTIN HEIDEGGER: Discourse on Thinking. *Translated with a Preface by John M. Anderson and E. Hans Freund. Introduction by John M. Anderson*
TB/1459

F. H. HEINEMANN: Existentialism and the Modern Predicament
TB/28

WERER HEISENBERG: Physics and Philosophy: *The Revolution in Modern Science. Intro. by F. S. C. Northrop*
TB/549

EDMUND HUSSERL: Phenomenology and the Crisis of Philosophy. § *Translated with an Introduction by Quentin Lauer* TB/1170

IMMANUEL KANT: Groundwork of the Metaphysic of Morals. *Translated and Analyzed by H. J. Paton*
TB/1159

IMMANUEL KANT: Lectures on Ethics. § *Introduction by Lewis White Beck* TB/105

WALTER KAUFMANN, Ed.: Religion From Tolstoy to Camus: *Basic Writings on Religious Truth and Morals*
TB/123

QUENTIN LAUER: Phenomenology: *Its Genesis and Prospect. Preface by Aron Gurwitsch*
TB/1169

MAURICE MANDELBAUM: The Problem of Historical Knowledge: *An Answer to Relativism*
TB/1338

GEORGE A. MORGAN: What Nietzsche Means
TB/1198

H. J. PATON: The Categorical Imperative: *A Study in Kant's Moral Philosophy* TB/1325

MICHAEL POLANYI: Personal Knowledge: *Towards a Post-Critical Philosophy* TB/1158

KARL R. POPPER: Conjectures and Refutations: *The Growth of Scientific Knowledge* TB/1376

WILLARD VAN ORMAN QUINE: Elementary Logic *Revised Edition*
TB/577

WILLARD VAN ORMAN QUINE: From a Logical Point of View: *Logico-Philosophical Essays*
TB/566

JOHN E. SMITH: Themes in American Philosophy: *Purpose, Experience and Community*
TB/1466

MORTON WHITE: Foundations of Historical Knowledge
TB/1440

WILHELM WINDELBAND: A History of Philosophy
Vol. I: Greek, Roman, Medieval TB/38
Vol. II: Renaissance, Enlightenment, Modern
TB/39

LUDWIG WITTGENSTEIN: The Blue and Brown Books °
TB/1211

LUDWIG WITTGENSTEIN: Notebooks, 1914-1916
TB/1441

Political Science & Government

C. E. BLACK: The Dynamics of Modernization: *A Study in Comparative History* TB/1321

KENNETH E. BOULDING: Conflict and Defense: *A General Theory of Action* TB/3024

DENIS W. BROGAN: Politics in America. *New Introduction by the Author* TB/1469

CRANE BRINTON: English Political Thought in the Nineteenth Century
TB/1071

ROBERT CONQUEST: Power and Policy in the USSR: *The Study of Soviet Dynastics °*
TB/1307

ROBERT A. DAHL & CHARLES E. LINDBLOM: Politics, Economics, and Welfare: *Planning and Politico-Economic Systems Resolved into Basic Social Processes*
TB/1277

HANS KOHN: Political Ideologies of the 20th Century
TB/1277

ROY C. MACRIDIS, Ed.: Political Parties: *Contemporary Trends and Ideas **
TB/1322

ROBERT GREEN MC CLOSKEY: American Conservatism in the Age of Enterprise, 1865-1910
TB/1137

MARSILIUS OF PADUA: The Defender of Peace. *The Defensor Pacis. Translated with an Introduction by Alan Gewirth*
TB/1310

KINGSLEY MARTIN: French Liberal Thought in the Eighteenth Century: *A Study of Political Ideas from Bayle to Condorcet* TB/1114

BARRINGTON MOORE, JR.: Political Power and Social Theory: *Seven Studies* || TB/1221
BARRINGTON MOORE, JR.: Soviet Politics—The Dilemma of Power: *The Role of Ideas in Social Change* || TB/1222
BARRINGTON MOORE, JR.: Terror and Progress—USSR: *Some Sources of Change and Stability*
JOHN B. MORRALL: Political Thought in Medieval Times TB/1076
KARL R. POPPER: The Open Society and Its Enemies *Vol. I: The Spell of Plato* TB/1101 *Vol. II: The High Tide of Prophecy: Hegel, Marx, and the Aftermath* TB/1102
CONYERS READ, Ed.: The Constitution Reconsidered. *Revised Edition, Preface by Richard B. Morris* TB/1384
JOHN P. ROCHE, Ed.: Origins of American Political Thought: *Selected Readings* TB/1301
JOHN P. ROCHE, Ed.: American Political Thought: *From Jefferson to Progressivism* TB/1332
HENRI DE SAINT-SIMON: Social Organization, The Science of Man, and Other Writings. || *Edited and Translated with an Introduction by Felix Markham* TB/1152
CHARLES SCHOTTLAND, Ed.: The Welfare State ** TB/1323
JOSEPH A. SCHUMPETER: Capitalism, Socialism and Democracy TB/3008
PETER WOLL, Ed.: Public Administration and Policy: *Selected Essays* TB/1284

Psychology

ALFRED ADLER: The Individual Psychology of Alfred Adler: *A Systematic Presentation in Selections from His Writings. Edited by Heinz L. & Rowena R. Ansbacher* TB/1154
ALFRED ADLER: Problems of Neurosis: *A Book of Case Histories. Introduction by Heinz L. Ansbacher* TB/1145
LUDWIG BINSWANGER: Being-in-the-World: *Selected Papers.* || *Trans. with Intro. by Jacob Needleman* TB/1365
ARTHUR BURTON & ROBERT E. HARRIS: Clinical Studies of Personality Vol. I TB/3075 Vol. II TB/3076
HADLEY CANTRIL: The Invasion from Mars: *A Study in the Psychology of Panic* || TB/1282
MIRCEA ELIADE: Cosmos and History: *The Myth of the Eternal Return* § TB/2050
MIRCEA ELIADE: Myth and Reality TB/1369
MIRCEA ELIADE: Myths, Dreams and Mysteries: *The Encounter Between Contemporary Faiths and Archaic Realities* § TB/1320
MIRCEA ELIADE: Rites and Symbols of Initiation: *The Mysteries of Birth and Rebirth* § TB/1236
HERBERT FINGARETTE: The Self in Transformation: *Psychoanalysis, Philosophy and the Life of the Spirit* || TB/1177
SIGMUND FREUD: On Creativity and the Unconscious: *Papers on the Psychology of Art, Literature, Love, Religion.* § *Intro. by Benjamin Nelson* TB/45
J. GLENN GRAY: The Warriors: *Reflections on Men in Battle. Introduction by Hannah Arendt* TB/1294
WILLIAM JAMES: Psychology: *The Briefer Course. Edited with an Intro. by Gordon Allport* TB/1034
C. G. JUNG: Psychological Reflections. *Ed. by J. Jacobi* TB/2001
KARL MENNINGER, M.D.: Theory of Psychoanalytic Technique TB/1144
JOHN H. SCHAAR: Escape from Authority: *The Perspectives of Erich Fromm* TB/1155

MUZAFER SHERIF: The Psychology of Social Norms. *Introduction by Gardner Murphy* TB/3072
HELLMUT WILHELM: Change: *Eight Lectures on the I Ching* TB/2019

Religion: Ancient and Classical, Biblical and Judaic Traditions

W. F. ALBRIGHT: The Biblical Period from Abraham to Ezra TB/102
SALO W. BARON: Modern Nationalism and Religion TB/818
C. K. BARRETT, Ed.: The New Testament Background: *Selected Documents* TB/86
MARTIN BUBER: Eclipse of God: *Studies in the Relation Between Religion and Philosophy* TB/12
MARTIN BUBER: Hasidism and Modern Man. *Edited and Translated by Maurice Friedman* TB/839
MARTIN BUBER: The Knowledge of Man. *Edited with an Introduction by Maurice Friedman. Translated by Maurice Friedman and Ronald Gregor Smith* TB/135
MARTIN BUBER: Moses. *The Revelation and the Covenant* TB/837
MARTIN BUBER: The Origin and Meaning of Hasidism. *Edited and Translated by Maurice Friedman* TB/835
MARTIN BUBER: The Prophetic Faith TB/73
MARTIN BUBER: Two Types of Faith: *Interpenetration of Judaism and Christianity* ° TB/75
MALCOLM L. DIAMOND: Martin Buber: *Jewish Existentialist* TB/840
M. S. ENSLIN: Christian Beginnings TB/5
M. S. ENSLIN: The Literature of the Christian Movement TB/6
ERNST LUDWIG EHRLICH: A Concise History of Israel: *From the Earliest Times to the Destruction of the Temple in A.D. 70* ° TB/128
HENRI FRANKFORT: Ancient Egyptian Religion: *An Interpretation* TB/77
MAURICE S. FRIEDMAN: Martin Buber: *The Life of Dialogue* TB/64
ABRAHAM HESCHEL: The Earth Is the Lord's & The Sabbath. *Two Essays* TB/828
ABRAHAM HESCHEL: God in Search of Man: *A Philosophy of Judaism* TB/807
ABRAHAM HESCHEL: Man Is not Alone: *A Philosophy of Religion* TB/838
ABRAHAM HESCHEL: The Prophets: *An Introduction* TB/1421
T. J. MEEK: Hebrew Origins TB/69
JAMES MUILENBURG: The Way of Israel: *Biblical Faith and Ethics* TB/133
H. J. ROSE: Religion in Greece and Rome TB/55
H. H. ROWLEY: The Growth of the Old Testament TB/107
D. WINTON THOMAS, Ed.: Documents from Old Testament Times TB/85

Religion: General Christianity

ROLAND H. BAINTON: Christendom: *A Short History of Christianity and Its Impact on Western Civilization. Illus.* Vol. I TB/131; Vol. II TB/132
JOHN T. MCNEILL: Modern Christian Movements. *Revised Edition* TB/1402
ERNST TROELTSCH: The Social Teaching of the Christian Churches. *Intro. by H. Richard Niebuhr* Vol. TB/71; Vol. II TB/72

RUDOLF BULTMANN and KARL KUNDSIN: Form Criticism: *Two Essays on New Testament Research. Trans. by F. C. Grant* TB/96
WILLIAM A. CLEBSCH & CHARLES R. JAEKLE: Pastoral Care in Historical Perspective: *An Essay with Exhibits* TB/148
FREDERICK FERRE: Language, Logic and God. *New Preface by the Author* TB/1407
LUDWIG FEUERBACH: The Essence of Christianity. § *Introduction by Karl Barth. Foreword by H. Richard Niebuhr* TB/11
C. C. GILLISPIE: Genesis and Geology: *The Decades before Darwin* § TB/51
ADOLF HARNACK: What Is Christianity? § *Introduction by Rudolf Bultmann* TB/17
KYLE HASELDEN: The Racial Problem in Christian Perspective TB/116
MARTIN HEIDEGGER: Discourse on Thinking. *Translated with a Preface by John M. Anderson and E. Hans Freund. Introduction by John M. Anderson* TB/1459
IMMANUEL KANT: Religion Within the Limits of Reason Alone. § *Introduction by Theodore M. Greene and John Silber* TB/FG
WALTER KAUFMANN, Ed.: Religion from Tolstoy to Camus: *Basic Writings on Religious Truth and Morals. Enlarged Edition* TB/123
JOHN MACQUARRIE: An Existentialist Theology: *A Comparison of Heidegger and Bultmann.* ° *Foreword by Rudolf Bultmann* TB/125
H. RICHARD NIERUHR: Christ and Culture TB/3
H. RICHARD NIEBUHR: The Kingdom of God in America TB/49
ANDERS NYGREN: Agape and Eros. *Translated by Philip S. Watson* ° TB/1430
JOHN H. RANDALL, JR.: The Meaning of Religion for Man. *Revised with New Intro. by the Author* TB/1379
WALTER RAUSCHENBUSCHS Christianity and the Social Crisis. ‡ *Edited by Robert D. Cross* TB/3059
JOACHIM WACH: Understanding and Believing. *Ed. with Intro. by Joseph M. Kitagawa* TB/1399

Science and Mathematics

JOHN TYLER BONNER: The Ideas of Biology. Σ *Illus.* TB/570
W. E. LE GROS CLARK: The Antecedents of Man: *An Introduction to the Evolution of the Primates.* ° *Illus.* TB/559
ROBERT E. COKER: Streams, Lakes, Ponds. *Illus.* TB/586
ROBERT E. COKER: This Great and Wide Sea: *An Introduction to Oceanography and Marine Biology. Illus.* TB/551
W. H. DOWDESWELL: Animal Ecology. *61 illus.* TB/543
C. V. DURELL: Readable Relativity. *Foreword by Freeman J. Dyson* TB/530
GEORGE GAMOW: Biography of Physics. Σ *Illus.* TB/567
F. K. HARE: The Restless Atmosphere TB/560
S. KORNER: The Philosophy of Mathematics: *An Introduction* TB/547
J. R. PIERCE: Symbols, Signals and Noise: *The Nature and Process of Communication* Σ TB/574
WILLARD VAN ORMAN QUINE: Mathematical Logic TB/558

Science: History

MARIE BOAS: The Scientific Renaissance, 1450-1630 ° TB/583
W. DAMPIER, Ed.: Readings in the Literature of Science. *Illus.* TB/512

STEPHEN TOULMIN & JUNE GOODFIELD: The Architecture of Matter: *The Physics, Chemistry and Physiology of Matter, Both Animate and Inanimate, as it has Evolved since the Beginnings of Science* TB/584
STEPHEN TOULMIN & JUNE GOODFIELD: The Discovery of Time TB/585
STEPHEN TOULMIN & JUNE GOODFIELD: The Fabric of the Heavens: *The Development of Astronomy and Dynamics* TB/579

Science: Philosophy

J. M. BOCHENSKI: The Methods of Contemporary Thought. *Tr. by Peter Caws* TB/1377
J. BRONOWSKI: Science and Human Values. *Revised and Enlarged. Illus.* TB/505
WERNER HEISENBERG: Physics and Philosophy: *The Revolution in Modern Science. Introduction by F. S. C. Northrop* TB/549
KARL R. POPPER: Conjectures and Refutations: *The Growth of Scientific Knowledge* TB/1376
KARL R. POPPER: The Logic of Scientific Discovery TB/576
STEPHEN TOULMIN: Foresight and Understanding: *An Enquiry into the Aims of Science. Foreword by Jacques Barzun* TB/564
STEPHEN TOULMIN: The Philosophy of Science: *An Introduction* TB/513

Sociology and Anthropology

REINHARD BENDIX: Work and Authority in Industry: *Ideologies of Management in the Course of Industrialization* TB/3035
BERNARD BERELSON, Ed., The Behavioral Sciences Today TB/1127
JOSEPH B. CASAGRANDE, Ed.: In the Company of Man: *Twenty Portraits of Anthropological Informants. Illus.* TB/3047
KENNETH B. CLARK: Dark Ghetto: *Dilemmas of Social Power. Foreword by Gunnar Myrdal* TB/1317
KENNETH CLARK & JEANNETTE HOPKINS: A Relevant War Against Poverty: *A Study of Community Action Programs and Observable Social Change* TB/1480
W. E. LE GROS CLARK: The Antecedents of Man: *An Introduction to the Evolution of the Primates.* ° *Illus.* TB/559
LEWIS COSER, Ed.: Political Sociology TB/1293
ROSE L. COSER, Ed.: Life Cycle and Achievement in America ** TB/1434
ALLISON DAVIS & JOHN DOLLARD: Children of Bondage: *The Personality Development of Negro Youth in the Urban South* ‖ TB/3049
ST. CLAIR DRAKE & HORACE R. CAYTON: Black Metropolis: *A Study of Negro Life in a Northern City. Introduction by Everett C. Hughes. Tables, maps, charts, and graphs* Vol. I TB/1086; Vol. II TB/1087
PETER E. DRUCKER: The New Society: *The Anatomy of Industrial Order* TB/1082
CORA DU BOIS: The People of Alor. *With a Preface by the Author* Vol. I *Illus.* TB/1042; Vol. II TB/1043
EMILE DURKHEIM et al.: Essays on Sociology and Philosophy: *with Appraisals of Durkheim's Life and Thought.* ‖ *Edited by Kurt H. Wolff* TB/1151
LEON FESTINGER, HENRY W. RIECKEN, STANLEY SCHACHTER: When Prophecy Fails: *A Social and Psychological Study of a Modern Group that Predicted the Destruction of the World* ‖ TB/1132

CHARLES Y. GLOCK & RODNEY STARK: Christian Beliefs and Anti-Semitism. *Introduction by the Authors* TB/1454

ALVIN W. GOULDNER: The Hellenic World TB/1479

ALVIN W. GOULDNER: Wildcat Strike: *A Study in Worker-Management Relationships* || TB/1176

CESAR GRANA: Modernity and Its Discontents: *French Society and the French Man of Letters in the Nineteenth Century* TB/1318

L. S. B. LEAKEY: Adam's Ancestors: *The Evolution of Man and His Culture. Illus.* TB/1019

KURT LEWIN: Field Theory in Social Science: *Selected Theoretical Papers.* || *Edited by Dorwin Cartwright* TB/1135

RITCHIE P. LOWRY: Who's Running This Town? *Community Leadership and Social Change* TB/1383

R. M. MACIVER: Social Causation TB/1153

GARY T. MARX: Protest and Prejudice: *A Study of Belief in the Black Community* TB/1435

ROBERT K. MERTON, LEONARD BROOM, LEONARD S. COTTRELL, JR., Editors: Sociology Today: *Problems and Prospects* ||
Vol. I TB/1173; Vol. II TB/1174

GILBERT OSOFSKY, Ed.: The Burden of Race: A Documentary History of Negro-White Relations in America TB/1405

GILBERT OSOFSKY: Harlem: The Making of a Ghetto: *Negro New York 1890-1930* TB/1381

TALCOTT PARSONS & EDWARD A. SHILS, Editors: Toward a General Theory of Action: *Theoretical Foundations for the Social Sciences* TB/1083

PHILIP RIEFF: The Triumph of the Therapeutic: *Uses of Faith After Freud* TB/1360

JOHN H. ROHRER & MUNRO S. EDMONSON, Eds.: The Eighth Generation Grows Up: *Cultures and Personalities of New Orleans Negroes* || TB/3050

ARNOLD ROSE: The Negro in America: *The Condensed Version of Gunnar Myrdal's An American Dilemma. Second Edition* TB/3048

GEORGE ROSEN: Madness in Society: *Chapters in the Historical Sociology of Mental Illness.* || *Preface by Benjamin Nelson* TB/1337

PHILIP SELZNICK: TVA and the Grass Roots: *A Study in the Sociology of Formal Organization* TB/1230

PITIRIM A. SOROKIN: Contemporary Sociological Theories: *Through the First Quarter of the Twentieth Century* TB/3046

MAURICE R. STEIN: The Eclipse of Community: *An Interpretation of American Studies* TB/1128

WILLIAM I. THOMAS: The Unadjusted Girl: *With Cases and Standpoint for Behavior Analysis. Intro. by Michael Parenti* TB/1319

EDWARD A. TIRYAKIAN, Ed.: Sociological Theory, Values and Sociocultural Change: *Essays in Honor of Pitirim A. Sorokin* ° TB/1316

FERDINAND TONNIES: Community and Society: *Gemeinschaft und Gesellschaft. Translated and Edited by Charles P. Loomis* TB/1116

SAMUEL E. WALLACE: Skid Row as a Way of Life TB/1367

W. LLOYD WARNER and Associates: Democracy in Jonesville: *A Study in Quality and Inequality* || TB/1129

W. LLOYD WARNER: Social Class in America: *The Evaluation of Status* TB/1013

FLORIAN ZNANIECKI: The Social Role of the Man of Knowledge. *Introduction by Lewis A. Coser* TB/1372

11